Ballads and Sea Songs
from Nova Scotia

LONDON : HUMPHREY MILFORD

OXFORD UNIVERSITY PRESS

RICHARD HINES
ABLE SEAMAN

Ballads and Sea Songs from Nova Scotia

COLLECTED BY

W. ROY MACKENZIE

Cambridge

HARVARD UNIVERSITY PRESS

1928

TO

PROFESSOR GEORGE LYMAN KITTREDGE

WHOSE FRIENDSHIP I CAN REPAY IN KIND
BUT WHOSE GENEROSITY HAS PLACED ME
UNDER A LASTING OBLIGATION

PREFACE

SEVERAL of the songs in this book were printed in an earlier work, *The Quest of the Ballad*. To the Princeton University Press, which published the *Quest*, and especially to the manager of the Press, Mr. Paul G. Tomlinson, I owe my thanks for a gracious and ready permission to reprint these songs in the present collection. In the pleasant but occasionally arduous business of collecting I have been helped by too many persons to mention in this brief notice, but I must make special acknowledgments to three of them: to my wife, whose good judgment and high enthusiasm have carried me into many a seemingly hopeless expedition; to my cousin Dr. Owen Cameron, who has a natural instinct for discovering ballad-singers and, better still, for inducing them to sing their ballads; and to my friend Mr. Harry Campbell, whose provocative violin has often supplemented my efforts. In the arranging of notes and texts for publication I have had the most valuable assistance from Miss Margaret Frances Johnson, and in several emergencies I have profited by the good services of Professor George D. Stout, who has transcribed and transmitted needful texts from the Harvard College Library. To Mr. Frances J. Audet, Chief of the Index and Information of the Public Archives of Canada, I am indebted for information relating to the loss of the *Cedar Grove*, and to Professor Archibald Mac-Mechan of Dalhousie University and Mr. Arthur R. Jewitt, formerly of the same university, for material dealing with the wreck of the *Atlantic*.

The forty-odd tunes which I have included at the end of this volume have had a somewhat casual history. Now that I have concluded this episode in my activities as a collector of folk-lore, I could wish that I had begun my labours with as keen an interest in the recording of music as I then had in the recording of texts, but the fact is that my only concern with the music at first was that I should be able to reproduce for my friends an occasional air that had made a special appeal to me, and for this I relied upon a somewhat exact ear and a tolerably retentive memory. Later I made rather more of a point of collecting music as well as words, but whether the airs were found early or late I can at least give full assurance that the ones which I have recorded are accurate reproductions of those used by the singers. To Mrs. Louise Brouster Young I am especially indebted for assistance in preparing these tunes for publication, and to Miss Eloise Frazier and to my colleague Professor Frank M. Webster I owe thanks for aid in this same enterprise.

My debt to Professor Kittredge is such that my hope of paying it is as small as his desire that it should be paid. There has been no time during my experience as a collector of ballads when I have not looked to him for counsel and support, and no time when I have not freely received these benefits from him. In the present case I have had the advantage of his comments on the ensuing text, which he read in manuscript before it went to press. The value of these comments can be realized only by those who have profited in a similar way, but, even so, it will be realized by a very large proportion of the readers of this book.

W. Roy Mackenzie

Washington University
    January 4, 1928

CONTENTS

CONTENTS

FOLK TUNES

CONTENTS

INTRODUCTION

ONCE a fellow-countryman of mine, having taken occasion to write an autobiography, set down a statement to the effect that he had on two occasions paid visits to the city of Boston, and then made haste to assure his readers that he was not saying so "for the sake of boast." I am now preparing to speak brave words about my collection of ballads, and I think that I, also, shall do well to issue a modest disclaimer of "boast" so far as my part in the collection is concerned. The folk-songs which I have encountered in Nova Scotia I have eagerly gathered and preserved, and it is due to no judgment or merit in me that these songs, in the sequel, array themselves in goodly fashion. That the assemblage is a fair one will not be denied, I believe, even by the casual overlooker of its numbers, and as for the interested student of such matters, he will agree with enthusiasm that it shows a range and variety of matter not often to be found in a regional collection. The peninsula of Nova Scotia is, or was, rarely adapted to the culture of a folk-song ranging from the traditional ballads of mediaeval England and Scotland to the improvised shanties of the nineteenth-century sailormen. No part of this narrow province is very far removed from the sea, and no member of the groups which, in the old days, chanted the folk-songs or listened to them, could fail to respond to the ballads which recorded the perils and the brave deeds which, in balanced measure, attended the lives of seagoing men or to the songs of labour which lightened and steadied their daily toil. This awareness of the sea and its romance is the factor which must lend to any representative collection from Nova Scotia a variety not to be found in the records of an inland state or province. The inhabitants of the hills in the southern states of America have preserved more variants of the old traditional ballads of Great Britain than have the scattered singers of Nova Scotia, but the latter have been richly compensated by the acquisition of songs, later in their composition, but steadily available by reason of the maritime cosmopolitanism of a province which, until the turn of the last century, sent many of its best singers a-questing on the seven seas.

In the collection that follows I have made a rough sort of grouping or arrangement of material. The casual reader could hardly be expected to notice this without the aid of a set of instructions, and since I have been at some pains to place each song where I think it should be I shall do myself no more than justice by explaining what the groups are and why they have been made.

The first group (1–16) includes the relics of the old English and Scottish popular ballads which came to Nova Scotia in the wistful memories of the Scottish settlers who migrated westward during the late years of the eighteenth and the early years of the nineteenth century. The story of these settlers and their songs I have told in *The Quest of the Ballad*, and if any chance reader of these lines should ever feel moved to provide himself with something like an adequate introduction to my songs and ballads I advise him very heartily to apply himself to that book, which was prepared expressly for the purpose of introducing the collection which I intended to publish in the course, if not in the fullness, of time. The few facts of the case I shall set down — briefly, as consorts with the expository rigour of a formal Introduction — and shall leave the limbs and outward flourishes of my history to be scanned at leisure by him who has the leisure, and the desire, to scan them. And now for the facts. The north coast of Nova Scotia, where I have done most of my collecting, was inhabited in the good days of ballad-singing by a composite population of Scotch, English, and French. The ancient and genuine ballads of this first group were, in the main, imported by the Scotch and preserved by the French. This, to be sure, is a very curt exposition of a leisurely process. When the Scotch settlers arrived in Nova Scotia with their songs they had no intention of turning them over to the members of an alien race. The evidence, which here as elsewhere in such matters is dim and faint, all suggests that they loved the mellowed growth of their national balladry and cherished it to keep it alive as lonely men will always cherish the customs which can take them on brief imagined excursions to the byres and the ingle-nooks of former days. But to the Scotchmen of Nova Scotia there came a time when all customs were to be subjected to the most rigorous standards that could be derived from or ascribed to the tenets of Holy Writ, — a time when all things which, so scrutinized, could not be adjudged as lovely and of good report must be consigned to the merely ungodly, where, it might secretly be hoped, they would remain as a visible sign of unregeneracy in the world. Fortunately for such as the reader and I, who may be supposed to be labouring still in the bonds of iniquity, by the time this crisis arrived many of the best songs of Scotland were being sung by the French neighbours of the men who were making up their minds to purge and live cleanly. These new-comers — of mingled French,

Alsatian, and Swiss parentage — were in a mood to acquire fresh traditions when they crossed the ocean. They and their forebears had suffered for the Protestant faith, and now, safely ensconced in a land of their own adoption, they lost little time in the exchange of their French dialect for an English speech often savouring richly of the Highland lilt; they as quickly absorbed the manners of their hospitable neighbours; and in the matter of allegiance few of their newly acquired fellow-countrymen could match their enthusiastic reverence for the British crown. They were a singing and a song-loving race, and their admiration of the Scotch ballads soon bred a familiarity with them which was as inevitable as it was fortunate. I have seemed to indicate something like a complete transference of the old ballads from one racial group to another, but in the affairs of men as distinguished from those of triangles no operation is likely to be as complete or as precise as that. There were unredeemed Scots who refused to subject themselves to the laws of Moses and the precepts of Saint Paul, and there were pious children of Huguenot fathers who believed that the cause of righteousness could be better served on earth by singing the songs of Zion than by entertaining their friends with ballads of profane love and adventure. But so much at least is certain: in my time the only districts in which the ancient ballads of Scotland have appreciably survived are those where the Huguenot settlers built their homes near those of the Scotch farmers. These districts are indented by the harbours and bays of the northern coast. In the upland region the case is sadly different. Here the Scotch alone cleared the land for their hamlets and farms in the early days, rejoicing sternly in the spectacle of hills that strangely materialized their recollections of the older Scotland. A regional song composed over a hundred years ago by Alexander McRae of the West River (and happily preserved in a broadside presented to me by Dr. George H. Cox of New Glasgow) ends with the significant lines:

> Now I'll pass on to the head of the river,
> For there I do mean for to dwell,
> For there it wants nothing but heather
> To make it like bonnie Dunkeld.

In those brave days the Scots of the West River could not only compose new songs about the country of their adoption but could also draw at will from a goodly store of old songs which had sprung from the soil of their parent land; and now the popular ballads which made glad their hearts have survived only as a vaguely remembered tradition or have failed to perpetuate even the faint record of a title or a name.

But I see no good reason for abandoning myself to the melancholy mood, as I seem likely to do if I continue much longer with this topic. I have, to be sure, been baffled many a time after catching eagerly at a name or a phrase from some old song of which no other remnant could be found, but I have also been blessed with a very fair increase of versions and variants of the true "English and Scottish popular ballads," and in the ordering of my groups in this book I have provided for a transition from them to the next main division, which will receive its comment when its turn comes. Numbers 17–20 are not specimens of the genuine popular balladry, but they are the next thing to it: they are songs, of a late vintage, but so similar in story to certain ballads of the older type that they make a proper space for themselves between these, which are their direct ancestors, and the typical broadside ballads that follow. Three out of the four can be traced easily enough: "The Turkish Lady" is an inferior later rendition of the "Lord Bateman" or "Young Beichan" story; "The Blaeberry Courtship" is a retelling of the old tale of "Lizie Lindsay"; and "The Sea Captain" is a version of the "Lady Isabel and the Elf Knight" story, one of the most familiar ballad motifs known to the remote forefathers of the English and Scottish peasantry — that of the beautiful and resourceful maid whose wits enable her to escape unharmed from a lover who is sometimes demonic and sometimes human, but whose designs upon her are never good. The fourth, "Sir Neil and Glengyle," can prove no such unmixed ancestry. It has affiliations with the family of "The Cruel Brother" and with that of "Sir James the Rose," it is an obvious and thwarted imitation of the strong old ballad manner, and, at any rate, it seems to belong here rather than elsewhere.

The next group is a main division indeed. I look over the titles in it, which range from "The Golden Glove" (No. 21) to "The Banks of Brandywine" (No. 71), and for the moment at least I do not know what to say about it. Numbers 21 to 71 were, however, arranged by me as a group, and as a group I must persuade the difficult reader to accept them. They are all songs of a familiar broadside type, but this same vague specification could be applied equally well to songs which I have chosen to place in others of my more or less arbitrary groups. The safest definition for me to hazard is probably this: all of the numbers in the present group are dramatic scenes illustrating, in some fashion or other, that strange thing which the Wisest Man himself could not understand — the way of a man with a maid. The first two scenes of this composite drama, indeed, ("The Golden Glove" and "The Lady's Fan") are concerned with an even harder thing to understand in the confusion of human relationships — the way of a maid with a man — but in these cases our perplexity may comfortably lose itself in gratification at the lovers' meetings which end the two brief journeys. In the group as a whole we shall find romantic comedy and tragedy commingled in about equal proportions. The old mediaeval ballad, when it deals with such persons and such events, is fairly certain to stir our emotions of pity and fear with the spectacle of such star-crossed pairs as Lord Thomas and fair Annet, who love deeply through all their strange vicissitudes, and who are as surely marked for death as are Romeo and Juliet; but the later ballad of the so-called broadside period is likely to be less sombre in tone, and happy illustrations of the fortunate dénouement are to be found here and there throughout the group which I am now labouring to define. I might have arranged matters differently here, with the sombre tales in one continuous series and the cheerful ones in another, but I believe that I shall have more chance of holding the reader's attention if I keep his emotions hovering between grief and satisfaction, and yield him the opportunity, while the kindly tear is still moistening his cheek by reason of his recollection of the woes of Mary and the death of her Constant Farmer's Son, to reanimate his faith in the essential happiness of a wholesome world by regarding the case of loyal Nancy, who is sailing over the main with her true lover William, both of them nourishing the reasonable hope that they shall presently return to shore and live happy ever after. Thus far, I think, the composition of the present group will justify itself without much difficulty. There are, however, sporadic examples here of ballads which do not easily find their places in these elemental schemes of tragedy and romantic comedy: there is the song of the mysterious Rinordine, who may, for all our baffled scrutiny can avail us in the Celtic night, be a faery lover or a merely human outlaw, and who — whether sorrowfully or cynically we cannot tell — reminds the infatuated maid who has followed him, that, if she should seek him again, "perhaps you'll not me find"; there is the tale of the brave lady who, out of pure love, disguises herself as a man and follows her unworthy Willie Taylor to sea, shoots him down when she finds him proceeding to the altar with another lady, and then, amid laughter and rejoicing, is nominated as "captain and chief commander" over the sailors with whom she has been toiling; and there is — to select one final illustration where more could be found — the case of the lover who proposes marriage to a "pretty fair maid" by the Chippewa Stream, and who, when the maiden exhibits a coyness which is surely her prerogative, informs her with an indifferent air that he has changed his mind and now thinks it "far better for single to remain." I could easily proceed with a more extended recital of my difficulties in choosing songs for this group, but I am sure that I have said enough to demonstrate that the only, and the sufficient, basis of agreement for these songs is their common presentation of the vicissitudes in the amatory affairs of young men and maidens.

A special explanation must now be given to cover the nine songs which conclude this division. "The Single Sailor" (No. 63) and the ensuing ballads ending with "The Banks of Brandywine" (No. 71) are all variations of one common theme, the return of the lover from the sea or from the wars and the testing of his sweetheart with the aid of some indeterminate disguise or behind the veil of night. His regular device is to pay court, unavailingly, to the faithful maiden and to assure her, without making the slightest impression upon her loyalty, that her absent lover is either a false young man or is dead in some foreign country. The "single sailor," for instance, after seven long years at sea comes riding by the garden where his sweetheart is walking, and, in full confidence that he will not be recognized with his altered "shape and colour," asks her a simple but searching question, "Fair maid, can you fancy I?" In the course of the dialogue that follows the maid convinces him that she can fancy one man only, her absent sailor who, living or dead, loyal or faithless, will continue to engross her thoughts to the end of her days. Then does the happy sailor put his hand down in his pocket and bring forth his half of the ring which he and this maid have divided, seven years ago, as a pledge of faith. What more need I say?

> To church they went and they both got married
> With their two hearts full of love and content.
> Now he stays at home and takes his ease,
> And he goes no more on the raging seas.

With the assurance that this happy dénouement is illustrative of the journey's end in each of the nine tales in this minor division, I may now conclude my remarks upon Group 21–71 and its recital of the joys and the woes of fifty men and fifty women.

My next main division begins five numbers hence with "The Battle of the Nile," which leads the van of my sea songs with a blare of trumpets and a thunder of ordnance. In the intervening space

I have inserted four songs which deal with victories of England on land — a small group which will serve as a prelude to the more stirring narratives of the ensuing battles at sea. Of these four songs two ("The Plains of Waterloo" and the "Heights of Alma") deal in comparatively plain fashion with the discomforts and dangers of the humbler sort of fighting man, but the other two ("The Bonny Bunch of Roses" and "Brave Wolfe") are ambitious attempts, not greatly successful, to build the lofty rhyme upon the epic of Napoleon's career and the vainly imagined romance of young General Wolfe. "The Plains of Waterloo" and "The Heights of Alma" have the great virtues of sincerity and unstrained realism, and one need not doubt that they were first sung by men who underwent the moving accidents by flood and field which are detailed in them. "The Bonny Bunch of Roses" and "Brave Wolfe" are lovely and pleasant to me by virtue of my recollection of the emotion which they stirred in the singers who gave them to me, but they are obviously composed of rumors and embellishments, and they have little of the stark quality which lends its unique value to the purer type of folk-song. I must be prepared for the criticism that my offering of ballads and songs is of no great value aside from its interest as a record of the material used in the self-entertainment of a humble society, but I am not even inclined to accept such a criticism as a valid one. In the careless and free process of oral transmission the songs of the folk are often strangely distorted, and we can have no recourse to authorized texts; but if intensity, vigour, and an utter sincerity in dealing with the subject in hand are attributes to be valued in literature I think it may be admitted that there is something to say in praise of such songs as "The Heights of Alma" and "The Plains of Waterloo."

The songs that follow, from the "Battle of the Nile" (No. 76) to "Charles Augustus Anderson" (No. 113), have to do in one fashion or another with the labours, the adventures, and the tragedies of seafaring men. Some of them are forecastle songs and some are shanties, and they have all in their time played their parts in the daily round of the sailor's life, whether by way of entertaining him when he was off duty or by regulating his efforts when he was tugging on the halliards or heaving at the capstan. A division as large as this one, and defined only by the generic term "sea songs," will naturally fall into several smaller groups, and the first of these includes the fighting songs, which begin with "The Battle of the Nile" and end with "As We Were A Sailing" (No. 84). With one exception these songs were composed to celebrate the prowess of the British fleet or of some doughty war-craft upon which for the nonce lay the responsibility of defending England's title on the seas. The exception is "Paul Jones" (No. 78), and I have never been able to figure to myself why an enemy so resourceful, so determined, and so successful in his opposition to the arms of England should have been made the hero of a song composed and enthusiastically sung by British people. I have asked myself if the ballad purveyors could, in this case, have made the odd mistake of confusing an enemy with a friend, — a foolish question, for the composers and singers of popular ballads do not make such mistakes, and, besides, Paul Jones enters the song in an American frigate, hailing from Baltimore or New York. I have made trial of the very tentative hypothesis that the British sense of sportsmanship is here displaying itself in a burst of admiration for a brave antagonist, and although I cannot quite rid myself of a lingering speculation to this effect I am not able to justify the speculation by means of analogy. When I attempt to do so my memory is persistently assailed by the concluding line of another of these fighting sea songs:

> We'll smother all those Frenchmen wherever we do meet.

The popular balladist is sometimes capable of pity for the widows and orphans of his slaughtered enemies, but he is not the man to congratulate a living and triumphant foe. Failing here, I remind myself that Paul Jones was a Scotchman, and that his victories, even though accomplished with base instruments, might be supposed to reflect glory upon the land of his birth; but whatever I personally may feel in such matters it is certain that the song gives me no warrant for this hypothesis. My last position is briefly occupied with the question, May not this song have been inspired by an obsessive terror for a Grendel-like antagonist who was likely at any moment to swoop down upon any point of the English coast? If there were the slightest indication of such terror in a line or phrase of any version of the song — if "Paul Jones" were even comparable to the French "Malbrook" — this position could be held indefinitely, but the fact is that after the first stanza the vicarious singer cheerfully takes his place in Paul Jones's crew, listens with admiration when the commander announces,

> "If we can't do no better let her sink alongside!"

and heartily drinks from the can after victory is made sure. The ancient who first sang the song for me was a loyal and true subject of the British crown, and yet he found no offence in it. Nothing could exceed the gusto with which he had delivered to me, a few minutes before, the triumphant song of "The *Chesapeake* and the *Shannon*." And when he had concluded and had drunk from the can to the success of "Captain Brookes" (no vicarious performance this time) he advised me as a friend to refrain from singing the song, good as it was, to my adopted American neighbors. "Ye might git a thrashing if ye do," he cautiously remarked, — "but here's one that they'll be very pleased to hear," and he proceeded lustily and without a sign of rancour through the sounding lines of "Paul Jones." 'S blood, there is something in this more than natural, if philosophy could find it out.

Of the other fighting songs in this group I can only say that if the reader should chance to find them as invigorating as I do he will be none the worse for running his eye over them, or, if he has a voice to carol withal, for trying two of them with the airs which I have set down in the Appendix. "The *Chesapeake* and the *Shannon*" has an uncommonly lively tune, and as for "Kelly the Pirate," I hope that I am not unduly influenced by my recollection of Dick Hines's victorious progress through the stately music of its verse and the impassioned minor of its chorus when I pronounce it one of the best folk-tunes that I have ever recorded.

The numbers that follow, from "The Old *Ramillies*" (No. 85) to "The Sailor's Tragedy" (No. 92), are concerned with misfortunes at sea or with the ultimate tragedy of the total wreck. Some of them, as I have shown in the head-notes, are of native Nova Scotian origin, and they are, alas, none the better for it. The ballad-singers of Nova Scotia I am willing to match against the ballad-singers of any other clime or region, but I have no inclination, and no warrant, to become boastful about the achievements of my fellow-country-men in the matter of ballad composition. The art of ballad-making, indeed, has never risen to any great heights in any part of this western continent, and if we have cause for gratulation in our dealings with folk-song, as I believe we have, this is due mainly to the affectionate persistence of our singers in cherishing the ballads which they and their forefathers brought to these shores from the British Isles. But, to return to the small group of songs which I should be discussing, there are, I believe, some numbers here that will be found to merit the reader's attention. If he is interested in story rather than in song he may abandon himself, in the safe retreat of his closet, to the supernatural terrors of "Captain Glen," "The New York Trader," and "The Sailor's Tragedy"; and if he is at one with the ballad-singers in holding that a song should be sung and not merely read or repeated he may take my word for it that "Green Beds" and "Frank Fidd" are worth the singing with the music which I have provided in the Appendix. "Green Beds" is a good and rollicking tale, and the music and the story go hand in hand; "Frank Fidd" in mere print seems no great matter, but when it was made complete in the singing of Dick Hines the sailor, it became a thing of vibrant magnificence. I cannot encourage the reader to suppose that he will ever be able to approach Dick's performance, but if he has a moderately strong baritone voice he will be the happier and the richer for making the assay.

We have now reached the sailors' shanties, for which, even in the abbreviated texts in which it is necessary for me to present them, I have a peculiar affection. It is a question whether this group should or should not include "Spanish Ladies" (No. 97), but, as I have explained in the head-note to my version, I have reasons for believing it to have been, not a shanty, or labour song, but a "forebitter," or forecastle song, employed by the sailors when they assembled, during the dog-watch, to sing, to dance, or to spin yarns. In that case the group begins with "We're All Away to Sea" (No. 98) and ends with "Lowlands" (No. 109). For those whose observation of sailors has been confined to a few brief glimpses of the silent efficiency of the workmen in our contemporaneous hotels of the sea it will be hard to realize how important in the routine of the seaman's activities, not many years ago, were these hearty and tuneful songs of labour. That they were actually of first-rate importance I shall presently show, and since, of all the types of folk-song that I present in this book, the shanty is the only one which I have not discussed at some length in *The Quest of the Ballad*, I shall, I hope, be pardoned for seeming to give it undue space here.

It may be assumed that any man who is much interested in the old seafaring custom of shanty-singing will now find himself rather puzzled in his efforts to realize exactly how this ritual was observed and what attributes the shanty possessed in the days when it mitigated the penalty of Adam for the sailorman. Not much more than a generation ago the ritual was still being practised and few questions were asked about it, but now that it has gone the way of the square-rigged ship we landlubbers are becoming aware of its importance in the history of communal song. We are writing books and articles of belated explanation, and we are in the habit of disagreeing vaguely with each other. Sometimes we convey the impression that every shanty had its fixed form, and even go so far on a false course as to state that a free and variable song like "Blow the Man Down" had nine specified verses. Sometimes we announce without reservations that each crew had its shantyman who took upon himself the duty of supplying all but the refrains and the choruses, and sometimes we proceed on the other tack to the extent of asserting that shanty-singing was the freest form of communal composition, where any sailor could supply a line or a verse as the inspiration seized him. It may be that a great deal of what we say is true, but it can hardly be that our explanations are all true for all occasions. For my own part I have lately been doing what I should have done long ago and have been resorting for information to the only true authorities, who are the surviving members of the old square-rigger crews. If I had been moved by this scientific impulse eight years ago I should now be in a position to record the decisions of my departed friend Dick Hines, who in his time had sailed the seven seas bearing his reputation as one of the most gifted and resourceful of shantymen; but the impulse came too late, and although I recorded those shanties which Dick, at his own good pleasure, chose to sing for me I never asked him for an explanation of the practice of shanty-singing. It is obvious that the best authority in this matter is the shantyman himself, but next to him stands the deep-sea man of the old days who was a singer even if he did not occupy the supreme position; and during the last two or three years I have been able to interview some sailor-men who in their time were forecastle singers and lusty bearers of the shanty chorus. Their evidence did not tally at every point, but they were all in hearty agreement in one matter, namely, the great virtue of the shanty in lightening their toil and in giving the crew a sense of unity and fellowship. "I've put in a good many hard years on ship-board," old Tom Shea told me, "and I've shipped with some queer-lookin' crews, but let me tell ye that when the shanties was started everything got jolly and cheerful at once, and the men that never seen each other before acted like wot they was old friends. — And ye needn't think," he added, "that the shanties was all noise and yellin'. There was some fine singers in them old crews, and it was great to hear them at the shanties."

It is now time for me to introduce my authorities. They fall into two groups exhibiting a measure of agreement and also some divergences on certain details of the ritual. The main spokesman for the first group is a sailor whom, for the convenience of the moment, I shall designate as George Creighton, and he is a scion of a family which sent all of its men down to the sea in the days when good men were needed to belay the sheets and keep the halliards from fouling. George is, and for many years has been, a singer, a fiddler, and an able seaman. It seems strange to me that, with his clear, strong voice and his easy knowledge of the old songs, he should never have been a shantyman himself, but the probable reason is that, with all his ability to reproduce, he was never what he himself would call "a good composer." Your first-rate shantyman must always be able to spin lines and stanzas out of the mere fabric of his brain and with no more time to serve him than is occupied in the roaring of the refrains. But, at any rate, George had no doubts about the way in which the shanties were made and delivered. He was as positive on this score as if he had been a scholar writing an article to disprove another scholar's theory. To begin with, in his sea-going days all group work was done to the accompaniment of songs. It was simply unthinkable that any crew should begin hoisting sails or heaving up the anchor without the appropriate shanties to ease and regulate the toil. At the beginning of each voyage the shantyman for that voyage was selected, and the process of selection was usually automatic and unobtrusive. The crew would get ready for work, one of their number would, without preliminary comment, start them off with a shanty, and the whole conduct of the ceremony was thus settled for that particular voyage. The man who first took the lead was the self-constituted and accepted shantyman to the end. Sometimes, however, the crew would be ready to start work but no potential leader would raise his voice. Then the mate would address the crew, calling for a shantyman to come forward and assume his high responsibilities. Such a man could always be found. Indeed, as George remarked, he had to be found, since the work could not go forward without the singing. But the task of finding him was not a difficult one, and it was a rare occasion when the mate was forced to engage in it. The shantyman did more than undertake a responsibility; he also received honours and enjoyed prerogatives. While the other men were pulling on the halliards or heaving at the capstan he stood by, a designated and distinguished figure, intent upon his high occupation of supplying the verses for the song which was necessary to sustain the work in hand. Sometimes he merely stood aside from the group or sat on the capstan head while the men were straining at the bars, and sometimes he "held the turn," that is, handled the end of the rope and took in the slack. Also, he bore no part in the refrain or chorus; he simply delivered his line, and then, when the sailors began to shout the refrain he fell silent, apparently utilizing this period for the composition of the next line. I asked George if the men never needed to be trained, at the start of the voyage, on the choruses. "Oh, no," he answered in the tone of quiet conviction that marked his testimony from beginning to end, "the men never needed any training. They would always know how to come in with the chorus." Obviously, according to this authority, the ceremonial was the smoothest and most automatic one that could be conceived. The crew assembled for work, a leader proclaimed himself by the simple act of starting a song, and the crew joined in, at the proper moment, with the chorus which was an organic part of the good seaman's knowledge in those days — as regular and as important a part of his equipment as the ability to tie a sailor's knot or to shake out a reef.

When I began my investigating I had a vague impression that any member of the crew might feel himself free to contribute a line or a verse as the shanty proceeded, but George made short work of clarifying my mind on this point. The contributing of the lines was the sanctified duty and privilege of the shantyman, and no one else ever thought of interfering. "If he had," said George in his quiet way, "he would soon have been called to account for it," — and I draw a merciful veil over any consideration of the form that this accounting might have taken. As for the length of the shanty that accompanied any particular piece of work the rule was simple and consistent: the singing began when the work began and lasted until that particular job was finished. George made no comment at this point on the shantyman's need of the old improvising faculty, and it is surely unnecessary for me to supply such a comment.

So ran the testimony of George Creighton, Able Seaman. I have received from other deep-sea labourers many statements corroborative of this and that detail in George's explanation, and it seems certain that we have here a true account of the ritual in its most strictly codified form. But a sailor, as I have remarked, is in some respects not unlike a scholar, and it is well known that the latter, when he is devoting himself to the elucidation of a theory, is too likely to treat with disdain or indifference any other theories which might interfere with the smoothness of his exposition. Other sailors have explained shanty-singing to me with a difference, which may be summed up briefly in the statement of Henry Shea, who followed the sea for eighteen years, and who should therefore have some notion of what he is talking about. The shantyman, according to Henry, was one of the gang or shift, and pulled on the halliards or heaved on the capstan like anyone else. Also, it was not necessary that one shantyman should continue as leader during the whole trip; there might be several good shantymen in a crew, and any one of them might, for any special occasion, assume the office of leadership. Concerning the manner of rendition of any individual shanty, however, Henry asserted as emphatically as George himself that the leader gave all the lines, or, to use his own conclusive words, "The shantyman made up the verses and the rest of the crew gave the choruses."

Obviously, then, one must allow for some differences when one is discussing the obsolete ritual of shanty-singing. The testimony that I have presented is all reliable, but the various parts of it do not apply to all cases, and there remains the necessity of distributing these parts over different voyages and among changing crews. The standard scheme I believe to have been the one outlined by George Creighton, but it seems probable that this scheme was subject to variations within certain carefully prescribed limits.

But, though the variations in the scheme were confined within the modest limits of prescribed order, those of the shanty which stood in the centre of that scheme were as boundless as the sea itself. I shall presently consider the question of lines and verses and occasional complete songs that were comparatively static, but the most familiar of these could at any time be discarded by a shantyman and replaced by his own improvisation. The one verbal element in the shanty that was supposed to remain static was the refrain. Even this varied occasionally to a slight degree, but it was conventionally regarded as the constant and inviolable part of the song. As for the lines, however, they depended solely upon the whim or the inspiration of the shantyman who was mitigating the rigours of the particular task which was engaging the energies of the crew at the particular moment. One day last June when I was making myself at home in George's cottage on the harbour front, as he had courteously entreated me to do, I received from my host and copied down on paper the following brief version of the old capstan shanty "Rio Grande":

> I shipped on a vessel the other day.
> > Way, Rio!
> O I shipped on a vessel the other day,
> > And we're bound for the Rio Grande.
>
> > Way, Rio!
> > Way, Rio!
> So fare you well, my bonny brown gal,
> > For we're bound for the Rio Grande.

This was not the only shanty that I heard that day, but it was all that I heard of that particular one. George, like other shanty-singing sailors, is likely to put the helm a-lee and lie to after a verse or so, with the remark that this is the way the shanty runs and any lines may be tacked on when the occasion arises for singing it. In September, however, when I chanced to be in his neighbourhood again

I dropped in to mingle smoke with him, and incidentally to learn a tune or two. I was not quite sure of the tune for "Rio Grande," and when I asked him to run it over for me he blew out one final vast cloud of tobacco smoke, settled himself in his chair, and lifted his robust baritone voice to the following effect:

> O Johnny came over the other day.
> Way, Rio!
> O Johnny came over the other day,
> For we're bound for the Rio Grande.
>
> Way, Rio!
> Way, Rio!
> Sing, Fare you well, my bonny brown gal,
> For we're bound for the Rio Grande.
>
> "Now give me your hand, my dear lily white.
> Way, Rio!
> If you will accept me I'll make you my wife,
> For we're bound for the Rio Grande."
>
> "O Johnny, I love you and don't want you to go,
> Way, Rio!
> And if you will stay I will love you so,
> For we're bound for the Rio Grande."

While George was rewarding himself for this effort by overhauling a trimly built vessel of a smaller size which lay at anchor between us on the table, I remarked that this was a longer shanty and a better one than the "Rio Grande" which he had sung for me in June. "I never heard," said George, as he felt around for a match, "that these shanties had any particular lines fitted to them. Ye have the chorus, and the lines come jist as the shantyman takes it into his head to give them to ye. I've heard the 'Rio Grande' sung a good many different ways in me time."

I shall return presently to the melodious and convivial atmosphere of George's land quarters, but in the meantime I must make a short excursion to the home of Henry Allen, retired seaman, for a line or two of the famous shanty "Blow the Man Down." Henry's version was in the familiar strain:

> Blow the man down, bullies, blow the man down.
> Way, hay, blow the man down!
> Blow the man down, bullies, blow the man down.
> O give me some time to blow the man down!
>
> As I was a walking down Manchester street,
> Way, hay, blow the man down!
> A nice little damsel I chanced for to meet.
> So give me some time to blow the man down!

Everyone who is familiar with the labour-songs of the sea will remember how this prelude is followed by a description of the damsel and a report of the conversation which she holds with the sailor who has chanced for to meet her. But when I went to George for a few staves of this classic he accommodated me with a robust version in which nice little damsels and casual love-making were completely and manfully ignored. This is the shanty according to George Creighton:

> Blow the man up and we'll blow the man down.
> To me way, hay, blow the man down!
> Blow the man up and we'll blow the man down.
> So give me some time to blow the man down!
>
> The Old Man is worried about us, you know.
> To me way, hay, blow the man down!
> He worries a lot, but he need worry no more.
> So give me some time to blow the man down!
>
> We got full last night and aboard we all came.
> To me way, hay, blow the man down!
> I told him we'd never do that again.
> So give me some time to blow the man down!
>
> For the Old Man's a good one, and so we all know.
> To me way, hay, blow the man down!
> He says, "We'll have a drink and all go below."
> So give me some time to blow the man down!
>
> Now he brought out a bottle and gave us a drink.
> To me way, hay, blow the man down!
> It was very kind of him, don't you think?
> So give me some time to blow the man down!
>
> Paddy West is my boarding-master, you know,
> To me way, hay, blow the man down!
> And I've got a record away back, you know.
> So give me some time to blow the man down!
>
> When we get to China we'll all let you know —
> To me way, hay, blow the man down!
> How the Old Man used us, and so and so.
> So give me some time to blow the man down!

George's only response to my remarks upon the originality of his song was, "O well, this one has been a favouryte of mine for a long while." There can be little doubt that he himself was one of the belated revellers who partook of the Old Man's bounty before they all went below on that night before the shanty came out of the skies and made light work of the business of hoisting the squaresails. The version is, I think, a peculiarly interesting one. It furnishes confirmation — if that is necessary — for the statement that "Blow the Man Down" was used to accompany the hoisting of sails when the ship was outward bound, and in spite of its crudities it has vividness and reality. The shantyman who composed it stands revealed before us, a fluent improviser, a wag, a shrewd rascal, — with his good words for the Old Man and his hint that a continuance of generosity on the long trip to China will merit an additional eulogy, — and a frankly confessed rascal withal, making no secret of his "record away back."

I seem to be labouring along in a general direction which would ultimately bring me into port with the conclusion that no shanty has any constant element except the refrain. As a matter of fact, I do not intend to do quite that. There were many shanties which, like "Blow the Man Down," could ordinarily be depended on to start off with a familiar stanza, although, as we have just seen, the shanty-man with a new story to tell might set his sails for an entirely different tack. There were others like "Santy Anna," the song which dealt with the campaigns of the Mexican general, sometimes hailing him as the conquering hero and again exhibiting him in precipitous flight before the Yankees, but invariably based on some phase of his military fortunes. And, most constant of all, were the shanties like "Reuben Ranzo" and "Whisky Johnny," which could be relied on for subject and, usually, for the form of the preluding stanza. The first of these, a halliard shanty, devoted itself to a frank recital of the attributes and exploits of the mythical protagonist, Reuben Ranzo, and regularly began with the simple formal stanza:

> Poor old Reuben Ranzo!
> Ranzo, boys, Ranzo!
> O, poor old Reuben Ranzo!
> Ranzo, boys, Ranzo!

After this sympathetic prelude, however, there is no telling what we may hear of the character and adventures of Reuben except that he was no sailor, and that for this reason — or in spite of this fact — he shipped on board a whaler. In my version he is reputed, notwithstanding his lack of seamanship, to have "lots of money," and in other versions he is said to have married the Captain's daughter and to be sailing the high seas with the lofty title of Captain Ranzo; but the truth of these reports is challenged by many shantymen who aver that he received thirty-five lashes "because he was so dirty" and that he ultimately came to a sad end. The famous old halliard shanty "Whisky Johnny" as regularly begins with the axiomatic statement, "Whisky is the life of man," and then proceeds to catalogue the virtues and accomplishments of this great sustaining fluid, with the shantyman more than ever on his mettle to find matter which will rise to the height of his argument.

There are other songs of sea labour which are as constant as these, but that is not to say much for the principle of constancy in the shanty. At most one can rely upon a central theme or an opening line in the shantyman's performance; and the crew, whose refrains were familiar and unchanging, could never be sure, as they heaved at the capstan bars or took a fresh grip on the halliards, whether they would be entertained next with an old remembered line or delighted with a fire-new one straight from the mint of the shantyman's invention. And herein consists the remarkable difference between the shanty and the other varieties of folk-song. Any true ballad will exhibit variations from time to time, from singer to singer, and from place to place, but these are for the most part comparatively slight variations in phraseology, unconsciously introduced, and they do not often lead us far from the familiar tale as it was in the beginning. The ballad of "Willie Taylor," which has been a solace to the illiterate for several generations in England and in this continent as well, shows about as many variations as one is likely to find in this species of song, and I shall cite some of these briefly for the purpose of contrast. Willie Taylor, who has been courting a gay lady, is suddenly interrupted in his courtship by the King's officers, who press him into service and send him to sea. His lady dresses in sailor's attire and follows in his wake, but when she is about to recover him she is informed by the captain of her ship that the recreant Willie is going to be married on the following morning to a lady of the foreign land at which they have just arrived. Then she calls for sword and pistol, confronts the wedding party, and shoots young Willie Taylor "and his bride at his right hand." The versions of the song practically all agree on these matters, but they disagree in a variety of ways about the dénouement which follows the lady's climactic revenge. An English text contributed to the *Journal of the Folk-Song Society* ends with a clear visualization — and audition — of Willie's last agonies:

> He rolled over, he rolled over,
>   He rolled over on every side.
> "Adieu, adieu to my true love Sally!
>   Once I thought you 'd have been my bride."

A broadside version (Such, No, 344) more pleasantly proceeds from the killing to the lady's reward for an act well and featly done:

> Then the Captain loved her dearly,
>   Loved her dearly as his life,
> And it was but three days after
>   Sarah became the Captain's wife.

The American versions hitherto collected, however, take a very gloomy view of the case. One from North Carolina does not even represent her as shooting her faithless lover, but invites us to believe that she threw herself overboard upon receiving the news of his defection; and a West Virginia text informs us that she was brought to trial after her accomplishment of a good revenge, crying for death to end her sorrows. I am happy to relate that in my version from Nova Scotia — or, rather, in the Widow Palmer's version, which she was graciously pleased to sing to me — resolution is not thus curbed with the rusty bit of old Father Antic the law. After the shooting is over the lady is heartily applauded by an intelligent bystander in the following wise:

> When the Captain saw this wonder
>   He laughed loudly at the fun,
> Saying, "You shall be captain and chief commander
>   Over my sailors every one."

And the approving singer adds a concluding apologia:

> If Willie Taylor was as constant a lover,
>   As constant a lover as he could pretend,
> She never would have been so cruel
>   As her true love's life to end.

In this ballad, then, whatever the time and the place of its rendition, the essence of the original story appears, and the differences which I have just cited are differences in opinion, or feeling, or tradition, among the various singers who know the song and who have no thought except to reproduce it as they learned it. "He that told the tale in older times," says Tennyson after he has finished the story of Sir Gareth,

> He that told the tale in older times
>   Says that Sir Gareth wedded Lyonors,
> But he that told it later says Lynette.

The ballad, while it lives, is subject to change. New details may be added and old details omitted, but always the essential story remains, and no singer has license to alter it. But the sailor's shanty, by virtue of its own tradition, might be one thing to-day and another to-morrow. The only part of it that tradition attempted to maintain was the chorus, and any set of lines, no matter how popular they might have become by repeated singing, could at any moment be thrown aside by any shantyman who was assailed by the divine urge to compose. There is one shanty which for a time I regarded as a clear exception to this rule — the one entitled "We're All Bound to Go," or, "We're all Away to Sea." In its usual form it has a marked resemblance to a certain type of broadside ballad, and as a matter of fact it has in Ireland been transformed into a ballad by the simple process of dropping the sailor's refrains. It may be found in my collection (No. 98) as it was sung to me by Dick Hines the shantyman, and in this form it resembles most of the other versions as much as one text of a ballad will resemble another. One might suppose that so good a song, with a narrative so picturesque, would retain at least as much of its original character as is permitted in the case of the popular ballad; but versions of it have been found, in England by Cecil Sharp and in America by Joanna C. Colcord, which have not an idea or a line in common with the old Black Baller version of Dick's rendition — nothing but that one constant element, the refrain. In those old sonorous days of packet boats and clipper ships any shanty — barring the chorus — could be what any shantyman, in the exercise of his great prerogative, at any time chose to make it.

If I have said too much about one of my varieties of songs of the sea, and one, furthermore, that is all too meagrely represented in my collection, I can only plead in my own defense that I have, in the title of this book, given some prominence to the deep sea and its melodies, and that I can in no wise convey the atmosphere of marine activity in the days of sailing-ships better than by discussing the songs which were an integrated part of the seaman's daily life. The weary reader may be comforted now by my assurance that there is little more that I need say for his guidance, and that I shall presently reach the comfortable haven of the period to this Introduction. "I'll tell ye," said Dan Thompson to me one day after we had weathered an August gale on the north coast and had rounded the cape which guarded the entrance to the harbor of our destination, — "I'll tell ye what I'm a goin' to do now. I'm a goin' to put a becket on the wheel and go below for coffee." As soon as I can clear away the litter that remains upon the deck I shall follow my good friend Dan.

And now let me explain, in some haste, that the remaining sea songs in this division record the last remorseful confessions of sinful seafaring men. The story of Captain Kidd I have told in outline in my head-note to the song which retails the episodes in his mis-

guided career, and the reader is, here and elsewhere, invited to consider the bare exposition of the head-note together with the richly
clad narrative of the song. The background of the ballads of George
Jones and Charles Augustus Anderson may be seen in *The Quest of
the Ballad* if the reader is not satisfied with the rather detailed stories
in the ballads themselves.

Next to this division stands the tale and confession of Jack Williams, who had something in common with the protagonists who are
arrayed immediately before him in my list. He is "by his trade" a
boatman, not a seaman, but he has sought other than legitimate
means of enrichment, and for doing so he is by way of paying a sore
penalty. Then, in due order, come a series of laments or complaints,
ending with the unrestrained outcries of the nameless one who sings
"The Prisoner's Song" (No. 121). In "Van Dieman's Land," which
follows, the lament is merely woven into the texture of a song which
has also strands of adventure sufficiently predatory in its character
to prepare us for the brave group of highway ballads that stand beyond it. We may now make, or renew, our acquaintance with such
heroes as Dick Turpin, Jack Donahue, and Will Brennan, who broke
their country's laws without, somehow, forfeiting the affectionate
and admiring regard which we, in common with the singers of their
fame, shall continue to accord them. It is to be noted that the pirates
who appear in folk-song are always regarded with fear or hostility,
though they sometimes receive the meed of a melodious tear when
they are captured and bound in Newgate, while the highwaymen,
even in the successful pursuit of their trade, are heroes to the folk.
The explanation is not far to seek. The pirate slew and plundered his
victims with a ferocity as indiscriminate as his greed, while the highwayman of legend was the terror only of those who could afford to
pay. The activities of the former with the ships that he has over-
hauled are characterized by the line, "Their crews he made them
walk the plank"; the selective dealings of the latter are summed up
in another line, traditional since the old days of Robin Hood: "He
robbed the rich to pay the poor."

I have now ended my introductory comment upon those songs that
will permit themselves to be sorted and labeled. The numbers that
follow, from the merry tale of "Kate and Her Horns" (No. 132) to
the ceremonious narrative of "The Building of Solomon's Temple"
(No. 159), are inserted, for the most part, as I chance to lift them
from my manuscript; and after these there are a few numbers which
should be in the earlier groups, but which came to my hand too late
for such consideration. In this heterogeneous list there are songs of

the invincible prize-fighter John Morrissey, jocund accounts of such Irish festivities as erstwhile took place at the Wedding of Bally-poreen, and complaints of the fickleness of such maids as Betsy Baker and Henrietta Bell and of the severity or indifference of wives who cause their sad husbands to exclaim, "I wish I was single again!" I would not have the reader fail to acquaint himself with Dave Rogers's tuneful rendition of that old story of "The Tailor and the Crow" which is a part of all true nursery lore, — and so I might proceed with commendations of the several numbers in this part of my list. But if a good wine needs no bush then a good song is found to be so in the savouring of it, and therefore, without more ado, I shall leave my ballads and sea songs to be judged by the qualities which may be found in them.

W. R. M.

ABBREVIATIONS

BARRY............. Phillips Barry, *Ancient British Ballads*, etc. (A privately printed list.)

BELDEN............ H. M. Belden, *A Partial List of Song-Ballads and Other Popular Poetry known in Missouri*. Second edition. 1910.

CAMPBELL AND SHARP Olive Dame Campbell and Cecil J. Sharp, *English Folk Songs from the Southern Appalachians*. New York, 1914.

CHILD............. Francis James Child, *The English and Scottish Popular Ballads*. Boston, 1883 ff.

COLCORD........... Joanna C. Colcord, *Roll and Go, Songs of American Sailormen*. Indianapolis, 1924.

COX............... John Harrington Cox, *Folk-Songs of the South*. Cambridge, 1925.

DEAN............. M. C. Dean, *The Flying Cloud, and 150 Other Old Time Poems and Ballads*. Virginia, Minnesota, 1922.

GRAY............. Roland Palmer Gray, *Songs and Ballads of the Maine Lumberjacks with Other Songs from Maine*. Cambridge, 1924.

JOURNAL........... *The Journal of American Folk-Lore.*

LOMAX............ John A. Lomax, *Cowboy Songs and Other Frontier Ballads*. New York, 1910, 1922.

O'CONOR........... Manus O'Conor, *Old Time Songs and Ballads of Ireland* (also called *Irish Com-all-ye's*). New York, 1901.

POUND (with page reference only) Louise Pound, *Folk-Song of Nebraska and the Central West, A Syllabus*. Nebraska Academy of Sciences, *Publications*, vol. ix, no. 3.

POUND (with number reference) Louise Pound, *American Ballads and Songs*. New York, 1922.

QUEST............. W. Roy Mackenzie, *The Quest of the Ballad*. Princeton, 1919.

RICKABY........... Franz Rickaby, *Ballads and Songs of the Shanty-Boy*. Cambridge, 1926.

SHEARIN AND COMBS Hubert G. Shearin and Josiah Combs, *A Syllabus of Kentucky Folk-Songs*. (*Transylvania Studies in English*, vol. ii.) Lexington, Kentucky, 1911.

SHOEMAKER........ Henry W. Shoemaker, *North Pennsylvania Minstrelsy*. Second edition. Altoona, Pennsylvania.

WILLIAMS.......... Alfred Williams, *Folk Songs of the Upper Thames*, 1923.

BROADSIDES........ Almost all the broadsides cited are in the Harvard College Library. References to broadsides by volume and page (as, "iv, 16") are to the bound collection numbered 25242.17.

Ballads and Sea Songs
from Nova Scotia

NOVA SCOTIA — A NEW BALLAD

To the tune of "King John and the Abbot of Canterbury"

Let's away to new Scotland, where Plenty sits queen
  O'er as happy a country as ever was seen;
And blesses her subjects, both little and great,
  With each a good house, and a pretty estate.

                                  Derry down, etc.

There's wood, and there's water, there's wild fowl and tame;
  In the forest good ven'son, good fish in the stream,
Good grass for our cattle, good land for our plough,
  Good wheat to be reap'd, and good barley to mow.

                                  Derry down, etc.

No landlords are there the poor tenants to teaze,
  No lawyers to bully, nor stewards to seize;
But each honest fellow's a landlord, and dares
  To spend on himself the whole fruit of his cares.

                                  Derry down, etc.

They've no duties on candles, no taxes on malt,
  Nor do they, as we do, pay sauce for their salt;
But all is as free as in those times of old,
  When poets assure us the age was of gold.

                                  Derry down, etc.

From the *Gentleman's Magazine*, February, 1750.

LADY ISABEL AND THE ELF-KNIGHT
(CHILD, No. 4)

A COMPOSITE version of this ballad, made up of a combination of the best stanzas from the following versions, has been printed by me in *Journal*, XXIII, 374, and in *The Quest of the Ballad*, pp. 93–95. In Nova Scotia the ballad is usually delivered without title, but in one case "Pretty Polly," a title which is also current in West Virginia, was suggested.

Many variants have been collected and printed, in recent years, both in Great Britain and in America. For later British references see *Journal*, XXXV, 338; Campbell and Sharp, p. 323. For American references see *Journal*, XXIX, 156–157; XXX, 286; Cox, p. 3.

A

No local title. From the singing and recitation of John Langille, River John, Pictou County.

1 There was a lord in Ambertown,
    He courted a lady gay,
And all he wanted of this pretty maid
    Was to take her life away.

2 "Go get me some of your father's gold,
    And some of your mother's fee,
And two of the best nags out of the stable,
    Where there stands thirty and three."

3 She went and got some of her father's gold,
    And some of her mother's fee,
And two of the best nags out of the stable,
    Where there stood thirty and three.

4 She mounted on the milk-white steed,
    And he on the rambling grey,
And they rode till they came to the salt seaside,
    Three hours before it was day.

5 "Light off, light off thy milk-white steed,
    And deliver it unto me,
For six pretty maids have I drownded here,
    And the seventh one thou shalt be."

6 "Take off, take off thy silken dress,
     Likewise thy golden stays.
  Methinks they are too rich and too gay
     To rot in the salt, salt seas."

7 "If I must take off my silken dress,
     Likewise my golden stays,
  You must turn your back around to me
     And face yon willow tree."

8 He turned himself around about,
     To face yon willow tree;
  She grasped him by the middle so tight,
     And she tumbled him into the sea.

9 "Lie there, lie there, you false-hearted man,
     Lie there instead of me,
  For six pretty maids thou hast drownded here;
     Go keep them company!"

10 So he rolléd high and he rolléd low,
     Till he rolléd to the seaside.
  "Stretch forth your hand, my pretty Polly,
     And I'll make you my bride."

11 "Lie there, lie there, you false-hearted man,
     Lie there instead of me,
  For six pretty maids thou hast drownded here,
     But the seventh hath drownded thee!"

12 She mounted on her milk-white steed,
     And she led her rambling grey,
  And she rode forward to her father's door,
     An hour before it was day.

13 The parrot being up so early in the morn,
     It unto Polly did say,
  "I was afraid that some ruffian
     Had led you astray."

14 The old man on his pillow did lie,
     He unto the parrot did say,
  "What ails you, what ails you, you pretty Poll parrot,
     You prattle so long before day?"

15 "The old cat was at my cage door,
　　And I was afraid he was going to eat me,
　And I was calling for pretty Polly
　　To go drive the old cat away."

16 "Well turned, well turned, my pretty Poll parrot!
　　Well turned, well turned!" said she.
　"Your cage it shall be of the glittering gold,
　　And the doors of ivory.

17 "No tales, no tales, my pretty Poll parrot,
　　No tales you will tell on me.
　Your cage it shall be of the glittering gold,
　　And hung on yon willow tree."

B

From the singing and recitation of David Rogers, Pictou, Pictou County.

1 There was a lord in Ambertown,
　　He courted a lady gay,
　And all he wanted of this pretty maid
　　Was to take her life away.

2 "Go get me some of your father's gold,
　　And some of your mother's fees,
　And two of the best horses out of the stable,
　　Where there stands thirty and three."

3 She got him some of her father's gold,
　　And some of her mother's fees,
　And two of the best horses out of the stable,
　　Where there stood thirty and three.

4 She mounted on the milk-white steed,
　　And he the rambling grey,
　And they rode till they came to the river side,
　　Two hours before it was day.

5 "Slack off, slack off, my pretty Polly,
　　Slack off, slack off," said he,
　"For six pretty maids I have drownded here,
　　And the seventh you shall be!"

6   "O turn your back, you villain," she said,
    "And face yon willow tree,
For you are not fit to see
    A naked woman like me."

7   "Take off, take off those silken gowns,
    Likewise those golden stays,
For they are too rich and costly
    To be rotting in the seas."

8   "If I've got to take off those silken gowns,
    And all those golden stays,
You must turn your back, you villain," she says,
    "And face yon willow tree."

9   And as he turned his back around
    To face yon willow tree,
She caught him by the waist so small
    And plunged him into the sea.

10   "Lie there, lie there, you villain," she says,
    "Lie there, lie there," says she,
"For six pretty maids you have drownded here,
    And the seventh has drownded thee!"

11   She mounted on the milk-white steed
    And led the rambling grey;
She rode till she came to her father's house,
    Two hours before it was day.

12   The parrot in the window high
    Heard what she had to say.
"Where have you been, my pretty Polly,
    That you're out so long before day?"

13   The old man in the tower high
    Heard what the parrot said.
"What's the matter, my parrot," he said,
    "That you're hooting so long before day?"

14   "The old grey cat was at my cage door,
    And swore she would devour me.
I was only calling for fair MacConnell
    To hiss the cat away."

15 "Well said, well said, my pretty parrot!
    Well said, well said!" said she,
Your cage shall be made of the glittering gold,
    And the door of the white ivory.

16 "Hush up, hush up, my pretty parrot,
    And don't tell tales on me.
Your cage shall be made of the glittering gold,
    And hung on yon willow tree."

C

"Pretty Polly." From the singing and recitation of Mrs. Levi Langille, Marshville, Pictou County.

1 There was a lord in Ambertown
    Courted a lady fair,
And all he wanted of this pretty fair maid
    Was to take her life away.

2 "Go get me some of your father's gold
    And some of your mother's fees,
And two of the best horses in your father's stall
    Where there stands thirty and three."

3 So she mounted on her steed white milk,
    And he on his dappling grey,
And they rode forward to the sea
    Two hours before it was day.

4 "Light off, light off thy steed white milk,
    And deliver it unto me,
For six pretty maids I have drownded here,
    And the seventh one thou shalt be.

5 "Take off, take off thy bonny silk plaid,
    And deliver it unto me.
Methinks they are too rich and gay
    To rot in the salt salt sea."

6 "If I must take off my bonny silk plaid,
    Likewise my golden stays,
You must turn your back around to me
    And face yon willow tree."

7 He turned himself around about
      To face yon willow tree;
   She grasped him by the middle so small,
      And she tumbled him into the sea.

8 So he rolléd high and he rolléd low
      Till he rolléd to the seaside.
   "Stretch forth your hand, my pretty Polly,
      And I'll make you my bride."

9 "Lie there, lie there, you false-hearted man,
      Lie there instead of me,
   For six pretty maids thou hast drownded here,
      But the seventh hath drownded thee!"

10 She mounted on her steed white milk,
       And she led her dappling grey,
    And she rode forward to her father's door
       An hour before it was day.

11 The old man he, it's being awoke,
       And heard all that was said.
    "What were you prittling and prattling, my pretty Polly,
       And keeping me awake all night long?"

12 "The old cat had got up to my littock so high,
       And I was afraid she was going to eat me,
    And I was calling for pretty Polly
       To go drive the old cat away."

13 "Don't prittle, don't prattle, my pretty Polly,
       Nor tell any tales on me.
    Your cage shall be made of the glittering gold
       Instead of the greenwood tree."

2

EARL BRAND

(CHILD, NO. 7)

THE Nova Scotia version of "Earl Brand" corresponds to Child B, the Scottish version which was published by Sir Walter Scott as "The Douglas Tragedy." It is in an excellent state of preservation, with only minor changes in phraseology, and it lacks little of Child B except a few lines at the beginning and the rose-and-briar motive at the end. This concluding motive appears in the text printed by Gavin Greig (*Folk-Song of the North-East*, LVII), but it has disappeared in the transition to a new land, and the disappearance is to me no cause for sorrow. I have read my version to American audiences, and they have been amused at what they have evidently regarded as a naïve suddenness in the ending of the tale; but a story which begins without preamble, and which proceeds with grim words to grim deeds, may not unfittingly show a laconic abstention at its close.

For references to American versions see Cox, p. 18.

"The Seven Brethren." From the singing and recitation of Robert Langille, Tatamagouche, Colchester County (printed, *Quest*, pp. 60–62).

1 "Arise, arise, ye seven brethren,
       And put on your armours bright.
   Arise and take care of your younger sister,
       For the eldest went away last night."

2 'T was on the road, 't was away they rode,
       'Twas all by the light of the moon,
   Until he looked over his left shoulder
       And saw her seven brethren drawing nigh.

3 "Lie down, lie down, Lady Margaret," he said,
       "And by my two steeds stand,
   Until I fight thy seven brethren
       And thy father who's nigh at hand."

4 She stood and saw her seven brethren fall
       Without shedding a tear,
   Until she saw her father fall,
       Whom she lovéd so dear.

5   "Withhold thy hand, Lord William," she said,
       "For thy stroke it is wonderful sore.
For it's many the true lover I might have had,
       But a father I'll never have more."

6   She took her white pocket-handkerchief
       That was made of the Hollands fine,
And wiped her father's bloody bloody wound
       That ran redder than wine.

7   "Choose ye, choose ye, Lady Margaret," he said,
       "Will you here abide?"
"O no, I must go wheresoever you go,
       For you have left me here no guide."

8   He mounted her on his milky-white steed,
       And he on his dappled grey.
The bugle-horn swung by his side,
       And slowly they rode away.

9   'T was on the road, 't was away they rode,
       'T was all by the light of the moon,
Until that they came to the Erint waters
       That was raging like the main.

10   He lighted down to take a drink
       Of the spring that run so clear;
And down the stream run his good heart's blood.
       Sore she begun to fear.

11   "Lie down, lie down, Lord William," she said,
       "For you are a slain man."
"O no, it is your scarlet red cloak
       That's reflecting on the main."

12   'T was on the road, 't was away they rode,
       'T was all by the light of the moon,
Until they came to his mother's chamber door
       And there they lighted down.

13   "Arise, arise, dear mother," he says,
       "Arise and let us in,
For by all the powers that is above,
       This night my love I've won.

14   "O mother, mother, make us a bed,
     And sheathe it with the holland fine,
  And lay Lady Margaret by my side,
     And sound sound sleep we'll take."

15   Lord William he died in the middle of the night,
     Lady Margaret ere it was day,
  And every true lovers that goes together
     I wish them more luck than they.

3

THE CRUEL MOTHER

(CHILD, No. 20)

THIS version follows Group I–L in Child, where the babes, who have prophesied only hell-fire for the mother in the preceding versions, now include in their prophecy a list of seven-year penances as a prelude to the eternity in hell. For references to American texts see *Journal*, XXX, 293; Cox, p. 29.

"The Greenwood Siding." From the singing and recitation of Mrs. Ellen Bigney, Pictou, Pictou County (printed, *Journal*, XXV, 183; *Quest*, pp. 104–106).

1 There was a lady came from York,
    Down alone in the lonely
  She fell in love with her father's clerk,
    Down alone by the greenwood siding

2 She loved him well, she loved him long,
  Till at length this young maid with child she did prove.

3 She leaned her back against an oak,
  When first it bowed and then it broke.

4 She leaned herself against a thorn,
  And then her two babes they were born.

5 She took her pen-knife keen and sharp,
  And she pierced it through their innocent hearts.

6 She dug a hole seven feet deep,
  She threw them in and bid them sleep.

7 It's when this young maid was returning home,
  She saw two babes a playing ball.

8 "O babes, O babes, if you were mine,
  I would dress you up in silks so fine."

9 "O mother, O mother, when we were thine,
  You did not dress us in silks so fine.

10 "But you took your pen-knife keen and sharp,
  And you pierced it through our innocent hearts.

11 "You dug a hole seven feet deep,
   You threw us in and bid us sleep."

12 "O babes, O babes, what shall I do,
   For the wicked crime I have done unto you?"

13 "O mother, O mother, it's us can tell:
   For seven long years you shall ring a bell.

14 "And seven more like an owl in the woods,
   And seven more like a whale in the sea.

15 "The rest of your time you shall be in hell,
   And it's there you'll be fixed for eternity!"

4

CAPTAIN WEDDERBURN'S COURTSHIP

(Child, No. 46)

The following text was published by me in *Journal*, XXIII, 377, and in *The Quest of the Ballad*, pp. 108–110. In *Journal*, XXIV, 335, Barry prints a version found in Boston, and sung by a native of County Down, Ireland. See also *Journal*, XXIX, 157–158, for a version from Illinois and references by Tolman and Kittredge.

"Six Questions." From the singing and recitation of John Adamson, Westville, Pictou County.

1 The Duke of Merchant's daughter walked out one summer's day;
   She met a bold sea captain by chance upon the way.
   He says, "My pretty fair maid, if it was n't for the law
   I would have you in my bed this night, by either stock or wa'."

2 She sighed and said, "Young man, O do not me perplex,

   .   .   .   .

   You must answer me in questions six before that I gang awa,
   Or before that I lie in your bed by either stock or wa'."

3 "O what is rounder than your ring? What's higher than the
        trees?
   Or what is worse than women's tongue? What's deeper than the
        seas?
   What bird sings first? What bird sings last? Or where does the
        dew first fall?
   Before that I lie in your bed by either stock or wall."

4 "The globe is rounder than your ring; sky's higher than the
        trees;
   The devil's worse than women's tongue; Hell's deeper than the
        seas;
   The roe sings first, the thirst sings last; on earth the dew first
        falls,
   Before that I lie in your bed by either stock or wall."

5 "You must get for me some winter fruit which in December
        grew;
   You must get for me a silken cloak that ne'er a waft went through;
   A sparrow's thorn, a priest new-born, before I gang awa,
   Before that I lie in your bed by either stock or wa'."

6 "My father's got some winter fruit which in December grew;
   My mother's got a silken cloak that ne'er a waft went through;
   A sparrow's thorns they're easy found — there's one on every
      claw;
   So you and I lie in one bed, and you lie next the wa'."

7 "You must get for my wedding supper a chicken without a bone;
   You must get for my wedding supper a cherry without a stone;
   You must get for me a gentle bird, a bird without a gall,
   Before that I lie in your bed by either stock or wall."

8 "O when the chicken's in the egg I'm sure it has no bone;
   And when the cherry's in full bloom I'm sure it has no stone;
   The dove it is a gentle bird — it flies without a gall,
   Before that I lie in your bed by either stock or wall."

9 He took her by the lily-white hand and led her through the hall;
   He held her by the slender waist for fear that she would fall;
   He led her on his bed of down without a doubt at all,
   So he and she lies in one bed, and he lies next the wall.

5

YOUNG BEICHAN

(CHILD, No. 53)

THE three variants of this ballad that were sung for me in Nova Scotia agree substantially in phraseology. They all specify India (instead of London, Northumberland, or England) as the home of the noble lord, and in no case do they mention the boring of his shoulder while he is in captivity (as in Child A, B, D, E, H, I, N, and in a version orally circulated in the United States) or the tree to which he was chained in his prison (as in Child L, and in the version in oral circulation in England). The status of the Nova Scotia version may therefore be readily determined by reference to Kittredge's notes on the ballad (*Journal*, XXX, 294–296): it corresponds to the "Lord Bakeman" of early American broadsides, which was printed also in *The Forget Me Not Songster* (New York, Nafis and Cornish, about 1840), pp. 171–174, and in *The Old Forget Me Not Songster* (Boston, Locke and Dubier), pp. 171–174.

For references to British and American texts and a discussion of their variations and peculiarities see notes by Kittredge referred to above; also, Cox, p. 36.

A

"Lord Bakeman." From the singing and recitation of Alexander Harrison, Maccan, Cumberland County.

1   In India there lived a noble lord,
      His riches was beyond compare.
   He was the darling of his parents,
      And of their estate an only heir.

2   He had gold and he had silver,
      And he had houses of high degree,
   But still he never could be contented
      Until a voyage he had been to sea.

3   He sailéd east and he sailéd west
      Until he came to the Turkish shore,
   Where he was taken and put in prison,
      Where he could neither see nor hear.

4   For seven long months he lay lamenting,
      He lay lamenting in iron bands,
   There happening to see a brisk young lady,
      Who set him free from his iron chains.

5   The gaoler had one only daughter,
       A brisk young lady gay was she;
     As she was walking across the floor,
       She chanced Lord Bakeman for to see.

6   She stole the keys of her father's prison,
       And said Lord Bakeman she would set free.
     She went unto the prison door
       And opened it without delay.

7   "Have you got gold, or have you got silver?
       Have you got houses of high degree?
     What will you give the fair lady,
       If she from bondage will set you free?"

8   "Yes, I've got gold and I've got silver,
       And I've got houses of high degree.
     I'll give them all to the fair lady,
       If she from bondage set me free."

9   "It's not your silver nor your gold,
       Nor yet your houses of high degree;
     All that I want to make me happy
       And all that I crave is your fair body.

10 "Let us make a bargain and make it strong,
       For seven long years it shall stand:
     You shall not wed no other woman,
       Nor I'll not wed no other man!"

11 When seven long years were gone and past,
       When seven long years were at an end,
     She packed up all her richest clothing,
       Saying, "Now I'll go and seek my friend."

12 She sailéd east, she sailéd west,
       Until she came to the Indian shore,
     And there she never could be contented
       Till for her true love she did inquire.

13 She did inquire for Lord Bakeman's palace
       At every corner of the street.
     She inquired after Lord Bakeman's palace
       Of every person she chanced to meet.

14   And when she came to Lord Bakeman's palace
    She knocked so loud upon the ring,
There's none so ready as the brisk young porter
    To rise and let this fair lady in.

15   She asked if this was Lord Bakeman's palace,
    "Or is the lord himself within?"
"Yes, yes," replied the brisk young porter,
    "He and his bride have just entered in."

16   "Ask him to send me one ounce of bread,
    And a bottle of his wine so strong,
And ask him if he's forgot the lady
    That set him free from his iron chains."

17   The porter went unto his master
    And bowed low upon his knees.
"Arise, arise, my brisk young porter,
    And tell me what the matter is."

18   "There is a lady stands at your gate,
    And she doth weep most bitterly.
I think she is as fine a creature
    As ever I wish my eyes to see.

19   "She's got more rings on her four fingers,
    And round her waist has diamond strings.
She's got more gold about her clothing
    Than your new bride and all her kin.

20   "She wants you to send one ounce of bread,
    And a bottle of your wine so strong,
And asks if you have forgot the lady
    That set you free from your prison chains."

21   He stamped his feet upon the floor,
    He broke the table in pieces three.
"Here's adieu to you, my wedded bride,
    For this fair lady I will go and see!"

22   Then up spoke his new bride's mother,
    And she was a lady of high degree:
"'Tis you have married my only daughter."
    "Well, she's none the worse for me!"

23   "But since my fair one has arrived,
            A second wedding there shall be.
        Your daughter came on a horse and saddle,
            She may return in a coach and three."

24   He took this fair lady by the hand,
            And led her over the marble stones.
        He changed her name from Susannah fair,
            And now she is the wife of Lord Bakeman.

25   He took her by the lily-white hand,
            And led her through from room to room.
        He changed her name from Susannah fair,
            And she is called the wife of Lord Bakeman.

B

"Lord Bateman." From the singing and recitation of David Rogers, Pictou, Pictou County.   Printed, *Quest*, pp. 115–118.   This text supplies (after B 15) one stanza that is not found in A:

> She wept, she wept and wrung her hands,
>   Crying, "Alas, I am undone!
> I wish I was in my native country,
>   Across the seas there to remain."

But B lacks some of the lines elsewhere that A preserves.

C

"Lord Bateman." From the singing and recitation of John Rogers, River John, Pictou County.   Though not quite so complete as A, C preserves the first two lines of the stanza quoted from B (above).

6

LORD THOMAS AND FAIR ANNET

(CHILD, No. 73)

THE two Nova Scotia versions are both closely related to Child's D. Cox prints several texts of the same version from West Virginia, pp. 46–64, and gives references for American texts, pp. 45–46.

A

"Lord Thomas and Fair Ellinor." From the singing and recitation of Alexander Harrison, Maccan, Cumberland County.

1 Lord Thomas he was a bold forester
   And a chaser of the king's deer.
Fair Ellinor was a fine woman
   And Lord Thomas he loved her dear.

2 "Come riddle my riddle, dear mother," he said,
   "And riddle us both in one,
Whether I shall marry with Fair Ellinor
   And let the brown girl alone."

3 "The brown girl she has got money,
   Fair Ellinor she has none;
Therefore I charge thee on my blessing,
   Bring the brown girl home."

4 And as it befell on a holiday
   As many more do beside,
Lord Thomas he went to Fair Ellinor,
   That should have been his bride.

5 But when he came to Fair Ellinor's home,
   He knockéd at the ring,
Then who was so ready as Fair Ellinor
   To let Lord Thomas in.

6 "What news, what news, Lord Thomas?" she said,
   "What news hast thou brought unto me?"
"I am come to bid thee to my wedding,
   And that is sad news for thee."

7 "O God forbid, Lord Thomas," she said,
    "That such thing should ever be done!
  I thought to have been thy bride myself,
    And thou to have been the bridegroom."

8 "Come riddle my riddle, dear mother," she said,
    "And riddle it all in one,
  Whether I shall go to Lord Thomas's wedding,
    Or whether I shall let it alone."

9 "There's many that are our friends, daughter,
    And many that are our foes;
  Therefore I charge thee on my blessing
    To Lord Thomas's wedding don't go."

10 "There's many that are our friends, mother,
    If a thousand were our foes.
  Betide me life, betide me death,
    To Lord Thomas's wedding I'll go!"

11 She clothed herself in gallant attire,
    And her merry men all was seen.
  As she rode through every place
    They took her to be some queen.

12 When she came to Lord Thomas's gate
    She knockéd at the ring,
  And who was so ready as Lord Thomas
    To let Fair Ellinor in.

13 He took her by the lily-white hand
    And led her through the hall,
  And he sat her in the noblest chair
    Among the ladies all.

14 "Is this your bride?" Fair Ellinor said,
    "Methinks she looks wondrous brown.
  Thou mightst have had as fair a woman
    As ever had trod the ground."

15 "Despise her not," Lord Thomas he said,
    "Despise her not unto me;
  For better I love her little finger
    Than all your whole body!"

16   This brown girl had a little pen-knife
        Which was both keen and sharp,
   And betwixt the short ribs and the long
        She pricked Fair Ellinor to the heart.

17   "O Christ now save me, Lord Thomas," she said,
        "Methinks you look wondrous wan;
   Thou usedst to look as good a colour
        As ever the sun shone on.

18   "O art thou blind, Lord Thomas," she said,
        "Or canst thou not very well see?
   O dost thou not see my own heart's blood
        Run trickling down my knee?"

19   "O dig my grave," Lord Thomas replied,
        "Dig it both wide and deep;
   And lay Fair Ellinor by my side,
        And the brown girl at my feet."

20   Lord Thomas he had a sword by his side
        As he walked about the hall;
   He cut his bride's head from off her shoulders
        And flung it against the wall.

21   He set his sword upon the ground
        And the point against his heart.
   There never was three lovers, sure,
        That sooner did depart.

B

"Lord Thomas."   From the singing and recitation of Mrs. Jacob Langille, Marshville, Pictou County.

1   Lord Thomas he was a worthy man,
        He wore a sword by his side;
   Fair Ellinor was a beautiful bride,
        Lord Thomas he loved her full well.

2   "Come riddle, come riddle, dear mother," he said,
        "Come riddle us all in one,
   Whether I'll marry Fair Ellinor
        Or bring the brown girl at home."

3 "The brown girl she's got house and land,
       Fair Ellinor has got none;
   My son, if you will take my blessing,
       O bring the brown girl at home."

4 Lord Thomas he was a worthy man,
       He wore a sword by his side;
   Fair Ellinor was a beautiful bride,
       Lord Thomas he loved her full well.

5 When he came to Fair Ellinor's door
       He knocked so loud at the ring;
   There was none so ready as Fair Ellinor
       To rise and let him in.

6 "What news, what news, Lord Thomas?" she said,
       "What news do you bring to me?"
   "I come to invite you to my wedding;
       It is bad news for thee."

7 "The Lord forbid, Lord Thomas," she said,
       "If any such things should be.
   I'm in hopes myself to be the bride
       And you to be the bride's groom."

8 "Come riddle, come riddle, dear mother," she said,
       "Come riddle us all in one,
   Whether I'll go to Lord Thomas's wedding
       Or will I stay at home."

9 "Many a one has been your friend
       Many more has been your foe;
   My girl, if you will take my blessing
       To Lord Thomas's wedding don't go."

10 .   .   .   .
    .   .   .   .
   "Betray my life, betray my death,
       To Lord Thomas's wedding I'll go."

11 She dressed herself in riches so gay,
       Her merry maids all in green;
   And every gate that she passed by
       They took her to be a queen.

12   When she came to Lord Thomas's door
      She knocked so loud at the ring,
  There was none so ready as Lord Thomas
      To rise and let her in.

13   He took her by the lily-white hand
      And led her through the hall;
  He set her on a golden chair
      Among the ladies all.

14   "Is this your bride, Lord Thomas?" she said,
      "I think she looks wonderful black.
  You might have had as fair a one
      As ever the sun rose on."

15   "Despise her not, Fair Ellinor," he said,
      "Despise her not to me,
  For better do I like your little finger
      Than all her whole body."

16   The brown girl she being standing by
      With a pen-knife in her hand,
  Betwixt the long rib and the short
      Pierced Fair Ellinor to the heart.

17   "O what is the matter?" Lord Thomas he said,
      "I think you look wonderful pale.
  You used to have as bright a colour
      As ever the sun rose on."

18   "Are you blind, Lord Thomas?" she said,
      "Or can you not very well see?
  Don't you see my own heart's blood
      Come dribbling down to my knees?"

19   Lord Thomas he was a worthy man,
      He wore a sword by his side;
  He off with his own bride's head
      And dashed it against the wall.

20   He ordered a coffin to be made,
      A coffin both wide and deep;
  He ordered Fair Ellinor at his right side,
      And the brown girl at his feet.

7

FAIR MARGARET AND SWEET WILLIAM

(CHILD, No. 74)

THE Nova Scotia version omits the preliminary stanzas which, in Child A and B, convey the sinister prophecy of a wedding in which the Lady Margaret is to bear no part; it omits, also, the bride's dream of a bower filled with swine and a chamber full of blood; and, by way of compensation, it adds two stanzas (2 and 3) introducing the mother and sister of Margaret. In other respects it is very much like Child B.

For references to American texts see Cox, p. 65. A great many versions have been found in the United States, and a text from Ontario is printed in *Journal*, XXXI, 74.

"William and Margaret." From the recitation of Mrs. George Forbes, Little Harbour, Pictou County. Learned at her former home in Stewiacke, Halifax County (printed, *Quest*, pp. 124–126).

1 As Margaret was in her pretty bouree
        A combing her locks so fair,
    She saw the rich wedding of William go by,
        Which struck her to the heart.

2 "O mother, come quickly, come bind up my head,
        O sister, come make up my bed;
    For I have a pain that lies at my heart,
        That will bring me to my grave."

3 Her mother she quickly came bound up her head,
        Her sister she made up her bed,
    And she had a pain that lay at her heart,
        That brought her to her grave.

4 In the middle of the night, about twelve o'clock,
        All people in bed and asleep,
    The ghost of Margaret rose up again
        And stood at William's bed feet.

5 "O how do you like your pillows?" she said,
        "And how do you like your sleep?
    And how do you like your widow lady,
        That sleeps in your arms so sweet?"

6 "Well do I like my pillow," he said,
　　"And well do I like my sleep,
　But ten thousand times better do I like the ghost
　　That stands at my bed feet."

7 Then William he quickly jumped up out of bed,
　　And ran to Margaret's hall.
　There's none so ready as Margaret's mother
　　To answer William's night call.

8 "Is Margaret in her pretty bouree,
　　Or is she in the hall?"
　"She is laid out in a long white robe,
　　With her lips as cold as clay."

9 He kissed her once, he kissed her twice,
　　He kissed her three times o'er;
　He made an oath, a solemn oath,
　　And never kissed woman more.

10 Margaret died on one good day,
　　And William died on the morrow;
　Margaret died with a heart full of love,
　　And William died for sorrow.

11 Margaret was buried at the chancel gate,
　　· And William was buried at the choir;
　Out of Margaret's grave grew a beautiful rose,
　　Out of William's there grew a sweet-briar.

12 The rose grew tall and the sweet-briar too,
　　Till they could grow no higher;
　They twined together in a true lover's-knot,
　　The rose wrapped around the sweet-briar.

8

LITTLE MUSGRAVE AND LADY BARNARD

(CHILD, No. 81)

THE versions in oral circulation in Nova Scotia correspond, on the whole, to Child A. They exhibit, however, the inevitable list of omissions and changes: Little Musgrave has become Little Matha Grove, and Lord Barnard is Lord Arnold (A) or Lord Daniel (B and C); after the duel between the husband and the lover the tale comes more swiftly to its conclusion; A has a final stanza which is an importation from "Lord Thomas and Fair Annet" (as in Child D, last stanza); in B, Little Matha Grove recognizes Lord Daniel's wife by the ring on her hand, a detail which is not in Child A, but which appears in Child D, E, F, H, J, K, and L.

A composite text, made up from the following versions, was published by me in *Journal*, XXIII, 371–374 (additional stanzas in *Journal*, XXV, 182–183), and in *Quest*, pp. 14–18. For references to versions found in the United States see Kittredge, *Journal*, XXX, 309; Cox, p. 94.

A

"Little Matha Grove." From the singing and recitation of Mrs. James Gammon, River John, Pictou County.

1 'T was on a day, a high holiday,
        The best day of the old year,
    When little Matha Grove he went to church
        The holy word to hear.

2 Some came in in diamonds of gold,
        And some came in in pearls,
    And among them all was little Matha Grove,
        The handsomest of them all.

3 Lord Arnold's wife was standing by.
        On him she cast an eye,
    Saying, "You little Matha Grove, this very night
        I invite you to lie with me.

4 "Lord Arnold is away to the New Castle,
        King Henry for to see,"

    .   .   .   .

        .   .   .   .

5   So the little foot-page was standing by,
       And he heard all that was said,
   And he took to his heels to the river side,
       And he bended his breast and he swum.

6   And when he came to Lord Arnold's bower
       He knocked so hard at the ring;
   There was none so ready as Lord Arnold
       For to rise and let him in.

7   "What news, what news, my little foot page,
       Do you bring unto me?"
   "This very night little Matha Grove
       Is in bed with your wedded lady!"

8   "If this be true, be true unto me,
       Be true you bring unto me,
   I have an only daughter dear
       And your wedded lady she shall be.

9   "If this be a lie, a lie unto me,
       A lie you bring unto me,
   I'll cause a gallows to be rigged
       And hangéd you shall be."

10 So he put the bugle to his mouth,
       And he sounded loud and shrill:
   "If there's any man in bed with another man's wife,
       It is time to be hastening away."

11 So Lord Arnold he ordered up all his men,
       And he placed them in a row.
       .   .   .   .
           .   .   .   .

12 "What's that? what's that?" said little Matha Grove,
       "For I know the sound so well.
   It must be the sound of Lord Arnold's bugle,"
       .   .   .   .

13 "Lie still, lie still, you little Matha Grove,
       And keep me from the cold.
   It's only my father's shepherd boy,
       That's driving the sheep down in the fold."

14 So they tossed and tumbled all that night
        Till they both fell fast asleep,
    And they never knew another word
        Till Lord Arnold stood at their bed's feet.

15 "How do you like my bed?" said he,
        "And how do you like my sheet?
    And how do you like my wedded lady,
        That lies in your arms and sleeps?"

16 "Well do I like your bed," said he,
        "Well do I like your sheet,
    Better do I like your wedded lady,
        That lies in my arms and sleeps."

17 "Get up, get up, you little Matha Grove,
        And some of your clothes put on,
    That it can't be said after your death
        That I slew a naked man."

18 "How can I get up," little Matha replied,
        "And fight you for my life,
    When you have two bright swords by your side,
        And I have ne'er a knife?"

19 "If I have two bright swords by my side,
        They cost me deep in purse,
    And you shall have the best of them,
        And I shall have the worst.

20 "And you shall have the very first blow,
        And I shall have the other.
    What more then could I do for you
        If you were my own born brother?"

21 The very first blow that Matha Grove struck,
        He wounded Lord Arnold sore.
    The very first blow Lord Arnold struck,
        Little Matha could strike no more.

22 "So curséd be my hand," said he,
        "And curséd be my bride!
    They have caused me to kill the handsomest man
        That ever trod England's ground."

23 He took his lady by the hand,
    He led her through the plain,
And he never spoke another word
    Till he split her head in twain.

24 He put his sword against the ground,
    The point against his heart.
There never was three lovers
    That sooner did depart.

B

"Little Matha Grove." From the singing and recitation of Mrs. Ellen Bigney, Pictou, Pictou County.

1 'T was on a day, a high holiday,
    The best day of the old year,
When little Matha Grove he went to church
    The holy word to hear.

2 Some came in in diamonds of gold,
    And some came in in pearls,
And among them all was little Matha Grove,
    The handsomest of them all.

3 Lord Daniel's wife who was standing by,
    On him she cast her eye,
Saying, "This very night, you little Matha Grove,
    You must come with me and lie."

4 "I would n't for the world, I would n't for my life,
    For fear Lord Daniel should hear,
For I know you are Lord Daniel's wife
    By the ring on your hand you do wear."

5 "Well, what if I am Lord Daniel's wife,
    As you suppose me to be?
Lord Daniel is away to the New Castle,
    King Henry for to see."

6 So the little foot-page was standing by,
    And he heard all that was said,
And he took to his heels to the river side,
    And he bended his breast and he swum.

7 And when he came to Lord Daniel's bower
    He knocked so hard at the ring,
There was none so ready as Lord Daniel
    For to rise and let him in.

8 "What news, what news, my little foot-page,
    Do you bring unto me?"
"This very night little Matha Grove
    Is in bed with your wedded lady!"

9 So he put his bugle to his mouth,
    And he sounded loud and shrill:
"If there's any man in bed with another man's wife,
    It is time to be hastening away."

10 So Lord Daniel ordered up all his men,
    And he placed them in a row.
  . . . .
    . . . .

11 "What's that? what's that?" said little Matha Grove,
    "For I know the sound so well.
It must be the sound of Lord Daniel's bugle,"
  . . . .

12 "Lie still, lie still, you little Matha Grove,
    And keep me from the cold.
It's only my father's shepherd boy,
    That's driving sheep down in the fold."

13 They rumbled and tumbled till they both fell asleep,
    And not a word did they say
Till Lord Daniel stood by the bedside,
    Little Matha for to slay.

14 "Get up, get up, you little Matha Grove,
    And fight me for your life!"
"How can I fight when you have two bright swords,
    And I've got scarcely a knife?"

15 "You shall have the best one,
    And I shall have the worst,
And you shall have the very first blow,
    And I shall have the next."

16 The very first blow that Matha Grove struck,
    He wounded Lord Daniel sore.
The very first blow Lord Daniel struck,
    Little Matha could strike no more.

17 "Curséd be my wife," said he,
    "And curséd be my hand!
They have caused me to slay the prettiest lad
    That ever trod England's land."

C

"Little Matha Grove." From the singing and recitation of Mrs. Levi Langille, Pictou, Pictou County.

1 'T was on a day, a high holiday,
    The best day of the old year,
When little Matha Grove he went to church
    The holy word to hear.

2 Some came in in diamonds of gold,
    And some came in in pearls,
And among them all was little Matha Grove,
    The handsomest of them all.

3 Lord Daniel's wife was standing by.
    On him she cast an eye,
Saying, "You little Matha Grove, this very night
    I invite you to lie with me.

4 "Lord Daniel is away to the New Castle
    King Henry for to see,"
. . . .
    . . . .

5 So the little foot-page was standing by,
    And he heard all that was said,
And he took to his heels to the river side,
    And he bended his breast and he swum.

6 And when he came to Lord Daniel's bower
    He knocked so hard at the ring,
There was none so ready as Lord Daniel
    For to rise and let him in.

7 "What news, what news, my little foot-page,
  Do you bring unto to me?"
"This very night little Matha Grove
  Is in bed with your wedded lady."

8 So he put the bugle to his mouth
  And he sounded loud and shrill:
"If there's any man in bed with another man's wife,
  It's time to be hastening away!"

9 So Lord Daniel ordered up all his men,
  And he placed them in a row.
  .   .   .   .
       .   .   .   .

10 "What's that? what's that?" said little Matha Grove,
   "For I know the sound so well.
It must be the sound of Lord Daniel's bugle,"
       .   .   .   .

11 "Lie still, lie still, you little Matha Grove,
   And keep me from the cold.
It's only my father's shepherd boy,
   That's driving sheep down in the fold."

12 So they hustled and they tumbled till they both fell asleep,
   And nothing more did they hear
Till Lord Daniel stood at their bedside,
       .   .   .   .

13 "How do you like my bed?" said he,
   "And how do you like my sheet?
And how do you like my wedded lady,
   That lies in your arms and sleeps?"

14 "Well do I like your bed," said he,
   "Well do I like your sheet,
Better do I like your wedded lady,
   That lies in my arms and sleeps."

15 "Get up, get up, you little Matha Grove,
   And some of your clothes put on,
That it can't be said after your death
   That I slew a naked man."

16 "How can I go and fight you

. . . .

When you have two bright swords lying down by your
    side,
And I've got scarcely a knife?"

17 The very first blow that Matha Grove struck,
    He wounded Lord Daniel sore.
The very first blow Lord Daniel struck,
    Little Matha could strike no more.

18 "So cursèd be my hand," said he,
    "And cursèd be my bride!
They have caused me to kill the handsomest man
    That ever trod England's ground."

D

"Little Matha Grove." Fragment contributed by John Langille, River
John, Pictou County.

Lord Daniel's away to the New Castle
    King Henry for to see,
And this very night Little Matha Grove
    Shall lie with his wedded lady.

. . . .

"Cursed be my wife," said he,
    "And cursed be my hands,
For I have slain the best-looking man
    That ever trod England's lands."

E

"Little Matha Grove." Fragment contributed by Mrs. Jacob Langille,
Marshville, Pictou County.

So he took to his heels to the river side
    And he bended his breast and he swum;
And when he came to the dry land
    He took to his heels and he run.

9

BONNY BARBARA ALLAN

(Child, No. 84)

Of the three Nova Scotia versions the first is based upon Child A, and the second and third are fairly good representatives of group B in Child. Version A, however, cannot be dismissed with the mere remark that it is based on Child A. It corresponds closely to that version in several stanzas, but in several others it departs for distant regions, charted and uncharted. To sum up the correspondences first: — stanza 1 represents Child A, stanza 1; stanza 11, with a slight change, represents Child A, stanza 3; stanza 12 corresponds in its first line to Child A, stanza 4, and then goes a-roving; stanzas 13, 14, and 18 correspond, respectively, to stanzas 5, 7, and 9 of Child A. Of the remaining twelve stanzas in my version A the most interesting — since they are the most eccentric — are 4 and 10. As for stanza 4, it may possibly be accounted for by the amplified version of the Buchan MS., in which the dying lover leaves the freights of nine ships to Barbara Allan, although there is no other evidence of connection with that version. As for stanza 10, it is a brief and strange excursion into the phraseology of "Sir Patrick Spens," or "Lord Derwentwater," or "Geordie." Version A from Nova Scotia, take it for all in all, is a queer and unaccountable composite.

Versions B and C present no special difficulties. Version B roughly resembles Child Bd (Percy's *Reliques*), though it differs in the following respects: it sends a letter, instead of a messenger, to Barbara Allan; it introduces the slighting of Barbara during the drinking of healths at the tavern, as in Child A; it adds the rose-and-briar motive at the end. As for Version C, it is remarkably reminiscent of Child Bd; it retains "yong Jemmye Grove" (slightly modified to "Young Jimmy Groves") as the lover, and in all other respects, except for the omission of a few stanzas, it corresponds closely to that version.

For references to American texts see *Journal*, XXIX, 160; XXX, 317; XXXV, 343; Cox, p. 96.

A

"Barbara Allan." From the singing and recitation of Alexander Harrison, Maccan, Cumberland County.

1 It fell about the Martinmas day
    When the green leaves were falling,
  Sir James the Graeme in the West Country
    Fell in love with Barbara Allan.

2 She was a fair and comely maid,
    And a maid nigh to his dwelling,
  Which made him to admire the more
    The beauty of Barbara Allan.

3 " O what's thy name, my bonny maid,
    Or where has thou thy dwelling?"
She answered him most modestly,
    "My name is Barbara Allan."

4 "O see you not yon seven ships,
    So bonny as they are sailing?
I'll make you mistress of them all,
    My bonny Barbara Allan."

5 But it fell out upon a day,
    At the wine as they were drinking,
They toasted their glasses round about
    And slighted Barbara Allan.

6 O she has taken it so ill out
    That she'd no more look on him,
And for all the letters he could send
    Still swore she'd never have him.

7 "O if I had a man, a man,
    A man within my dwelling,
That will write a letter with my blood,
    And carry it to Barbara Allan,

8 "Daring her to come here with speed,
    For I am at the dying,
And speak one word to her true love,
    For I'll die for Barbara Allan."

9 His man is off with all his speed
    To the place where she is dwelling:
"Here's a letter from my master dear,
    Give ye to Barbara Allan."

10 O when she looked the letter upon,
    With a loud laughter gi'ed she;
But ere she read the letter through,
    The tears blinded her eye.

11 O hasty, hasty rose she up,
    And slowly gaed she to him,
And slightly drew the curtains by:
    "Young man, I think you're dying!"

11 "Father dear, dig me a grave,
    Go dig it deep and narrow!
My true love died for me today,
    I'll die for him tomorrow."

12 So in the churchyard they were laid,
    Those two and only lovers.
On her grave there grew a rose,
    On his there grew a briar.

13 They grew, they grew to the steeple's top,
    Till they could grow no higher,
Then they formed a true love's-knot
    For the lovers to admire.

C

"Barbary Ellen." From the singing and recitation of Mrs. Jacob Langille,
Marshville, Pictou County.

1 It was the very month of May,
    And the green buds they were swelling.
Young Jimmy Groves on his death-bed lay
    For the love of Barbary Ellen.

2 He sent his man down to the town
    In the place where she was dwelling:
"Make haste and come to my master's house,
    If your name is Barbary Ellen."

3 Slowly, slowly she got up,
    And so slowly she came nigh him.
"I cannot keep you from your grave;
    Young man, I think you're dying."

4 He turned his back unto her then,
    A deadly swound he fell in;
He bid adieu to all his friends,
    And adieu to Barbary Ellen.

5 As she was walking in the plain
    She heard the death-bell tolling,
And every stroke it seemed to say,
    "O cruel Barbary Ellen."

6   As she was walking on the road
        She met the corpse a coming.
    "Lay down, lay down the corpse," she said,
        "That I may look upon him."

7   The more she looked the more she laughed
        For the love that he had for her,
    While all of her friends cried out, "For shame,
        O cruel Barbary Ellen!"

8   When he was dead and laid in grave
        Her heart was struck with sorrow:
    "O mother, mother, make me a bed,
        For I will die to-morrow.

9   "Hard-hearted creature that I was,
        Who lovéd me so dearly.
    O that I had more kinder been
        When he was alive and near me.

10   "Come young and old, both great and small
        And shun the fall I fell in;
    Henceforth take warning by the fall
        Of cruel Barbary Ellen."

10

YOUNG JOHNSTONE

(CHILD, No. 88)

THE two interesting texts found in Nova Scotia differ markedly in form, and are obviously derived from two distinct traditions. Version A does not follow any of the Child versions closely, nor does it seem to have been influenced by the altered text in Pinkerton's *Select Scotish Ballads* (I, 69) or the free version in Chambers's *Twelve Romantic Scottish Ballads* (p. 293). In the absence of the dream, and in the description of the hawk, hound, and steed (coloured, respectively, dark gray, light gray, and milk-white), it is reminiscent of Child C, but in most respects it is very unlike that version. As for Version B, it is clearly enough a variant of Child D, which begins: "Johnston Hey and Young Caldwell." It has the same dreams of swine and the bride's bed, and of lions and ravens (the latter strangely transformed, through the medium of corbies, to "corbet"), and the same evasive explanation from the slayer, to account for his absence, that he has been at "yon state house" — a corruption of "yon slate house" in Child D. Here, however, there is a curious composite of influence in the lines

> I have been at yon state house,
> Learning young Clark to write.

In Child B Johnstone tells his sister,

> I hae been at the school, sister,
> Learning young clerks to sing,

repeating the explanation, later, to his sweetheart. In Child D he tells his mother, his sister, and his sweetheart, in answer to their successive questions,

> O I hae been at yon new slate house
> Hearing the clergy speak.

A

"Johnson and the Colonel." From the singing and recitation of John Henderson, Tatamagouche, Colchester County (printed, *Quest*, pp. 120–124).

1   As Johnson and the young Colonel
      Together were drinking wine,
   Says Johnson to the young Colonel,
      "If you 'll marry my sister, I 'll marry thine."

2   "No, I 'll not marry your sister,
      Nor shall you marry mine,
   For I will keep her for a miss
      As I go through the town."

3 Young Johnson has drawn his broad bright sword
  Which hung low down to the ground,
 And he has given the young Colonel
  A deep and deadly wound.

4 Then mounting on his milk-white steed,
  He swiftly rode away
 Until he came to his sister's house
  Long, long ere the break of day.

5 "Alight, alight, young Johnson," she said,
  "And take a silent sleep,
 For you have crossed wide wide waters,
  Which are both wide and deep."

6 "I cannot light, I cannot light,
  Nor neither sleep can I,
 For I have killed the young Colonel,
  And for it I did fly."

7 "O have you killed the young Colonel?
  O woe be unto thee!
 To-morrow's morn at eight o'clock
  It's hangéd you shall be."

8 "O hold your tongue, you cruel woman,
  O hold your tongue," said he,
 "How can I trust to a strange lady
  If I cannot trust to thee?"

9 He's mounted on his nimble steed
  And swiftly rode away,
 Until he came to his own true love
  Long, long ere break of day.

10 "Alight, alight, young Johnson," she said,
  "And take a silent sleep,
 For you have crossed the stormy waters,
  Which are both wide and deep."

11 "I can't alight, I cannot stop,
  Nor either sleep can I,
 For I have killed the young Colonel
  And for it I must fly."

12 "O have you killed my brother?" she said,
   "O what shall now be done?
   But come into my chamber,
   I'll secure you from all harm."

13 She's lockéd up his hawks
   And she's lockéd up his hounds,
   And she's lockéd up the nimble steed
   That bore him from the ground.

14 She's lockéd one, she's lockéd two,
   She's lockéd three or four,
   And then she stood for his life-guard
   Behind the entry door.

15 On looking east and looking west
   She happened for to see
   Four and twenty of the King's Life Guards
   Come riding merrily.

16 "O did you see young Johnson?" they said,
   "Or did he pass by this way?
   For he has killed the young Colonel,
   And for it he did fly."

17 "What color was his hawk?" she said,
   "And what color was his hound?
   And what color was his nimble steed
   That bore him from the ground?"

18 "A dark gray was his hawk," they said,
   "And a light gray was his hound,
   And a milk-white was the nimble steed
   That bore him from the ground."

19 "Then ride away, O ride away,
   And quickly ride, I pray;
   Or I fear he'll be out of London Town
   Long, long ere the dawn of day."

20 She went into his chamber
   For to tell him what she had done,
   And he has pierced his lovely dear
   That ne'er did him any wrong.

21 Young Johnson being in a silent sleep
And dreaming they were near,
He has drawn his bright broad shining sword
And pierced his lovely dear.

22 "What cause for this, dear Johnson?" she said,
"O what is this you've done?
For you have pierced your dearest dear
That ne'er did you any wrong."

23 "O can you live? O can you live?
Can you live but one single half hour?
And all the doctors in London Town
Shall be within your bower."

24 "I cannot live, I cannot live!
O how can I live?" said she,
"For don't you see my very heart's blood
Come trickling down from my knee?

25 "O ride away, you ride away,
And quickly get over the plain,
And never let it once enter your mind
That your own true love you've slain."

B

"Johnson and Coldwell." From the singing and recitation of David Rogers, Pictou, Pictou County.

1 As Johnson and the young Coldwell
Was a drinking of their wine
Says Johnson unto young Coldwell,
"If you marry my sister I'll marry thine."

2 "I'll not marry your sister,
Or you'll not marry mine,
But as I go through yonder town
I'll make her my Clementine."

3 Johnson had a broadsword by his side,
Which was both keen and bright,
And 'twixt the long ribs and the short
He pierced young Coldwell's heart.

4   He got up and he rode down
       By the clear light of the moon,
    Until he came to his mother's tower,
       And there he lighted down.

5   "Where have you been, dear son," she said,
       "So far and so late in the night?"
    "I've been down to yon state house,
       Learning young Clark to write."

6   "I dreamt a dream, dear son," she said —
       "And I hope it may be for your good —
    That the lions were nopping your noble blood,
       And corbet be your flesh for food."

7   "To dream of lions, dear mother," he said,
       "Is the losing of a friend,
    For I have murdered young Coldwell,
       And I'm afraid in my heart I'll be slain."

8   He got up and he rode down
       By the clear light of the moon,
    Until he came to his sister's tower,
       And there he lighted down.

9   "Where have you been, dear brother," she said,
       "So far and so late in the night?"
    "It's I've been down to yon state house,
       Learning young Clark to write."

10 "I dreamt a dream, dear brother," she said —
       "I hope it may be for your good —
    That the lions were nopping your noble blood,
       And corbet be your flesh for food."

11 "To dream of lions, dear sister," he said,
       "Is the losing of a friend,
    For I have murdered young Coldwell,
       And I'm afraid in my heart I'll be slain."

12 He got up and he rode down
       By the clear light of the moon,
    Until he came to his true love's tower,
       And there he lighted down.

13   "Where have you been, my dear," she said,
    "So far and so late in the night?"
"It's I've been down to yon state house,
    Learning young Clark to write."

14   "I dreamt a dream, my dear," she said —
    "And I hope it may be for your good —
That your bride's bed was covered with young swine,
    And the sheets were stained with blood."

15   "To dream of swine, my dear," he said,
    "Is the losing of a friend,
For I have murdered your brother Coldwell,
    And I'm afraid in my heart I'll be slain."

16   "Lie down, lie down, my dear," she said,
    "And your guard I now will be,
For I love your little finger better
    Than my brother's whole body."

17   She went unto her tower window
    To see what she could see.
There she spied four and twenty young English lords
    Come riding towards her tower.

18   "Did you see the murderer?" they said,
    "Or did he pass this way?
White was the steed that he rode on,
    And blue was the clothes that he wore."

19   "O yes, I saw the murderer," she said,
    "He passed about twelve in the day.
If that be the description you give of him,
    He's near to London Town."

20   She went unto her own true love
    With good tidings for to bring,
And with a penknife in his hand
    He pierced her to the heart.

21   "Can you live at all?" he said.
    "Can you live one half hour?
I'll have all the doctors in this land
    To come within your tower."

22 "I cannot live at all," she said,
      "I cannot live one half hour.
  I tried your precious life to save
      To the utmost of my power."

23 He stuck his sword all in the ground,
      And the point fornent his heart,
  And for the sake of his own true love
      He pierced his faithful heart.

11

SIR JAMES THE ROSE

(Child, No. 213)

The two substantially similar versions that follow represent "Sir James the Ross," an unacknowledged adaptation, by Michael Bruce, of the old Scottish ballad "Sir James the Rose" (Child, No. 213). It first appeared in *The Weekly Magazine or Edinburgh Amusement*, September 20, 1770, IX, 371–373, with the superscription "Sir James the Ross, an Ancient Historical Ballad." See Grosart, *The Works of Michael Bruce*, pp. 197–205, for a reprinted copy, and the same work, pp. 257–260, for notes and a copy of Bruce's ballad as it was published, with alterations, by Logan in 1770. Child remarks that this adaptation "has perhaps enjoyed more favor with 'the general' than the original" (*English and Scottish Popular Ballads*, IV, 156). The current title in Scotland, apparently, was not "Sir James the Ross," but "Sir James the Rose" (see, for instance, Whitelaw's *Book of Scottish Ballads*, p. 41). The Nova Scotia versions, derived from Scottish tradition, regularly employ this older title and the corresponding designation of the hero throughout the ballad.

A

"Sir James the Rose." From the singing and recitation of Robert Reid, River John, Pictou County.

1   Of all the Scottish northern chiefs
      Of high and warlike name,
    The bravest was Sir James the Rose,
      A knight of muckle fame.

2   His growth was like the youthful oak
      That crowns the mountain brow,
    And waving o'er his shoulders broad
      The locks of yellow flew.

3   Wide were his fields, his herds were large,
      And large his flocks of sheep,
    And numerous were his goats and deers
      Upon the mountains steep.

4   In bloody fight thrice had he stood
      Against the English keen,
    Ere two and twenty opening springs
      The blooming youth had seen.

5 The fair Matilda dear he loved,
  A maid of beauty rare;
Even Margaret on the Scottish throne
  Was never half so fair.

6 Long had he wooed, long she refused
  With seeming scorn and pride.
At length her eyes confessed the love
  Her fearful words denied.

7 Her father, Buchan's cruel lord,
  Their passion disapproved;
He bade her wed Sir John the Graeme,
  And leave the youth she loved.

8 One night they met as they were wont,
  Down by a shady wood,
Where on the bank beside the burn
  A blooming saught tree stood.

9 Concealed beneath the underwood
  The crafty Donald lay,
A brother to Sir John the Graeme,
  To hear what they might say.

10 And thus the maid began, "My sire
   Our passion disapproves.
He bids me wed Sir John the Graeme,
   So here must end our loves.

11 "My father's will must be obeyed,
   Naught boots me to withstand.
Some fairer maid in beauty's bloom
   Shall bless thee with her hand.

12 "Soon will Matilda be forgot
   And from thy mind effaced,
But may the happiness be thine
   Which I can never taste."

13 "What do I hear? Is this thy vow?"
   Sir James the Rose replied,
"And will Matilda wed the Graeme,
   Though sworn to be my bride?"

14   "His sword shall sooner pierce my heart
        Than reave me of my charms" —
     Then clasped her to his throbbing breast,
        Fast locked within his arms.

15   "I spoke to try thy love," said she,
        "I'll ne'er wed man but thee.
     The grave shall be my bridal bed
        Ere Graeme my husband be.

16   "Take then, dear love, this faithful kiss
        In witness of my troth.
     May every plague become thy lot
        The day I break my oath!"

17   They parted thus, the sun was set,
        Up hasty Donald flies;
     Then, "Turn thee, turn thee, beardless youth!"
        He loud, insulting cries.

18   Then turned about the fearless chief,
        And soon his sword he drew,
     For Donald's blade before his face
        Had pierced his tartans through.

19   "'T is for my brother's slighted love,
        His wrongs sit on my arm."
     Three paces back the youth retired,
        And saved himself from harm.

20   Returning swift his sword he reared
        Fierce Donald's head above,
     And through the head and crashing bone
        The furious weapon drove.

21   Life issued at the wound. He fell
        A lump of lifeless clay.
     "So fall my foes!" quoth valiant Rose,
        And stately strode away.

22   Through the green woods in haste he passed
        Unto Lord Buchan's hall,
     Beneath Matilda's window stood,
        And thus on her did call:

23   "Art thou asleep, Matilda dear?
      Awake, my love, awake!
  Behold, thy lover waits without,
      A long farewell to take.

24   "For I have slain fierce Donald Graeme,
      His blood is on my sword;
  And far, far distant are my men,
      Nor can assist their lord.

25   "To Skye I will direct my flight,
      Where my brave brothers bide,
  To raise the mighty of the Isles
      To combat on my side."

26   "Oh do not so," the maid replied,
      "With me till morning stay,
  For dark and dreary is the night,
      And dangerous is the way.

27   "All night I'll watch you in the park,
      My faithful page I'll send
  In haste to raise the brave clan Rose
      Their master to defend."

28   He laid him down beneath a bush,
      And wrapped him in his plaid,
  While trembling for her lover's sake
      At distance stood the maid.

29   Swift ran the page o'er hill and dale,
      Till in a lonely glen
  He met the furious John the Graeme
      With twenty of his men.

30   "Where goest thou, little page?" he said,
      "So late who didst thou send?"
  "I go to raise the brave clan Rose,
      Their master to defend.

31   "For he has slain fierce Donald Graeme,
      His blood is on his sword,
  And far, far distant are his men
      Nor can assist their lord."

32 "And he has slain my brother dear,"
   The furious chief replied;
"Dishonour blast my name, but he
   By me ere morning dies!

33 "Say, page, where sleeps Sir James the Rose,
   And I'll thee much reward."
"He sleeps in Lord Buchan's park,
   Matilda is his guard."

34 They spurred their steeds and furious flew
   Like lightning o'er the lea;
They reached Lord Buchan's lofty towers
   By dawning of the day.

35 Matilda stood without the gate
   Upon a rising ground,
And viewed each object in the dawn,
   All ear to every sound.

36 "Where sleeps the Rose?" began the Graeme,
   "Or has the villain fled?
This hand shall lay the wretch on earth
   By whom my brother's bled."

37 At this the valiant knight awoke,
   The virgin shrieking heard.
Straight he rose and drew his sword
   When the fierce band appeared.

38 "Your sword last night my brother slew,
   His blood yet dims its shine,
But ere the sun shall gild the morn
   Your blood shall reek on mine."

39 "Your words are brave," the chief replied,
   "But deeds approve the man.
Set by your men, and hand to hand
   We'll try what valour can."

40 Four of his men, the bravest four,
   Fell down beneath his sword,
But still he scorned the poor revenge,
   But sought their haughty lord.

41 Till basely behind him came the Graeme
    And pierced him in the side;
Out spouting came the purple stream,
    And all his tartans dyed.

42 But yet his hand dropped not the sword,
    Nor sank he to the ground,
Till through his enemy's heart the steel
    Had pierced a mortal wound.

43 Graeme like a tree by wind o'erthrown
    Fell breathless on the clay,
While down beside him sank the Rose,
    Who faint and dying lay.

44 Matilda saw and fast she ran.
    "Oh spare his life!" she cried.
"Lord Buchan's daughter begs his life;
    Let her not be denied."

45 Her well-known voice the hero heard,
    And raised his death-closed eyes,
And fixed them on the weeping maid,
    And weakly this replies:

46 "In vain Matilda begs a life
    By death's arrest denied.
My race is run. Adieu, my love!"
    Then closed his eyes and died.

47 The sword yet warm from his left side
    With frantic hand she drew.
"I come, Sir James the Rose," she cried,
    "I come to follow you!"

48 The hilt she leaned against the ground
    And bared her snowy breast,
And fell upon her lover's face,
    And sank to endless rest.

B

"Sir James the Rose." From the singing and recitation of George Forbes,
Little Harbour, Pictou County.

1 Of all the northern Scottish chiefs
    Of high and warlike fame,
The bravest was Sir James the Rose,
    That knight of muckle fame.

2 His growth was like the tifted fir
    That crowns the mountain's brow,
And waving o'er his shoulders broad
    His locks of yellow hue.

3 The chieftain of that brave clan Rose,
    A firm undaunted band,
Five hundred warriors drew their swords
    Beneath his brave commands.

4 In bloody fights thrice had he stood
    Before the English keen,
Ere two and twenty opening springs
    That blooming youth had seen.

5 One fair Matilda dear he loved,
    A maid of beauty rare;
Even Margaret on the Scottish throne
    Was never half so fair.

6 Long had he wooed, long she refused
    With seeming scorn and pride.
After her eyes convinced her love
    Her faithful tongue denied.

7 One day they met as they had wont
    Down by a shady wood,
All on a bank beneath the blawn
    A blooming saw-tree stood.

8 Concealed beneath the underwood
    The crafty Donald lay,
A brother to Sir John the Graeme,
    To hear what they would say.

9 With this the maid began, "My sire
    Our passion disapproves,
And bids me wed Sir John the Graeme,
    So here must end our love.

10 "My father's will must be obeyed,
    Naught puts me to withstand.
Some fairer maid of beauty rare
    Will bless you with her hand."

11 "What's this I hear? Is this thy vow?"
    Sir James the Rose replied,
"And will Matilda wed the Graeme
    Though sworn to be my bride?

12 "My sword will sooner pierce my heart
    Than reft me of thy charms."
Then clasped her to his beating breast,
    Fast locked up in his arms.

13 "I only spoke to try your love,
    No one I'll wed but thee.
My grave shall be my bridal bed
    Ere Graeme my husband be."

14 The sun being set, they parted thus;
    Up hastily Donald flies.
"O turn! O turn, you beardless youth!"
    He bold insulting cries.

15 Then turned about the fearless chief,
    And quick his sword he drew,
For Donald's blade before his breast
    Had pierced his tartan through.

16 "This for my brother's slighted love!
    His wrongs lie on my arm."
Three paces back the youth retired,
    And saved himself from harm.

17 Then turning round, his sword he reared
    O'er Donald's head above,
And through his brains and shattering bone
    His sharp-edged weapon drew.

18   Graeme like a tree by wind o'erthrown
     Fell breathless on the clay.
  "There falls my foe!" said valiant Rose,
     And quickly strode away.

19   Then through the greenwood quick he hied
     Without the least delay.
  He reached Lord Buchan's lofty bowers
     And softly then did say:

20   "Art thou asleep, Matilda dear?
     Awake, my love! Awake!
  A luckless lover calls on thee
     A long farewell to take.

21   "For I have slain Sir Donald Graeme,
     His blood yet dims my sword,
  And far, far distant are the men
     That would me help afford.

22   "To Skye I'll now direct my way
     Where my bold brethren bide.
  I'll raise the chiefest of that isle
     To combat on my side."

23   "O, do not so!" the maid replied,
     "With me till morning stay;
  For dark and dismal is the night
     And dreary is the way.

24   "All night I'll watch thee in the park.
     My faithful page I'll send
  To run and raise the Rose's men,
     Their master to defend."

25   Swift runs the page o'er hill and dale,
     Till in a lonely glen
  He met the furious Sir John Graeme
     With twenty of his men.

26   "Where run you so, my little page?
     Who did thee so late send?"
  "I run to raise the Rose's men
     Their master to defend.

27 "For he has slain Sir Donald Graeme,
      His blood yet dims his sword,
  And far, far distant are the men
      That should him help afford."

28 "O has he slain my brother dear?"
      The furious Graeme replies.
  "Dishonour blast my name but he
      By me ere morning dies!

29 "Tell me where is Sir James the Rose?
      I will thee well reward."
  "He lies into Lord Buchan's park,
      Matilda is his guard."

30 They swiftly pricked their sweating steeds,
      And scoured along the lea,
  And reached Lord Buchan's lofty bowers
      By dawning of the day.

31 Matilda stood without the gate,
      To whom the Graeme did say,
  "Saw ye Sir James the Rose last night,
      Or did he pass this way?"

32 "Last night at noon," Matilda said,
      "Sir James the Rose passed by.
  He furious pricked his sweating steed
      And onward past did ride.

33 "He's by this time in Edinboro Town
      If horse and man hold good."
  "Your page then lies who said he was
      A sleeping in this wood!"

34 She wrung her hands and tore her hair.
      "Brave Rose, thou art betrayed,
  And ruined by those very means
      By which I hoped thine aid."

35 With this the hero he awoke,
      Her well-known voice he heard,
  He quickly rose and drew his sword
      Ere the fierce band appeared.

36 "Last night your sword my brother slew,
    His blood yet dims its shine,
But ere the rising of the sun
    Your blood shall shine on mine."

37 "You 're worded well," the youth replies,
    "But it 's deeds that prove the man.
Lay by your men and, sword to sword,
    We 'll try what valour can."

38 Then forward trod with dauntless steps
    And dared him to the fight,
But Graeme gave back and feared his sword,
    For well he knew its might.

39 Four of his men, the bravest four,
    Sank down beneath his sword,
But still he scorned that poor revenge
    And sought their haughty lord.

40 Then basely came the Graeme behind
    And stabbed him in the side;
Out spurting came the purple gore,
    And all his tartans dyed.

41 His hand yet never quit the grip,
    Nor fell he to the ground,
Till through his enemy's heart his sword
    Had pierced a mortal wound.

42 Graeme staggered, reeled, and tumbled down,
    A lump of breathless clay;
Then down beside him sank the Rose,
    And faintish dying lay.

43 The sad Matilda saw him fall.
    "O spare his life!" she cried,
"Lord Buchan's daughter begs a life.
    Let her not be denied!"

44 Her well-known voice the hero heard
    And raised his death-closed eyes.
He fixed them on the weeping maid,
    And weakly thus replies:

45 "Matilda begs a life in vain,
    Denied by death's arrest."
Then bowed his head and closed his eyes,
    And sank to endless rest.

46 His sword yet warm by his right side
    With frantic hand she drew.
"I come, Sir James the Rose," she cried,
    "I come to follow you!"

47 She put the hilt unto the ground,
    Then bared her snow-white breast,
And fell upon her lover's sword,
    And sank to endless rest.

I 2

ANDREW LAMMIE

(CHILD, No. 233)

THE three stanzas of the following fragment are all that I have been able to collect of a ballad that was once current among the Scotch people in the northern counties of Nova Scotia. The first of these was given to me by John Henderson of Tatamagouche, Colchester County, a veteran who had sung this song and many others in his youth, but who, when he tried to go beyond the first verse of "Andrew Lammie" for me, was estopped by the weariness and the mere oblivion of a hundred years. The second and third stanzas were contributed by Alexander Sutherland of Toney River, Pictou County, who could almost, but not quite, recollect a good many others. The resultant constitutes a slight fragment of Child C, the first stanza corresponding to stanza 1 of the Child version, the second combining stanzas 37 and 38, and the third corresponding to stanza 40, but modified by the influence of a stanza from "Barbara Allan."

Versions of the ballad are printed by Whitelaw (*Book of Scottish Ballads*, pp. 265–267), and by Greig (xv, xvi, xxxiv). It is also in the following chapbook collections in the Harvard College Library: 25263.23, No. 13; 25252.19 (second chapbook in collection made by John Bell, Newcastle; printed by R. Hutchison, Glasgow).

1   In Mill o' Tiftie there lived a man,
        In the neighbourhood of Fyvie.
    He had an only daughter fair,
        Her name was bonny Annie.

. . . .

2   Her father beat her wondrous sore
        With heavy strokes a many.
    Her mother did her daily scorn,
        But woe be to her brother!

. . . .

3   "O mother dear, make me my bed,
        And make it soft and bonny.
    My true love died for me today,
        I'll die for him tomorrow."

13

HENRY MARTYN

(CHILD, No. 250)

ONE of the songs that Little Ned Langille sang for me before he left this world was "Bolender Martin," and the only excuse that I can offer for my shameful inability to reconstruct more than the following fragment is that of my extreme youth and unawareness at the time of the singing. When I began my work of collecting (after Ned's death) I made special efforts to recover some version of this ballad, and, failing in these efforts, I present the bit that I can recollect with certainty as a remnant and reminder of an old Nova Scotia tradition. The tune I remember clearly enough, and I shall set it down in the Appendix. As for the title "Bolender Martin," it is, pretty obviously, a corruption (introduced by Little Ned himself or by some of his singing predecessors) of "Bold Andrew Martin." The ballad, which was probably derived from the older "Sir Andrew Barton," was current both as "Henry Martyn" and as "Andrew Bartin," and the process of fusion and corruption which resulted in Little Ned's title will be readily imagined by the student of such matters.

For references to American and recent English versions see Kittredge, *Journal*, XXX, 327. Cox prints a version from West Virginia (pp. 150–151), and Gray reproduces a text from *Journal*, XVIII, 302–303 (pp. 80–81).

1 There lived three brothers in fair Scotland,
      In Scotland there lived brothers three.
   And they drew lots to see which would go
      A robbing all on the salt sea.

2 The lot it fell on Bolender Martin,
      The youngest of the three,
   That he should turn robber all on the salt sea
      To maintain his two brothers and he.

3 .   .   .   .
      .   .   .   .
   "I am the rich merchant from fair Engeland,
      And I pray you to let me pass by."

4 "Oh no, oh no," says Bolender Martin,
      "That thing can never be,
   For I have turned robber all on the salt sea,
      To maintain my two brothers and me."

14

OUR GOODMAN

(CHILD, No. 274)

THE following version, so far as it goes, corresponds pretty closely to Child A.
The song used to be a great favourite in the Scotch communities in the north
of Nova Scotia, but the Scotch inhabitants of Nova Scotia for the most part
gave up their ballads many years ago. The fragment which I present was
recollected by my mother from the singing of a maid in her home at Durham,
Pictou County.

For references see *Journal*, XXIX, 166; XXX, 328; XXXV, 348; Cox, p. 154.
Cox presents three variants of Child A from West Virginia.

1   O hame came our goodman at e'en,
        And hame came he,
    And there he saw a horse
        Where nae a horse should be.

2   "O how came this horse here?
        And how came he here?
    O how came this horse here
        Without the leave o' me?"

3   "O ye puir blind doted body,
        Blinder mat ye be!
    It's but a bonny milk cu
        Me mither sent to me."

4   "A milk cu?" quo' he.
    "Aye, a milk cu," quo' she.

5   "O lang hae I ridden,
        And muckle hae I seen,
    But a saddle on a milk cu
        Saw I never nane."

6   O hame came our goodman at e'en,
        And hame came he,
    And there he saw a coat
        Where nae a coat should be.

7   "O how came this coat here?
        And how came it here?
    O how came this coat here
        Without the leave o' me?"

8   "O ye puir blind doted body,
      Blinder mat ye be!
  It's but a bonny blanket
      Me mither sent to me."

9   "A blanket?" quo' he.
  "Aye, a blanket," quo' she.

10   "O lang hae I ridden,
      And muckle hae I seen,
  But buttons on a blanket
      Saw I never nane."

11   O hame came our goodman at e'en,
      And hame came he,
  And there he saw a sword
      Where nae a sword should be.

12   "O how came this sword here?
      And how came it here?
  O how came this sword here
      Without the leave o' me?"

13   "O ye puir blind doted body,
      Blinder mat ye be!
  It's but a bonny parritch stick
      Me mither sent to me."

14   "A parritch stick?" quo' he.
  "Aye, a parritch stick," quo' she.

15   "O lang hae I ridden,
      And muckle hae I seen,
  But tassels on a parritch stick
      Saw I never nane."

15

THE FARMER'S CURST WIFE

(CHILD, No. 278)

THE following version is fairly similar to Child A. Several versions and fragments of the song have been found in the United States: see *Journal*, xxx, 329; Cox, p. 164.

"The Devil's Song." From the singing of David Rogers, Pictou, Pictou County.

1   It 's of a farmer who lived in York,
He had an old wife and he wished her in hell.

Chorus
Sing fal the di daddy
Sing fal the di daddy
Sing fal the di daddy
Sing fal the di day

2   The devil came to him when he was at plough,
Saying, "One of your family I must have now."

3   "O take her, O take her with all of my heart,
I hope you two devils you will never part!"

4   The devil he took her, put her into a sack;
He off to hell with her onto his back.

5   She saw three little devils all dancing in chains.
She off with her cloak to knock out their damn brains.

6   The three little devils to their father did bawl,
"This old devil will murder us all!"

7   The women, they say, are ten times worse than the men,
For when they 're in hell they 're kicked out again.

16

THE MERMAID

(CHILD, NO. 289)

THIS slight fragment is all that I have been able to recover in Nova Scotia of the true folk rendition of "The Mermaid." The ballad is well known there and elsewhere as a college song, and it has been printed times without number in broadsides and song-books both in Great Britain and in America. As a sailor song it is reproduced in such collections as Davis and Tozer's *Sailor Songs or "Chanties"* (pp. 92–93) and Ashton's *Real Sailor-Songs* (pp. 41–42). The old man who sang the fragment for me is not himself a sailor, but he has spent a good part of his life working in and about the vessels at the wharves of his native town, and there he acquired this bit and other snatches of the sailors' songs.

For references to British and American texts see Kittredge, *Journal*, XXVI, 175; Cox, p. 172. Add Spaeth, *Read 'em and Weep*, 1927, pp. 81–83.

"The *Royal George*." From the singing and recitation of Ephraim Tattrie, Tatamagouche, Colchester County.

1 "O I thought more of my greasy pots and pans
     As you did of your three wives,
     All three, all three, all three,
  As you done of all your three wives."

2 O the *Royal George* turned round three times,
     And down to the bottom she did go,
     She did go, she did go, she did go,
  All down to the bottom of the sea.

17

THE TURKISH LADY

THE title of this song is sometimes used for "Young Beichan" ("Lord Bate-man"), and one may suppose that the song itself, with its jingling lines and rather colourless narrative, is simply an inferior retelling of the tale in the old ballad. Logan (*A Pedlar's Pack*, p. 11) conjectures that it was composed about the middle of the seventeenth century, and compares it with "The Spanish Lady's Love to an Englishman."

"The Turkish Lady" has been printed many times in England, and it appeared in some of the American songsters of the last century. For references see Kittredge, *Journal*, XXX, 296–297.

A

"The Turkish Lady." From the singing and recitation of Peter Hines, Tatamagouche, Colchester County.

1   Young virgins all, I pray draw near,
     A pretty story you shall hear.
     'Twas of a Turkish lady brave
     That fell in love with an English slave.

2   A merchant ship at Bristol lay
     As we were sailing o'er the sea.
     By a Turkish slaver took were we,
     And all of us made slaves to be.

3   They bound us down in irons strong,
     They whipped and lashed us all along;
     No tongue can tell, I'm certain sure,
     What we poor sailors could endure.

4   Come set you down and listen a while,
     And hear how Fortune did on me smile.
     It was my fortune for to be
     A slave unto a rich lady.

5   She dressed herself in rich array,
     And went to view her slaves one day.
     Hearing the moan the young man made,
     She went to him and thus she said:

6   "What countryman, young man, are you?"
     "An Englishman, and that is true."
     "I wish you were some Turk," said she,
     "I would ease you of your misery.

7 "I'll ease you of your slavish work
   If you'll consent and turn a Turk.
   I'll own myself to be your wife,
   For I do love you as my life."

8 "No, no," then said he,
   "Your conscience slave, madam, I'll be.
   I'd sooner be burnt at a stake
   Before that I'd my God forsake!"

9 This lady to her chamber went,
   And spent that night in discontent.
   Little Cupid with his piercing dart
   Did deeply wound her to the heart.

10 She was resolvéd the next day
   To ease him of his slavery,
   And own herself to be his wife,
   For she did love him as her life.

11 She dressed herself in rich array
   And with the young man sailed away;
   Unto her parents she bade adieu.
   By this you see what love can do.

B

"The Turkish Lady." From the singing and recitation of Alexander Harrison, Maccan, Cumberland County.

1 Young virgins all I pray draw near,
   A pretty story you shall hear.
   'T is of a Turkish lady brave,
   Who fell in love with an English slave.

2 A merchant's ship at Bristol lay
   As they were sailing o'er the sea.
   By a Turkish rover took were we
   And all of us made slaves to be.

3 They bound us down in irons strong,
   They whipped and lashéd us along.
   No tongue can tell, I'm certain sure,
   What us poor souls did endure.

4 Come, sit you down and listen a while,
  And hear how Fortune did on me smile.
  It was my fortune for to be
  A slave unto a rich lady.

5 She dressed herself in rich array,
  And went to view her slaves one day.
  Hearing the moan the young man made,
  She went to him and thus she said:

6 "What countryman, young man, are you?"
  "I am an Englishman, that's true."
  "I wish you was a Turk," said she,
  "I'd ease you of your misery.

7 "I'll ease you of your slavish work,
  If you'll consent to turn a Turk.
  I'll own myself to be your wife,
  For I do love you as my life."

8 "No, no, no," then said he,
  "Your constant slave, madam, I'll be.
  I'd sooner be burnt there at the stick
  Before that I'll my God forsake!"

9 This lady to her chamber went,
  And spent that night in discontent.
  Little Cupid with his piercing dart
  Had deeply wounded her to the heart.

10 She was resolvéd the next day
  To ease him of his misery,
  And own herself to be his wife,
  For she did love him as her life.

11 She dressed herself in rich array,
  And with the young man sailed away.
  Unto her parents she bid adieu.
  Now you see what love can do.

12 She is turned a Christian brave,
  And is wed to her own slave
  That was in chains and bondage too.
  By this you see what love can do.

18

THE BLAEBERRY COURTSHIP

THIS romantic Scots ballad is remarkably reminiscent of "Lizie Lindsay" (Child, No. 226), and Professor Tolman suggests (*Journal*, XXXV, 345) that it is founded on the older ballad. There is a chapbook copy, printed in 1810 by T. Johnston, Falkirk, in the collection by John Bell of Newcastle (25252.19 in Harvard College Library). For references to other Scottish and English texts and for a version procured in the United States from "an aged Scotchwoman, who learned the words from her mother," see *Journal*, XXXV, 345–346. Add Christie, *Traditional Ballad Airs*, I, 150–151.

A

From the singing and recitation of John Henderson, Tatamagouche, Colchester County (printed, *Quest*, pp. 230–234).

1 "Will ye gang to the Highlands, my jewel, wi' me?
   Will ye gang to the Highlands my flock for to see?
   It is health to my jewel to breathe the fresh air,
   And to pu' the blaeberries in the forest sae fair."

2 "To the Highlands, my jewel, I 'll no gang wi' thee,
   For the road it is lang and the hills they are hie,
   For I love these low valleys and the sweet cornfields
   Before all the blaeberries your wild mountains yields."

3 "O the hills are bonny when the heather's in bloom.
   'T would cheer a fine fancy in the month o' June
   To pu' the blaeberries and carry them home,
   And set them on your table when December comes on."

4 Then up spake her faither, that saucy old man:
   "Ye might 'a' chosen a mistress amang your ain clan.
   It 's but poor entertainment for our Lowland dames,
   For to promise them berries when the wild heather blooms.

5 "Tak up your green plaidie, walk over yon hill,
   For the sight o' your Hielan' face does me much ill.
   I 'll wed my own daughter, and spend pennies too,
   To whom my heart pleases, and what 's that to you?"

6 He called on his daughter, he gave her advice,
   Saying, "If ye 'll gang wi' him I 'm sure ye 're not wise.
   He 's a poor Hielan' fellow, he 's as poor as a crow,
   Of the clan o' the caterans for aught we may know.

7 "But if ye gang wi' him I'm sure ye'll gang bare,
Ye'll get naething that faither or mither can spare;
Of all ye possess I'll deprive ye for aye,
If ower the hills, lassie, ye gang away."

8 "Keep back your hand, faither, ye're no willin' to give,
But I'll fain go wi' him as sure as I live!
What signifies gold or treasure to me
When the Highland hills is 'tween my love and me?"

9 Now she's awa wi' him in spite o' them a',
Awa to a place which her eyes never saw.
He had no a steed for to carry her on,
But aye he said, "Lassie, think na the road long."

10 In a short time thereafter they came to a glen.
The lass being weary she sat hersen doon.
"Rise up, my brave lassie, and let us gang on,
For the sun will be gane doon before we get hame."

11 "My shoes are all torn and my feet are all rent,
I'm weary wi' travellin' and like to faint.
Were it not for the sake o' your kind companie
I wad lie in this desert until I wad dee."

12 In a short time thereafter they cam to a grove
Where the flocks they were feeding in numberless droves.
While Alan stood musing his flocks for to see,
"Step on," said the lassie, "that's na pleasure to me."

13 Twa bonnie laddies wi' green tartan trews
And twa bonnie lassies were butting the yoes:
"Ye're welcome, honoured master, ye're welcome again,
This while we've been lookin' for ye comin' hame."

14 "Put in your yoes, lassies, and gang awa hame.
I hae brought a swan frae the north to tame.
Her feathers are fallen, and where can she fly?
The best bed in all the house, there shall she lie."

15 The laddies did whistle and the laddies did sing,
And they made to the lassie a broad bed of down.
The lassie's heart was doon and couldna' well raise
Till mony a lad and lass came in wi' mony a phrase.

16 Early next morning he led her to the high,
And bade her look round her as far as she could spy:
"These lands and possessions — I have no debt to pay —
Ye scarce can walk round them in a long summer's day."

17 "O Alan, O Alan, I'm indebted to thee,
A debt, dear Alan, I never can pay.
O Alan, O Alan, how cam ye to me?
Sure I'm not worthy your bride for to be."

18 "Why call ye me Alan when Sandy's my name?
Why call ye me Alan? Ye're surely to blame.
For don't ye remember, when at school wi' me,
I was hated by all the rest, lovéd by thee?

19 "How oft have I fed on your bread and your cheese
When I had naething else but a handful o' peas.
Your hard-hearted faither did hunt me wi' dogs;
They rave all my bare heels and tore all my rags."

20 "Is this my dear Sandy whom I lovéd so dear?
I have not heard of you for mony a year.
When all the rest went to bed, sleep was frae me
For thinkin' whatever had become o' thee."

21 "In love we began and in love we will end,
And in joy and mirth we will our days spend;
And a trip once more to your faither we'll go
To relieve the old farmer of his toil and woe."

22 Wi' men and maidservants to wait them upon
Awa in a chaise to her faither they've gone.
The laddie went foremost, that brave Highland loon,
Till they cam to the gate that leads to the toon.

23 When they cam to the gate he gave a loud roar:
"Come doon, gentle farmer, Katherine's at your door!"
He looked out at the window and saw his daughter's face;
Wi' his hat in his hand he made a great phrase.

24 "Haud on your hat, faither, and don't let it fa'.
It's not for the peacock to bow to the craw!"
"O haud your tongue, Sandy, and don't taunt me,
My daughter's nae worthy your bride for to be!"

25   Then he's held the bridle-rein until he came doon,
       And then he conveyed him into a fine room.
       Wi' the best o' Scotch whisky they drunk o' a toast
       And the son and the faither drunk baith in one glass.

B

"The Blaeberry Courtship." From the singing and recitation of Alexander Sutherland, Toney River, Pictou County.

1   In the Highlands of Scotland there lived a young man,
      He was well situated with houses and lands;
      He's away to the Highlands to look for a bride,
      And he's dressed himself up in a braw suit of Clyde.

2   "Will ye gang to the Highlands, bonny lassie, with me?
      Will ye gang to the Highlands, bonny lassie?" said he.
      "It's good for your health, love, to breathe the fresh air,
      And go gathering blueberries on our wild mountain plains."

3   "I'll nae gang to the Highlands, bonny laddie," said she,
      "I'll nae gang to the Highlands, bonny laddie, with you;
      I would rather stop home in those low cornfields,
      Nor go gathering blueberries on your wild mountain plains."

4   Then down came her father, a saucy old man:
      "Could n't you get a mistress in all your Highlands?
      It's a poor invitation for Lowlander dame
      To go gathering blueberries on your wild mountain plains."

5   Then up spake the young man and said,
      "If you be a farmer, as farmer you are,
      Some of your spare pennies with her you must share,
      Or you'll ne'er see your daughter gang o'er the hill there."

6   "Gang awa wi' your tartan plaid ower yon hill
      One sight of my daughter will do you no ill;
      You'll not get my daughter nor spare pennies three.
      I will wed her to whom I like. What's that to thee?"

7   Then down came her mother her child to advise,
      Saying, "If you do take him I'm sure you're not wise.
      He's a poor naked fellow, as bare as a crow;
      He has fled from his country, and that you'll soon know."

8 But this lassie gang awa to a place she ne'er knew,
From her dadda and mamma now she's gang awa.
And he had no steed for to carry her on,
Saying, "Gang on, bonny lassie, to sweet Milltown."

9 It's they gang along till they came to a glen.
This lassie being weary she sat herself down,
Saying, "If it was fit for your sweet company,
I would lie in these deserts until break of day."

10 "Rise up, bonny lassie, the sun's gangin' down.
Gang on, bonny lassie, unto sweet Milltown;
It's there we'll get lodgings for you and me."
And she wished for a barn or a byre to lay in.

11 It's they gang along till they came to Milltown,
Where drovers were driving their drove after drove.
This young man stood viewing his flocks passing by,
Saying, "Gang on, bonny lassie, to sweet Milltown."

12 It's they gang along till they came to Milltown,
Where two pretty maidens were milking their cows,
Saying, "You're welcome home, master, with your Lowland
   dame,
For it's long we've been waiting for your coming hame."

13 Now this lassie is home to her place of abode,
And she is much weary of her lonesome road.
With rum, gin, and brandy they drunk their health round,
And they made for this lassie a braw bed of downs.

14 'T was early next morning he led her to the high;
He bade her look round her as far as she could see:
"This is my lands and possessions, my debts they're all paid,
And you would not ride round them on a long summer's day."

19

THE SEA CAPTAIN

THIS tuneful ballad, which has much more of the pure lyrical quality than is usual in narrative folk-song, is one of the numerous developments of the motive of "Lady Isabel and the Elf Knight." It is rather closely related to "The Broomfield Hill" (Child, No. 43), a ballad still orally current in England: see *Journal of the Folk-Song Society*, III, 69; IV, 110–116; VII, 31–33; Gillington and Sellers, *Songs of the Open Road*, No. 8, pp. 18–19; Williams, p. 75; cf. Barry, *Journal*, XXIV, 14–15.

A

"The Sea Captain." From the singing and recitation of Mrs. James Campbell, River John, Pictou County (printed, *Quest*, p. 129).

1 It was of a sea captain that followed the sea.
     Let the winds blow high or blow low O.
  "I shall die, I shall die," the sea captain did cry,
     "If I don't get that maid on the shore O,
     If I don't get that maid on the shore."

2 This captain had jewels, this captain had gold,
     This captain had costly a ware O.
  And all he would give to this pretty fair maid,
     If she'd please take a sail from the shore O,
     If she'd please take a sail from the shore.

3 With great persuasions they got her on board,
     The weather being fine and clear O.
  She sang so sweet, so neat and complete,
     That she sang all the seamen to sleep O,
     That she sang all the seamen to sleep.

4 She took all his jewels, she took all his gold,
     She took all his costly a ware O.
  She took his broadsword to make her an oar,
     And she paddled her way to the shore O,
     And she paddled her way to the shore.

5 "O were my men mad or were my men drunk,
     Or were my men deep in despair O,
  To let her away with her beauty so gay
     To roam all alone on the shore O,
     To roam all alone on the shore?"

6 "Your men were not mad, your men were not drunk,
    Your men were not deep in despair O.
I deluded your men as well as yourself.
    I'm a maid again on the shore O,
    I'm a maid again on the shore!"

𝓑

"The Sea Captain." From the singing and recitation of Miss Greta Brown,
River John, Pictou County.

1 There was a sea captain that followed the sea.
    Let the winds blow high or blow low, boys.
"I will die, I will die," was the seaman's reply,
    "If I don't get that maid from the shore, shore,
    If I don't get that maid from the shore!"

2 One night at the ocean he took her on board,
    The captain he gave her a share O.
He gave her big gun from the cabin below.
    And farewell all sorrow and care, care,
    And farewell all sorrow and care.

3 The night being so still and the water so calm,
    She sat on the stern of the ship O.
Her voice was so sweet, so neat and complete,
    She sang seamen and captain to sleep, sleep,
    She sang seamen and captain to sleep.

4 She took off his jewels, she took off his ring,
    She took off his gosbear to wear O.
She took his broadsword for to make her an oar,
    And she paddled her way to the shore, shore,
    And she paddled her way to the shore.

5 "O was your men mad, or was your men drunk?
    Or was your men deep in despair O?
But to let me roam all alone by the shore,
    I'm a maid most again on the shore, shore,
    I'm a maid most again on the shore!"

20

SIR NEIL AND GLENGYLE

PETER BUCHAN, in *Ancient Ballads and Songs of the North of Scotland* (1828),
II, 16–20, printed "Sir Niel and MacVan," which is substantially reproduced
in the Nova Scotia version. He remarks (p. 307): "I have read of a Sir Niel
Campbell who followed the fortune of Sir William Wallace, and, along with
that brave champion, shared much of his hardships and toil; but I cannot
say, to a certainty, that he was the man so dishonourably slain by one of his
own clansmen, Campbell of Glengyle. This tragical affray originated in laying both their loves on one lady, a rich heiress in Argyleshire."

For other versions see Greig, CIX ("Sir Niel and M'Van"); Christie, *Traditional Ballad Airs*, I, 82–83 ("Sir Niel and MacVan"); Whitelaw, *Book of
Scottish Ballads*, pp. 289–290; No. 4 of a collection of Chap-book Ballads
(25263.23 in the Harvard College Library).

"Sir Neil and Glengyle." From the singing and recitation of Robert Langille, Tatamagouche, Colchester County (printed in part, *Quest*, pp. 237–238).

1   In yonder isle beyond Argyle
    Where flocks and herds were plenty,
  Lived airy squire [1] whose sister fair
    Was the flower of all that country.

2   The knight Sir Neil had wooed her long,
    Expecting soon to marry.
  A Highland laird his suit preferred,
    Young, handsome, brisk, and airy.

3   Long she respected brave Sir Neil
    Because he wooed sincerely,
  But as soon as she saw the young Glengyle
    He won her most entirely.

4   Till some lies unto her brother came
    That Neil had boasted proudly
  Of favours from that lady young,
    Which made him vow thus rudely:

5   "I swear by all our friendships past
    This hour again next morning
  This knight or me shall lose our lives.
    He shall know whom he's scorning!"

---

[1] Probably a corruption of *a rich squire*.

6 To meet on the shore where the proud billows roar
    In a challenge he defied him.
Ere the sun was up these young men met,
    No living creature nigh them.

7 "What ails, what ails my dearest friend?
    Why want you to destroy me?"
"I want no flattery, base Sir Neil,
    But draw your sword and fight me."

8 "Why should I fight with you, MacVaughn?
    You've never me offended;
And if I aught to you have done
    I'll own my fault and mend it."

9 "Is this your boasted courage, knave?
    Who would not now despise thee?
But if thou still refuse to fight,
    I'll like a dog chastise thee."

10 "Forbear, fond fool, tempt not thy fate,
    Presume not now to strike me.
There's not a man in all Scotland
    Can wield a broadsword like me."

11 "Combined with guilt thy wondrous skill
    From fate shall not defend thee.
My sister's wrongs shall brace my arms.
    This stroke to death shall send thee."

12 But this and many a well-aimed blow
    The generous baron warded;
Being loath to harm so dear a friend
    Himself he only guarded.

13 Till mad at being so rebused,
    A furious push he darted
Which pierced the brains of bold MacVaughn,
    Who with a groan departed.

14 "Curse on my skill, what have I done!
    Rash man, but thou wouldst have it.
Thou'st forced a friend to take a life
    Who would have bled to save it."

15 But turning round his mournful eyes
        To see if one was nigh them,
    There he espied the young Glengyle,
        Who like the wind came flying.

16 "I'm come too late to stop the strife,
        But since thou art victorious,
    I'll be revenged or lose my life.
        My honour bids me do this."

17 "I know your bravery, young Glengyle,
        Though of life I am regardless.
    Why am I forced my friends to kill?
        See bold MacVaughn lies breathless."

18 "Does it become so brave a knight?
        Does blood so much affright thee?
    Glengyle shall never disgrace thy sword;
        Unsheathe it then and fight me."

19 Again with young Glengyle he closed,
        Intending not to harm him.
    Three times with gentle wounds him pierced,
        But never did disarm him.

20 "Yield up thy sword to me, Glengyle,
        Whereon is our quarrel grounded?
    I could have pierced thy dauntless breast
        Each time I thee have wounded.

21 "But if thou thinkest me to kill,
        In faith thou art mistaken,
    And if thou scorn'st to yield thy sword
        In pieces straight I'll break it."

22 While talking thus he quit his guard.
        Glengyle in haste advancéd
    And pierced his generous manly heart;
        The sword right through him glancéd.

23 And down he fell and cried, "I'm slain!
        Adieu to all things earthly!
    Adieu, Glengyle, this day's thine own,
        But thou hast won it basely!"

24 When tidings came to Lady Ann
    Time after time she fainted.
She ran and kissed their clay-cold lips,
    And thus their fate lamented:

25 "Illustrious, brave, but dauntless men,
    This horrid sight does move me,
My dearest friends rolled in their blood,
    The men that best did love me.

26 "Oh thou, the guardian of my youth,
    My dear and only brother,
For this thy most untimely fate
    I'll mourn till life is over!

27 "Thou, Sir Neil, how art thou fallen
    And withered in thy blossom!
No more I'll love that trait'rous man
    That pierced thy erest [1] bosom.

28 "A kind and generous heart was thine
    Thy friendship was abuséd.
A braver man ne'er faced a foe
    Had thou been fairly uséd.

29 "For thee a maid I'll live and die,
    Glengyle shall ne'er espouse me.
And for the space of seven long years
    The dowie black shall clothe me."

[1] Probably *dearest*.

21

THE GOLDEN GLOVE

In England, where this song has enjoyed an unusual popularity for well over
a century, the title is either "The Golden Glove" or "The Squire of Tamworth."
It was printed as a broadside in the United States early in the nineteenth century, and in recent years versions have been collected in many parts of the
country. See *Journal*, XXIX, 171–172; Cox, p. 384. The title most often
found in the United States is "Dog and Gun."

No local title. From the singing and recitation of Robert Langille, Tatamagouche, Colchester County.

1 'T was of a young squire in Yarmouth did dwell.
   He courted a nobleman's daughter so fair,
   And for to be married was all their intent,
   When friends and relations had given their consent.

2 A farmer was chosen to give her away,
   To wait on the squire and give him his bride;
   But as soon as the farmer the lady she espied,
   "My heart is all inflamed, dear jewel!" she cried.

3 In place of being married she went to her bed,
   Thoughts of the farmer still ran in her head,
   Thoughts of the farmer still ran in her mind,
   And a way for to gain him she quickly did find.

4 Coat, waistcoat, and breeches the lady she put on,
   And she has gone a hunting with her dog and her gun.
   She hunted all round where the farmer he did dwell,
   And often she fired, but nothing did kill.

5 At length the young farmer appeared in the field,
   .   .   .   .
   "I thought you'd been at the wedding," the lady she cried,
   "To wait on the squire to give him his bride!"

6 "O no," said the farmer, "the truth and I must tell,
   I won't give her away, for I love her too well."
   This pleaséd the lady to hear him so bold,
   And she gave him a glove that was flowered with gold.

7 She said she had found it in coming along
   As she was a hunting with her dog and her gun;
   So this lady goes home with her heart full of love,
   And she put out a speech that she had lost her glove.

8 "The man that does find it and bring it to me,
   The man that does find it his loving bride I'll be."
   This pleaséd the farmer to hear of the news.
   With his heart full of love to the lady he goes.

9 Saying, "Honourable lady, I have picked up your glove,
   If you should be pleased to grant to me your love."
   "'T is already granted," the lady she said,
   "For I love the sweet breath of a farmer," she cried.

10 "While I'll be mistress of my dairy and a milking of my cows
   My brisk young farmer will go whistling at his plough."
   'T was after they were married she told of her fun,
   How she had hunted out the farmer with her dog and her gun.

11 "'T is now I have got him so fast in my snare,
   And forever I'll enjoy him, I vow and declare!"

2 2

THE LADY'S FAN

THE story of the ensuing song has been known and has been recorded in a variety of ways throughout Europe since the sixteenth century. Schiller's *Der Handschuh*, Leigh Hunt's *The Glove and the Lions*, and Browning's *The Glove* are only the most familiar of a great many versions. The relation of the folk ballad to the more literary versions is one of the minor mysteries in a subject where mysteries abound. Kittredge points out (*Modern Language Notes*, XXVI, 167) that the earliest text of the ballad is in one of Bishop Percy's broadsides. In this and in the other recorded English versions the lady's suitors are a Captain and a brisk Lieutenant from the *Tiger:*

> One of them had been made a Captain
> And was commanded by brave Colonel Carr;
> The other was a brisk Lieutenant
> On board the *Tiger*, a Man-of-War.

(See Christie, *Traditional Ballad Airs*, II, 126.) The Captain proves to be a timid creature, and the brisk Lieutenant rescues the fan and wins the lady. In all of these matters my version agrees. In the Kentucky version published by Shearin (*Modern Language Notes*, XXVI, 113) the Tiger has disappeared and the lady is won by the Captain, not the Lieutenant.

For references and texts see Kittredge (as above), and Shearin, *The Sewanee Review*, April, 1911.

From the singing and recitation of Miss Greta Brown, River John, Pictou County.

1   Come and sit down and I'll sing you a ditty
    Concerning a pretty fair maid.
She was fair, fair-agéd beauty,
    Worth ten thousand pounds a year.

2   Many a young man came for to see her,
    Many a one she did adore.
She had two lovers, and they were brothers,
    And one of them she did adore.

3   One of them was a great sea captain
    That sailed the largest ship that sailed,
The other of them was a lieutenant
    Of the *Tiger* man-of-war.

4   As they were seated by the dinner table,
    A woman unto them made this reply,
"Us three take a walk out together,
    Content our hearts with them must try."

5   As they were walking down by the river,
      Where there was a lion's den,
  She threw her fan into the den,
      And one like that she held right there.

6   "Anybody here for to do me a favour,
      Anybody here my heart to win,
  Anybody here for to do me a favour,
      Will return my fan again."

7   Up speaks the faint-hearted captain,
      And unto the lady made this reply,
  "In the den there lies great danger;
      Life and death I dare not try."

8   Up speaks the bold lieutenant,
      And unto the lady made this reply,
  "In the den there lies great danger;
      I'll return your fan or die."

9   Into the den he quickly bolted
      Where the lions drew fierce and strong.
  For his sword for his protection,
      He returned the fan again.

10   When she saw that her true lover was coming,
      And no harm was done to him,
  She threw her head into his bosom:
      "You're the one my heart did win."

11   Up speaks the faint-hearted captain,
      And unto the lady made this reply,
  "Many a desert lands I've travelled;
      For your life I'll repent and die."

23

THE BANKS OF SWEET DUNDEE

ROBERT FORD (*Vagabond Songs and Ballads of Scotland*, First Series, p. 77) wrote in 1898, "It [*i.e.*, "The Banks of Sweet Dundee"] cannot be less than a hundred years old. Fifty years ago, when harvest work in Scotland was almost wholly done by the hand-hook, it was a common song among the bands of shearers in the Carse of Gowrie and thereabout when songs went round in the bothies at night." We may suppose, then, that the song has been in existence for well over a century, and during a considerable part of that time, at least, it has been a particular favourite in England and Scotland. It has appeared frequently in songbooks and broadsides in both England and America. For references see Kittredge, *Journal*, xxxv, 355. Cox prints two versions from West Virginia, pp. 379–381.

From the singing and recitation of Robert Langille, Tatamagouche, Colchester County (printed, *Quest*, pp. 47–48).

1 'T was of a beautiful young damsel, as I have heard it told,
Her father died and left her five thousand pounds in gold.
She livéd with her uncle as you may plainly see,
And she lovéd a ploughboy on the banks of sweet Dundee.

2 Her uncle had a ploughboy, young Mary loved him well,
And in her uncle's garden her tale of love would tell.
. . . .
. . . .

3 One morning very early just at the break of day
Her uncle came to Mary and then to her did say,
"Arise, young lovely Mary, and come along with me,
For the young squire's waiting for you on the banks of sweet
Dundee."

4 "A fig for all your squires, your dukes and lords besides,
For young William he appears to me like diamonds in mine eyes."
"Hold on," said her uncle, "for revenged on you I'll be,
For I will banish William from the banks of sweet Dundee."

5 The press-gang came on William as he was all alone.
He boldly fought for liberty though there was ten to one.
The blood did flow in torrents, he fought so manfully;
He'd rather die for Mary on the banks of sweet Dundee.

6 One morning as young Mary was lamenting for her love,
She met the wealthy young squire down by her uncle's grove.
He put his arms around her. "Stand off, base man," said she,

. . . .

7 He put his arms around her and strove to throw her down.
Two pistols and a sword she spied beneath his morning-gown.
Young Mary took the pistols, the sword she handled free;
She fired and shot the squire on the banks of sweet Dundee.

8 Her uncle overheard the noise and hastened to the ground:
"Now since you've killed the squire I'll give you your death-
wound."
"Keep off," then says young Mary. "Undaunted I shall be."
She fired and shot her uncle on the banks of sweet Dundee.

9 A doctor he was sent for, a man of noted skill,
Likewise there came a lawyer for him to sign his will.
He signed all his gold to Mary who fought so manfully,
He closed his eyes no more to rise on the banks of sweet Dundee.

10 Young William he was sent for and speedily did return.
As soon as he arrived upon the shore young Mary ceased to
mourn.
The banns were quickly published, their hands were joined so
free,
She now enjoys her ploughboy on the banks of sweet Dundee.

24

THE LOST LADY FOUND

THERE are many titles for this song in the English collections. The ordinary broadside title is "The Lost Lady Found." The song was a very popular one throughout England.

For English versions see M. H. Mason, *Nursery Rhymes and Country Songs*, p. 56 ("'T is of a Young Damsel"); Reynardson, *Sussex Songs*, pp. 20–21 ("Gipsy Song"); Broadwood, *English Traditional Songs and Carols*, pp. 86–91 (with music); Gillington, *Eight Hampshire Folk Songs*, No. 6, pp. 12–13 ("As Down in a Valley"; with music); R. V. Williams, *Folk-Songs from the Eastern Counties*, pp. 12–15 (with music); Barrett, *English Folk-Songs*, No. 43, pp. 74–75; *Proceedings of the Dorset Natural History and Antiquarian Field Club*, XXVII, 33; *Journal of the Folk-Song Society*, II, 99–101. See also broadsides: Catnach (VII, 185); Bebbington, Manchester, No. 396 (X, 139); Such, No. 22 (XI, 22); T. Butchelar, London, No. 376 (with "Lovely Ann"); Catnach (with "The Fox Chase"); W. Fortey, Catnach Press (with the same); Pitts; imprint obliterated, No. 396 (with "Bonny Jean" and "The Old Oak Table").

No local title. From the singing and recitation of Alexander Sutherland, Toney River, Pictou County.

1 It's of a rich lady in England did dwell.
  She lived with her uncle, I know it right well.
  It's down in the valley by lowlands so sweet
  The gypsies betrayed her and stole her away.

2 She had been missing and could not be found.
  Her uncle had searched the country all round,
  Till he met with a trustee, a trustee of old.
  The trustee replied him that she had not been there.

3 Then up speaks the trustee with courage so bold,
  "I'm afraid she's been murdered for the sake of her gold,
  So we'll have life for life," the trustee did say,
  "We'll send you to prison and there you may stay."

4 But she had a rich squire who loved her right well.
  . . . .
  Saying, "My mind is tormented, and great is my fear.
  If I had the wings of a dove I would fly to my dear."

5 I traveled through England, through France, and through
    Spain,
  I ventured my life o'er the deep raging main,
  Brought up, came on shore, came took lodgings one night,
  And in that same room felt my own heart's delight.

6 I gazed on her features, she flew in my arms,
  I gazed on her features, I told her the charm,
  Saying, "What brought you to Dublin, my dear?" he did say.
  "The gypsies betrayed me and stole me away."

7 "Your uncle in England in prison do lie,
  And for your sweet sake he's condemned for to die."
  "O carry me to England, my dear," she did say,
  "Ten thousands I'll give you, and I'll be your bride."

8 The cars being running, as it happened to be,
  The cars being under the high gallows tree,
  "O pardon, O pardon, O pardon," cried she,
    Don't you see I'm alive your sweet life for to save!"

9 It's then from the gallows he quickly was led.
  The drums they did beat and sweet music did play.
  Every house in the valley did murmur with sound
  As soon as they heard the lost lady was found.

25

THE PRENTICE BOY

THIS favourite English song is sometimes entitled "The Prentice Boy" and sometimes "Cupid's Garden." The *Journal of the Folk-Song Society* (II, 195–196) has a version with the title "Covent Garden," which begins: "It was in Covent Garden in sweet pleasure I did walk." See also *The Cheerful Songster* (Boswell Chapbooks, Harvard College Library, XVII, No. 17); Pitts broadside, etc. The song occurs in two of Coverly's Boston broadsides (about 1814): see Ford, *Massachusetts Broadsides*, No. 3308, and *The Isaiah Thomas Collection*, No. 216 ("The Prentice Boy"). It is common in American song books: see, for example, *The Echo, or Columbian Songster* (Brookfield, Massachusetts), 2d ed., pp. 154–155; Kenedy, *The American Songster* (Baltimore, 1836), pp. 248–250; *The Forget Me Not Songster* (New York, Nafis and Cornish), pp. 197–198; *The New American Singer's Own Book* (Philadelphia, 1841), pp. 55–56; *The American Songster* (Philadelphia, 1850), p. 79; *Home Sentimental Songster* (New York, T. W. Strong), pp. 224–225. See also Shearin and Combs, p. 11; Shearin, *Sewanee Review*, July, 1911 ("Cubeck's Garden"); Pound, No. 31 ("The Prentice Boy"); *Journal*, XXVI, 363–364.

There is another broadside song (Such, No. 385) entitled "Down in Cupid's Garden" and beginning in the same fashion: "As down in Cupid's Garden for pleasure I did go." It must not, however, be confused with "The Prentice Boy." It is, in fact, an entirely different type of song, setting forth the toot ing of a maid's faith by her sailor lover, her satisfactory response, and the consequent beatification of both. The only correspondence between the two songs is in the title and introductory lines. See Chappell, *Popular Music of the Olden Time*, II, 727–729; *Vocal Library*, p. 539; R. Brimley Johnson, *Popular British Ballads*, II, 246; Hullah, *The Song Book*, 1866, pp. 94–95; Greig, CLV ("Covent Garden"); *Notes and Queries*, 9th Series, XI, 6; broadsides of Catnach ("The Lovers' Meeting," VII, 152) and H. Such, No. 385 ("Down in Cupid's Garden," XIII, 79).

"The Prentice Boy." From the singing and recitation of Alexander Harrison, Maccan, Cumberland County.

1 As down in Cupid's garden for pleasure I did walk,
I heard two loyal lovers most sweetly for to talk.
It was a brisk young lady and her prentice boy,
And in private they were talking, for he was all her joy.

2 He said, "Dear honoured lady, I am your prentice boy;
However can I think a fair lady to enjoy?"
His cheeks as red as roses, his humour kind and free.
She said, "Dear youth, if e'er I wed, I'll surely marry thee."

3 But when her parents came this to understand,
   They did this young man banish to some foreign land.
   While she lay broken-hearted, lamenting she did cry,
   "For my honest charming prentice a maid I'll live and die."

4 This young man to a merchant a waiting-man was bound,
   And by his good behaviour great fortune there he found.
   He soon became his butler, which prompted him to fame,
   And for careful conduct the steward he became.

5 For a ticket in a lottery his money he put down,
   And there he gained a prize of twenty thousand pounds.
   With store of gold and silver he packed up his clothes indeed,
   And to England returned to his true love with speed.

6 He offered kind embraces, but she flew from his arms:
   "No lord, duke, or nobleman shall e'er enjoy my charms,
   The love of gold is cursed, great riches I decry;
   For my honest charming prentice a maid I'll live and die!"

7 He said, "Dear honest lady, I have been in your arms.
   This is the ring you gave for [toying] [1] in your charms.
   You vowed if ever you married, your love I should enjoy.
   Your father did me banish, I was your prentice boy."

8 When she beheld his features, she flew into his arms;
   With kisses out of measure, she did enjoy his charms.
   Then so through Cupid's garden a road to church they found,
   And there in virtuous pleasure in Hymen's bands were bound.

[1] Word supplied from text in *The Forget Me Not Songster*.

26

THE CONSTANT FARMER'S SON

In both England and America the story which has been familiarized by Boccaccio's *Decameron* and Keats's *Isabella* is current in two ballad variants. One of these is known in England as "In Bruton Town" and in America as "The Bramble Briar"; the other, in England occasionally called "The Merchant's Daughter," is ordinarily, in both countries, entitled "The Constant Farmer's Son." For a discussion of the background and associations of the ballads see Belden's article, "Boccaccio, Hans Sachs, and The Bramble Briar (*Publications of the Modern Language Association*, XXXIII, 327). See also *Journal*, XXIX, 168; XXXV, 359; Cox, p. 305; Pound, No. 22 (two versions of "The Bramble Briar") and No. 32 ("The Constant Farmer's Son").

From the singing and recitation of John Adamson, Westville, Pictou County (printed in part, *Quest*, p. 154).

1 In London there lived a pretty fair maid.
  She was comely, fair, and handsome, her parents loved her well.
  She was courted by lords and noblemen, but all their love was in vain.
  There was but one, the farmer's son, poor Mary's heart could gain.

2 Long time young William courted her; they fixed the wedding day.
  Her parents they did give consent. Her brothers they did say,
  "There is a lord has pledged his word, and him she shall not shun.
  First we 'll betray and then we 'll slay the constant farmer's son."

3 There was a fair not far from town, her brothers they did say.
  They asked young William's company to spend with them the day,
  But back returning home again they swore his race had run,
  And with a stake the life did take of the constant farmer's son.

4 These villains returning homewards, to Mary they did say,
  "O think no more of your false love, but let him go his way.
  O think no more of your false love. He 's courted some other one,
  And we the same have come to tell of the constant farmer's son."

5 As Mary on her pillow lay she dreamt a shocking dream,
  She dreamt she saw her own true love down by a purling stream.
  So Mary rose, put on her clothes, to meet her love did run.
  In yonder vale lies cold and pale her constant farmer's son.

6 She kissed him once, she kissed him twice, she kissed him ten
times o'er,

. . . .

She gathered green leaves from the trees to keep him from the
sun.
A night and a day she passed away with her constant farmer's
son.

7 At length her hunger grew very great. Poor maid, she sicked for
woe,
And home unto her parents poor Mary she did go,
Saying, "Parents dear, you soon shall hear the dreadful deed's
been done, —
In yonder vale lies cold and pale my constant farmer's son."

8 It's up and speaks her oldest brother and swore it was not he,
And so did the younger one, and swore most bitterly.
"You need n't turn so red," says she, "nor try the law to shun.
You've done the deed and you shall bleed for my constant
farmer's son."

9 Those villains confessed the murder and for the same did die.
Young Mary she did fade away but never ceased to cry.
Her parents they did fade away. The glass of life had run.
Poor Mary sighed and then she died for her constant farmer's son.

27

YOUNG EDMUND

THE hero of this humble tragedy is variously known as Young Edwin, Young Edward, and Young Edmund, and any given version of the song will appear under a corresponding title. The song has been current in England, Scotland, and Ireland, and several versions have been found in the United States. For references see *Journal*, XX, 274; XXXV, 421–423. Add Campbell and Sharp, No. 46; Cox, No. 106; Wyman and Brockway, *Twenty Kentucky Mountain Songs*, pp. 42–45.

"Young Edmund." From the singing and recitation of Carl Langille, River John, Pictou County (printed, in part, *Quest*, p. 155).

1 Young Emily was a servant maid,
 She loved a sailor bold;
And for much gain he crossed the main,
 For love as I've been told.

2 Seven long years or better
 Since Edmund's been at home,
He came unto young Emily's house
 And she was all alone.

3 He came unto young Emily's house
 His gold all for to show,
That he had gained upon the main.
 He plowed the Lowlands low.

4 "My father keeps a public house
 Down yonder by the shore,
And you this night shall enter in
 And there to morning dwell.

5 "You'll meet me in the morning.
 Don't let my parents know
That your name it is young Edmund
 That plowed the Lowlands low."

6 Young Emily in her chamber
 She dreamt a dreadful dream:
She dreamed she saw young Edmund
 Float in yon crystal stream.

7   She rose at day in the morning,
        To meet her love did go,
    Because she loved him dearly.
        He plowed the Lowlands low.

8   "O mother, where's that stranger
        Came here last night to dwell?"
    "He is dead," and says her father,
        "And you no tales shall tell."

9   Saying, "Father, cruel father,
        You will die a public show
    For the murdering of young Edmund
        That plowed the Lowlands low!"

10 She went unto the justice,
        And there her case made known.
    He is taken on suspicion,
        His trial soon comes on.

11 The jury found him guilty,
        And hanged he was also
    For the murdering of young Edmund
        Who plowed the Lowlands low.

12 "I'll build myself a little house
        Down yonder by the shore.
    The ship that's on the ocean
        The wind tossed to and fro,
    Reminds me of young Edmund
        That plowed the Lowlands low."

28

CAROLINE OF EDINBORO TOWN

THIS song has appeared in many song books and broadsides in Great Britain and America: see *Journal*, xxxv, 362; Cox, pp. 362–363; Dean, p. 53; Shoemaker, pp. 206–207.

The following version was recollected by my mother from the singing of a maid in her father's house at Durham, Pictou County.

1 Come all young men and maidens, attend unto my rhyme.
'T is of a young damsel that was scarcely in her prime.
She beat the blushing roses, admired by all around
Was comely young Caroline of Edinboro Town.

2 Young Henry was a southern man a courting to her came,
But when her parents came to know they did not like the same.
Young Henry was offended and unto her did say,
"Arise, my dearest Caroline, and with me run away.

3 "We will both go to London and there we'll wed with speed,
And then young Caroline shall have happiness indeed."
Enticed she was by Henry, put on her other gown,
And away went young Caroline of Edinboro Town.

4 O'er hills and lofty mountains together they did roam,
In time arrived at London far from her happy home.
She said, "My dearest Henry, pray never on me frown,
Or you'll break the heart of Caroline of Edinboro Town."

5 They had not been in London not more than half a year
When hard-hearted Henry proved to be severe.
Said Henry, "I'll go to sea. Your friends did on me frown,
So beg your way, without delay, to Edinboro Town."

6 Oppressed with grief, without relief, this maiden she did go
Into the woods to eat such fruit as on the bushes grow.
Some strangers they did pity her, and some did on her frown,
And some did say, "What made you stray from Edinboro
    Town?"

7 Beneath a lofty spreading oak this maid sat down to cry,
A watching of the gallant ships as they went passing by.
She gave three shrieks for Henry, then plunged her body down,
And away went young Caroline of Edinboro Town.

8 .   .   .   .
.   .   .   .
And fast asleep while in the deep, the fishes watching round,
Lies comely young Caroline of Edinboro Town.

9 And now, ye tender parents, ne'er try to part true love;
You're sure to see in some degree the ruin it will prove.
Likewise, young men and maidens, ne'er on your lovers frown;
Think on the fate of Caroline of Edinboro Town.

29

THE GASPARD TRAGEDY

EBSWORTH (*Roxburghe Ballads*, VIII, 143, 173) reproduces the text of "The Gosport Tragedy, or, Perjured Ship Carpenter," a garland of about 1750, "Printed and Sold at the Printing Office in Bow Church-yard, London." This is the earliest known text of the song. The Nova Scotia version has twenty-three stanzas as against the thirty-five in the Garland, but, aside from that difference, it is in substantial and interesting agreement with the old text.

For references to texts, British and American, see Kittredge, *Journal*, XX, 261; Cox, p. 308. Add Wyman and Brockway, *Twenty Kentucky Mountain Songs*, pp. 110–115. Cox prints three short versions from West Virginia under the titles "Come, Pretty Polly," "Polly and Sweet William," and "Young Beeham" (pp. 308–310). These texts represent "Polly's Love, or, The Cruel Ship Carpenter," an English song in eleven stanzas which is a condensation of the original "Gosport Tragedy."

"The Gaspard Tragedy." From the singing of Mrs. Margaret Curry, Tatamagouche, Colchester County (printed, *Quest*, pp. 55–58).

1 In Gaspard of late a young damsel did dwell,
   For wit and for beauty few did her excel.
   A young man did court her for to be his dear,
   And he by his trade was a ship carpenter.

2 He said, "Dearest Mary, if you will agree
   And give your consent, dear, to marry me,
   Your love it can cure me of sorrow and care;
   Consent then to wed with a ship carpenter."

3 With blushes as charming as roses in bloom
   She answered, "Dear William, to wed I'm too young,
   For young men are fickle, I see very plain;
   If a maiden is kind, her they quickly disdain."

4 "My charming sweet Mary, how can you say so?
   Thy beauty is the heaven to which I would go.
   And if there I find channel if I chance for to steer,
   I there will cast anchor and stay with my dear."

5 But yet 't was in vain she strove to deny,
   For he by his cunning soon made her comply,
   And by base deceptions he did her betray;
   In sin's hellish path he led her astray.

6 Now when this young damsel with child she did prove,
She soon sent her tidings to her faithless love,
Who swore by the heavens that he would prove true,
And said, "I will marry no damsel but you."

7 Things passed on a while. At length we do hear
His ship was a sailing, for sea he must steer, —
Which pained this poor damsel and wounded her heart,
To think with her true love she must part.

8 Cried she, "Dearest Will, ere you go to sea
Remember the vows you have made unto me.
If at home you don't tarry I never can rest;
Oh, how can you leave me with sorrows oppressed?"

9 With tender expressions he to her did say,
"I'll marry my Mary ere I go to sea,
And if that to-morrow my love can ride down,
The ring I can buy our fond union to crown."

10 With tender embraces they parted that night
And promised to meet the next morning at light.
William said, "Mary, you must go with me
Before we are married our friends for to see."

11 He led her through groves and valleys so deep.
At length this young damsel began for to weep,
Crying, "Willie, I fear you will lead me astray
On purpose my innocent life to betray."

12 He said, "You've guessed right. All earth can't you save,
For the whole of last night I was digging your grave."
When poor Mary did hear him say so,
The tears from her eyes like a fountain did flow.

13 "Oh, pity my infant! Oh, spare my poor life!
Let me live full of shame if I can't be your wife.
Oh, take not my life lest my soul you betray,
And you to perdition be hurried away."

14 "There is no time disputing to stand," —
But instantly taking a knife in his hand,
He pierced her fair breast, whence the blood it did flow,
And into the grave her fair body did throw.

15 He covered her body and quick hastened home,
 Left nothing but the small birds her fate for to moan.
 On board ship he entered without more delay,
 And set sail for Plymouth to plough the salt sea.

16 A young man named Stuart, of courage most bold,
 One night happened late for to go in the hold,
 Where a beautiful damsel to him did appear,
 And she in her arms held an infant most dear.

17 Being merry with liquor he went to embrace,
 Transported with joy at beholding her face,
 When to his amazement she vanished away,
 Which he told to the captain without more delay.

18 The captain soon summoned his jovial ship's crew,
 And said, "My brave fellows, I'm afraid some of you
 Have murdered some damsel ere you came away,
 Whose injuréd ghost now haunts on the sea.

19 "Whoever you be, if the truth you deny,
 When found out you'll be hanged on the yard so high;
 But he who confesses, his life we'll not take,
 But leave him on the first island we make."

20 Then William immediately fell to his knees.
 The blood in his veins quick with horror did freeze.
 He cried, "Cruel murderer, what have I done!
 God help me, I fear my poor soul is undone.

21 "Poor injuréd ghost, your full pardon I crave,
 For soon must I follow you down to the grave!"
 No one else but this poor wretch beheld this sad sight,
 And raving distracted he died that same night.

22 Now when her sad parents these tidings did hear
 Soon searched for the body of their daughter so dear.
 In the town of Southampton in a valley so deep
 Her body was found, which caused many to weep.

23 In Gaspard's green churchyard her ashes now lie,
 And we hope that her soul is with God in the sky.
 So let this sad tale be a warning to all
 Who dare a young innocent maid to enthrall.

30

WHO IS AT MY BEDROOM WINDOW?

THIS is one of a large group of English and Scottish songs on the "Night Visit" (see Baskervill, *Publications of the Modern Language Association*, XXXVI, 565–614). It is, as Kittredge points out (*Journal*, XX, 260), a variant of a song known, in a Nithsdale version, to Allan Cunningham, and cited in part in a note to "O my luve's like a red, red rose" in his edition of Burns, 1834, IV, 285.

For English and Scottish references see *Journal*, XX, 260; XXX, 338; XXXV, 356; Campbell and Sharp, p. 330; Hudson MS. of Irish Airs, Vol. I, No. 181 (Boston Public Library). For American references see Cox, No. 108.

"Who Is at My Bedroom Window?" From the singing of Miss Greta Brown, River John, Pictou County.

1   "O who is at my bedroom window,
     Disturbing me from my night's rest?"
  "It is, it is your own true lover,
     The very one that you love best."

2   "Go, Maggie dear, go ask your father,
     See if our wedding bride may be.
  If he says 'No,' love, come and tell me,
     And I'll no longer troubled be."

3   "It is no use of asking father,
     For he is on his bed of rest,
  And by his side a silver dagger
     To stab the one that he loves best."

4   "Go, Maggie dear, go ask your mother,
     See if our wedding bride may be.
  If she says 'No,' love, come and tell me,
     And I'll no longer troubled be."

5   "It is no use of asking mother,
     For she is on to set us free.
  You'd better go and court some other,
     For you cannot marry me."

6   "I can climb the highest mountains,
     I can rob the eagle's nest,
  I can go and court some other,
     But you're the one that I love best."

7   She drew the dagger from her pocket
        And buried it deep, deep in her breast,
    Sang adieu to her cruel parents:
        "I'll die with the one that I love best."

8   He drew the dagger from her bosom
        And buried it deep, deep in his breast,
    Sang adieu to her cruel parents,
        And she died with the one that she loved best.

31

BESSIE OF BALLINGTON BRAE

M. C. DEAN prints a version of this song, entitled "Ballentown Brae," in *The Flying Cloud*, pp. 44–45. It tells the story of the betrayal of Bessie by the Lord of Morelands, of her death, and of her appearance (or that of her ghost) before her betrayer during the night. At this point the fragment which I present, and which is all that I have been able to find of a song once popular in Nova Scotia, takes up the tale.

An English broadside (without printer's imprint) on file in the Harvard College Library contains a song entitled "Sweet Ballenden Braes" — a lament by a deserted maiden who is going back to Ballenden Braes to die. It is in the same measure and stanza form as the song under discussion, and is, I think, quite certainly to be connected with it. The first stanza is:

> 'T was down in a glen where the holly grows green
> I espied a young lassie, tears fell frae her een,
> And thus she lamented — how wretched my days
> Since I was decoyed from sweet Ballenden Braes.

"Bessie of Ballington Brae." From the recitation of Frank McNeil, Little Harbour, Pictou County.

1 . . . . then he saddled his steed
  And o'er hills and high mountains he rode with great speed,
  Until he arrived at the noontide of day,
  Where he courted pretty Bessie of Ballington Brae.

2 Then out from the scabbard his short sword he drew,
  And without repenting he pierced his heart through.
  . . . .
  . . . .

3²

RINORDINE

In *Irish Country Songs*, I, 4–6, Herbert Hughes prints the following fragment, entitled "Reynardine":

> If by chance you look for me
> Perhaps you'll not me find,
> For I'll be in my castle.
> Enquire for Reynardine.
>
> Sun and dark I followed him,
> His eyes did brightly shine.
> He took me o'er the mountains,
> Did my sweet Reynardine.

This is described by Hughes as a "fragment of an Ulster ballad," and the following explanation is added: "In the locality (*i.e.*, Donegal) where I obtained this fragment Reynardine is known as the name of a faery that changes into the shape of a fox."

In *Notes and Queries*, 10th Series, IX, 12, John I. Crone surmises that the story refers to an attachment formed by a member of an English or Scottish "planter's" family for one of the original Celtic owners early in the seventeenth century: — "These latter being the original Tories, and frequently outlawed, would require 'concealment' from the edict of the judges."

The *Journal of the Folk-Song Society* prints a fragment, with music (I, 271–272), and the song is to be found on several English broadsides in the Harvard College Library: — H. Such, London, No. 109 (25242.17, XI, 109; here the title is "The Mountains High," and the hero is called Randal Rhine); broadside without imprint, numbered 885; T. Batchelar, London (with "The Monkey Turned Barber"); Catnach (with "The Monkey Turned Barber"). See also *Notes and Queries*, 10th Series, VIII, 468, 518; IX, 12, 33.

For American texts see Combs, *Folk-Songs du Midi des États-Unis*, 1925, pp. 165–166 ("Ryner Dine," West Virginia); *The American Songster* (Baltimore, collected and published by John Kenedy, 1836), pp. 191–193; *The Forget Me Not Songster* (New York, Nafis and Cornish), pp. 199–200; the same (Philadelphia and New York, Turner and Fisher, pp. 25–26; *The Old Forget Me Not Songster* (Boston, Locke and Dubier), pp. 199–200; *The American Singer's Own Book* (Philadelphia, M. Kelly, 1841), pp. 47–49; *The American Songster* (New York, Nafis and Cornish), pp. 191–193; *The American Vocalist* (New York, Richard Marsh, 1856), pp. 47–49; *Howe's 100 Old Favorite Songs* (Boston, Elias Howe Co.), p. 266. The song occurs in a Boston broadside of about 1813: "N. Coverly, Jr., Printer" (see Ford, *Massachusetts Broadsides*, No 3316, and *The Isaiah Thomas Collection of Broadsides*, No. 218; cf. another broadside in the same collection, No. 1). Cf. Belden, No. 34.

"Rinordine." From the singing and recitation of Alexander Harrison, Maccan, Cumberland County.

1 One evening as I rambled two miles below Pomroy,
  I met a farmer's daughter all on the mountain high.
  I said, "My pretty fair maiden, your beauty shines most clear,
  And upon these lofty mountains I'm glad to meet you here."

2 She said, "Young man, be civil, my company forsake,
  For to my great opinion I fear you are a rake;
  And if my parents should know, my life they would destroy
  For keeping of your company all on the mountains high."

3 I said, "My dear, I am no rake, but brought up in Venus' train,
  And looking out for concealment all in the judge's name.
  Your beauty has ensnared me, I cannot pass you by;
  And with my gun I'll guard you all on the mountains high."

4 This pretty little thing she fell into a maze,
  With her eyes as bright as amber upon me she did gaze,
  Her cherry cheeks and ruby lips they lost their former dye,
  And then she fell into my arms all on the mountains high.

5 I had but kissed her once or twice till she came to again.
  She modestly then asked me, "Pray sir, what is your name?"
  "If you go in yonder forest my castle you will find,
  Wrote in ancient history — my name is Rinordine."

6 I said, "My pretty fair maiden, don't let your parents know,
  For if you do they'll prove my ruin and fatal overthrow.
  But when you come to look for me perhaps you'll not me find;
  But I'll be in my castle, and call for Rinordine."

7 Come all ye pretty fair maidens, a warning take by me,
  And be sure you quit night walking and shun bad company,
  For if you don't you'll surely rue until the day you die;
  And beware of meeting Rinor all on the mountain high.

33

THE GAY SPANISH MAID

Cox prints a short version of this song from West Virginia (p. 371).
From the singing and recitation of Mrs. James Campbell, River John, Pictou County.

1   A gay Spanish maid at the age of sixteen
    O'er meadow did roam far and wide,
And under a beech tree she sat down to rest
    With a gay gallant youth by her side.

2   "Our ship sails to-night, O my darling Onette,
    And with you I can't wander no more;
But when all in the cottage retire to rest,
    Will you meet me to-night on the shore?"

3   When all in the cottage retired to rest,
    Onette she crept out the hall door.
With her hat in her hand she went down the dry sand,
    And she sat on a rock by the shore.

4   The moon was fast rising far over the lake,
    Where the water and sky seemed to meet,
And from over the lake came a murmuring wave,
    And it broke on the shore at her feet.

5   The moon was fast rising far over the lake,
    And their sorrows no one can tell.
He kissed her once more as they sat on the shore,
    And he bade her a sad farewell.

6   That night passed away with a wild crushing storm,
    And the rain in great torrents did fall.
Onette she awoke from her long troubled dreams,
    And she offered a prayer to her God.

7   Attention we'll turn to that ship in the storm
    As the wind through her rigging did moan.
There was nothing to cheer the sad hearts of the crew,
    And the ship she was lost in the storm.

8 All through that night I was out in the storm,
    And the ship riding wave after wave.
I jumped on a plank to escape from the wreck,
    While the rest found a watery grave.

9 All through the night found me out on a plank,
    And for safety I prayed in despair.
I thought of the maid I had left on the shore,
    And a thousand times wished myself there.

10 Early next morning a sail I espy,
    And for safety I prayed to my God.
My signal they spy and so bore down on me,
    And so joyfully took me on board.

11 Attention we'll turn to the maid on the shore
    When she heard of the ship in the storm:
She died like a rose that was bit by the storm,
    And she left him in sorrow to mourn.

34

JOHNNY DOYLE

THIS was once a popular broadside song in England and Ireland. In the United States several texts have been published. For British versions see Greig, C II; *Journal of the Folk-Song Society*, V, 142–146; *Journal of the Irish Folk-Song Society*, I, 66 (air only); broadsides in Harvard College Library, 25242.17, X, 98 (Bebbington, Manchester, No. 354); XIII, 3 (Such, No. 310). For texts published in the United States see: The *"Love Among the Roses"* Songster (New York, Robert M. De Witt, 1869), p. 26; *"The Rovin' Irish Boy"* Songster (De Witt, 1870), p. 22; *The Singers' Journal*, I, 53; De Marsan broadside, List 11, No. 50; O'Conor; Campbell and Sharp, pp. 281–283. Reported by Shearin and Combs, p. 27. Professor Hudson has found the song in Mississippi.

"Johnny Doyle." From the singing and recitation of John Brown, River John, Pictou County.

1 It's of a Saturday evening as we made up the plan
Early Monday morning to be jogging on.
Our waiting-maid being listening and heard all we did say,
She went unto my mother and told tales on me.

2 Early Sunday morning when my mother then arose,
She conveyed me unto her own bedroom;
My clothes she made ready for me to put on,
This fair maid being slowly of putting them on.

3 A coach and a postilion for her they did provide,
And six gallant horsemen to ride alongside.
They rode and they rode till they came to the upper town,
They rode and they rode till they lighted themselves down.

4 She says, "You've got pleasure, but me, I've got my toil.
My heart lies at home with my own Johnny Doyle."
. . . .
. . . .

5 The church door being opened the minister walked in,
Her earrings broke and fell unto the ground,
And to excuse the matter her father made this reply,
"My daughter is an innocent and harmless young bride."

6 The marriage being over and then returning home
On a soft downy pillow she hove herself down.
Sick, sore, and tired, and like unto die,
On a soft downy pillow her body they found.

7 "Shut the door, dear mother, don't let Tom Moore come in;
Shut the door, dear mother, don't let him see the ring;
For on this very night I shall surely end my life.
He shall never enjoy me nor call me his wife!"

8 "I would send for Johnny Doyle if I thought he was home;
I would send for Johnny Doyle if I thought that he would come.

. . . .

. . . .

9 "You need not send for Johnny Doyle, for now it is too late;
Far, far is the distance, and death is my fate.
You need not send for Johnny Doyle, for now it is too late,
And now I will die for my own Johnny's sake."

35

WILLIAM AND NANCY

EBSWORTH (*Roxburghe Ballads*, VII, 55) prints a song entitled "The Undaunted Seaman, who resolved to fight for his King and Country; Together with His Love's Sorrowful Lamentation at their Departure"; date, about 1690. It begins:

> My Love, I come to take my leave, yet prithee do not sigh and grieve;
> On the wide ocean I will fight, for to maintain the Nation's Right.
> Under noble chief Commanders I resolve to take my chance;
> On Board I'll enter, hope I'll venture, to subdue the Pride of France.

A little later it introduces the following conversation, the substance of which, with infinite changes in form, is common to all versions of the ballad:

> With sighs and tears this Damsel said, "If you resolve to go to Sea,
> In Sailor's Robes I'll be array'd, and freely go along with thee;
> Life and Fortune I will venture, rather than to stay on shore;
> Grief will oppress me, and possess me, that I ne'er shall see thee more.
>
> Said he, "My Dearest, stay on Land, such idle fancies ne'er pursue,
> Thy soft and tender milk-white Hand a Seaman's labour cannot do;
> Here I leave both Gold and Treasure, to maintain my Dear on shore."
> But still she crying, and replying, "I shall never see thee more."

In this early version the story ends with the lover's departure and the maid's lament. Many of the later versions have the same conclusion, and one special group, with the title "The Banks of the Nile," exhibits it consistently. But in many others, with varying titles, the maid's pleading breaks down the lover's scruples, and she dons her male attire and accompanies him to sea. Aside from this detail, the versions fall into two main groups: the first a loosely constituted one, with a great variety of titles and many differences in details, in which the lover is preparing to go to sea, sometimes with Lisbon as the destination; the second a fairly integrated one, with a common title ("The Banks of the Nile") and only minor differences in phraseology and detail, in which the lover is preparing to sail for the Nile. The two groups are represented, respectively, by the two Nova Scotia versions.

A version of this song is printed in a chapbook entitled *Five Excellent New Songs*, printed by J. Morren, Edinburgh (42d in series of chapbooks collected by John Bell, Newcastle — No. 25252.19 in Harvard College Library), and another in a chapbook entitled *The Jaunting Car* (52d in the same series). For other British texts see Greig, *Folk-Song of the North-East*, xxv ("The Banks of the Nile"); *The Newcastle Song Book*, I, section entitled *The Canary*, pp. 10–11 ("William and Nancy's Parting"); *Journal of the Folk-Song Society*, II, 22–23 ("Lisbon"), VI, 17–18 ("The Hills and Dales"); Ashton, *Modern Street Ballads*, pp. 253–255 ("Young Henry of the Raging Main"; here Emma goes to sea with Henry, and almost half of the ballad is devoted to an account of her life on board ship). See also the following broadsides: Harkness, Preston, No. 231 (with "The Braes o' Gleniffer"); Harkness, No. 250 (with "Oxford City"); Harkness, No. 313 (with "The Wandering Boy"); J. Catnach (with "The Gallant Maid"); Pitts; P. Brereton, Dublin; T. Pearson, Manchester, No. 227; John Ross, Newcastle, No. 100 (IV, 130); Bebbington, Manchester, No. 4 (IX, 4); Bebbington, No. 227 (IX, 219); Such, No. 191 (XII, 37). A text of "The Banks of the Nile" from a broadside (Taylor, Bethnal Green) was printed in the *Boston Transcript*, December 14, 1907, p. 8.

For American versions see Campbell and Sharp, No. 68; Dean, pp. 105–106; Belden, No. 15 ("William and Polly"); and *Journal*, XXV, 9–10.

A

No local title. From the singing and recitation of Robert Langille, Colchester County (printed, *Quest*, pp. 135–137).

1   'T was in one summer season,
        The twentieth of May,
    That we hoisted up our English colours,
        And we did make for sea.

2   The sun did shine most glorious,
        To Lisbon we were bound;
    The hills and dales were covered
        With pretty maids all around.

3   I spied a handsome sailor
        Just in his blooming years,

    .   .   .   .   .   .

        .   .   .   .   .   .

4   Just coming to his true love
        To let her understand
    That he was going to leave her
        And sail for some foreign land.

5   "The King has wrote for seamen,
        And I for one must go,
    And for my very life, my love,
        I dare not answer no."

6   "O stay at home, dear Willie,
        And I will be your wife;
    For the parting with you, Willie,
        Is the parting of my life."

7   "But if I was to stay at home
        Another would take my place;
    And that would be a shame for me,
        Likewise a sad disgrace."

8   "My yellow hair I will cut off,
      Men's clothing I'll put on,
I'll be thy body-servant,
      Likewise thy waiting-man."

9   "Thy waist it is too slender, love,
      Thy fingers are too small
To wait on me in battle
      Where many a man does fall,

10   "Where cannon they do rattle,
      And bullets they do fly,
And silver trumpets they do sound,
      To drown the dismal cries."

11   "My yellow hair I will cut off,
      Men's clothing I'll put on,
No storms or dangers do I fear,
      Let the winds blow high or low!"

12   "But if I was to meet some other
      In sweeter charms than thee,
And she was to please my fancy,
      What would my Nancy say?"

13   "What would I say, dear Willie?
      And I would love her too,
And I would gently step aside
      While she would be talking to you."

14   "Dear Nancy, all these words
      They are enough to break my heart;
Pray let us now be married
      Before that we depart!"

15   Now this young couple's married,
      And they sail o'er the main.
I hope good luck may attend them
      Till they return again.

B

"The Banks of the Nile." From the singing and recitation of Robert Reid, River John, Pictou County.

1   "Our corporal drums are beating,
    So I must away;
The bugle horns are sounding,
    No longer can I stay.

2   "We're ordered off to Portsmouth,
    'T is manys a weary mile,
To fight like British heroes
    On the banks of the Nile."

3   "O Willie, dearest Willie,
    Don't leave me here to mourn,
Or I will curse and rue the day
    That ever I was born.

4   "For parting with you, my love,
    Is parting with my life;
So stay at home, dear Willie,
    And I will be your wife.

5   "I'll put on my velveteen
    And go along with you,
I'll cut off my yellow locks
    And I'll see Egypt too.

6   "We'll stand by our banner
    While kind Fortune seems to smile,
And we'll comfort one another
    On the banks of the Nile."

7   "Your waist it is too slender,
    And your fingers are too small,
Your cheeks too red and rosy
    To face a cannon ball.

8   "Your delicate constitution
    Would not bear the unwholesome clime
Of the dark and sandy desert
    On the banks of the Nile."

9   "O curse be to the cruel wars
         Since first that they began!
     They've robbed us of our country
         And manys a clever man.

10   "They've robbed us of our sweethearts,
         The protectors of our soil,
     And their bodies feed the lions
         On the banks of the Nile."

36

DIXIE'S ISLE

THIS song is obviously an American adaptation of the previous number, "The Battle of the Nile" (No. 35 B). New Orleans and Dixie's Isle are substituted for Egypt and the banks of the Nile, New York and Boston are inserted for local colour, and that is about all. The other differences between "Dixie's Isle" and my version of "The Banks of the Nile" are as ordinary as the differences that one expects to find between any two versions of a folksong that has adapted itself to successive generations and changing communities.

"Dixie's Isle." From the singing and recitation of Harry Sutherland, River John, Pictou County.

1   "'The drums and fifes are a beating,
         No longer can I stay;
     The trumpet it doth loudly roar
         That calls me far away.

2   "We're ordered down to New Orleans
         To that unfruitful soil,
     To go fight those Southern soldiers
         Way down upon Dixie's Isle."

3   "O Willie dear, to leave me here,
         How could you be so cruel?
     For I will curse and rue the day,
         The hour that I was born.

4   "O I'll cut off my curly locks
         And go along with you,
     I'll cut off my golden locks
         And go to Orleans too.

5   "We'll fight the enemy man for man,
         May the heavens upon us smile!
     And we'll comfort one another
         Way down upon Dixie's Isle."

6   "The parting from you, Jennie dear,
         It will only be for a while,
     To go fight those Southern soldiers
         Way down upon Dixie's Isle.

7 "The captain he gave orders
    The women they were to go;
The captain he gave orders,
    And his orders they remain so.

8 "The scorching suns of New Orleans
    Would your tender rest spoil,
Among those swamps and deserts
    Way down upon Dixie's Isle."

9 "O may the curse be on New Orleans
    And the day the war began!
It robbed New York and Boston
    Of manys a gallant son.

10 "It robbed them from their sweethearts
    And from their native soil,
And the bloody stain doth yet remain
    Way down upon Dixie's Isle."

11 And now the war is over
    And home we will return
To our wives and sweethearts
    And those we left behind.

12 We'll kiss them and caress them,
    May the heavens upon us smile!
And we'll go no more a fighting
    Way down upon Dixie's Isle.

37

THE ROSE OF BRITAIN'S ISLE

THOUGH this song was often printed in English broadsides, its absence from the more recent collections would indicate that it was not widely sung in the later years of the nineteenth century. The broadside song of "The Constant Pair, or The Pretty Prentice Boy" (W. Taylor) is remarkably similar to this one. The two songs have many phrases in common, and present the same story, including the enmity of the father, the following by the maid of her lover to sea, and the repentance and reconciliation of the father.

Broadside copies of "The Rose of Britain's Isle" were issued by George Walker, Durham, No. 104 (II, 9); Catnach (VII, 102); W. Taylor (with "We Parted"; here the song is ascribed to "J. Morgan"); another without imprint, numbered 14 (with "The Wild Rover").

"The Rose of Britain's Isle." From the singing and recitation of Mrs. James Palmer, Waldegrave, Colchester County.

1   Come all you people far and near,
        It's quickly you shall hear;
    It's of a lady tall and slim,
        That lived in Cankershire.

2   Her cheeks like blooming roses
        All in her face did shine;
    This maiden's name was lovely Jane,
        She was the rose of Britain's Isle.

3   Her father was a farmer,
        And Jane his only child;
    At sweet sixteen she fell in love
        With her father's servant boy.

4   It's when her father came to know
        This couple a courting were,
    He in a fatal passion flew.
        How he did stamp and swear!

5   Saying, "If you bring disgrace on me
        I'll send you manys a mile.
    With great disdain you'll cross the main
        From the rose of Britain's Isle!"

6   Young Edward he was taken
      And sent across the main,
    While Jane at home did sigh and mourn,
      Her bosom swelled with pain.

7   She dressed herself in men's attire,
      And in a little while
    On board with Edward she was shipped,
      The rose of Britain's Isle.

8   They had not been very long at sea
      Till a storm it did arise,
    And when young Edward went aloft
      Jane stood with watery eyes.

9   It's when they came to the coasts of Spain
      The enemy gave the alarm,
    And by a ball young Jane did fall
      And sprainéd her left arm.

10   The seamen ran to lend her aid,
       While Jane with an innocent smile
    To Edward said, "Behold your maid,
       She's the rose of Britain's Isle!"

11   It's when they came to shore,
       It's married they was with speed.

      .   .   .   .

       .   .   .   .

12   And when they came unto him
       It's on them he did smile,
    To Edward said, "You're welcome home
       With the rose of Britain's Isle.

13   "Five hundred pounds I'll give you
       If you but stay with me,
    And when that I do come to die
       My heiress you shall be."

14   Young Edward lives contented,
       And on each other smile
    Young Edward he is happy now
       With the rose of Britain's Isle.

38

ERIN'S LOVELY HOME

THIS is probably an Irish song, but it has been current in many parts of England also, and during the sixties and seventies of the last century it appeared in many of the popular songsters published in the United States.

For British versions see: Gavin Greig, *Folk-Song of the North-East*, XLVII; Sharp and Marson, *Folk-Songs from Somerset*, II, 24–25; *Journal of the Folk-Song Society*, I, 117; II, 167–168, 211; *Journal of the Irish Folk-Song Society*, I, 11–12; Sharp, *One Hundred English Folk-Songs*, pp. 124–125 (with music). The following broadside copies are in bound collections in the Harvard College Library: 25242.17, IV, 71 (John Gilbert, Newcastle, No. 26); IV, 159 (John Ross, Newcastle); V, 217 (Ryle); VI, 73 (Cadman, Manchester, No. 239); IX, 95 (Bebbington, Manchester, No. 99); XI, 31 (Such, No. 31). The following broadside sheets containing the song are on file in the Harvard College Library: J. Harkness, Preston, No. 457 (with "The Landing of Royal Charlie"); Ryle & Co., London (with "Don't be too Particular").

For texts published in America see: *The "We Parted By the River Side" Songster* (New York, American News Co., 1869), p. 38; *Dan Bryant's "Shaun the Post" Songster* (New York, Robert M. De Witt, 1870), p. 168; *The "When the Corn is Waving, Annie" Songster* (New York, The American News Co.), p. 35; *Wehman's Irish Song Book, No. 1*, 1887, pp. 107–108; Wehman broadside, No. 181; J. H. Johnson (Philadelphia) broadside; Manus O'Conor, p. 25.

"Erin's Lovely Home." From the singing and recitation of David Rogers, Pictou, Pictou County.

1 When I was young and in my prime, my age being twenty-one,
　I hired as a servant unto a gentleman.
　I served him true and honest, and very well, it's known,
　And lately he banished me from Erin's lovely home.

2 The reason that he banished me I soon shall let you know —
　I owned I loved his daughter, and she loved me as well.
　She had a very large portion, and riches I had none,
　And that's the reason he banished me from Erin's lovely home.

3 It was in her father's garden all in the month of June,
　A viewing of the roses all in their youthful bloom.
　She says, "My dearest Willie, if with me you will roam,
　We'll bid adieu to all our friends in Erin's lovely home."

4 He gave consent that very night away with her to go.
　Far from her father's dwelling they both set off alone.
　The night being bright by the moonlight they both set off alone
　And thinking to get safe away from Erin's lovely home.

5 It's when they got to Belfast about the break of day
My love she got ready our passage for to pay.
Five hundred pound she counted, saying, "Love, make this your
    own,
And do not grieve for those you leave in Erin's lovely home."

6 It's when they thought all danger past the old man did appear,
Which soon did separate me from the arms of my dear.
He marched me back to Homeford jail in the county of Tibrone,
It's there I was confinéd in Erin's lovely home.

7 As I lay in confinement, it grieved my heart full sore,
But the parting with my own true love did grieve me ten times
    more.
There's seven links all in my chain and every link a year
Before that I return again to the arms of my dear.

39

MY FATHER'S SERVANT BOY

THE Harvard College Library has broadsides of this song by Such, No. 346 (XIII, 39), Catnach, and Pitts.

"My Father's Servant Boy." From the singing and recitation of Richard Hines, River John, Pictou County.

1 Come all you old, both great and small, attend unto my fame;
There's none of you will pity me but those who felt the same.
I lived between Duncannon and the town of Duncalloy,
And now I'm in America with my father's servant boy.

2 My father he would have me wed unto a gentleman;
Next day in church we were to meet to join in wedlock band.
The night before, I stole from them unto a village nigh,
Where I did meet my own true love, my father's servant boy.

3 I took my love along with me, I cared for nothing more;
I bid farewell to all my friends, likewise to the Shamrock shore.
To Belfast town we both went down and soon found Captain
    Coy,
And in his ship I sailed away with my father's servant boy.

4 When we got to America our money we did spend,
And some time was supported by a true Irish friend,
Till a gentleman from Ireland he did my love employ.
Two pounds a week I do receive from my father's servant boy.

5 They wrote me a letter to Philadelphia town:
If I would go home again I would get five hundred pound.
This news I sent to them from Philadelphia town:
Where they are worth a shilling there, here I am worth one pound.

40

MARY RILEY

THE following text, after the fourth stanza, corresponds to the Maine version printed by Gray, pp. 82–83, ("Mary Aclon"); but in Gray's text there is no mention of the ring or of the father's eavesdropping; the lover is betrayed by Venus and Cupid, and is, on a more rational count, arrested and imprisoned for making love to the squire's daughter.

"Mary Riley" is probably a modified version of that most popular of Irish folk-songs, "Willy Reilly." The story has all the elements of the longer narrative in "Willy Reilly": the courting of the lady, the enmity of her father, the arrest and imprisonment of the lover and his trial on the two charges of making love to the squire's daughter and of stealing her ring (and, in "Willy Reilly," her money and jewels also), the appearance of the lady at the trial, and the freeing of the lover by virtue of her testimony. "Willy Reilly" may be found in O'Conor, p. 86, and in many Irish and American song books. It is also common in English broadsides (Bebbington, No. 367, Harkness, No. 69, etc.), usually with the title "Riley and Colinban" — a modification of the title "Reilly and his Colleen Bawn." Cf. Cox, p. 336.

"Mary Riley." From the singing and recitation of David Rogers, Pictou, Pictou County.

1   One evening as I went a walking,
       Conversing with me and my dear,
     Her old agéd father stood in ambush
       And heard the fond words that we said.

2   A gold ring she put on my finger,
       Saying, "Johnny, keep me in your mind,
     And if ever you roam from this island,
       I hope you 'll not leave me behind."

3   They kissed and shook hands and they parted,
       Expecting to meet the next noon;
     But hard was the heart of her father,
       He locked my love up in her room.

4   With a coach of police he got ready,
       He swore to the ring on my hand.
     And for the squire's young daughter
       I'm afraid a hard trial I'll stand.

5   But Mary being constant and loyal,
       Straightway to my trial she came;
     She was dressed like some lady of honour,
       The best of gold robes she had on.

6 Which made all the nobles to wonder,
   And all the grand jury to stare,

   .   .   .   .

     .   .   .   .

7 It's then she addresséd the jury,
   Those words unto them she did say:
   "In case you love a young female,
   Why should you be banished away?

8 "It's seven long years we've been courting;
   I own that I gave him my heart;
   And there's nothing but death will relieve me
   If Jimmy and I has to part."

9 Now this young couple are married,
   Their fortune on both sides paid down;
   They live on the banks of the Shannon,
   Although they've caused manys a frown.

10 They live on the banks of the Shannon
    In love and sweet unity.
    Here's a health unto young Mary Riley,
    For loyal she's provéd to be!

41

ELLEN THE FAIR

THIS song is also known as "Helen the Fair." It was a common broadside ballad, but is not included in the recent English collections. See broadsides: R. Evans, Foregate Street, Chester (25242.18, collected in 1831); T. Birt, London (25242-62); J. Kendrew, York (III, 89); M. S. Dodds, Newcastle, No. 110 (III, 129); W. Forth, Bridlington, No. 131 (III, 171); J. Cadman, Manchester, No. 390 (V, 4); Bebbington, Manchester, No. 147 (IX, 142); Ann Batchelor, London (with "Down in Our Village"); no imprint (with "The American Stranger" and "March to the Battle Field"); T. Birt, London, No. 188; another without imprint (with "If I had a thousand a year").

For American texts see: *The Forget Me Not Songster* (New York, Nafis and Cornish), p. 141; the same (Philadelphia and New York, Turner and Fisher), p. 32; *The Old Forget Me Not Songster* (Boston, Locke and Dubier), p. 141; *The "Low Backed Car" Songster* (New York, Richard Marsh), pp. 61-62; *The New American Song Book and Letter Writer* (Louisville, Ky., C. Hagan & Co., 1847), pp. 129-130.

"Ellen the Fair." From the singing and recitation of Alexander Harrison, Maccan, Cumberland County.

1 Fair Ellen one morn from her cottage had strayed;
To the next market town tripped the beautiful maid.
She looked like a goddess, so charming and fair.
"Come buy my sweet posies!" cried Ellen the Fair.

2 "I've cowslips and jessamines, and harebells so blue,
Wild roses and eglantines, glistening with dew,
And the lily, the queen of the valley, so rare.
Come buy my sweet posies!" cried Ellen the Fair.

3 Enraptured I gazed on this beautiful maid,
For a thousand sweet smiles on her countenance played;
And while I stood gazing, my heart I declare
A captive was taken by Ellen the Fair.

4 Oh, could I but gain this fair nymph for my wife
How gladly would I change my condition in life.
I'd forsake the gay follies of the town and repair
To dwell in a cottage with Ellen the Fair.

5 But what need I care for the lordly or great!
My parents are dead, I've a noble estate;
And no lady on earth, nor a princess shall share
My hand and my fortune with Ellen the Fair.

6 In a little time after, this nobleman's son
Did marry the maid his affections had won.
When presented at Court, how the Monarch did stare,
And the ladies all envied sweet Ellen the Fair.

42

THE MAID OF THE MOUNTAIN BROW

M. C. DEAN prints a version of this song from Minnesota in *The Flying Cloud and 150 Other Old Time Poems and Ballads*, pp. 83–84, under the title "The Maid of the Logan Bough."

"The Maid of the Mountain Brow." From the singing and recitation of John Brown, River John, Pictou County.

1 Come all ye men and maidens and listen to my song,
   And if you'll pay attention I'll not detain you long.
   'T was of a wealthy young man I'm going to tell you now,
   And he's lately become a member of the Maid of the Mountain
     Brow.

2 He said, "My lovely fair maid, if you'll come along with me now
   We'll go and we'll get married and it's happy we will be.
   We'll join our hands in wedlock bands if you'll come along with
     me now.
   I will labour late and early for the Maid of the Mountain
     Brow."

3 She being a wigglesome young thing she did n't know what to say.
   Her eyes did sparkle like diamonds and as merrily she did play:
   "Kind sir, I would rather be excused, I can't go with you now.
   I will tarry another season at the foot of the Mountain Brow."

4 He said, "My lovely fair maid, how can you answer no?
   Look down in yonder valley where my crops do gently grow.
   Look down in yonder valley stands my horses and my plow.
   They work both late and early for the Maid of tho Mountain
     Brow."

5 "If they work both late and early, kind sir, it's not for me."
   Your conduct it is none of the best, for I can plainly see.
   There is an inn where you call in, for I've heard the people say,
   Where you rap and call and pay for all, and go home at the break
     of day."

6 "If I rap and call and pay for all, my money it is my own,
   I'll spend none of your fortune, for I've understood you have
     none.
   You thought you had my poor heart gained by happening on me
     now,
   But I'll leave you where I met you at the foot of the Mountain
     Brow."

7 "O it's Jimmy dear, it's Jimmy, how can you be so unkind!
   To a girl you loved so dearly how quickly you've changed your
     mind,
   To a girl you loved so dearly, and you're going to leave me now.
   O don't leave me broken-hearted at the foot of the Mountain
     Brow!"

43

REILLY'S FAREWELL

THE unfortunate hero of this ballad had, like Shakspere, a name that could be represented by a practically infinite variety of spellings, and the recorders of his tragedy have overlooked few of the possibilities. The title of the ballad also can be, and has been, varied to an almost equal degree. The Irish versions (published, for the most part, in America) are usually "O'Reilly [or O'Riley] the Fisherman." The English versions may have this caption or any other one including the name Reilly or O'Reilly spelled in any manner whatsoever. Some of the variants will be noted below. In the Nova Scotia text the hero is consistently referred to as "Young Reilly," and this phrase would seem to be the natural one to employ as a title. There is, however, another broadside song, entirely independent of this one, entitled "Young Reilly," and I am avoiding unnecessary confusion by borrowing one of the more distinctive English titles. For a brief discussion of "Young Reilly" see my note on "Waterloo," pp. 182–183.

For British versions of the song see: Greig, CX ("John Rylie"); G. B. Gardiner, *Folk-Songs from Hampshire*, pp. 9–11 (with music); Ashton, *Modern Street Ballads*, pp. 390–391 ("Riley's Farewell"); *Journal of the Folk-Song Society*, I, 256–257 ("Young Riley the Fisherman"); V, 147–148 ("John Riley"); *Journal of the Irish Folk-Song Society*, I, 5 ("One Evening Fair"; fragment, with music). See also the following broadside copies: Manchester, "Riley's Farewell" (25242.71); W. R. Walker, Newcastle-on-Tyne, No. 20 (IV, 17); J. Cadman, Manchester, No. 265 (VI, 192); Ryle (VII, 32); Bebbington, Manchester, No. 22 (IX, 22); Such, No. 121 (XI, 121); John Harkness, Preston, No. 262 (with "The Sailor Boy's Farewell to his Mother"); Bebbington, Manchester, No. 22 (with "Youth and Bloom").

For texts published in America see: The *"We Parted By the River Side" Songster* (New York, American News Co., 1869), p. 6; *Dan Bryant's "Shaun the Post" Songster* (New York, Robert M. De Witt, 1870), p. 119; *Paddy's Own Song Book* (De Witt), pp. 23–25; De Marsan broadside, List 6, No. 91; Wehman broadside, No. 782; *Delaney's Irish Song Book No. 3*, p. 24; O'Conor, p. 49; Pound, No. 39 ("Jack Riley").

No local title. From the singing and recitation of John Adamson, Westville, Pictou County.

1 As I walked out one evening down by a river clear,
   I overheard a fair maid and the tears fell from her eye,
   Saying, "This is a dark and a stormy night — " these words
      I heard her say —
   "My love is on the raging main bound to America.

2 "My love he is a sailor bold. His age is scarce nineteen.
   He is as fine a young man as ever you have seen.
   My mother took me by the hand, these words to me did say,
      'If you are fond of Reilly let him leave this country.'

3 "'O mother dear, don't be severe. How can I part my love?
For his very heart lies in my breast as constant as a dove.'
'O daughter dear, I'm not severe; here is one thousand pound.
Send Reilly to America to purchase there some ground.'"

4 As soon as Ellen received the money, to Reilly she did run,
Saying, "This very night for to take your life my father has
charged his gun.
Here is one thousand pound in gold my mother sent to you.
You will sail away to America and I will follow you."

5 In two or three days after, young Reilly sailed away,
And when he put his foot on board, these are the words he said:
"Here is a token of true love. I'll break it fair in two.
You have my heart, so take this ring till I will find out you."

6 In two or three months after I was walking down the gate.
Young Reilly he came back again and took his love away.
The ship was wrecked, all hands were lost, her father wept full
sore.
Young Reilly and his true love were found dead on the shore.

7 And on her breast a letter was found, and it was wrote with blood,
Saying, "Cruel was my father when he thought to shoot my love.
Let this be as a warning to all young maidens gay
For not to let the lads they love sail to America."

44

JIMMY AND HIS OWN TRUE LOVE

THIS song has been printed on broadsides with various titles — sometimes "The Sailor and his Truelove," and sometimes "Jemmy's Farewell": 25242.4, I, 63 (J. Jennings, London); II, 62 (Pitts); also, on file, Pitts; "Printed and sold at 60 Old Street."

"Jimmy and His Own True Love." From the singing and recitation of Mrs. James Campbell, River John, Pictou County.

1 As Jimmy and his own true love went walking out one day
 To view the hills and the valleys, for they were young and gay,
 It was in the spring when the birds did sing, and the larks sang
  loud on high,
 It was so sweet and charming to hear their melody.

2 The very first time she saw her love she called out, "Jimmy, my
  dear,
 I hear you are going to leave me in sorrow to lament."
 She hung down her head and her rosy cheeks with many a tear
  that fell:
 "You 're bound for the West Indies, dear Jimmy, I fare you
  well."

3 "O now, my weeping Annie, why do you so remind?
 What makes it run in your fancy that I will never return?
 If I were away for seven long years, it 's faithful I would be;
 I 'll never forsake the girl I love while I sail on the sea."

4 She took the rings from her fingers, and diamonds they were
  three,
 Saying, "Lovely Jimmy, take these while you sail on the sea,
 For on the sea there is many a league and many a foaming roar.
 You will think of lovely Annie, the girl whom you adore.

5 "My father and my mother chastising me full sore
 For keeping of your company, but I will keep it more.
 The chastisement they gave to me will never change my heart,
 For I will go and meet you, love, though the night be ever so
  dark."

6 "O now, my weeping Annie, I can no longer stay.
  Our topsails they are hoisted, our anchor waits array."
  She hung down her head and her rosy cheeks with many a tear
    that fell:
  "May the Heavens above protect you, dear Jimmy, I fare you
    well."

45

THE JOLLY PLOUGHBOY

THIS song — variously entitled "The Simple Ploughboy," "The Pretty Ploughboy," and "The Jolly Ploughboy" — was once a very popular one in England and Scotland. Robert Ford, writing in 1901, says: "In the rural districts of Perthshire, I am sure, no song was better known fifty years ago, and it is still occasionally sung, I am told, both in Aberdeenshire and Roxburghshire" (*Vagabond Songs and Ballads of Scotland*, Second Series, p. 150).

For English and Scotch texts see Baring-Gould, *Songs of the West*, 5th edition, No. 59, pp. 122–123; Greig, CXVII; Ford, *Vagabond Songs and Ballads of Scotland*, II, 150–152; Sharp, *Folk-Songs from Somerset*, V, No. 111, 20–23 ("The Pretty Ploughing-Boy"); Broadwood, *English Traditional Songs and Carols*, pp. 72–73 ("The Valiant Lady, or the Brisk Young Lively Lad"); Merrick, *Folk-Songs from Sussex*, pp. 10–11; Baring-Gould and Sharp, *English Folk-Songs for Schools*, No. 29, pp. 60–61; *Journal of the Folk-Song Society*, I, 132–133; II, 146–147; IV, 303–310. See also the following broadside copies: Harkness, No. 488 (II, 133); Catnach (VII, 70); Bebbington, Manchester (X, 93); Such (XII, 74); James Paul & Co. (with "The Old Girl at Home"); W. S. Fortey, at the Catnach Press (with "The Spotted Cow" and "Canadian Boat Song"); Such (with "Young Edwin in the Lowlands Low").

In America a version has been published by Campbell and Sharp, No. 49, p. 178.

"The Jolly Ploughboy." From the singing and recitation of Mrs. James Campbell, River John, Pictou County.

1 Jack, the jolly ploughboy, was ploughing up his land;
     His horses lie beneath the shady tree.
   He did whistle, he did sing, caused the valleys for to ring;
     His intentions were to court a pretty maid.

2 When thus her old father the news came to hear
     That his daughter was a courting on the plain,
   He rose and oppressed and sent him off to sea,
     And sent him to the war to be slain.

3 She dressed herself up in full sailor's array
     With a sword and bright pistol by her side.
   She rode down the street, the tears rolled down her cheeks,
     She looked just like a jovial sailor bold.

4 The first man she met was in sailor's array.
     "O where is my ploughboy?" cried she.
   "He is in yonder fleet ploughing up the deep;
     Pass along, my pretty fair maid, pass along!"

5 She went to the harbour where'er the fleet did lay,
    And thus to the captain did say,
"You have stolen away my ploughboy to send him off to sea,
    And sent him to the war to be slain.

6 "O here, O here is my purse full of gold,
    And this I will freely give o'er."
She threw it on the deck, threw her arms around his neck,
    And she rowed him in her arms to the shore.

7 O happy are they when true lovers do meet,
    When their troubles, their trials are all o'er.
She did whistle, she did sing, caused the valleys for to ring,
    When she gained the love of him whom she adore.

46

WILLIE TAYLOR

UNDER the slightly varying titles "William Taylor," "Bold William Taylor," and "Willie Taylor," this song has had remarkable currency in Great Britain. Several versions, also, have been collected in the United States. It seems a work of supererogation to parody a ballad which might itself serve as a travesty of the Lovers' Separation theme, but about the end of the eighteenth century "Willie Taylor" was given a slightly different garment of phraseology, including a "Toll de loll" chorus, and was thus presented as an avowedly comic song with the title "Billy Taylor." This production served its turn chiefly on the stage, while the original song continued on its round among the singers of the people.

The versions of "Willie Taylor" exhibit a good many variations in the treatment of the last phase of the story, and some of these I have discussed in the Introduction. It is quite certain that the original ending was the triumphant one that is retained in the Nova Scotia version, but occasionally this is turned into tragedy of a sentimental sort.

For references see *Journal of the Folk-Song Society*, v, 163–164; Cox, p. 382.

"Willie Taylor." From the singing and recitation of Mrs. James Palmer, Waldegrave, Colchester County.

A

1   Willie Taylor, brisk young sailor,
        Courted by a lady gay,
    A day or two before the marriage,
        Pressed he was and sent away.

2   She dressed herself in men's attire,
        Boldly entered for Jacky Tar.
    Her lily white hands and slender fingers
        Daubed they were with pitch and tar.

3   When she came to the field of battle,
        There she stood among the rest
    A silver button flew off her waistcoat;
        There appeared her milk-white breast.

4   When the captain saw this wonder,
        He said, "What wind has blown you here?"
    "I am in search of my true love,
        Whom you pressed and I love dear."

5 "If you 're in search of your true lover,
    Tell me your true lover's name."
"My true lover's name is Willie Taylor,
    Whom you pressed to the Isle of Man."

6 "If your true love is William Taylor,
    I find he is a false young man,
For he is to be married to-morrow
    To a lady of this land.

7 "If you rise early in the morning,
    Early by the break of day,
There you 'll see young Willie Taylor
    Walking with his lady gay."

8 She rose early in the morning,
    Early by the break of day,
And there she saw young Willie Taylor
    Walking with his lady gay.

9 She called out for sword and pistol,
    Sword and pistol at her command,
And then she shot young Willie Taylor
    And his bride at his right hand.

10 When the captain saw this wonder,
    He laughed loudly at the fun,
Saying, "You shall be captain and chief commander
    Over my sailors every one!"

11 If Willie Taylor was as constant a lover,
    As constant a lover as he could pretend,
She never would have been so cruel
    As her true love's days to end.

B

"Willie Taylor." From the singing and recitation of Robert Reid, River
John, Pictou County.

1 Willie Taylor was a brisk young sailor,
    Courted by a lady gay.
A little before they were to be married,
    Pressed he was, and sent to sea.

2 She dressed herself in man's apparel,
  And boldly entered for Jack Tar.
Her lily-white hands and her long slender fingers
  Daubed they were with pitch and tar.

3 It 's when she came to the front of battle,
  O she fought most manfully,
Till a silver button flew from her waistcoat
  And her milk-white breast was seen.

4 When the captain saw this wonder,
  Says he, "What winds have blown you here?"
"O I am in search of my own true lover,
  Whom you pressed the other year."

5 "If you 're in search of your true lover,
  Pray tell to me his name."
"His name is Willie Taylor,
  Whom you pressed from the Isle of Man."

6 "If Willie Taylor is your true lover,
  He 's a false young man,
For he 's to be married to-morrow
  To a lady of this land."

7 She rose up in the morning early,
  Gaily at the break of day,
And there she saw young Willie Taylor
  Walking with his lady gay.

8 Then she called for sword and pistol,
  Sword and pistol at her command,
And there she shot false Willie Taylor
  And his bride at his right hand.

9 When the captain heard this wonder
  () he laughed at the fun,
Saying, "I 'll make you captain chief commander
  Over the sailors every one!"

47

THE GREEN MOSSY BANKS OF THE LEA

IT seems probable that this is an English song, not an Irish one, in spite of the presumptive evidence of the line "I quickly sailed over to Ireland"; and the Lea of the refrain may be the river which joins the Thames near the Isle of Dogs. In the English versions, which appear in a great many broadsides, this line usually reads, "We quickly sailed over to England."

For English texts see: Sharp and Marsan, *Folk-Songs from Somerset*, III, 34–38; *Journal of the Folk-Song Society*, II, 150–151; IV, 91; VII, 24; broadside copies: Walker, Durham (25242.71); John Ross, Newcastle, No. 62 (IV, 20); Cadman, Manchester, No. 126 (V, 70); no imprint (VII, 172); Bebbington Manchester, No. 125 (IX, 120); Such, No. 130 (XI, 130); Harkness, Preston, No. 88 (with "The Banks of Sweet Dundee"); Walker, Durham, No. 5 (with "Child of Good Nature"); Elias Keys, Devonport (with "The Croppy Boy"); another, without imprint (with "Masonic Hymn").

In America the song was published in *Wehman's Irish Song Book No. 1*, pp. 9–10, and in *Delaney's Irish Song Book No. 5*, p. 24. It appeared also as a Wehman broadside (No. 924). Barry has published a melody, *Journal*, XXII, 81.

From the singing and recitation of Richard Hines, River John, Pictou County.

1 When first from my country, a stranger, curiosity caused me to
    roam,
  Over Europe I resolved to be a ranger, when I left Philadelphia
    my home.
  I quickly sailed over to Ireland, where forms of great beauty
    doth shine.
  It was there I beheld a fair damsel, and I wished in my heart she
    was mine.

2 One morning I careless did ramble where the sweet wind's pure
    breezes did blow;
  'T was down by a clear crystal river where the sweet purling
    waters doth flow.
  It was there I beheld a fair damsel, some goddess appearing to be,
  As she rose from the reeds by the waters on the green mossy
    banks of the Lea.

3 I stepped up and bid her good morning; her fair cheeks did blush
    like the rose.
  Said I, "These green banks looks charming; your guardian I'll
    be if you choose."

She says, "Sir, I ne'er wants a guardian; young man, you're a
    stranger to me;
For yonder's my father a coming on the green mossy banks of
    the Lea."

4   I waited till up came her father; I picked up my courage once
      more;
   Said I, "Sir, if this be your daughter, she's a beautiful girl I
      adore.
   Ten thousand a year is my fortune; a lady your daughter shall
      be;
   She'll ride in her chariot and horses on the green mossy banks of
      the Lea."

5   They welcomed me home to their cottage; soon after in wedlocks
      did join.
   I quickly created a cottage with splendour and grandeur to
      shine.
   So now the American stranger great pleasure and pastime can see
   With his adorable gentle Matilda on the green mossy banks of
      the Lea.

6   Come all you pretty fair maids, take warning, no matter how
      poor you may be,
   There's many a poor girl that's handsome as those that's got
      large property.
   By flattery let no man deceive you, no matter how poor you may
      be,
   Like adorable gentle Matilda on the green mossy banks of the
      Lea.

48

THE NEW RIVER SHORE

THIS strange composite ballad is interesting chiefly because of its echoes, here and there, of lines and stanzas from a variety of other songs.

The first stanza corresponds to the final stanza of the broadside ballad "Can't You Love Whom You Please," printed by J. Evans, Long Lane, London. See also stanzas 1 and 2 of "The Green Laurels" (Cox, p. 417). Cox's note refers to other songs which have this motive: "The Orange and Blue," "The Irish Transport," "The Wagoner's Lad," "Forsaken," and "The Rue and the Thyme."

The second and last stanzas correspond to stanzas 3 and 4 of the version of "The Wagoner's Lad" printed in *Journal*, xx, 268–269. See also Shearin and Combs, p. 27.

The last stanza corresponds to the final stanza of Version B of "The Wagoner's Lad" in Campbell and Sharp, No. 64, pp. 215–219, and to the first stanza of "Loving Nancy" in Wyman and Brockway, *Lonesome Tunes*, pp. 62–64. It is really the first stanza of the following brief song ("The Ladies' Case"), which dates from early in the eighteenth century:

> How hard is the Fortune of all Womankind,
> For ever subjected, for ever confined;
> The Parents controul us until we are Wives,
> The Husband enslaves us the rest of our lives.
>
> If fondly we love, yet we dare not reveal,
> But Secretly languish, compell'd to conceal;
> Deny'd every freedom of Life to enjoy,
> We're sham'd if we're kind, we're blam'd if we're coy.

This two-stanza song was published (with the music) about 1734 in *The British Musical Miscellany, or, The Delightful Grove*, I, 5 (London, I. Walsh), with the heading "The Ladies Case. Sung by Miss Raftor at the Theatre Royal. The Words by Mr. Carey. The Tune by Mr. Gouge"; and, with the same heading, in *The Universal Musician: or Songster's Delight* (London, Printed and Sold by the Booksellers, ca. 1734), p. [113]. Miss Raftor's first appearance was in 1728; she became Mrs. Clive in 1732. "Mr. Carey" is, of course, Henry Carey, the author of "Sally in Our Alley." The song may be found also in *A Compleat Collection of Old and New English and Scotch Songs*, I (1735), 105; *The Robin* (London, 1749), Song 103; *The Muses Delight* (Liverpool, 1754), p. 143; *The Busy Bee, or, Vocal Repository* [17–], II, 186; *The Goldfinch* (Glasgow, ca. 1782), p. 55; *The Nightingale*, 1791, pp. 22–23 (with six additional lines); Dalrymple, *A Collection of English Songs*, 1796, p. 20 (with "The Other Side"; "How happy's the State of Fair Womankind"); *The British Melodist, or, National Song Book*, 2d ed., ca. 1819, pp. 251–252; *The Vocal Library*, 1822, No. 107, p. 36. It occurs in an early nineteenth-century American broadside as "A Married Woman's Lamentation" (Ford, *Massachusetts Broadsides*, No. 3261a), and in De Marsan's *Singer's Journal* (New York), II, 34. The *Massachusetts Mercury* for August 19, 1800 (a Boston newspaper), contains an imitation or adaptation entitled "Woman's Hard Fate. — By a Lady." This begins, "How wretched is poor woman's fate."

"The New River Shore," as it is called in Nova Scotia, has been sung, though perhaps not widely, in the United States with the title "The Green-briar Shore." There is a version, corresponding fairly closely to mine, in the Sharp MS. of *Songs from the Southern Appalachians* (Harvard College Library), fol. 616, and the song is reported by Shearin and Combs, p. 27. For an interesting variant ("The New River Shore") see Frank Moore, *Anecdotes, Poetry and Incidents of the War: North and South*, 1866, pp. 180–181.

"The New River Shore." From the singing and recitation of Mrs. James Palmer, Waldegrave, Colchester County (printed, *Quest*, p. 162).

1　O can you love little? O can you love long?
　　Can you love an old sweetheart till the new comes on?
　　Can you tell them you love them their minds for to ease?
　　And when their backs is turned to you, you can love who you
　　　　please.

2　Yes, I can love little, I can love long;
　　I can love an old sweetheart till the new comes on.
　　I can tell them I love them their minds for to ease,
　　And when their backs is turned to me, I can love who I please.

3　As I was a walking one morning in spring
　　To hear the birds whistle and the nightingales sing,
　　I saw a pretty fair maid, she's the one I adore.
　　I'll be her own true love on the New River shore.

4　It's when my love's parents they came for to hear,
　　They pressed me away from my dearest dear.
　　They sent me away where loud cannons did roar,
　　And left her lamenting on the New River shore.

5　It was three months after a letter she sent,
　　.　　.　　.　　.　　.　　.　　.　　.　　.　　.
　　"Come back, my dearest Jimmie, you're the lad I adore.
　　And straight I'll go with you from the New River shore."

6　I picked up my broadsword; it glittered all round;
　　A short time after laid seven to the ground,
　　Some bleeding, some dying, some wounded full sore:
　　I gained my own true love on the New River shore.

7　O hard is the fortune of all womenkind;
　　They're always controlled, they're always confined,
　　Controlled by their parents until they're married wives,
　　Then slaves to their husbands all the rest of their lives.

49

THE SUNNY SOUTH

Cox prints a version of this song, found in Kentucky, under the title "The Bright Sunny South" (p. 280). This version, however, exhibits in the last two stanzas affiliations with "The Rebel Soldier" (Cox, p. 279), whereas the Nova Scotia version ignores the proffered aid of the latter song and introduces a reference to the Fenians — a palpable Canadian modification.

"The Sunny South." From the singing and recitation of Alexander Murphy, Cape John, Pictou County.

1 In the sweet sunny south there was peace and content,
In the days of my boyhood I quietly spent,
Near a broad flowing river and a bright flowing stream,
Ever fresh in my memories and sweet in my dreams.

2 I pondered a while and I counted the cost;
I buckled my sword and I mounted my horse;
For I must away for I can't no longer stand.
I am going in defense of my own native land.

3 Oh father, dear father, oh for me do not weep,
For all your kind advice I will forever keep.
You thought me to be loyal from a boy up to a man;
I will go in defense of my own native land.

4 Oh mother, dear mother, oh for me do not weep,
For on some lonely mountain I longing to sleep,
With my knapsack for my pillow and my rifle in my hand.
I am going in defense of my own native land.

5 My dear and loving sister stood pale into her woe.
She kissed me and embraced me, she bade me for to go;
So I must away for I can't no longer stand;
I will go in defense of my own native land.

6 My dear and loving sweetheart, the girl I love the best,
In sorrow and anguish she clasped me to her breast:
"For you must away for you can't no longer stand;
You must go in defense of your own native land."

7 Time points the way when this conflict will be over,
When from Yankees and Fenians our country will be free.
When this cruel war is over and this bloody work is done,
I will return to my loved ones that is weeping at home.

50

THE ROCKS OF SCILLY

THIS song is fairly common in English broadsides, and before the middle of the nineteenth century it was being reproduced in American song-books.

For English versions see Baring-Gould, *Songs of the West*, No. 52 ("The Wreck off Scilly"); *Journal of the Folk-Song Society*, V, 173 ("Scilly Rocks"); and the following broadsides: Pitts (25242.4, II, 46); Spencer, Bradford (25242.17, I, 140); George Walker, Durham, No. 133 (II, 114); W. Dickinson, York (II, 196); no imprint (VI, 166); Pitts (with "Kelvin Grove"); James Paul & Co. (with "The Trysting Tree"); F. Jennings, Sheffield (with "The Soldier's Wives' Complaint for the Loss of their Husbands"); T. Birt, London, No. 75.

For American texts see: *The Forget Me Not Songster* (New York, Nafis and Cornish), pp. 51–53; the same (Philadelphia and New York, Turner and Fisher), pp. 155–157; *The Old Forget Me Not Songster* (Boston, Locke and Dubier), pp. 51–53; *Uncle True Songster* (Philadelphia, etc., Fisher & Brother), pp. 75–77.

"The Rocks of Scilly." From the singing and recitation of Alexander Harrison, Maccan, Cumberland County.

1 Come all you jolly sailors bold
    That plough the raging main,
  And listen to my tragedy
    Whilst I relate the same.

2 I parted with my wedded wife
    Whom I did still adore.
  To the seas we were commanded
    Where the lofty billows roar.

3 To the East Indies we were bound,
    Our course we then did steer,
  And all alone I still thought o'er
    My lovely Molly dear.

4 Sometimes on deck, sometimes aloft,
    Sometimes I am below;
  But Molly she's still in my eye,
    Fond love commands me so.

5 She's charming, beautiful, and fair;
    She's all my soul's delight;
  The brightest day appears to me
    Like the shades of night.

6 By myself alone I sigh and moan
    Whilst others sport and play;
Were Molly she along with me,
    It would be always day.

7 My very heart's lodged in her breast,
    Which does increase my pain,
But night and day I do think still
    We shall never meet again.

8 When we our loading had received,
    And when to England bound,
We little thought it was our fate
    On Scilly rocks to drown.

9 On the rocks of Scilly we were cast
    By the tempest of the main;
Of all our good ship's jolly crew
    But few could reach the shore.

10 We had not sailed a day but seven
    When the storm began to rise;
The swelling seas run mountains high
    And dismal were the skies.

11 "Aloft, aloft!" our boatswain cries,
    "Each man to his post observe,
And reef your sails both fore and aft,
    Our ships and lives to save."

12 "To the top!" then cried our captain bold,
    "And he that first sees land,
For his reward he shall receive
    Full fifty pounds in hand."

13 "To the top!" then our boatswain's mate,
    "To the maintop so high!"
He looked around on every side,
    But no land could he spy.

14 In head of us a light he saw,
    Which did his spirits cheer.
"Take courage, hearts of oak," he cried,
    "Some harbour we are near."

15 "Sail on, sail on," the captain cried,
   "We're right before the wind,
For by the light which I have seen,
   The land we soon shall find."

16 But as we sailed before the wind
   And thought all dangers past,
On the rocks of Scilly we poor souls
   That fatal night were cast.

17 The first stroke that our ship did get,
   Our captain he did cry,
"The Lord have mercy on our souls,
   For in the deep we die."

18 Of eighty jolly sailors bold,
   But four could reach the shore;
Our gallant ship in pieces went
   And never was seen more.

19 When Molly heard the fatal news
   Her tender heart did break,
And like a faithful lover
   She died for her true love's sake.

51

THE PAISLEY OFFICER

Version A corresponds pretty closely to the English song of "The Paisley Officer," which may be found in a broadside issued by Walker, Newcastle, No. 169 (IV, 101). The text printed by Gray, pp. 85–87, is also similar to the broadside copy. Version B — with its plunge *in medias res* and its additional stanzas at the end — has less the appearance of a fragment than of a separate version.

A

"Bonny Scotland." From the singing and recitation of Robert Reid, River John, Pictou County.

1 In bonny Scotland blithe and gay,
  Where bluebells they do grow,
There lived a shepherd's daughter
  Down in the valley low.

2 She herded sheep the whole day long
  Upon the banks of Clyde;
Although her lot in life was low,
  She was called the village pride.

3 An officer down from Paisley town
  Came hunting down that way;
He hunted on these lowland glens
  Where Mary's cottage lay.

4 A long and loving eye he bent
  Upon her form so fair;
He wondered how so fair a flower
  Could blow and flourish there.

5 It's many a day young Henry came
  A hunting down that way;
It's many a day young Henry came
  To hide his grief and woe.

6 He hunted on those Lowland glens,
  And on the banks so gay,
Still thinking that his lonely hours
  Would pass the time away.

7   Young Henry came to Mary,
      His heart oppressed with woe,
   Saying, "Mary, lovely Mary,
      Far from you I must go.

8   "Our regiment has got the rout,
      While I must give command
   To leave these bonny Highland glens
      For India's burning sand.

9   "O Mary, lovely Mary,
      I love you in my heart.
   I wish you were my wedded bride
      This night before we part."

10   "All for to go along with you
      Would be my whole desire,
   And I will pass as your servant
      Dressed up in men's attire."

11   As they marched up through Paisley town,
      They were wondered much at there,
   To see there such a fine recruit
      So beautiful and fair.

12   The ladies all admired her
      While she stood on parade,
   But little they knew that a soldier's coat
      Concealed so fair a maid.

13   So Henry and his Mary
      Across the sea did go,
   But little they knew the hardships great
      They had to undergo.

14   She fought her way right manfully,
      While Henry done his best,
   But while she strove to heal his wounds
      A ball went through her breast.

15   Young Henry came to Mary
      And unto her did say,
   "I'm afraid you're deadly wounded, love,
      Your lips are like the clay."

16 "The very first time that I saw you
 'Twas you I did adore."
And she closed her eyes, no more to rise,
 On India's burning shore.

B

No local title. From the singing and recitation of Mrs. James Campbell,
River John, Pictou County.

1 Young Henry came to Mary
 His heart being full of woe,
Saying, "Mary, lovely Mary,
 Far from you I must go.

2 "Our regiment they are on the road,
 And I have got command
To leave these lovely hills and dales
 For India's burning sands."

3 "O Henry, lovely Henry,
 Those words will break my heart;
I wish I were your wedded wife
 Before tonight we part.

4 "For me to go along with you
 'Twould be my real desire,
For me to be your waiting-maid
 Dressed up in men's attire."

5 When they arrived at Paisley town,
 The people wondered there
For to see a young recruit
 So beautiful and fair.

6 The ladies all admired him
 As he stood on parade;
But little they thought a soldier's coat
 Concealed so fair a maid.

7 Now to cross the ocean
 Young Henry's forced to go,
But little knows the danger
 He has to undergo.

8　Young Henry fought right manfully
　　　While Mary did her best,
　　And when she stooped to dress his wounds
　　　A bullet pierced her breast.

9　"I fear you're deadly wounded, love,"
　　　Young Henry he did say,
　　"I fear you're deadly wounded, love,
　　　Your lips are like the clay.

10　"'T was ever since I first saw you,
　　　'T was you I did adore."
　　They closed their eyes, no more to rise,
　　　On India's burning shore.

11　With gentle hands the soldiers laid
　　　These fair ones in their grave,
　　Side by side young Henry
　　　So manful and so brave.

12　A simple hill now marks the spot
　　　Where their remains doth lie.
　　May the Lord have mercy on their bones,
　　　Young Henry and his bride.

52

MARY ON THE SILVERY TIDE

THE song of faithful Mary and her sad passage down the silvery tide was fairly common in broadsides, and it has remained in currency in England. In the United States it is practically unknown. The English broadside title is usually "Poor Mary in the Silvery Tide."

For English texts see Sharp, *Folk Songs from Somerset*, 5th Series, No. 112, pp. 24–28; *Journal of the Folk-Song Society*, I, 216; and broadsides: Walker, Newcastle, No. 23 (IV, 74); Catnach (VII, 57); Bebbington, Manchester, No. 144 (IX, 139); Such, No. 303 (XII, 148); without imprint, No. 41 (with "The Black Band's Downfall"); Catnach (with "The Blessings of a Good Little Wife"). See also *Notes and Queries*, 5th Series, VIII, 344–418.

A version from Michigan has been printed by R. W. Gordon in the *Adventure* magazine.

"Mary on the Silvery Tide." From the singing and recitation of Paul Brown, River John, Pictou County.

1 There was a fair young creature who lived by the seaside,
 Who was handsome in form and feature, she was called the village
  pride.
 It was a young sea-captain who Mary's heart did win,
 And true she was to Henry while he was on the raging main.

2 It was in Henry's absence another mener came
 A courting pretty Mary, but she refused the same.
 "Your vows are vain while on the main has won my heart," she
  cried,
 "And then begone, I love but one, and he is on the silvery tide."

3 This nobleman went walking all out to take the air,
 When he spied pretty Mary down on the silvery tide.
 "Now," says this heartless villain, "Consent and be my bride
 Or I'll send your body a floating down on the silvery tide!"

4 "O no, no, dear captain, my vows I'll never break,
 For it's Henry I love dearly; I'll die for his sweet sake!"
 With his handkerchief he bound her hands and threw her o'er the
  side,
 And screaming she went floating down on the silvery tide.

5 Shortly afterwards young Henry returned from the sea,
 Expecting to be happy and appoint the wedding day.
 "Young Mary she is murdered," her wretched parents cried,
 "She has proved her own destruction down on the silvery tide!"

53

THE SAILOR AND THE SHEPHERDESS

In broadsides this song is usually entitled "The Sailor's Courtship." The Harvard College Library has copies, on file, by Pitts, London; T. Birt, London; Catnach, London; Henson, Northampton; Forth, Pocklington, No. 51. The Forth broadside is entitled "The Pretty Young Shepherdess."

"The Sailor and the Shepherdess." From the singing and recitation of Alexander Murphy, Cape John, Pictou County.

1 It's of a bonny shepherdess
　　A watching of a flock,
　Down by the seaside all alone;
　　Chance there came that way
　Was a bright young sailor gay,
　　And he fain would make her his bride.

2 The weather it being warm
　　As she laid on the grass,
　She caused the young sailor to draw nigh;
　　He kissed her ruby lips
　While she lay fast asleep,
　　Saying, "My dear, you have stolen my heart away."

3 She woke in surprise,
　　She opened her eyes,
　She saw the young sailor standing by.
　　"Sailor," said she,
　"What brought you here by me?"
　　And by that she began to cry.

4 "I'm lately come
　　From that little ship you see.
　I have landed on a rock all alone."
　　And he says, "My dearest dear,
　I must find some comfort here,
　　Or else I am forever undone."

5 "O sailor," said she,
　　"How can this ever be,
　Or how can I give my consent?
　　For while you're on the sea
　My mind will have no ease,
　　It will cause me to sigh and lament."

6 "O maiden," said he,
   "If you will but marry me,
You'll have gold and silver in store.
   The sea I will forsake,
And the promise I will make
   To be true to you forevermore."

7 This couple joined in peace
   To love and increase.
The sailor and the shepherdess I'll adore.
   Take a sailor for your life
If they'll have you for their wife,
   For sailors are blessed forevermore.

54

THE CHIPPEWA STREAM

From the singing and recitation of Miss Greta Brown, River John, Pictou County.

1   As I went a walking one evening in June,
A viewing the roses — they were in full bloom —
I met a pretty fair maid as I passed along;
She was washing some linens by the Chippewa Stream.

2   I went up beside her and I made a low bow,
And what I said to her I'll tell to you now:
"It's been twelve months or better my mind's been on thee,
And it's now we'll get married if you will agree."

3   "O to marry, to marry, kind sir, I'm too young;
Besides all you young men have a false flattering tongue.
How cross would my mother and my father would be
If I was to wed with a rover like thee."

4   He turned around quickly, knowing well what to say:
"I wish you a good man, a good man I pray.
The sky it looks heavy, I think we'll have rain." —
So they shook hands and parted on the Chippewa Stream.

5   "O come back, love, come back, love, you've quite won my heart;
It is now we'll get married and never depart.
'T is now we'll get married and happy I'll be,
And live happy together till the day we do die."

6   "O the last words you spoke, love, was far out of tune.
O the last words you spoke, love, I've quite changed my mind.
I think it's far better for single to remain
Than to court some pretty fair maid on the Chippewa Stream."

55

POLLY OLIVER

THIS popular English broadside song is usually entitled either "Polly Oliver" or "Polly Oliver's Ramble." For references to English and American texts see Cox, p. 387.

The fragment which is all that I have hitherto been able to find in Nova Scotia breaks so abruptly into the middle of a good tale that I must supply the introductory stanzas. Bebbington's broadside (No. 267) proceeds as follows to the point where my fragment takes up the story:

> One night as Polly Oliver lay musing in bed
> A comical fancy came into her head:
> "Neither father nor mother shall make me false prove;
> I'll list for a soldier and follow my love."
>
> Early next morning this fair maid arose,
> She dressed herself in a suit of men's clothes;
> Coat, waistcoat, and breeches, and sword by her side,
> On her father's black gelding like a dragoon she did ride.
>
> She rode till she came to fair London town,
> She dismounted her horse at the sign of the Crown;
> The first that came to her was a man from above,
> The next that came down was Polly Oliver's true love.
>
> "Good evening, good evening, kind captain," said she;
> "Here's a letter from your true love Polly Oliver," said she.
> He opened the letter and a guinea was found —
> "For you and your companions to drink her health round."

No local title. From the singing and recitation of Mrs. James Campbell, River John, Pictou County.

1 And Polly being drowsy she hung down her head;
   She called for a candle to light her to bed.
   "Upstairs," said the captain, "I lie at my ease.
   You may lie with me too, countryman, if you please."

2 "To lie with a captain is an unbecoming thing.
   I am a poor soldier who fights for my king;
   I fight for my king on land or at sea.
   Begone, pretty captain, and bother not me."

3 Early next morning young Polly arose;
   She dressed herself up in her old former clothes.
   Coming downstairs she appeared like a dove,
   Saying, "Here's your Polly, your old loyal love."

56

THE DAWNING OF THE DAY

In story, and to some extent in phraseology, there is a noticeable resemblance between this song and the stall ballad of "The Shannon Side." In each the maiden is seduced by a stranger, is deserted, and ends the song with a warning to other maidens who may find themselves in circumstances like those at the beginning of the episode. The maid of "The Shannon Side" thus exhorts her sisters, in words almost identical with those at the conclusion of "The Dawning of the Day":

> Now may I be a warning to all young maids beside,
> And never trust a man again upon the Shannon side.

For texts of "The Shannon Side" see broadsides by Such (No. 77), Bebbington (No. 263), Walker (No. 119), Forth (No. 90), Harkness (No. 589), etc.

For English versions of "The Dawning of the Day" see Gillington, *Eight Hampshire Folk Songs*, No. 5, pp. 10–11 (with music); and broadsides: Pitts (25242.4, II, 72); Forth, Pocklington, No. 50 (25242.17, III, 57); John Gilbert, Newcastle, No. 31 (IV, 139); Forth, Pocklington, No. 115 (IV, 204); J. Cadman, Manchester, No. 113 (VI, 130); Ryle (VII, 104); Bebbington, Manchester, No. 108 (IX, 104); Such, No. 232 (XII, 78); Harkness, Preston, No. 59 (with "Future Prospects of Taxation"); Hurd, Shaftesbury (with "The Wife Well Managed"); Pitts, No. 159. For a tune see *Journal*, XXV, 282.

In America the song was published in *The Forget Me Not Songster* (New York, Nafis and Cornish), pp. 178–180; *The Popular Songster* (Philadelphia and New York, Fisher & Brother). A fragmentary text appeared in a Wehman broadside (No. 998).

From the singing and recitation of Harry Sutherland, River John, Pictou County.

1 As I walked out one morning fair all in the month of June,
   Each bush and tree was decked in green and the flowers were in
      their bloom.
   Returning home all from a walk through a field I took my way;
   I chanced to see a pretty fair maid at the dawning of the day.

2 No shoes or stockings, hat or cloak did that pretty fair maiden
      wear;
   Her hair in golden ringlets hung down o'er her shoulders fair.
   Two milking-pails were in her hands so jovial and so gay;
   She seemed to me like Venus fair at the dawning of the day.

3 "O where are you going, my pretty fair maid? O where are you
      going so soon?"
   "I'm going a milking, sir," she said, "all in the month of June.
   Those pasture fields that I go to are so, so far away
   That I have to be there each morning fair at the dawning of the
     day."

4 "O there's time enough, my pretty fair maid, suppose it were a
    mile.
  Come sit down on those primrose banks and chat with me a
    while."
  "O no, O no," replied this maid, "to that I can't obey.
  Look around, the skies are breaking clear, 'tis the dawning of the
    day."

5 Those words she spoke. My arms entwined around her slender
    waist.
  I laid her on the primrose banks and her I did embrace.
  "Leave off your freedom, kind sir," she said, "and let me go my
    way.
  Look around, the sky is breaking clear, 'tis the dawning of the
    day."

6 We arose, shook hands and parted, and I crossed o'er the way.
  In the course of seven months after, I met her on my way.
  She appeared to me quite dropsical as I crossed o'er the way,
  And carelessly I passed her by at the dawning of the day.

7 The tears rolled down her lily-white cheeks and bitterly she did
    cry,
  "I hope you'll gain no credit, sir, by thus deluding me,
  That I may be a warning to all other maids so gay
  To never trust a lad they meet at the dawning of the day."

8 "For to marry you, my pretty fair maid, 'tis a thing that cannot
    be.
  To join our hands in wedlock bonds, to that I can't agree,
  For I've been lately married to a girl from Bathly Bay,
  Of whom I gained ten thousand pounds, at the dawning of the
    day."

9 The tears rolled down her lily-white cheeks and bitterly she did
    cry,
  "I hope you'll gain no credit, sir, by thus deluding me,
  That I may be a warning to all other maids so gay,
  To ne ver trust a lad they meet at the dawning of the day."

57

THE INDIAN LASS

THERE is so close a similarity between this song and the one that follows it ("The Lass of Mohee") that I have hesitated between the alternatives of printing them separately or including them under one title.

For English versions see Kidson, *Traditional Tunes*, pp. 109–111 (with two airs); *Journal of the Folk-Song Society*, II, 262 (fragment, with music); broadsides: Forth, Pocklington, No. 146 (III, 100); John Gilbert, Newcastle, No. 74 (IV, 70); no imprint (VI, 213); Bebbington, Manchester (X, 124); Such, No. 36 (XI, 36); Nichols, Wakefield (with "The Rose of Ardee"); Such (with "The Banks of Inverness"); Bebbington, No. 380 (with "The Jolly Light Dragoon").

The song has been found in oral circulation in North Carolina (Minish MS.) and was printed as a De Marsan broadside (New York), List 14, No. 40.

"The Indian Lass." From the singing and recitation of John Adamson, Westville, Pictou County.

1   As I went a walking by yon far distant shore
     I went into an ale-house to spend half an hour,
     And as I was musing and taking my glass,
     By chance there came in a fair Indian lass.

2   She sat down beside me, she squeezéd my hand:
     "Kind sir, you're a stranger and not of this land.
     It's I've got good lodgings, so with me you'll stay;
     My portion you'll have then without more delay."

3   With a glass of good liquor she welcomed me in:
     "Kind sir, you are welcome to everything."
     And as I embraced her it was all of her moan:
     "You are a poor sailor and far from your home."

4   We tossed and tumbled in each other's arms;
     All night I enjoyed her sweet lovely charms.
     With love and enjoyment time soon passed away;
     I did not go and leave her till nine the next day.

5   The day was arrived, we were going to sail,
     For to leave this fair maid on the beach to bewail.
     She pulled out her handkerchief and wipéd her eye,
     Saying, "Don't go and leave me, my sailor," she cries.

6   Our anchors being weighed, away then we flew;
     With a sweet pleasant gale parted us from her view.
     And now we are over, and taking our glass,
     And here's a good health to the Indian lass.

58

THE LASS OF MOHEE

KITTREDGE suggests (*Journal*, XXXV, 408) that "The Lass of Mohee" is a chastened American remaking of "The Indian Lass." The latter song, although it appeared on a De Marsan broadside (List 14, No. 40), has had little circulation in the United States, while the former has been found in North Carolina, Kentucky, Virginia, West Virginia, Mississippi, Missouri, Michigan, Iowa, Montana, and Minnesota. For references see *Journal*, XXXV, 408; Cox, p. 372; Dean, pp. 17–18; Pound, No. 91; Henry, *New Jersey Journal of Education*, (1926), XV 5 (North Carolina). The song is known by various titles, the most common of which is "The Pretty Mohee [or Mohea]."

"The Lass of Mohee." From the singing and recitation of Mrs. James Campbell, River John, Pictou County.

1   As I went a walking one evening in June,
      A viewing the roses — they were in full bloom —
  As I was a sitting down on the green grass,
      Who did I happen to spy but a young Hindoo lass.

2   She stepped up towards me, she gave me her hand.
      Said she, "You're a stranger from some foreign land.
  If you will follow, you're welcome to come;
      I live by myself in a snug little home."

3   The sun was a setting all o'er the salt sea
      As I rambled along with that pretty Mohee.
  Together we rambled, together we roamed,
      Till we came to the cot where the cocoanut grew.

4   With fondest expression she said unto me,
      "If you will consent to live here with me
  And go no more rambling across the salt sea,
      I will teach you the language of the lass of Mohee."

5   "O fairest of creatures, that never could be!
      I have a dear girl in my own counteree.
  I'll never forsake her for her poverty,
      For her heart is as true as the lass of Mohee."

6   'Twas early the next morning as the sun it arose;
      She seemed much surprised and these words I did say,
  "I'm now going to leave you, so farewell, my dear.
      Our ship hoist her anchor and homeward must steer."

7   The last time I saw her was down on the sand.
    As the boat passed by her, she waved her hand,
And that was a signal to bid me adieu.
    She still kept a waving till the boat lost her from view.

8   So now we're safe landed on our native shore;
    My friends and relations gather round me once more.
They all gather round me but none can I see
    Whose heart was as true as the lass of Mohee.

9   This Hindoo was beautiful, she was loving and kind,
    She acted her part in a heavenly design.
I being a stranger she took me to her home;
    I'll remember the Mohee as I ramble along.

59

THE BUTCHER BOY

THIS song, which has had an enormous circulation in Great Britain, Canada, and the United States, seems to be mainly the result of a combination of two songs, "The Squire's Daughter" (also known as "The Cruel Father, or, Deceived Maid") and "There is an Alehouse in Yonder Town." The latter, modified to "There is a Tavern in the Town," is a widespread college song. As for the heartless butcher boy, he seems to have that divinity in his nature "of here and everywhere." In the English versions he usually makes his home "in London city" or "in London town" (though a version in the *Journal of the Folk-Song Society*, II, 159, begins, "In Jessie's city, oh, there did dwell"). In Ireland he courts his successive maids "in Dublin city." In the United States he is claimed by "New York City" (Shearin, p. 24; Cox, p. 431), and by "Jersey City," or "New Jersey City" (Belden, No. 21; Cox, p. 430; Tolman, *Journal*, XXIX, 169), although even here he is sometimes reported as living "in London city" (Barry, No. 41; Cox, p. 432).

I remember once hearing the ballad sung in Nova Scotia with the following stanza included:

> I wish my baby it was born,
> And sitting on its father's knee,
> And I myself was in my grave.
> Perhaps he then would think of me.

A variant of this stanza may be found in the version of "A Brisk Young Sailor Courted Me" printed in the *Journal of the Folk-Song Society*, V, 181–187. For references to versions of this ballad, which has close affiliations with "The Butcher Boy," see Cox, p. 353 ("Sweet William"). The stanza in the following form is the concluding one in the beautiful song "Waly, waly, but love is bonny," first published in *A New Miscellany of Scots Sangs* (London, Printed for A. Moore, 1727), p. 182:

> Oh, oh, if my young babe were born,
> And set upon the nurse's knee,
> And I mysell were dead and gane!
> For a maid again I'll never be.

It occurs also in "Arthur's Seat shall be my Bed," a song thought to have been printed in the seventeenth century (see Child, IV, 93, 105).

For references to British and American versions of "The Butcher Boy" see *Journal*, XXIX, 169–170; XXXI, 73; XXXV, 360–361; Cox, p. 430.

A

From the singing and recitation of Mrs. Ellen Bigney, Pictou, Pictou County (printed, *Quest*, pp. 9–10.)

> 1 In London town where I did dwell,
> A butcher boy I loved him well.
> He courted me for many a day;
> He stole from me my heart away.

2   There is an inn in that same town,
     And there my love he sits him down;
     He takes a strange girl on his knee
     And tells her what he wouldn't tell me.

3   The reason is, I'll tell you why,
     Because she's got more gold than I.
     But gold will melt and silver fly,
     And in time of need be as poor as I.

4   I'll go upstairs and make my bed.
     "There is nothing to do," my mother said.
     My mother she has followed me,
     Saying, "What is the matter, my daughter dear?"

5   "O mother dear, you little know
     What pains or sorrow or what woe!
     Go get a chair and sit me down,
     With pen and ink I'll write all down."

6   She wrote a letter, she wrote a song,
     She wrote a letter, she wrote it long;
     On every line she dropped a tear,
     At every verse cried, "Willy dear!"

7   Her father he came home that night
     Enquiring for his heart's delight;
     He went upstairs, the door he broke,
     He found her hanging on a rope.

8   He took a knife and cut her down,
     And in her bosom these lines he found:
     "O what a foolish girl was I
     To hang myself for a butcher's boy.

9   "Go dig my grave both wide and deep,
     Put a marble stone at my head and feet,
     And on my grave place a turtle dove
     To show the world that I died for love."

B

"The Butcher Boy." Contributed by Mrs. Willard Thompson, Cape John, Pictou County.

1 In Dublin city where I did dwell,
    A butcher boy I loved him well.
He courted me for many a day,
    He courted me my life away.

2 I remember the time not long ago
    He would follow me through rain and snow.
But oh, he changed his mind since then;
    He passes my door and he ne'er looks in.

3 There is a house all in this town —
    And take a chair and set ye down —
And he'll take a strange girl on his knee,
    And he'll tell to her what he ne'er told me.

4 But oh, I know the reason why,
    Because she's got more gold than I;
But her gold will melt and her silver fly.
    She'll see the day she's as poor as I.

5 She went upstairs to make her bed,
    And never a word to her mother said.
Her mother following after, inquiring,
    "What's the matter, my darling girl?"

6 "O mother dear, if you only knew!
    My trials and troubles I cannot tell you,
But take you a chair and set ye down.
    With pen and ink I'll write it down."

7 She wrote a letter, she wrote a song,
    She wrote a letter and she wrote it long;
And every line she dropped a tear,
    And every word cried, "Johnny dear!"

8 Her father coming home that night,
    Inquiring for his heart's delight,
He ran upstairs and the door he poked,
    He found her hanging to a rope.

9 He took his knife and cut her down,
    And in her bosom found these few lines:
"O was n't I a foolish girl,
    To hang myself for a butcher boy.

10 "O dig my grave both wide and deep,
    Place a marble stone at my head and feet,
And on my breast place a turtle dove,
    Let the wide world know that I died for love."

60

YOUNG CHARLOTTE

A FULL account of this song, with texts and tunes, is given by Phillips Barry, *Journal*, XXII, 367, 442; XXV, 156. He places it before 1833, and ascribes it to William Lorenzo Carter of Benson or Bensontown, Vermont. For many years it has been current in practically every part of the United States and also in Canada. Cox prints two versions from West Virginia, pp. 286–291, and gives references, p. 286. See also the version from Michigan in Rickaby, pp. 135–138.

"Young Charlotte." From the singing and recitation of John Brown, River John, Pictou County.

1   Young Charlotte lived on the mountain side
      On a very lonely spot;
  There was no friends for miles around
      Except her father's cot.

2   On manys the cold and frosty night
      Kind friends would gather there,
  For Charlotte's people were sociable folks,
      And she was very fair.

3   Her father loved to see her dressed
      As gay as a city belle,
  For she was the only child he had,
      And he loved his darling well.

4   One New Year's Eve as the sun went down
      Beneath the starry sky,
  The moon into the window peeped
      As the merry sleighs passed by.

5   In yonder village sixteen miles away
      There is a ball tonight,
  And though the air is piercing cold,
      Our hearts are warm and light.

6   Her anxious look and her roguish eye
      As she darted here and there,
  And rattling to the cottage door
      Young Charlie's sleigh appeared.

7　"O Charlotte dear," her mother said,
　　"Those blankets round you fold,
For it is a bitter cold night abroad,
　　And you'd get your death of cold."

8　"O no, O no, mamma," she said,
　　As she looked like a gypsy queen,
"To drive in blankets muffled up,
　　I never could be seen.

9　"My silken cloak is warm enough,
　　You know it's well lined through,
And then I have a silken scarf
　　To fold around me too."

10　Her bonnet was on, her gloves were off
　　As they jumped into the sleigh,
And away they drove on the mountain side
　　Far over the hills away.

11　Young Charlie said, "It's a bitter cold night,
　　For the reins I can scarcely hold."
Young Charlotte low a murmuring,
　　"I am exceeding cold."

12　He cracked the whip and the steed flew on
　　Much faster than before,
And away they drove on the mountain side
　　Far over the hills away.

13　Young Charlie said, "It's a bitter cold night,
　　For the frost glistens on my brow."
Young Charlotte murmuring replied,
　　"I'm getting warmer now."

14　He cracked the whip and the steed flew on
　　Still faster than before,
Till the village drew near and the lights appeared,
　　And the ballroom hove in view.

15　When they reached the door young Charlie jumped out
　　And offered her his hand:
"Why sit you there like a monument?
　　You'll neither speak nor stand!"

16 He called her once and he called her twice,
  But she answered ne'er a word.
He called her once and he called her twice,
  But still she never stirred.

17 He took her by the lily-white hand,
  It was as cold as ice,
And rushing to the ballroom door
  He screamed out for a light.

18 A lifeless corpse young Charlotte was,
  For she froze with him in the sleigh.
A lifeless corpse young Charlotte was,
  For she froze by the mountain way.

19 Young Charlie sat down by the ballroom fire
  And the bitter tears did flow:
"You're there, my own, my blooming maid,
  You never more will go."

20 He clasped his arms around her neck
  And kissed her marble brow,
And his thoughts did wander when she said,
  "I'm getting warmer now."

61

MARY OF THE WILD MOOR

ACCORDING to the proportion of one's sensibilities this will be regarded as an affecting song or as a merely sentimental one. Obviously it has been accepted in the former character by a great many people both in Great Britain and in America. Few songs have appeared more frequently in broadsides and in song-books. Kidson remarks, in his note on the text which he prints in *Traditional Tunes* (p. 77): "I have found that the song is known in the North and East Ridings. . . . Both air and song appear to be not much earlier than the beginning of the present [*i.e.*, the nineteenth] century. It is often seen on ballad sheets of this and of later date."

The song was printed in many English broadsides; for example: Such, No. 73, Debbington, Manchester, No. 44; Harkness, Preston, No. 60 (with "William of the Man of War"); Barr, Leeds, No. 110 (with "Flora the Lily of the West").

In America it was printed, together with "The Waterman," in a broadside "Sold, wholesale and retail, by T. Deming, 62 Hanover St., Boston." See also: *The Shilling Song Book* (Boston, Oliver Ditson & Co., 1860), p. 41; *The "Waiting for a Broadway Stage" Songster* (New York, Robert M. De Witt, 1868), p. 29; *The "Up In A Balloon" Songster* (De Witt, 1869), p. 50; *The "Sweet Genevieve" Songster* (De Witt, 1869), p. 46; *Jennie Engel's "Courting in the Rain" Songster* (De Witt, 1872), p. 36. For further references see *Journal*, XXIX, 185; XXXV, 389; Cox, p. 437.

"The Village Pride." From the singing and recitation of Mrs. Ellen Bigney, Pictou, Pictou County.

1 'Twas one cold winter's night when the winds
        They blew bitter across the wild moor,
    When poor Mary she came with a child in her arms
        Wandering home to her own father's door.

2 "O why did I leave this fine cot,
        Where once I was happy and free?
    Now doomed for to roam without friends or a home,
        O father, take pity on me!

3 "O father, O father," she cries,
        "Pray come down and open your door,
    Or this child at my bosom will perish and die
        From the winds blown across the wild moor."

4 But her father was deaf to her cry,
        Not a sound of his voice reached her ear;
    But the watch-dogs did bark and the village bells rang,
        And the winds blew across the wild moor.

5 But what did her old father say
      When he came to the door the next morn,
   Where he found Mary dead but her child still alive,
      Fondly clasped in its dead mother's arms?

6 With grief the old man pined away,
      And the child to its mother went soon,
   And there's none that is left to this very day,
      For the cottage is going to ruin.

7 But the village points out the spot
      Where the willows weep over the door,
   Where Mary died, once the village pride,
      From the winds blown across the wild moor.

62

THE FATAL SNOWSTORM

I HAVE found no exact equivalent of this song in the recent collections and song-books. There is on file in the Harvard College Library a Pitts broadside containing the three songs "The Fatal Snowstorm," "Poor Rose," and "The Letter," the first of which is so similar to the following song in motive and, to a lesser degree, in phraseology that I have adopted its title. In the broadside the mother, wandering in a snowstorm, comes to a house, knocks at the door, is denied admission, and dies. Some of these harrowing circumstances are presented indirectly, in my version, but the stories, at least, are alike. The song in the Pitts broadside is ascribed to John Embleton.

In *Journal*, XXVIII, 170, there is a song ("The Orphan Girl"), contributed by E. C. Perrow from North Carolina, which has a good deal in common with the present one. The girl comes through the snowstorm to the rich man's door, is denied entrance, and dies. It is not the same song, but it bears marks of relationship.

No local title. From the singing and recitation of Mrs. Ellen Bigney, Pictou, Pictou County.

1 'Twas on a winter evening,
    When the frost came down like snow
Over hill and valley,
    Where wintry winds do blow,

2 I spied a female form
    All in a depth of snow
With an infant in her arms;
    She knew not where to go.

3 "O cruel was my father,
    Who barred the doors on me;
And cruel was my mother —
    She might have pitied me.

4 "And cruel was the wintry wild
    That pierced my heart with cold,
And cruel was the young man
    That sold his heart for gold.

5 "But still, my pretty baby,
    I'll fold you to my breast.
It's little does your father know
    This night we're in distress.

6   "It's little does your father know
      What we must undergo.
  I'll fold you to my bosom, love,
      Through this cold frost and snow.

7   "Come all you pretty fair maids,
      And a warning take by me:
  Don't believe a young man
      Or anything he'll say.

8   "For they'll court you and they'll kiss you
      Until your love they'll gain:
  And then they'll go and leave you
      In sorrow, grief, and shame.

9   "I'll go to some lonely valley
      And then kneel down and pray;
  I'll ask of the almighty God
      To have mercy on my soul."

10 She kissed her baby's cold white lips,
      She laid him by her side,
  She raised her hands to heaven
      And then lay down and died.

63

THE SINGLE SAILOR

UNDER such varying titles as "The Broken Token," "A Pretty Fair Maiden," "The Young and Single Sailor," and "The Sailor's Return," this song has been current in Great Britain and has been printed repeatedly in broadsides and song collections. Many versions have also been found in circulation in the United States. It is representative of a fairly large group of ballads (including the eight ensuing numbers in this collection) in which the lover, after being absent for some time at sea or in the wars, returns and tests the fidelity of his sweetheart, who for some reason or other fails to recognize him, while he pretends to be a stranger and plies her with requests to accept his advances and forget the absent Johnny or William. Only when he proclaims his identity is he recognized by the maiden, and as a rule the tellers of the tale make no attempt to motivate the preliminary deception. One version of "The Single Sailor" mentions the lapse of seven years and the change in "shape and colour," and "The Banks of Claudie" regularly includes one explanatory line, — "I own she did not know me, I being in disguise," — but in most cases we are simply to infer that the dim light of evening or the shadows of night enable the lover to maintain his assumption of strangeness until his test is completed and his faith in the maiden established. In the Percy Collection of Broadsides and Garlands (Harvard College Library), III, fol. 64, there is an interesting earlier ballad of this type, entitled "The Valiant Seaman's Return to his Love," which definitely mentions a disguise, employed by the sailor while he is testing the maiden and thrown off when he is convinced of her faithfulness. Another broadside in this same collection (III, fol. 79) is equally interesting for a different reason: it transforms, or rather develops, Gay's "Black-Eyed Susan" into a Return and Test ballad series, beginning with Gay's song under the title "William and Susan," proceeding to "Sweet William's Return to his Dear Susan," and ending with "Sweet Susan's Loyalty."

For references to British texts of "The Single Sailor" see Campbell and Sharp, p. 334; Cox, p. 316. Cox adds American references.

A

No local title. From the singing and recitation of John Brown, River John, Pictou County. The last two stanzas were added by John Adamson, Westville, Pictou County.

1 As a maid was walking in her garden,
    A single sailor came riding by.
  He stepped up to her, he thought he knew her;
    He said, "Fair maid, can you fancy I?"

2   "You appear to me like some man of honour,
     Like some noble lord you appear to me.
  How can you impose on a poor young creature,
     Who is not fitted your servant to be?"

3   "If you're not fitted to be my servant
     I have some great reward for thee.
  I'll marry you, I'll make you my lady,
     And I'll have servants to wait on thee."

4   "I have a true love all of my own, sir,
     And it's seven long years he has been to sea.
  And it's seven long years I'll wait all on him,
     If he's alive he'll return to me."

5   "How can you fancy a roving sailor?
     How can you fancy such a slave?
  He may be dead in some foreign country,
     Or else the ocean has proved his grave."

6   "If he's alive I'd hope to see him,
     And if he's dead I hope he's blest.
  'Tis for his sake I'd never marry,
     For he's the man that I love best."

7   "Such a girl as you I do admire,
     Such a girl as you to be my wife.
  You shall have gold and silver plenty,
     And treasures flowing on every side."

8   "O what care I for your gold and silver?
     O what care I for your birth and land?
  O what care I for your old maid-servant,
     If my own sailor returns to me?"

9   He slipped his hand into his pocket,
     His fingers were both slim and small;
  He pulled out a ring that was broken between them.
     Soon as she seen it she down did fall.

10   He picked her up into his arms,
     And kisses he gave her, one, two, by three,
  Saying, "I am your young and your single sailor;
     I've just returned to marry thee."

11 "If you're my true and my single sailor
   Your shape and colour do not agree.
   But seven years makes a great alteration,
   And sure there's seven since I did you see!"

12 To church they went and they both got married
   With their two hearts full of love and content.
   He stays at home and he takes his ease,
   And he goes no more on the raging seas.

B

"The Single Sailor." From the singing and recitation of Miss Greta Brown, River John, Pictou County.

1 A maid was walking in her garden,
   A single sailor came gliding by.
   He stepped up towards her, he thought he knew her;
   And said, "Fair maiden, do you fancy I?"

2 "You seem to me like a man of honour,
   A noble lord you appear to be.
   How could you ask a lonely creature,
   Fit enough your servant to be?"

3 "A girl like you I'd like to marry,
   A girl like you to be my wife.
   I'll marry you, make you my lady,
   Have maid-servants to wait upon you."

4 "What care I for your gold and silver?
   What care I for your wealth and worth?
   What care I for your maids of honour,
   If my true love will return?

5 "Seven long years he has been to ocean,
   Seven long years he's got to stay,
   Seven long years I'll wait upon him,
   And if he's alive he'll return to me.

6 "And if he's dead he'll have my blessing;
   We'll meet on that other shore.
   'Twas for his sake I'd never marry,
   Treasures blooming on every side."

7 He put his right hand in his pocket,
   His fingers were both long and slim.
He brought out a ring they had broken between them,
   And when she saw it, down did fall.

8 He picked her up in his arms
   And gave her kisses one by two:
"I am your own true lonely sailor;
   I just came back to marry you."

64

THE DARK-EYED SAILOR

THIS song has been popular both in England and in America, and it has appeared in several song-books and broadsides in both countries. The regular English title is "Fair Phœbe and her Dark-eyed Sailor." For references see Cox, p. 319. Add: broadsides by Harkness, Preston (No. 53), Forth, Pocklington (No. 78), Willey (No. 17), and H. Disley, London; *The "That's the Style for Me" Songster* (New York, Robert M. De Witt, 1869), and *The "Oh, How is That for High" Songster* (De Witt, 1870).

"The Dark-eyed Sailor." From the singing and recitation of Richard Hines, River John, Pictou County.

1 As I walked out one evening fair
  Down by the river to take the air,
  I met a female upon my way,
  And I paid attention to hear what she would say.

2 Said William, "Lady, why roam alone?
  The night is coming and the day is gone."
  She said, while tears from her eyes did fall,
  "It's my dark-eyed sailor that proved my downfall.

3 "It's seven years since he left the land.
  He took a gold ring from off his hand;
  He broke it in two. Here's one half with me,
  And the other's rolling in the bottom of the sea."

4 Said William, "Lady, shake him from your mind;
  Some other sailor as good you'll find.
  Love turns aside and cold doth grow
  Like a winter's morning when the lands are clothed with snow."

5 "His coal-black eyes and his curly hair,
  His flattering tongue did my heart ensnare.
  Gentle he was, but no rake like you,
  To advise a maiden to slight the jacket blue."

6 Then half of the ring William he did show.
  She seemed distressed with joy, not woe.
  "You're welcome, William, I've got lands and gold
  For my dark-eyed sailor who's manly, true, and bold."

7 They joined in wedlocks and did well agree.
  They live in a cottage down by the sea.
  So, maids, be true while your love's away,
  For a cloudy morning ofttimes brings a pleasant day.

65

JOHNNY GERMAN

A TEXT of this song, from West Virginia, is printed by Cox (pp. 328–329), and another, from Missouri, by Belden in Herrig's *Archiv*, CXX, 63. For references see Cox, p. 328.

From the singing and recitation of John Rogers, River John, Pictou County.

1 As I walked out one morning
 All for to take the air,
It's there I spied a pretty fair maid;
 Her countenance looked quite sad.

2 I says, "My pretty fair maid,
 What's the cause of your sad woe?"
"My true love's gone and left me,
 And where I do not know.
He's left me no true token
 Whether he'll return or no."

3 "Perhaps I've seen your true love
 The last time I've been to sea.
He was proper, tall, and handsome.
 They call him Handsome John.

4 "He sails aboard of the *Rainbow*,
 And under Captain Roe;
His name is Johnny German —
 Is that the lad or no?"

5 When this fair maid heard this news
 She fairly jumped for joy,

. . . .

. .

6 "Come tell to me immediately
 Whether he's alive or no."
"Your true love Johnny German
 Just died five months ago."

7 When this fair maid heard this news
 She fell in deep despair,
A wringing of her lily-white hands,
 And a tearing of her hair.

8   She betook unto her chamber,
        And on her bed did lie
    With a sad lamentation,
        And wishing she could die.

9   When her true love came to know
        How he'd treated her severe,
    How he'd treated her
        Although she loved him so dear,

10 He dressed himself in scarlet,
        And to pretty Polly did go
    With a kind resolution
        To welcome her sad woe.

11 "Open the door, pretty Polly,
        And leave your tears behind,

        .   .   .   .

        .   .   .   .

12 "I only done it to try you,
        To see if you'd prove true,
    For I never met with a pretty fair maid
        Could gain my heart but you!"

13 She's lovelier than the morning,
        She's beautiful as the rose;
    On Polly's lovely bosom
        There lies a sweet repose.

14 Adieu to the gallant *Rainbow*
        Since Polly has won my heart.
    We'll be joined together
        That nothing but death can part.

66

JANIE ON THE MOOR

This broadside song appeared sometimes with the above title and sometimes with the title "Sweet Jenny of the Moor." See broadsides by Such, No. 121 (XI, 121); H. Disley (with "Sally in Our Alley"); W. S. Fortey (with "Wait for the Waggon").

For texts published in America see: *Jennie Hughes' Rose of Erin Songster* (New York, Robert M. De Witt, 1874), p. 54; *Delaney's Irish Song Book No. 4*, p. 22; De Marsan broadside, List 16, No. 81.

A

"Janie on the Moor." From the singing and recitation of Mrs. James Campbell, River John, Pictou County.

1 One morning for recreation as I roamed by the seaside
   The hills all were covered with flowers bedecked with pride.
   I spied a handsome fair maid as she roamed along the shore;
   Like roses blooming were the cheeks of Janie on the Moor.

2 Said I, "My handsome fair maid, why thou so early rise?"
   "'Tis for to breathe the morning air while the larks are in the
     skies;
   I love to roam the beach alone where loud the billows roar
   That make the bosom of the deep," cried Janie on the Moor.

3 We both sat down together on yonder mossy side.
   Said I, "My handsome fair maid, I will make you my bride.
   I have both gold and silver brought from some foreign shore,
   And with me you may tarry, dear Janie on the Moor."

4 "I have a true love of my own. Long since he's gone from me,
   But with pleasure I'll wait on him till he'll return from sea.
   I'll wait on him without a doubt till he'll return on shore.
   We'll join our hands in wedlock bands," cried Janie on the Moor.

5 "If your true love was a sailor pray tell to me your name."
   "His name was Dennis Ryan, from New York town he came;
   But with pleasure I'll wait on him till he returns on shore,
   And we'll join our hands in wedlock bands," cried Janie on the
     Moor.

6 "If your true love was a sailor I know the young man well.
 He was in the battle at Vendons Town, by an angry ball he fell.
 Here is a token of true love which he on his finger wore."
 She fell a fainting in his arms, dear Janie on the Moor.

7 When he saw she was tender-hearted, "Behold, my love," he
   cried,
 "This is your Dennis Ryan a standing by your side!
 So come and we'll get married and be happy evermore.
 We'll join our hands in wedlock bands, dear Janie on the Moor."

B

"Janie on the Moor." From the recitation of Alexander Brown, River
John, Pictou County.

1 One morning for recreation as I strolled the beach seaside,
 The hills and all were covered with flowers decked with pride.
 I overheard a damsel, as she strolled along the shore;
 It's blooming roses were the cheeks of Janie on the Moor.

2 Says I, "My lovely fair maid, why do you so early rise?"
 "For to breathe the morning air while the lark sings in the sky;
 I love to roam the beach along where so loud the breakers roar;
 It would wake the bosom of the deep," cried Janie on the Moor.

3 We both sat down together down yonder moss seaside.
 Says I, "My lovely fair one, I will make you my bride.
 It's I've got gold and silver fetched from a foreign shore,
 And with me you may tarry, sweet Janie on the Moor."

4 "I've got a true love of my own, long time he's gone to sea,
 And with pleasure I'll wait on him till he returns to me.
 I'll wait on him without a doubt till he returns on shore,
 And we'll join our hands in wedlock bands," cried Janie on the
   Moor.

5 "If your true love be a sailor lad, pray tell to me his name."
 "His name is Dennis Riley, from New York town he came."

 . . . .
 . . . .

6 "If his name be Dennis Riley I know the young man well.
It was in a fearful battle by an angry bullet fell;
And here's a ring of true love, which he on his finger wore."
She fell and fainted in his arms, sweet Janie on the Moor.

7 When he saw she was tender-hearted, "Behold your love!" he
    cried.
"Your dearest Dennis Riley is standing by your side.
Arise and we'll get married, live happy on the shore.
We'll join our hands in wedlock bands and go to sea no more."

67

THE LADY OF THE LAKE

THIS song is preserved in broadsides: J. Cadman, Manchester, No. 356 (VI, 202); Bebbington, Manchester, No. 172 (IX, 166). Greig also prints a version (LXXXVIII). Apparently the song was current chiefly in the south of Scotland and in the northern counties of England.

From the singing and recitation of Mrs. James Palmer, Waldegrave, Colchester County (printed in *Journal*, XXV, 185–186).

1 As I walked out one evening down by the river side,
Along the banks of sweet Dundee, a lovely lass I spied.
First she sighed, and then did say, "I fear I'll rue the day,
. . . .

2 "Once I had a kind sweetheart, his name was Willie Brown,
And in the *Lady of the Lake* he sailed from Greenwich town,
With full five hundred immigrants bound for America,
And on the banks of Newfoundland I am told they were cast away."

3 When she made mention of my name, I to myself did say,
"Can this be you stands by my side, my own dear Liza Gray?"
I turned myself right round about, my tears for to conceal,
And with a sigh I then begun my mournful tale to tell.

4 "I own this loss of Greenock Quay, for I in that vessel went;
Along with your true love Willie Brown some happy hours I spent.
Along with your true love Willie Brown some happy hours spent we;
He was my chief companion upon the raging sea.

5 "We tossed upon the raging main five hundred miles from shore,
The nor'west winds and fields of ice down on our vessel bore.
That night the *Lady of the Lake* to pieces she was sent,
And all the crew but thirty-two down to the bottom went."

6 She said, "Kind sir, if that be true, what you relate to me,
Unto all earthly pleasures I'll forever bid adieu.
And in some lonely valley I'll wander for his sake,
And I'll always think of the day he sailed in the *Lady of the Lake*."

7 "O Liza, lovely Liza, from weeping now refrain,
For don't you see the Lord spared me to see your face again?
For don't you see what you gave me when I left Greenock Quay?"
In his hand he bore the likeness of his own dear Liza Gray.

68

DONALD'S RETURN TO GLENCOE

THIS song is frequently entitled "McDonald's Return to Glencoe." It is assigned by Gavin Greig to the early part of the nineteenth century. The style is a little more bookish and a little less picturesque than that of the average folk ballad, but the song seems to have had a wide currency in both Great Britain and Ireland, and it was especially popular in Scotland.

For British versions see Ford, *Vagabond Songs and Ballads of Scotland*, II, 64–66; Greig, LV ("Glencoe"); *Journal of the Folk-Song Society*, II, 171 (music only); V, 100–103. See also the following broadside copies: no imprint (25242. 71); "Sold at Dalton's Public Library, York," No. 49 (III, 172); J. Gilbert, Newcastle, No. 47 (IV, 113); Forth, Pocklington, No. 127 (IV, 181); no imprint (VI, 181); Ryle (VII, 118); Bebbington, Manchester (IX, 119); Such, No. 108 (XI, 108); Walker, Durham, No. 24 (with "The Moon is on the Water"); Hodges (late Pitts); J. Paul & Co.; another, without printer's imprint, No. 424 (with "The Deserter").

In America the song has been published as a De Marsan broadside (List 5, No. 87) and as a Wehman broadside (No. 437). See also O'Conor, p. 136.

"The Pride of Glencoe." From the singing and recitation of John Adamson, Westville, Pictou County.

1 As I went a walking one evening of late
  Where Flora's gay mantle did the fields decorate,
  I carelessly wandered where I didn't go,[1]
  To the foot of a fountain that lies in Glencoe.

2 Like the pride of Mount Aetna the prize he had won,
  There approached me a damsel as fair as the sun,
  With ribbon and tartans that round her did flow,
  Was one Miss MacDonald, the pride of Glencoe.

3 I said, "My gay lassie, your enchanting smiles
  And comely sweet figure doth my heart beguile;
  If you'll place your affections you'll on me bestow,
  You'll bless the happy hour we met in Glencoe."

4 "Young man," she made answer, "your suit I disdain,
  For I once had a lover, young Donald by name.
  He is gone to the war about ten years ago,
  And a maid I'll remain till he returns to Glencoe."

---

[1] Should be *know*.

5   "It's perhaps that young Donald regards not your name,
But has placed his affections on some foreign dame.
He might have forgotten for all that you know
The bonnie Scotch lassie that he left in Glencoe."

6   "It's young Donald would never from his true love depart,
For love, truth, and honour are found in his heart;
And if never I see him then single I'll go
And mourn for MacDonald, the pride of Glencoe."

7   It's finding her true-hearted, he pulled out a glove
That in parting she gave him as a token of love.
She flew in his arms and the tears down did flow,
Saying, "O you MacDonald, you've returned to Glencoe!"

8   "Cheer up, my gay lassie, your sorrow's all o'er;
Since we have once met, love, we'll never part more.
The French and the Spaniards at the distance may blow,
But in peace and contentment we'll reside in Glencoe!"

69

WATERLOO

THE spirited old lady who sang this ballad for me, entitling it "Waterloo," prefaced her performance by assuring me, with a sort of demoniacal glee, that I had never heard the song before and would never hear it again, for the simple reason that the unique copy of it existed in her own proper brain. Since then I have been inclined more than once to accept her pronouncement as authoritative, and have had to remind myself that the investigator must not be overruled by prophecies. The hypothesis that I have finally excogitated is that "Waterloo" is a fragmentary and modified version of the early nineteenth-century English ballad entitled "The Mantle So Green," and that "The Mantle So Green" is in its turn a modified version of the late eighteenth-century English ballad "George Reilly."

The background of "George Reilly" is a sea-fight between the British and the French; that of "The Mantle So Green" is the Battle of Waterloo, as it is in my "Waterloo" fragment. The name of the hero is variable within certain limits: in "George Reilly" it corresponds to the title, in "The Mantle So Green" it is William Reilly, and in "Waterloo" it is William Smith. The theme (return of the lover in disguise and testing of the sweetheart's loyalty) is the same for all three, but since it is common also to several other ballads I mention this similarity only to establish a foundation for the special evidence which it will be necessary for me to present. It is in the details of the common story (aside from the battle, which is not the same for all three), and in the phraseology at important points, that the correspondence of the three songs becomes manifest. I shall cite a few instances of these (using Cox's version of "George Reilly," O'Conor's version of "The Mantle So Green," and my own mysterious fragment entitled "Waterloo").

1. "George Reilly":

   Then said the gallant sailor: "What is your true love's name?
   Both that and the description, I wish to know the same."

   "Mantle So Green":

   "Since you are not married tell me your love's name.
   I have been in battle, I might know the same."

   "Waterloo":

   "Can I but be so bold as to ask your true love's name?
   For I have been in battle where cannons loudly rattle,
   And by your description I might have known the same."

2. "George Reilly":

   "Three years we spent together on board the old Belflew,
   And such a gallant comrade before I never knew."

   "Mantle So Green":

   "He was my chief comrade in famed Waterloo."

   "Waterloo":

   "Through Portugal and Russia we often marched together,
   He was my loyal comrade through France and through Spain."

3. "George Reilly":

". . . . ."

"Your true love he fell by a French cannon ball.
Whilst wallowing in his blood your generous lover lay,
With faltering voice and broken sighs, these are the words I heard him say:
'Farewell, my dearest Nancy! were you but standing by,
To gaze your last upon me, contented would I die.'"

"Mantle So Green":

"We fought so victorious where bullets did fly,
And in the field of Nervon your true lover does lie;
We fought for three days to the fourth afternoon,
He received his death summons on the 18th of June.

"As he was a dying I heard his last cry:
'Were you here, lovely Nancy, contented I would die'" —

"Waterloo":

"As by the French we were all surrounded,
Like bold British heroes we did them subdue.
We fought three days together until we did subdue them,
Like bold Napoleon Boney on the plains of Waterloo.

. . . .

"By French soldiers your true love was slain.
It's there I saw him lie, there I saw him bleed and die.
With his low faltering voice he bid me adieu."

"George Reilly" and "The Mantle So Green" exhibit the same scheme of metre and rhyme and the same story with the one difference which I have noted (*i.e.*, a sea-fight in the former and the Battle of Waterloo in the latter), while "The Mantle So Green" and "Waterloo," with a difference in rhyme scheme, have exactly the same story. As for the passages that I have cited for comparison, they all exhibit, not ballad commonplaces, but special phraseology and special narrative details. It is certainly not unreasonable to conclude that the three songs are related.

A version of "George Reilly" is printed by Greig (cxxxviii). Cox prints a version from West Virginia (pp. 323–325) and gives American references.

"The Mantle So Green" appears in the following English broadsides: J. Cadman, Manchester, No. 166 (v, 40); Ryle (vii, 40); Such (xii, 63); without imprint, No. 197 (with "The Happy Tar"). For texts published in the United States see *The Ten Cent "Clodoche" Songster* (New York, Robert M. De Witt, 1869), p. 24; *The "That's the Style for Me" Songster* (De Witt, 1869), p. 59; De Marsan broadside, List 14, No. 51; Wehman broadside, No. 438; *Delaney's Irish Song Book No. 3*, p. 7; O'Conor, p. 38.

Campbell and Sharp print a different song under the title "George Reilly" (No. 82). It must not be confused with the "George Reilly" of the trio which I have been discussing. Both it and the song printed as "John Riley" by Wyman and Brockway (*Lonesome Tunes*, pp. 34–37) are versions of the common broadside song "Young Riley." For references to this song see Cox, p. 323.

"Waterloo." From the singing and recitation of Mrs. James Palmer, Waldegrave, Colchester County.

1 As I walked out on a fine summer's evening,

. . . .

There I overheard a damsel make a sad lamentation
About her absent lover on the plains of Waterloo.

2 I said, "My pretty fair maid, ye pride of all nations,
Can I but be so bold as to ask your true love's name?
For I have been in battles where cannons loudly rattle,
And by your description I might have known the same."

3 "O, William Smith's his name, he's a hero of fame."
"Many's the battle him and I have been in.
Through Portugal and Russia we often marched together,
He was my loyal comrade through France and through Spain."

4 "And ere that he left me he gave me a token,
A gold diamond ring that was broken in two.
'You have my heart and ring, dear lovely Sally,
To remember your dear Willy when he's far at Waterloo.'"

5 "As by the French we were all surrounded
Like bold British heroes we did them subdue;
We fought three days together until we did subdue them
Like bold Napoleon Boney on the plains of Waterloo.

6 .   .   .   .
" By French soldiers your true love was slain.
It's there I saw him lie, there I saw him bleed and die,
With his low faltering voice he bid me adieu."

7 When he found her so loyal he pulled out the token,
The gold diamond ring that was broken in two,
Saying, "You have my heart and ring, dear lovely Sally,
To remember your dear Willy, but he's far from Waterloo."

70

THE BANKS OF CLAUDIE

THIS song has been widely sung in Great Britain and Ireland, and also in Canada and the United States. For references see *Journal*, XXVI, 362; XXXV, 351; Cox, p. 321.

"The Banks of Claudie." From the singing and recitation of Mrs. James Palmer, Waldegrave, Colchester County.

1 As I walked out one evening down by the river side
I overheard a damsel, the tears fell from her eyes,
Saying, "This is a dark and stormy night" — those very words
    did say —
"And my love is on the raging seas bound for America."

2 I stepped up to this fair maid and put her in surprise;
I own she did not know me, I being in disguise.
I said, "My pretty fair maid, my joy and heart's delight,
How far do you wander this dark and dreary night?"

3 "Kind sir, the way to Claudie would you be pleased to show?
And pity the distressèd, for there I have to go.
I am in search of a young man, and Johnny is his name,
And upon the banks of Claudie I am told he does remain."

4 "This is the banks of Claudie, the ground whereon you stand,
But do not trust young Johnny, for he's a false young man.
O do not trust young Johnny, for he'll not meet you here.
Come along with me to yonder banks, no danger need you fear."

5 "If Johnny he was here this night he'd shed me from all harm;
He's dressed in his readiness all in his uniform;
He's gone to plough the ocean, his foes he will defy.
Like a rolling king of honour he fought in the wars of Troy."

6 When he found her so loyal he could no longer stand;
He jumped into her arms, saying, "Betsy, I'm the man.
O Betsy, I'm the young man that caused you all your pain,
And since we're met on Claudie banks we'll never part again."

7 "Ye purling streams of Claudie, ye waters that roll by,
And all ye little small burns that prove your destiny,
Had I a tongue to flatter I'd tell ye some love tale
About a bonny boy from Claudie that in my mind remains."

71

THE BANKS OF BRANDYWINE

The Nova Scotia version of this ballad corresponds pretty closely to the texts in the following collections: *The American Songster* (Baltimore, collected and published by John Kenedy, 1836), pp. 240–242; *The Forget Me Not Songster* (New York, Nafis and Cornish), pp. 158–160; the same (Philadelphia and New York, Turner and Fisher), pp. 22–24; *The Old Forget Me Not Songster* (Boston, Locke and Dubier), pp. 158–160; *The American Singers' Own Book* (Philadelphia, M. Kelly, 1841), pp. 52–54; *The American Songster* (New York, Nafis and Cornish, 1847), pp. 240–242; *The New American Song Book and Letter Writer* (Louisville, C. Hagan & Co., 1847), p. 134; *Leary's American Songster* (Philadelphia, W. A. Leary and Co., 1850), p. 9; *The American Star Songster* (New York, Richard Marsh; published also as vol. III of *Marsh's Selection, or, Singing for the Million*, 1854), pp. 9–12; *The American Vocalist* (New York, Richard Marsh, 1856), pp. 52–54; *The Singer's Journal*, I, 221; *Wehman's Irish Song Book No. 1*, 1887, pp. 56–57; De Marsan broadside, List 3, No. 87; Wehman broadside, No. 358; J. Wrigley broadside (New York), No. 230.

"The Banks of Brandywine." From the singing and recitation of Mrs. Ellen Bigney, Pictou, Pictou County.

1 One morning very early, in the pleasant month of May,
  As I walked out to take the air, all nature being gay,
  The moon had not yet veiled her face, but through the trees did
    shine,
  As I wandered forth to take the air on the banks of Brandywine.

2 At such an early hour I was surprised to see
  A lovely maid with downcast eyes upon those banks so gay.
  I modestly saluted her, she knew not my design,
  And requested her sweet company on the banks of Brandywine.

3 "I pray, young man, be civil, my company forsake,
  For in my real opinion I think you are a rake.
  My love's a valiant sailor, he's now gone to the main,
  While comfortless I wander on the banks of Brandywine."

4 "My dear, why do you thus give up to melancholy cries?
  I pray give up your weeping and dry those lovely eyes,
  For sailors in each port, my dear, they do a mistress find.
  He will leave you to wander on the banks of Brandywine."

5 "O leave me, sir, do leave me! Why do you me torment?
My Henry wont to see me, therefore I am content.
Why do you thus torment me, and cruelly combine
To fill my heart with horror on the banks of Brandywine?"

6 "I wish not to afflict your mind, but rather for to ease.
Such dreadful apprehensions, they soon your heart will seize.
Your love, my dear, in wedlock bands another one has joined."
She swooned into my arms on the banks of Brandywine.

7 The lofty hills and craggy rocks reëchoed back her strains;
The pleasant groves and rural shades were witness to her pains.
"How often has he promised me in Hymen's chains to join!
Now I'm a maid forsaken on the banks of Brandywine."

8 "O no, my dear, that ne'er shall be. Behold your Henry now!
I clasp you to my bosom, love, I've not forgot our vow.
It's now I know you're true, my dear, in Hymen's chains we'll
join,
And bless the happy morn we met on the banks of Brandywine."

72

THE BONNY BUNCH OF ROSES

THIS was a very popular stall ballad in the earlier days of the nineteenth century. Christie, in *Traditional Ballad Airs*, prints a version which he took down in 1850 from the recitation of a native of Aberdeenshire, who learned it from his father, a Peninsular veteran. The broadside copies usually have a double title, "Young Napoleon, or The Bonny Bunch of Roses," but in later times the second phrase has been used alone. The ancients who sang the ballad for me took pains in each case to elucidate the symbolism of the "bunch of roses" (*i.e.*, England, Scotland, and Ireland) before beginning the performance, and I suspect that this is a traditional circumstance accompanying the rendition of the song. "The Bonny Bunch of Roses" is composed in the stanza form of an older broadside song, "The Bunch of Rushes," and, as was sometimes indicated on the broadsides, could be sung to the same tune. "The Bunch of Rushes" begins:

> As I walked out one morning, it was to take some sport
> Down by a crystal fountain, where few people did resort.
> It was there I saw a fair maid apparently a-going astray
> With a bunch of rushes in her hand that she'd been gathering all the day.

For British texts of "The Bonny Bunch of Roses" see Greig, XCIV; Christie, *Traditional Ballad Airs*, II, 232–233; Baring-Gould, *Songs of the West*, No. 27; Herbert Hughes, *Irish Country Songs*, II, 92–100 (with music); *Journal of the Folk-Song Society*, II, 276–277 (a fragment to which is appended the Fortey broadside version); and III, 56–57 (music only); *Journal of the Irish Folk-Song Society*, XV, 31 (fragment, with air). See also the following broadsides: G. Jaques, Manchester (I, 79); George Walker, Durham, No. 179 (II, 98); W. R. Walker, Newcastle, No. 13 (IV, 153); Forth, Pocklington, No. 79 (IV, 209); Cadman, Manchester, No. 150 (VI, 135); Catnach (VII, 67); Bebbington, Manchester, No. 23 (IX, 23); Such, No. 30 (XI, 30); Harkness, Preston, No. 106 (two copies, each with a "Plaintive Pastoral"); W. Taylor (with "Within a Mile of Edinboro' Town"); Catnach (with "Adventures of Little Mike"); W. S. Fortey (with the same song); Pitts (with "The Frolicksome Farmer"); Paul (with "The British Man of War"); Hillat & Martin, London.

For texts printed in America see *The Forget Me Not Songster* (New York, Nafis and Cornish), pp. 222–223; the same (Philadelphia and New York, Turner and Fisher), pp. 120–122; *The Old Forget Me Not Songster* (Boston, Locke and Dubier), pp. 222–223; *The Forget Me Not Songster* (New York, D. J. Sadlier & Co., 1847), pp. 90–92; *Leary's American Songster* (Philadelphia, W. A. Leary & Co., 1850), p. 42; *The American Star Songster* (New York, Richard Marsh; published also as vol. III of *Marsh's Selection, or Singing for the Million*, 1854), pp. 42–44; *The "Low Backed Car" Songster* (Marsh), pp. 55–57; *Wehman's Irish Song Book, No. 1*, 1887, pp. 49–50; De Marsan broadside, List 9, No. 5; Wehman broadside, No. 411; O'Conor, p. 127.

A

"The Bonny Bunch of Roses O." From the singing and recitation of
Robert Langille, Tatamagouche, Colchester County.

1   By the dangers of the ocean,
    In the bonny month of June,
    Those little warbling songsters
    Their notes so cheerfully did tune.
    'Twas there I spied a damsel,
    All seemingly in grief and woe,
    Conversing with young Buonaparte
    Concerning the bonny bunch of roses O.

2   Then up steps young Napoleon
    And took his mother by the hand,
    Saying, "Mother, pray have patience
    Till I am able to command,
    For I'll raise a terrible army
    And through tremendous dangers go,
    And in spite of all the universe
    I'll gain you the bonny bunch of roses O."

3   "O son, don't speak so venturesome,
    For England is a heart of oak.
    There is England, Scotland, and Ireland,
    Their unity has never been broke.
    Now, son, look at your father,
    In Saint Helena his body lies low,
    And you might follow after him,
    So beware of the bonny bunch of roses O!

4   "He took three hundred thousand men,
    And likewise kings to join his throne.
    He was so well provided,
    Enough to sweep the world along.
    He took a terrible army,
    And over frozen realms did go.
    He swore he'd conquer Moscow,
    Then to the bonny bunch of roses O.

5   .   .   .   .
        .   .   .   .
        .   .   .   .
        .   .   .   .

"But when he came to Moscow,
Near overpowered by driven snow,
All Moscow was a blazing;
Then he lost the bonny bunch of roses O."

6   Then up spake young Napoleon,
Saying, "Mother, adieu forever now,
For if I had lived I should have been clever,
But now I drop my youthful head.
But while our bones do moulder,
And weeping willows over us grow,
By the deeds of great Napoleon
We'll stain the bonny bunch of roses O."

B

"The Bonny Bunch of Roses." From the singing and recitation of Alexander Harrison, Maccan, Cumberland County.

1   By the borders of the ocean
One morning in the month of June,
For to hear those warlike songsters
Their cheerful notes and sweetly tune,
I overheard a female
Who seemed to be in grief and woe,
Conversing with young Buonaparte
Concerning the bonny bunch of roses O.

2   Then up steps young Napoleon
And takes his mother by the hand,
Saying, "Mother dear, have patience,
Until I am able to command;
Then I will take an army,
Through tremendous dangers I will go.
In spite of all the universe
I will conquer the bonny bunch of roses O!"

3   The first time I saw young Buonaparte
Down on his bended knees fell he;
He asked the pardon of his father,
Who granted it most mournfully.
"Dear son," he said, "I'll take an army
And on the frozen Alps will go;
Then I will conquer Moscow,
And return to the bonny bunch of roses O."

4   He took five hundred thousand men,
With kings likewise to bear his train.
He was so well provided for
That he could sweep this world alone.
But when he came to Moscow
He was overpowered by the driven snow,
When Moscow was a blazing,
So he lost his bonny bunch of roses O.

5   "Oh, son, don't speak so venturesome,
For in England are the hearts of oak.
There is England, Ireland, Scotland;
Their unity was never broke.
Oh, son, think of thy father —
On the isle of Saint Helena his body lies low,
And you must soon follow after him,
So beware of the bonny bunch of roses O."

6   "Now do believe me, dearest mother,
Now I lie on my dying bed;
If I had lived I would have been clever,
But now I droop my youthful head.
But whilst our bodies lie mould'ring,
And weeping willows over our bodies grow,
The deeds of great Napoleon
Shall sing the bonny bunch of roses O."

73

THE PLAINS OF WATERLOO

THIS song is plainly derived from the English song "The Plains of Waterloo," which begins:

On the sixteenth day of June, my boys, in Flanders where we lay,
Our bugles the alarm did sound before the break of day.
The British, Belgians, Brunswickers, and Hanoverians too,
All Brussels left that morning for the plains of Waterloo.

(Ford, *Vagabond Songs and Ballads of Scotland*, I, 59–63). There is no invocation or introduction, as in my version A, but the account of the battle is much more detailed. See also *The Linnet* (J. Marshall, Newcastle, 25276.1.6, No. 10), pp. 17–20; Logan, *A Pedlar's Pack of Ballads and Songs*, pp. 106–109; Kidson, *Traditional Tunes*, pp. 120–123; Christie, *Traditional Ballad Airs*, I, 266–267; *Notes and Queries*, 7th Series, V, 106; Greig, LXXIX (with an introductory "Come all" stanza). Most of the texts designate "the sixteenth day of June," but one of Kidson's begins:

On the eighteenth day of June, my boys,
Eighteen hundred and fifteen.

Apparently the song, in some form or other, and with a regular iteration of "the plains of Waterloo," was composed very soon after the event and sung by the veterans. Greig remarks that it "is said to have been written by John Robertson, a bugler in the 92nd Highlanders."

The text printed by Dean, pp. 118–119, corresponds fairly closely to version A.

A

"The Plains of Waterloo." From the singing and recitation of Harry Sutherland, River John, Pictou County (printed, in part, in *Quest*, pp. 165–166).

1 Come all you brisk and lively lads, come listen unto me,
   While I relate how I have fought through the wars of Germany.
   I have fought through Spain, through Portugal, through France
        and Flanders too;
   But it's little I thought I'd be reserved for the plains of Waterloo.

2 On the eighteenth day of June, brave boys, as you shall now soon
        hear,
   And the drums and fifes they played so sweet, we knew the
        French were near.
   There was Boney with his gallant troops, his numbers being not
        few;
   He boldly went and pitched his tents on the plains of Waterloo.

3 There was Wellington our countryman, he commanded us that
    day;
  While Boney commanded the Prussian troops, he swore would
    gain the day.
  The French they gained the first two days, and would the third
    one too,
  While Blucher deceived poor Buonaparte on the plains of
    Waterloo.

4 It would fill your heart with grief, brave boys, for to see those
    Frenchmen's wives,
  Likewise their little children with tears flowing from their eyes,
  Crying, "Mother dear, O mother, we shall forever rue
  The day we lost our dear fathers on the plains of Waterloo."

5 It's manys the river I've crossed o'er through water and through
    mud;
  And it's manys the battle I've fought through with my ankles
    deep in blood.
  But Providence being kind to me in all that I've come through,
  'Twas there we pitched our last campaign on the plains of
    Waterloo.

B

"Wellington and Waterloo." From a broadside printed by James Barry at
Six Mile Brook, Pictou County.

      The eighteenth day of June, my boys,
        Napoleon did advance,
      With the choicest troops that he could raise
        Within the bounds of France.
      With the glittering eagles showing all around,
        And proud to face the foe;
      But the British lines they tore their wings
        On the plains of Waterloo.

          Chorus

      So with Wellington we'll go,
      So with Wellington we'll go,
      For Wellington commanded us
      On the plains of Waterloo.

The fight did last from ten o'clock
    Until the close of day;
When limbs, and blood, and cannon balls
    In thick confusion lay.
Their cuirassiers did so furious charge,
    Their squares to overthrow,
Whilst Britainers maintained their ground
    On the plains of Waterloo.

It's now the cheering of the charge
    Was heard amidst the fight;
Whilst Belgium's troops in confusion stood,
    And like cowards took their flight;
And left bold Britons in the field,
    All single with the foe;
Whilst Britainers undaunted stood
    On the plains of Waterloo.

And now the dreary night comes on,
    Comes creeping o'er the plain;
The Prussians with the English join
    Amidst the heaps of slain;
The Prussians with the English join
    All ready for the foe;
And Buonaparte's Imperial crown
    Was lost at Waterloo.

O peace be to those honoured souls
    That fell that glorious day;
And may the plough never raise their bones,
    Nor cut that sacred clay.
But may this place remain a waste,
    And a terror to the foe;
Whilst trembling Frenchmen pass that way,
    They will think of WATERLOO.

74

THE HEIGHTS OF ALMA

AFTER the Crimean War this apparently became a popular street song throughout Great Britain. Robert Ford prints a version (*Vagabond Songs and Ballads of Scotland*, II, 73–76) which has a few more stanzas than the one which I present, but the latter may be considered as compensated by the addition of a rousing chorus.

For a text from Minnesota see Dean, pp. 40–41. For a Canadian fragment (with tune) see *Journal*, XXXI, 163–164.

"The Heights of Alma." From the singing and recitation of Alexander Murphy, Cape John, Pictou County (*Quest*, pp. 5–6).

1 Come all you Britons, I pray give ear
To those few lines I've brought you here,
To those few lines I've brought you here,
    The victory gained at Alma.

Chorus

Sing tantinaray ri til di day
Sing tantinaray ri til di day
To those few lines I've brought you here,
    The victory gained at Alma.

2 It was on September the twentieth day,
In spite of all salt dash and spray
We landed safe on the Crimea,
    All on the route for Alma.

Chorus

Sing tantinaray ri til di day
Sing tantinaray ri til di day
We landed safe on the Crimea,
    All on the route for Alma.

3 All night we lay on the cold ground,
No shade nor shelter to be found,
And while with rain we were almost drowned,
    To cheer our hearts for Alma.

Chorus

Sing tantinaray ri til di day
Sing tantinaray ri til di day
And while with rain we were almost drowned,
    To cheer our hearts for Alma.

4 Next morning a burning sun did rise
Beneath the eastern cloudless skies,
When our great chief, Lord Raglan, cries,
    "Prepare your march for Alma!"

Chorus

Sing tantinaray ri til di day
Sing tantinaray ri til di day
When our great chief, Lord Raglan, cries,
    "Prepare your march for Alma!"

5 When Alma's heights did heave in view,
The stoutest hearts it would subdue
To see the Rooshians' monstrous crew
    On the towering heights of Alma.

Chorus

Sing tantinaray ri til di day
Sing tantinaray ri til di day
To see the Rooshians' monstrous crew
    On the towering heights of Alma.

6 But when the heights we did command,
We boldly fought them hand to hand;
The Rooshians could no longer stand
    Our British charge at Alma.

Chorus

Sing tantinaray ri til di day
Sing tantinaray ri til di day
The Rooshians could no longer stand
    Our British charge at Alma.

7 The Rooshians to Sebastopol fled,
They left their wounded and their dead;
They thought next day the river run red
    With the blood was spilt at Alma.

Chorus

Sing tantinaray ri til di day
Sing tantinaray ri til di day
They thought next day the river run red
    With the blood was spilt at Alma.

8 The English I have heard them say
 They lost ten thousand men that day,
 While thirteen thousand Frenchmen lay
  In their bloody gore at Alma.

   Chorus
   Sing tantinaray ri til di day
   Sing tantinaray ri til di day
   While thirteen thousand Frenchmen lay
    In their bloody gore at Alma.

75

BRAVE WOLFE

In both England and America the death of young General Wolfe in 1759 stimulated the ballad-makers to the production of songs of admiration and sorrow. The sample which follows is evidently of American composition. It occurs in Boston broadsides of the eighteenth and the early nineteenth century (see Ford, *Massachusetts Broadsides*, Nos. 1157–1160, 3049–3052, and *Isaiah Thomas Collection*, Nos. 55, 58). It may be found also in *The Echo, or Columbian Songster* (Brookfield, Massachusetts), pp. 152–154; *The Forget Me Not Songster* (New York, Nafis and Cornish), pp. 45–47; the same (Philadelphia and New York, Turner and Fisher), pp. 133–135; *The Old Forget Me Not Songster* (Boston, Locke and Dubier), pp. 45–47; *The New American Song Book and Letter Writer* (Louisville, C. Hagan & Co., 1847), pp. 118–121; *Home Sentimental Songster* (New York, T. W. Strong), pp. 242–243; *The Soldier's Companion* (New York, Leavitt and Allen), pp. 8–10; Baker and Southard, *The Boston Melodeon*, III (1850), 42 (with music); *Uncle True Songster* (Philadelphia and New York, Turner and Fisher), pp. 100–102; McCarty, *Songs, Odes, and other Poems on National Subjects*, 1842, III, 8–10; *Howe's 100 Old Favorite Songs* (Boston, Elias Howe Co.), p. 242; Stevenson, *Poems of American History*, pp. 122–123; Shoemaker, pp. 105–107.

The English song entitled "Bold General Wolfe" (see Williams, *Folk-Songs of the Upper Thames*, pp. 162–163) has nothing in common with this one except subject and sentiment.

"Quebec." From the singing and recitation of Richard Hines, River John, Pictou County.

<blockquote>
1   Come all you old men all,
     Let me delight you.
   Come all you young men all,
     Let naught affright you.
   Nor let your courage fail
     When it comes to trial,
   And do not be dismayed
     At the first denial.

2   I walked out with my love
     Thinking to move her,
   I sat down by her side
     And gazed upon her.
   But when I looked on her
     My tongue did quiver;
   I could not speak my mind
     When I was with her.
</blockquote>

3 "Love, here's a diamond ring,
      Long time I've kept it
   All for your sake alone,
      If you'll accept it.
   When you view the roses red
      Think on the giver;
   All for your sake alone
      I'm done forever."

4 This brave undaunted youth
      Went on the ocean,
   Crossed to America
      To seek promotion;
   And landing at Quebec
      With all his party
   The city to attack,
      Being brave and hearty.

5 He landed on the beach
      And the heights he mounted;
   When marching on the plain
      His men he counted.
   "I've got an army strong
      Who fight for honour;
   Brave Wolfe here at their head,
      We're bound to conquer."

6 Brave Wolfe called out his men
      In a line so pretty
   On the plains of Abraham
      Before the city.
   The French came marching down
      In hopes to meet them,
   With men three to one
      Resolved to beat them.

7 Each man fell in the ranks
      At brave Wolfe's desire;
   The French went running down
      And poured in their fire.
   Brave Wolfe received a shot;
      His days were ended.
   By all his valiant men
      He was sore lamented.

8   Brave Wolfe lay on the ground
     Where the drums did rattle,
And raising up his head,
     "How goes the battle?"
"Quebec is all our own
     And they can't prevent it."
He said without a groan,
     "I die contented."

76

THE BATTLE OF THE NILE

THERE are several English songs and ballads dealing in one fashion or another with Nelson's victory at the Nile, but most of them differ markedly from the one presented here. The closest correspondence seems to be in the song entitled "The Battle of the Nile" in a chapbook printed by C. Randall, Stirling, included in the "Ballads collected by John Bell, Newcastle" (Harvard College Library, 25252.19, No. 11).

"Nelson's Victory." From the singing and recitation of John Henderson, Tatamagouche, Colchester County.

1 'Twas on the ninth day of August in the year ninety-eight,
  We'll sing the praise of Nelson and the bold British fleet,
  For the victory we've gained o'er the rebellious crew,
  And to the Mediterranean Sea, brave boys, we'll bid adieu.

   Chorus
   So come, you British tars, let your hands and hearts agree
   To protect the lives and liberties of the mother country.

2 At four o'clock that evening he brought that fleet in sight,
  And like undaunted heroes we were eager for the fight.
  They were lying at an anchor near the Egyptian shore,
  Superior to our British fleet, and to take us they made sure.

3 Our noble captain he was slain soon after we began;
  Brave Cuthbert in succession he boldly took command.
  For full four hours that evening we engaged them on the main,
  And early the next morning we renewed the fight again.

4 Full fifty seamen we had slain, which grieved our hearts full
      sore;
  Two hundred more were wounded, lay bleeding in their gore.
  But early the next morning most glorious for to see,
  Our British ships of war, brave boys, were crowned with victory.

5 Buonaparte's pride we demolished, and that very soon;
  We made his crew to rue the day that ever they left Toulon.
  But now he's got among the Turks where he'll be forced to stay,
  And besides he has lost the title of The Conqueror of Italy.

6 A building castles in the air and doing these great feats,
  And threatening of Albania's plans in our united states,
  Planting the Tree of Liberty all on our native shore;
  But Nelson's stars have nipped the bud will never flourish more.

7 And now the fight is over and we have gained the day.
  Nine sail we took and four we burnt, the rest they ran away.
  But when we come home to England so loudly we will sing,
  "Success to our *Majestic* boys and long live George the King!"

77

NELSON'S VICTORY AT TRAFALGAR

Logan (*A Pedlar's Pack of Ballads and Songs*, pp. 67–69) has a song entitled "Nelson's Glorious Victory at Trafalgar," which is palpably a sister version of this song. It has the same metre and a good deal of the same phraseology, though there are also many verbal variations. My version corresponds pretty closely to that in Ashton's *Modern Street Ballads*, pp. 298–299. See also chapbook printed by R. Hutchison, Glasgow, 12th in set of chapbooks collected by John Bell, Newcastle, Harvard College Library, 25252.19 ("Arise, Brave Britons"); 96th chapbook in the same set ("Tak' your Auld Cloak about Ye, etc."); broadsides: H. Andrews, Leeds, No. 323 (XIV, 26); Harkness, Preston, No. 81 (with "The Prentice Boy"); another by Harkness, containing this song alone.

"Nelson's Victory at Trafalgar." From the singing and recitation of Richard Hines, River John, Pictou County.

1 We got ready for the battle
To face the daring foe.
Our ships were numbered twenty-seven
To shake the Spanish shore.
Lord Nelson on the poop stood high,
And to his men he then did cry,
"My lads we'll conquer them or die!"
    Said brave Nelson.

2 He formed a line of battle,
He struck the fatal blow,
When some went into the air,
And others sank below.
When victory was on his side
A fatal ball his life destroyed;
In the midst of glory he did die,
    Did brave Nelson.

3 To view the hero dying,
He prayed for England's fame;
He prayed for Britain's glory
Till his last breath was drawn.
He said, "My lads, my glass is run,
This day it is my setting sun,
The victory I know is won,"
    Said brave Nelson.

4 There was Collingwood and Hardy,
They fought for England's fame;
Collingwood in the *Royal Sovereign*,
He well deserved the name.
Now Buonaparte will boast no more,
Nor land upon our British shore,
Unless he goes in London Tower,
    Though Nelson is no more.

78

PAUL JONES

APPARENTLY several folk-songs with Paul Jones as the hero sprang up in England and Scotland during the days when he was a potential figure of danger off any part of the coast. Maidment, in the *North Countrie Garland*, reproduces one of these. But by far the most popular of the Paul Jones songs was the one which is represented here. It appeared in innumerable broadsides in England and in many song-books in the United States.

In Ebsworth's *Roxburghe Ballads*, VIII, 332, there is a version which begins: "A noble fine frigate, called *Percy* by name," and the English ship, which is defeated, is the *Richards*. In most of the versions, however, Paul Jones's leaky but victorious ship is the "*Richard* by name." See also for English versions: Firth, *Naval Songs and Ballads*, pp. 259–260 (a composite text); Logan, *A Pedlar's Pack of Ballads and Songs*, pp. 32–38 ("Paul Jones the Pirate"); W. A. Barrett, *English Folk-Songs*, pp. 56–57; *Journal of the Folk-Song Society*, III, pp. 206–213; Baring-Gould, *Songs of the West*, No. 108. For broadside copies see: Forth, Pocklington, No. 114 (III, 192); W. R. Walker, Newcastle, No. 119 (IV, 60); John Ross, Newcastle-on-Tyne, No. 119 (IV, 128); Catnach (VII, 99); Bebbington, Manchester, No. 287 (X, 35); Such, No. 10 (XI, 10); T. Birt (with "Pretty Star of the Night"); Catnach (with "The Wandering Savoyard" and "I Love Her, How I Love Her"); another, without imprint (with "The Shannon Side" and "My Mother's Voice"); W. S. Fortey, at the Catnach Press (with "Woodman, Spare that Tree"; here the *Richard* has become "the *Rachel* by name"); Such (with "Catch 'em Alive"). See also *Notes and Queries*, 9th Series, II, 306, 353, 495; III, 34, 296.

For early American broadside texts see Ford, *American Broadsides*, Nos. 3004, 3005, 3094 and *The Isaiah Thomas Collection*, Nos. 202, 204. See also for American texts *The Forget Me Not Songster* (New York, Nafis and Cornish, pp. 24–25); the same (Philadelphia and New York, Turner and Fisher), pp. 204–205; *The Old Forget Me Not Songster* (Boston, Locke and Dubier), pp. 24–25; *The American Sailor's Songster* (New York, Philip J. Cozans), pp. 200–202; *The New American Song Book and Letter Writer* (Louisville, C. Hagan & Co., 1847), pp. 100–102; *Leary's American Songster* (Philadelphia, W. A. Leary & Co., 1850), p. 159; *The Rough and Ready Songster* (New York, Nafis and Cornish, 1851), pp. 84–87; *The American Star Songster* (New York, Richard Marsh; published also as vol. III of *Marsh's Selection, or, Singing for the Million*, 1854), pp. 159–161; McCarty, *Songs, Odes, and Other Poems on National Subjects* (New York, 1842), II, 85–86; *Journal*, XXXI, 171–173 (Quebec version); S. B. Luce, *Naval Songs*, 2d ed., pp. 44–45; Eggleston, *American War Ballads*, I, 83–86; B. E. Stevenson, *Poems of American History*, pp. 224–225.

A

"Paul Jones." From the singing and recitation of Alexander Murphy, Cape John, Pictou County.

1 It's American frigate from Baltimore came,
Mounted guns forty-four, called the *Richard* by name,
Came to cruise in the Channel of old England's fame,
With a noble commander, Paul Jones was his name.

2 We had not sailed far till there we espied
A large forty-four and a twenty likewise,
Those two noble warships well laden with store.
We'll toss up the can to our country once more.

3 At the hour of twelve, Pierce came alongside.
With a fond speaking-trumpet, "Who are you?" he cries,
"Come answer me quickly! I shall hail you no more,
Or else a broadside into you I will pour."

4 Our carpenter being frightened to Paul Jones did say,
"Our ship she leaks water from fighting to-day."
Paul Jones he made answer in the height of his pride,
"If we can't do no better let her sink alongside!"

5 We fought them four glasses, four glasses so hot,
Till fifty bold seamen lie dead on the spot,
When fifty-five wounded and bleeding in gore,
While the thundering loud cannons of Paul Jones did roar.

6 Come now, my brave boys, we have taken a prize,
A large forty-four and a twenty likewise.
Those two noble warships well laden with store.
We'll drink of the can to our country once more.

7 God help the poor widow who shortly must weep
For the loss of her husband now sank in the deep.
We will drink to Paul Jones with his sword in his hand,
Who showed us an action and give the command.

B

"Paul Jones." From the singing and recitation of Nelson Langille, River John, Pictou County.

1 There was a flash frigate, from New York she came,
Mounted guns forty-four, called the *Richard* by name,
For to cruise in the Channel of old England's fame
With a noble commander, Paul Jones was his name.

2 We had not cruised long when two sail we spied,
A large forty-four and a twenty likewise,
And fifty bright ships well loaded with store,
Whilst the convicts stood in for the old Yorkshire shore.

3 About twelve in the day we came up alongside.
With a loud speaking-trumpet, "Whence come you?" we cried,
"Come answer us quickly! I will hail you no more,
Or else into you a broadside I will pour."

4 Paul Jones then he smiled, unto his men did say,
"Let every man stand the best of his play."
Then broadside for broadside we fought on the main;
Like true buckskin heroes we returned it again.

5 Our carpenter being frightened unto Paul Jones did say,
"Our ship she leaks water since fighting to-day."
Paul Jones then made answer in the height of his pride,
"If we can't do no better we'll sink alongside!"

79

THE *CHESAPEAKE* AND THE *SHANNON*

THIS song was a product of the War of 1812, and one need not doubt that it was composed very soon after June 1, 1813, which was the date of the fight between the *Shannon* and the *Chesapeake*. On August the 19th of the preceding year the American frigate *Constitution* had encountered the British frigate *Guerrière*, and after a two-hour fight the *Guerrière* surrendered and was burned. Out of the celebrations over this victory grew the American song "The *Constitution* and the *Guerrière*" (see Cox, No. 60), which began:

It oftimes has been told
How the British seamen bold
Could flog the tars of France so neat and handy O;
But they never found their match
Till the Yankees did them catch.
O the Yankee boys for fighting are the dandy O!

Now the case was reversed with a literal vengeance, and it may be supposed that the time was short before the British tars began to sing their reprisal-song neatly fashioned on the model of the American song of triumph. This was received with enthusiasm in a good many quarters. Thomas Hughes, apparently from personal recollection, represents the Rugby boys as singing it in the course of an evening's jollification (*Tom Brown's School Days*, chap. vi). It is possible, of course, that the British song was composed first and was imitated, sarcastically, by the Americans. The question of priority has not been settled.

For texts see Logan, *A Pedlar's Pack*, pp. 69–72; Firth, *Naval Songs and Ballads*, pp. 311–312; Whall, *Sea Songs and Shanties*, pp. 44–46; Sharp, *Folk-Songs from Somerset*, v, 56–57, and *Folk-Songs from Somerset* (in Novello's School Song Series), Set 4, pp. 4–5; E. E. Hale, *New England History in Ballads*, pp. 135–136; B. E. Stevenson, *Poems of American History*, pp. 301–302. See also *Notes and Queries*, 6th Series, VIII, 374; IX, 156; 9th Series, v, 435 (J. K. Laughton holds that the English song preceded the American); 11th Series, XI, 454, 500; XII, 58.

"The *Chesapeake* and the *Shannon*." From the singing and recitation of Alexander Murphy, Cape John, Pictou County.

1   The *Chesapeake* so bold
Out of Boston as we're told,
Came to take the British frigate neat and handy O.
The people all in port
They came out to see the sport,
And their music played up Yankee Doodle Dandy O.

2   Before this action it begun
    The Yankees made much fun,
    Saying, "We'll tow her up to Boston neat and handy O;
    And after that we'll dine,
    Treat our sweethearts all with wine,
    And we'll dance a jig of Yankee Doodle Dandy O."

3   Our British frigate's name
    All for the purpose came
    In so cooling Yankee's courage neat and handy O,
    Was the *Shannon*, Captain Brookes,
    And his crew all hearts of oaks,
    And in fighting they were allowed to be the dandy O.

4   The action scarce begun
    When they flinchéd from their guns.
    They thought they had worked us neat and handy O;
    But Brookes he wove his sword,
    Saying, "Come, my boys, we'll board,
    And we'll stop this playing up Yankee Doodle Dandy O."

5   When Britons heard this word
    They all sprang on board;
    They hauled down the Yankees' ensign neat and handy O.
    Notwithstanding all their brags
    The British raised their flags
    On the Yankees' mizzen-peak was quite the dandy O.

6   Brookes and all his crew
    In courage stout and true
    They worked the Yankee frigate neat and handy O.
    O may they ever prove
    In fighting or in love
    That the bold British tars will be the dandy O!

80

THE BATTLE OF THE *SHANNON* AND *CHESAPEAKE*

THE fragment which follows is all that I have been able to find of this broad-side version of the famous sea-fight. It carries us into the battle, and then, with a delicate international courtesy, suppresses that part of the narrative which might be painful to the sensibilities of a defeated foe. The preceding "*Chesapeake and Shannon*" song is not so much a narrative as a triumphant lyric. The present one is, in its entirety, a fairly straightforward recital, and it apparently has not retained its popularity as has the other song, with its rollicking jingle and its ear-capturing refrains. In the earlier part of the nineteenth century, however, it appeared on several broadsides, always with the title "The Battle of the *Shannon* and *Chesapeake*." This title, although it was not used by the Nova Scotia singer, I have borrowed as an aid in the somewhat difficult task of distinguishing the one song from the other.

Broadsides containing the song are: Pitts (25242.4, II, 72); Catnach (v, 206); Such, No. 154 (XII, 1); reprinted by Firth, *Naval Songs and Ballads*, pp. 312–313.

"The *Chesapeake* and the *Shannon*." From the singing and recitation of Peter Hines, Tatamagouche, Colchester County (printed, *Quest*, pp. 139–140).

1 'T was of the *Shannon* frigate in the merry month of May;
To watch those bold Americans off Boston light she lay.
The *Chesapeake* lying in harbour, a frigate stout and fine,
She had four hundred and sixty men on board, and her guns was
    forty-nine.

2 Captain Brooke he commanded us; a challenge he did write
To the captain of the *Chesapeake* to bring her out to fight.
He says, "My noble Lawrence, don't think it's through enmity,
For it's to show to all the world that Britain rules the sea."

3 The challenge being accepted, the *Chesapeake* she bore down,
And she was as fine a frigate as belonged to the British crown.
Yard-arm and broadside for a quarter of an hour,
When that enemy's ship drove up alongside, and her yards got
    locked in ours.

81

KELLY THE PIRATE

A COMPARISON of Version A with Versions B and C suggests a rather interesting problem: Are they, all three, variants of the same ballad, or does A represent one "Kelly the Pirate" song and B another, with C coming in as a variant of B? Version A corresponds to the texts in English broadsides (which are entitled either "The Bold Pirate" or "Kelly the Pirate"). Versions B and C are similar to the texts (entitled "Kelly the Pirate") in the American songsters, which, however, have no chorus. The verbal correspondences between A on the one hand, and B and C on the other, are so slight that it is hardly possible that all three can be variants in the proper sense of the word. It seems much more reasonable to suppose that Version A alone represents the original English song, and that B and C represent an American song, derived from and reproducing several of the lines of the English original, but apart from this relationship to be regarded as an independent composition.

For the English song see, for example, *A New Garland, containing three Choice Songs* (Preston, E. Sergent, *ca.* 1793), and broadsides: Ryle (VII, 129); C. Croshaw, York (with "The Hardy Tar").

The American song was printed in *The Forget Me Not Songster* (New York, Nafis and Cornish), p. 75; the same (Philadelphia and New York, Turner and Fisher, about 1840), pp. 205–206, in *The Old Forget Me Not Songster* (Boston, Locke and Dubier), p. 75, and in *Uncle Sam's Naval and Patriotic Songster* (New York, Philip J. Cozans), p. 29.

A

"Kelly the Pirate." From the singing and recitation of Robert Langille, Tatamagouche, Colchester County.

1   Come all ye jolly tarsmen, come listen to my song;
    If you pay good attention I'll not keep you long.
    'T was of the *Stag* frigate, that ship of great fame,
    That fought the arch-pirate, bold Kelly by name.

2   It was on the first of January all on the fifth day
    That we spied a large cutter, to the leeward she lay.
    The man on the masthead so loudly did cry,
    Saying, "There's a sail and she seems to lie by."

3   Our captain he viewed her all round,
    Saying, "That's Kelly the pirate, I'll bet fifty pound.
    So it's keep up undaunted, keep all snug and tight,
    For I mean to abide with bold Kelly to-night.

4 "Keep all up undaunted, make all snug and clear.
   Around with your helm and after him steer."
   We steadied a little till we came within shot,
   But this bold sassy pirate seemed to value us not.

5 We steadied a little till we came within hail,
   Then a few English pills we let fly in his tail.
       .   .   .   .
       .   .   .   .

6 Bold Captain Kelly on the deck he did stand,
   Saying, "Boys, be brave, valiant, and stout,
   For if we are taken you plainly must see
   Like dogs on the gallows we hangéd must be!"

7 Bold Captain Cooper on the deck he did stand;
   With a voice like the thunder he gave the command:
       .   .   .   .
   "Point your guns, blow your matches, and fire away."

8 With a round of large metal we did them so gall
   That down came the mainmast, their colours, and all.
   With canister-shot we did pepper them so
   That down to the bottom they quickly did go.

9 'T was of that sassy frigate if you — your name,
   She's a foe to Great Britain, from Dunkirk she came,
   To rob our rich merchant-ships all on the wave,
   But bold Captain Cooper her soon did invade.

B

"Kelly the Pirate." From the singing and recitation of Richard Hines,
River John, Pictou County (printed, *Quest*, pp. 142–143).

1 Admiral Kelly gave orders on the first of May
   To cruise in the Channel for our enemy,
   To protect our commerce from that daring foe,
   And all our merchant-ships where they would go.

Chorus
   Then it's O Britons, stand true,
   Stand true to your colours, stand true!

2 It was early one morning, by the wind we did lie,
  A man from the masthead a sail he did spy.
  "A sail! O a sail!" he loudly did cry,
  "She is a large cutter and seems to lay by."

3 Our noble commander he pulled out his glass,
  So did our lieutenant to see what she was.
  Our captain stepped up and he viewed her all round,
  Says, "That's Kelly the pirate, I'll bet fifty pound!"

4 "Don't you see that villain?" he cried, "Make sail!
  We'll soon overtake him, my boys, I'll give bail.
  Lay aloft, shake your reefs out, make everything clear,
  And up with the helm and for him we'll steer."

5 We sailed till we came within gunshot,
  Bold Kelly he seemed for to value us not.
  With a loud voice like thunder, Kelly did say,
  "Load your guns, light your matches, and fire away!"

6 We engaged with that cutter four hours and more,
  Till the blood from our scuppers like water did pour.
  With round and grape metal we peppered his hull,
  Till down came his mizzenmast, colours, and all.

7 We towed him in Portsmouth that very same day,
  And then on to Newgate sent Kelly away.
  Here's a health to our captain and officers too!
  Here's a health to *Stag* frigate and all of her crew!

C

"Kelly the Pirate." From the singing and recitation of Alexander Harrison, Maccan, Cumberland County.

1 Our Admiral gave orders on the same day
  To cruise in the Channel for our enemy,
  To protect all our merchants from the brave foe,
  And all interlopers, as you may suppose.

2 On the twenty-first of January so clear was the day,
  A man from our masthead a sail he spied.
  "A sail! O a sail!" he loudly did cry,
  "She is a large cutter, and seems to lay by."

3 Our noble commander he pulled out his glass,
   So did our lieutenant to see what she was.
   Our captain jumped up and surveyed her all round:
   "It's Kelly the pirate, I'll lay fifty pounds!

4 "Do you see that proud villain?" he cried, "Make sail!
   "We'll soon overhaul him, my boys, I'll give bail!
   Jump up and shake out your bags all snug and clear,
   And up with your helm, and after them steer."

5 We sailed till we came within gunshot.
   Bold Kelly he seemed to value us not.
   With a loud voice like thunder bold Kelly did say,
   "Board your guns, blow your matches, my boys, and fire
       away!"

6 We engaged this cutter for four hours and more,
   Till the blood from the scuppers like water did pour.
   With round and grape metal we peppered his hull
   Till down came her ensign, staff, colours, and all.

7 We have taken this prize all on the same day,
   And straight to our prison sent Kelly away.
   Here's a health to our captain, and lieutenant too,
   Likewise the *Hart* frigate and all her crew!

82

THE LITTLE FIGHTING CHANCE

THE Nova Scotia version of this militant song corresponds to the English version printed by Reynardson, *Sussex Songs*, pp. 18–19 ("The Fourteenth of July"). The English song ends: "We will smother all those Frenchman wherever we do meet." The transfer of the ultimate threat to the "Yankee dogs" of my version was probably made in Nova Scotia itself.

"The Little Fighting Chance." From the singing and recitation of Robert Langille, Tatamagouche, Colchester County.

1 On the fourteenth of July once so clear was the sky,
 . . . . came bearing down so nigh,
 Came bearing down upon us as we sailed out of France.
 The name that she was called was the *Little Fighting Chance*.

> *Chorus*
> So cheer up, my lively boys, let it never be said
> That the sons of old Britannia would ever be afraid.

2 We gave to them a gun and the battle had begun;
 The cannons they did roar and the bullets they did fly.
 It was broadside for broadside, we showed them gallant sport;
 And to see the lofty yards and topmasts they came rolling overboard.

3 We fought them four hours, the battle was so hot,
 Till four of our foremost men lay dead upon the spot.
 Sixteen were wounded, made twenty in all,
 And down with the French lily, boys, the Frenchmen one and all!

4 O now, my brave boys, since the prize is our own,
 What shall we do for jury-masts, for spars we have none?
 So we tore in with a sweet and pleasant gale,
 And early the next morning at the head of our king sail.[1]

5 O now, brave boys, since we have gotten safe to shore,
 We'll make the ale-houses and the taverns for to roar.
 Here's a health unto King George and all his gallant fleet.
 We'll smother all the Yankee dogs that ever we do meet!

[1] Reynardson: "at the head of Old Kinsale."

83

BOLD DIGHTON

THE Nova Scotia versions correspond, with a few variations, to the texts found in American songsters, under the title "Bold Dighton." See *The Forget Me Not Songster* (New York, Nafis and Cornish), pp. 67–71; the same (Philadelphia and New York, Turner and Fisher), pp. 219–223; *The Old Forget Me Not Songster* (Boston, Locke and Dubier), pp. 67–71; *The American Sailor's Songster* (New York, Philip J. Cozans), pp. 89–93.

The original title of this piece was "The Escape from Basseterre." The author was P. Russel. The Harvard College Library has two broadside copies of the early nineteenth century. One is headed: "The Escape from Bassaterre. Being the account of an action fought off Guadaloupe, in 1805, where ninety-five Americans, and near three hundred Britons made their escape at that place. — Composed by P. RUSSEL, while lying in irons in the Moro Castle, who received two wounds in the action." The other is headed: "The Escape from Basseterre SOLD by the AUTHOR only: who COMPOSED the FOLLOWING LINES while in the MORO CASTLE.

☞ From WOUNDS which the Author received in BATTLE, he is unable to obtain a LIVELIHOOD in the ordinary pursuits of life: — And it is hoped that every GENEROUS AMERICAN will be ready to participate in the SUFFERINGS of the UNFORTUNATE as well as to APPLAUD the BRAVE."

Other poems by Russel are extant in broadsides of about the same date: "Filial Affection. Composed while the author was lying in irons in the Moro Castle, with an intention of sending it to his mother"; "Russell's Reflections. Occasioned by a retrospective review of the events of his own life, while lying in irons in the Moro Castle. — Tune — Mouldering Cave"; "Capt. Lawrence's Victory, or The Capture of the Peacock" and "Death of Lawrence" — both in one broadside with the following introductory note: "The lines of this sheet, were composed by the unfortunate RUSSELL, who has been prevented from obtaining a livelihood in the ordinary pursuits of life from wounds received in battle" (Ford, *Massachusetts Broadsides*, No. 3328); "Love and Misfortune. Sold by the Author only, who composed the FOLLOWING LINES while suffering in a loathsome PRISON; at a time when he had reason to consider himself on the verge of ETERNITY."

The last of these is autobiographical. For example,

> They took us on board, we at Guadaloupe landed,
>   And there was I gall'd by the French Tyrant's chains,
> I thought on my love, whilst my heart it expanded;
>   While sickness and famine augmented my pains
>
> Escap'd from the French, being wounded full sorely;
>   The Spaniards a prisoner soon made me once more,
> In the Castle call'd Moro, I suffer'd severely,
>   From pain, thirst and hunger, ere I left their sad shore.
>
> . . . .
>
> Releas'd from those foes, I arrived in Columbia;
>   And there I experienced misfortune and pain,
> For wants then oppress'd, whilst mankind seem'd to shun me;
>   But shrinking at trifles is what I disdain.

By falsehood imprison'd forlorn and neglected;
  On straw now I rest, but no longer can sleep;
Such heart rending pangs I could ne'er have expected,
  But yet at life's troubles, I scorn'd for to weep.

A

"Bold Dighton." From the singing and recitation of Alexander Harrison, Maccan, Cumberland County.

1 Come all you bold heroes that plough the rough main,
  Give ear to our story, the truth I'll explain.
  It was our misfortune which happened in great war,
  And how we escaped from the French at Bastar.

2 We were then confined on the Guadaloupe shore,
  Of true valiant seamen four hundred or more,
  Shut up in a small compass being greatly distressed,
  With painful disease and famine oppressed.

3 A gallant young hero, from Saint Lucia he came,
  Both generous and wealthy, called Dighton by name.
  He had the heart of a lion, the soul of a prince,
  And friendship's kind impulse to us did evince.

4 He came to our prison, he mourned our sad fate,
  He launched out his gold to relieve our sad state.
  Five hundred bright guineas he gave, I am sure,
  Which did greatly relieve us in this distressed hour.

5 At this generous action the French did complain.
  They soon did confine him with fetters and chains
  With us in the prison, it was them we might see,
  But from his chains and fetters we soon set him free.

6 Says Dighton, "My boys, if you'll take my advice,
  Now if you'll prove constant it is done in a trice.
  Down by the *Umpire* the *Tiger* doth lie,[1]
  A stout and fine coaster, she is fit for the sea.

7 "The captain's on shore and we have all things on board,
  A plenty of cannons, pikes, pistols, and swords.
  Now if you will prove constant and stand by my side,
  We will board her, my boys, and we will sail the next tide."

---

1 The broadsides read, "*For 'tis down by yon pier, the Tyger does lay.*"

8 Then at this adventure we all did agree,
Each breast loaded with ardor to fight and be free.
"Come give us your signal," each sailor replied,
"We are ready to conquer, or die by your side."

9 "Prepare for the conflict, no longer delay.
But keep yourselves cool, boys, my orders obey."
Three gallant young seamen as seconds he chose.
Our signal for freedom was, "Death to our foes!"

10 Then out of prison we all rushed amain.
The three guns were fired, the French guards were slain.
On board of the *Tiger* we soon rushed our way.
We cut both her cables and stood out to sea,

11 Which caused a sad rumpus, it being midnight.
The Frenchmen bawled out in a terrible fright,
"Mon Dieu, fracter engie!" [1] Drums beat and bells toll,
Our hero shouts, "Freedom!" to each valiant soul.

12 Their fortress was open, their cannon did play,
Their shot flew like hail as we got under way.
They shattered our spars as we sailed from the shore.
To bid them good-bye we a broadside let pour.

13 Then out of all danger we thought ourselves clear,
But for this mistake we did pay very dear.
Next morning at daylight it was there we espied
The *Lion*, a corvette, hang down on our side.

14 She plied us with grapeshot with broadside so sore,
Which caused the *Tiger* to make her guns roar.
With thirty-six eighteens the *Lion* did growl,
And eighteen brass nines the fierce *Tiger* did howl.

15 Yard-arms and broadsides, for three glasses we lay,
At length our broadside cut her mainmast away.
Says Dighton, "My boys, if you are tired of this fun
You now have your choice, to fight or to run!"

16 To spare blood and slaughter the crew did incline.
To run down the corvette it was our design.
But at this same moment she grappled us fierce,
And then sword in hand was our only resource.

[1] An attempt to reproduce phonetically a phrase unintelligible to the singer. The broadsides read, "*Mon Dieu! footer Engla.*"

17 To board and to slaughter they were fully bent.
To give us no quarters was their sole intent.
To board us thrice over they tried with this view,
But they were repulsed by the *Tiger's* bold crew.

18 Then Dighton cried out as each hero should feel,
Whose eyes transferred fury like bright burnished steel,
"There is death to each man on the point of my sword.
Come all my bold heroes, let us jump overboard!"

19 Then over the bulwark he jumped like a roe.
One stroke from his sabre laid two Frenchmen low.
On board of the corvette we all rushed so fierce
That soon from their quarters the French did disperse.

20 Steel sparkle, pikes rattle, and swords loudly clash,
And the blood on her decks like salt water did dash.
Her scuppers with huge streams of crimson did pour,
And the blue seas all round us rolled purple with gore.

21 Three hundred brave seamen were slain of their crew,
When the Frenchmen gave out and they cried, "Mon Dieu!"
They fell on their knees and their weapons let fall,
And then our bold hero for quarter did call.

22 We soon gave them quarter and then we did hear
That for to engage us they did volunteer.
They trebled our metal with e'en two for one,
But Fortune's kind favor saved Freedom's bold son.

23 Then Dighton cried out, "Now the battle is o'er,
Let the French learn this lesson and teach it on shore,
Go back to their country and friends and take care
To treat well in future each prisoner of war!"

24 To conduct the French back we the *Tiger* then gave,
Our seamen were generous and valiant and brave;
Then down to Antigua with our corvette we bore,
And on the next morning we all jumped ashore,

25 Drink a health to each seaman that ploughs the rough main.
May each crowned with laurels return home again.
May the fair of our country some gratitude show
To the sons of the ocean that fight the proud foe.

26 And as for brave Dighton, our true valiant friend,
   May glories pursue him while honors attend,
   And when he does die may each seaman draw near,
   Come kneel at his tombstone and let fall a tear.

B

"The *Tiger* and the *Lion*." From the singing and recitation of Richard Hines, River John, Pictou County (printed, *Quest*, pp. 71–74).

1 Come all you bold seamen that ploughs the rough main,
   Give ear to my story, the truth I'll explain.
   There was a misfortune in sad time of war,
   And how we escaped from the French at Bastar.

2 There were seamen bold three hundred and more
   Was shut up in prison on Guadeloupe shore;
   They were chained down in prison and sorely oppressed,
   By painful diseases and famine oppressed.

3 There was a bold seaman, from St. Lords he came;
   He was generous in action, called Dighton by name.
   He had the heart of a lion, the soul of a prince,
   Through honour and friendship to us did advance.

4 He came to the prison to bemoan our sad fate,
   He launched out his gold to relieve our sad state;
   Five hundred guineas he paid down, and more,
   Which much did relieve us in that distressed hour.

5 At this generous action the French did complain.
   It was then they bound him in fetters and chains.
   They threw him in prison with us, you may see.
   From his fetters and chains, boys, we soon set him free.

6 "Come all you bold seamen, if you take my advice,
   Stand true to my side, it is done in a trice.
   Down in yon portway the *Tiger* she lays;
   She's a well-found staunch cruiser, she's fit for the sea.

7 "The captain's on shore and all things on board,
   There's plenty of cannon, pikes, pistols, and swords.
   And if you prove valiant and stand by my side
   Never fear but we'll board her and sail the next tide."

8 At this generous action we all did agree
  To break out of prison to die or be free.
  Two gallant young sailors as his seconds he chose,
  And a signal of freedom was, "Death to his foes!"

9 Then out of the French prison we all rushed amain,
  Two big guns was fired, the French guard was slain,
  And down to the *Tiger* we all took our way,
  We slipped both her cables and steered out for sea.

10 Their ports being opened, right on us did play.
  The shot flew like hail as we got under way.
  They shattered our spars as we sailed from the shore.
  To bid them a good-night a broadside did pour.

11 Then early next morning we thought ourselves clear,
  But for our mistake, boys, we paid very dear.
  'T was early next morning just as day we spied
  The *Lion* of Pervert bearing down alongside.

12 She supplied us with broadsides, which grieved our hearts sore,
  Which caused the bold *Tiger* to make her guns roar.
  With twenty-six eighteens the *Lion* did howl.
  With eighteen brass fours the *Tiger* did growl.

13 'T was yard-arm and broadside together did lay
  Till a shot from the *Tiger* took his mizzen away.
  "Now," said bold Dighton," if you're tired of the fun,
  You have got your choice, to fight or to run."

14 To shun blood and slaughter we all did incline.
  To run from the *Tiger* it was our design.
  But to our misfortune and our sad distress,
  That very same moment they grappled us fast.

15 They tried for to board us thrice over in view,
  But they were opposed by the *Tiger's* bold crew.
  They thribled our metal with men three to one,
  But Fortune still favoured old Britain's bold sons.

16 Then up speaks bold Dighton, like a hero did feel.
  His eyes glanced like fury like the bright varnished steel.
  "Come each of you seamen on the point of your sword!
  It's death, boys, or freedom! We'll all jump on board!"

17 Then over the bulwarks we crushed on our foe.
   One clip from his sword laid the French captain low.
   Then down on the decks, boys, their weapons let fall,
   And on us brave heroes for mercy did call.

18 Swords rattled, pikes, pistols, the swords loud did clash,
   The blood on our decks like water did splash.
   The huge streams of crimson from our scuppers did pour,
   And the blue sea around us ran purple with gore.

19 "It's now," says bold Dighton, "since the battle is o'er,
   Let the French learn a lesson, go teach it on shore.
   Let them go home to their country and tell them beware
   For to treat well in future the prisoners of war!"

20 We cleared our decks that very same day.
   The wind from the sou'west, we got under way,
   And down to Antigua away then we bore,
   And early next morning we all went on shore.

21 Here's a health to bold Dighton, a true valiant friend.
   May honour protect him and glory attend!
   And when he is dead I pray you'll draw near
   And kneel at his tombstone and let fall a tear.

84

AS WE WERE A-SAILING

IT may be that this ballad derives in some fashion from "Captain Ward and the Rainbow" (Child, No. 287). In Kidson's *Traditional Tunes* there is a fragment, obtained on the coast of Yorkshire, in which the ship is the *Rainbow*. It ends thus:

> Good health unto this damsel who fought all on the main,
> And here's to the royal gallant ship called *Rainbow* by name.

A version in Williams's *Folk Songs of the Upper Thames* ends,

> Here's a health to the girl, she's a girl of great fame,
> She's on board the ship that's called *Newrion* by name —

which helps to explain the transmutation of the ship to the *Union* of some of the later versions, including my own. It is to be noted that the ship is the "*Union* by name" in the American texts cited below.

For British versions see Kidson, *Traditional Tunes*, pp. 99–100 (with music); Williams, p. 261 ("Aboard the *Resolution*"); Christie, *Traditional Ballad Airs*, II, 176–177 ("The Bold Damosel"). Among the broadsides on file in the Harvard College Library there is one containing a version of this song with the title "Down by the Spanish Shore" (on the same sheet with "The Brave Collier Lads"), issued by W. Harris, Birmingham.

For American texts see *The American Songster*, collected and published by John Kenedy (Baltimore, 1836), pp. 245–246; *The American Songster* (New York, Nafis and Cornish, 1847), pp. 245–246.

No title. From the singing and recitation of Robert Langille, Tatamagouche, Colchester County (printed, *Quest*, p. 52).

1 As we were a sailing down by the Spanish shore,
   Our drums they did beat and the guns loudly roar.
   We spied a lofty admiral ship come plowing down the main,
   Which caused us to hoist our topsails again.

2 Come boys, let us be hearty! come boys, let us be true!
   And after our enemy we quickly shall pursue.
   Soon as we overtake them upon the ocean wide,
   And with foresail we'll give them a broadside.

3 They gave to us another as good as we sent.
   For to sink each other was our whole intent.
   At the very second broadside our captain he was slain.
   Up steps a damsel his place for to maintain.

4 "Oh quarters, oh quarters, my brave British boys."
"No quarters, no quarters," the damsel she replies,
"You have the best of quarters I can to you afford.
You must fight, strike, or sink, my boys, or jump overboard!"

5 Now since we gained the victory we'll drink a glass of wine.
Drink to your own true love here, and I'll drink to mine.
Here's a health unto the damsel, the damsel of Ame,[1]
So boldly she fought on the *Union* by name!

[1] Kidson: "*Who fought all on the main.*"

85

THE OLD *RAMILLIES*

H. M. S. Ramillies was wrecked off the south coast of Devon on the 15th of February, 1760, and of several hundred men on board only twenty-six were saved. Various songs were composed in commemoration, but to the printed texts of these the Nova Scotia version is related only in subject-matter, not in phraseology. One of the songs, entitled "The Fatal *Ramillies*," is in a Pitts broadside. See also Williams, *Folk-Songs of the Upper Thames*, p. 144 ("The Fate of the *Ramillies*"); *Journal of the Folk-Song Society*, III, 286–287.

"The Old *Ramillies*." From the singing and recitation of Richard Hines, River John, Pictou County.

1 It happened to be on the first of May
   While the *Ramillies* to her anchor lay.
   At twelve o'clock a gale came on,
   And she from her anchor cut and run.

2 The storm increaséd more and more,
   The billows was rolling on the shore.
   Our close-reefed tops'ls we quickly spread
   In hopes to weather the old Ram Head.

3 The rain poured down in a dreadful shock,
   While the sea beat over our forc-top.
   She would neither stay nor wear,
   Nor yet gather way enough to steer.

4 The bos'n on the deck did stand,
   He blowed his call and gave command:
   "Launch out the boats your lives to save,
   Or the sea this night will be your grave."

5 Some in one place, some in another,
   Five hundred men they all got smothered.
   There was only four saved to tell the tale
   How the *Ramillies* behavéd in the gale.

6 When the news to Plymouth came
   That the *Ramillies* was lost and all her men,
   All Plymouth town was flowing in tears
   To hear the dreadful sad affair.

7 Come, all you pretty fair maids, weep with me,
   Who lost your loves in the *Ramillies*.
   There was only four saved to tell the tale
   How she behavéd in the gale.

86

BY THE LIGHTNING WE LOST OUR SIGHT

THERE is an eighteenth-century English song, quite different from this, which records a similar misfortune: "The Blind Seaman's Lamentation, Addressed to his Brother Sailors" (in a chapbook printed by E. Sergent, Preston, *ca.* 1793: Harvard College Library, 25276.43.58, No. 21). The sailor was struck blind at the wheel. The song begins:

> Good people all I pray draw near,
> Till I relate my misery,
> Of the misfortune to me befel,
> How I was blinded on the Sea.

From the singing and recitation of Harry Sutherland, River John, Pictou County.

1 Come all you lads bound over the deep, I hope you will attend,
And listen unto those few lines which I have lately penned.
I was once as hardy a sailor lad as ever furled a sail,
Till by the lightning I lost my sight in that tremendous gale.

2 On the eighteenth of September last from Cork we did set sail.
We were bound for Gibraltar in a fair and pleasant gale.
The weather being fine, our course did steer our ship before the wind,
And still my love grew warmer for the girl I left behind.

3 Scarce had we reached our distant port, we lay a few days there,
When our orders ran for old England with the wind still blowing fair.
We shoved our good ship out to sea, and on her did crowd sail,
While a storm arose, the sun eclipsed, it blew a hurricane.

4 The storm it still continued, and then it blew a gale.
Our captain cried, "My heroes bold, close reef your main top-sail!"
Scarce had he those words uttered when like tars aloft did they,
Like hardy tars through storm and wind his orders to obey.

5 Scarce had we reached the main top when a heavier flash rolled
    by.
  Dear God, I ought to remember it, the last sight with my eyes!
  Our to'gallantmast to pieces went all by a ball of light,
  Which leaves me and four sailors more, by the lightning we lost
    our sight.

6 Next morning when the sun arose we were a sight to view.
  Our chief mate was washed overboard, and four more of the
    crew.
  The storm it still continued, the lightning sharp did flash,
  The foaming seas washed over her, and on her sides did smash.

87

NEWFOUNDLAND

THIS song is of Nova Scotian composition. The singer who delivered it to me stated that it was made by Captain Cale White of Maitland, Colchester County.

From the singing and recitation of Peter Hines, Tatamagouche, Colchester County (printed, *Quest*, pp. 199–201).

1 Saint Patrick's day in 'sixty-five from New York we set sail.
Kind Providence did favor us with a sweet and pleasant gale.
We bore away from America, as you shall understand.
With courage brave we rode the waves bound down to New-
foundland.

2 When two days out, to our distress our captain he fell sick,
And scarcely was enabled to show himself on deck.
The fever raged, which made us fear that death was near at hand.
For Halifax we bore away bound down to Newfoundland.

3 The land we made, but knew it not, for strangers we were all,
Our captain not being able to come on deck at all.
So we were all obliged again to have her off from land.
With saddest hearts we put to sea bound down to Newfoundland.

4 All that night we run our brig till early the next day.
"Our captain's getting worse," we all with one accord did say.
"We'll square away for Cape Canso. My boys, now bear a
hand."
In Arishat that afternoon we anchored safe, bound down to
Newfoundland.

5 Unto the board of health we then for medical aid did go.
Our captain near the point of death, that symptoms it did show.
The small-pox now was breaking out, for that it proved to be,
And eight days after we arrived, at God's just command,
He breathed his last in Arishat, bound down to Newfoundland.

6 Both day and night may we lament for our departed friend,
And pray to be protected from what has been his end.
Be with us and protect us, God, by Thy almighty hand,
And guide us safe while on the seas bound down to Newfound-
land.

88

THE WRECK OF THE *ATLANTIC*

On March 20, 1873, the *Atlantic*, a crack ship of the new White Star fleet, left Liverpool for New York with about one thousand people, including passengers and crew, on board. She was a four-masted barque-rigged iron vessel of 3707 tons gross, and was classed A1 on the Liverpool register. During this voyage she was battered by westerly gales, and after ten days at sea the engineer reported a shortage of coal, whereupon the Captain, James Agnew Williams, decided to change her course and put into Halifax. On the night of March 31st she was steaming through heavy seas on a course intended to take her about five miles east of the Sambro light, which marks the outer entrance of Halifax Harbour. About two hours after midnight the ship struck a ledge off the settlement of Prospect, seven miles west of Sambro light. Many of the passengers were trapped in their berths and drowned when the ship heeled over ten minutes after the first shock. The rigging and bow remained awash, and the surviving passengers and members of the crew sought a precarious refuge there, but many of them were caught by the waves, which were rising higher with an increasing wind, and by noon 535 persons had perished by drowning or from exposure. In the meantime, however, the fisher folk of Prospect had gone bravely to work with their dories, and during the morning they succeeded in rescuing some 450 survivors from the wave-beaten spars and rigging. Some notable acts of heroism were performed, and these are duly — and truly — set forth in the following ballad, which, as I was informed by the singer who introduced me to it, was brought out in broadside form shortly after the event.

For another song on the "Wreck of the *Atlantic*" see *Delaney's Song Book No. 12*, p. 26.

"The Wreck of the *Atlantic*." From the singing and recitation of Robert Langille, Tatamagouche, Colchester County.

1   Dear friends, come listen to the tale,
     The loss which we deplore,
  Of the gallant ship *Atlantic* lost
     On Nova Scotia's shore.

2   The most terrific accident
     Befell that fated ship,
  As she approached those rocky shores
     On her way across the deep.

3   The sun had set behind the hills,
     Night spread her wings around,
  A night that will remembered be
     For many a year to come.

4 Alas, a ship, a noble ship,
       That had the ocean crossed,
   And on the lonely Prospect shores
       That night was wrecked and lost.

5 With full a thousand souls on board,
       Her captain had no fear,
   And heeded not the rocky coast
       Which he was drawing near.

6 Till, oh, alas, it was too late!
       The final shock was given.
   That noble ship had struck the rock,
       Amidships she was riven.

7 The terror-stricken souls on board,
       Oh, who could give them aid?
   Unto each other looked for help,
       Each praying to be saved.

8 Numbers overboard were washed,
       And perished in the deep,
   While others frozen with the cold,
       Died on the sinking ship.

9 Poor helpless women down below,
       Of whom not one was saved,
   Dear little children too,
       All met a watery grave.

10 Amongst the women there were two
        Who down the waves that night
    Had each of them a little babe
        That scarce had seen the light.

11 A lady with her babe in arms
        Had reached the deck, we're told,
    With nothing but her night-clothes on
        To shield her from the cold.

12 To save her life her slender form
        Was fastened to a mast,
    Where ten long hours she there remained
        Before she breathed her last.

13 But ere she died her little babe
    Was swept into the sea.
What misery did that mother bear
    In her hours of agony!

14 Third officer Brodie, a brave man,
    Swum over to the shore,
And quickly got a rope on board
    To help the others o'er.

15 The kind-hearted fishermen
    Did kindly them receive,
Giving them freely of their stores,
    Supplying all their needs.

16 Next morning when the sun arose
    And the angry billows swelled,
The people on the Prospect shore
    A dreadful sight beheld.

17 The rocks around were strewn with dead,
    And as each wave broke o'er,
Bearing its burden to be laid
    With sorrow on the shore,

18 Both men and women, young and old,
    With flesh and clothes all torn
Upon the sharp and craggy rocks
    The angry waves had borne.

19 A lady with her little babe
    Clasped tightly to her breast
Upon the tangled seaweed lay,
    Gone to her long, long rest.

20 All who came there to see the sight
    With heartfelt grief bemoaned
The fate of those who left their homes
    To cross the ocean foam.

21 And far away from friends and home
    In a foreign land to die,
A stranger's home their burial place,
    No friend to close an eye.

22 Amongst the men on Prospect shore
   Who risked a watery grave,
   And spurred the men around him
   The shipwrecked men to save,

23 Was their kind and loving clergyman,
   Mr. Ancient was his name;
   His name deserves to be enrolled
   Upon a list of fame.

24 He said, "My friends, come take the boats,
   And try whom we can save,"
   And boldly took the foremost part,
   The bravest of the brave.

25 Those hardy men who gave such help
   Deserve the highest praise.
   Oh, never forget their noble deeds
   When thankful songs we raise!

26 The captain in that trying hour
   Spoke kindly to the men,
   Saying, "Be calm, good men," while angry waves
   Swept angry over them.

27 One Mr. Street, a gentleman,
   Quite frantic with despair,
   From cabin came, and in his arms
   His little daughter bare.

28 And to one Ellery he said,
   "Pray, Charlie, take my child,
   That I may go my wife to seek,
   The billows raging wild!"

29 And as the steward gazed on the child
   And saw her face so fair,
   His thoughts went quickly to his home —
   He had one like her there.

30 The father did the mother seek,
   But neither one came back;
   The angry waves soon swept them off
   From off the sinking wreck.

31 Poor suffering little innocent,
        It cried, "Papa, come!"
    Its clothes were then just taken from
        Its little bed so warm.

32 It cried, "Papa!" a short time,
        But papa never came,
    Expiring in the steward's arms
        In agony and pain.

33 Its little soul to heaven flew
        To call its papa there.
    I hope they hand in hand will walk
        Through heavenly mansions fair.

34 Amongst those rescued from the wreck
        Was John Andrew, a brave lad,
    Who boldly struggled to the wreck
        Bereft of all he had.

35 Father, mother, brother too,
        Had sunk to rise no more,
    But he with help from some strong men
        Got safely to the shore.

36 Kind friends then took him to their homes,
        His wants they did supply.
    Strangers with pity in their hearts
        Beheld the orphan boy.

37 When he arrived in Halifax
        Warm welcome he received,
    And now we have him journeying home
        With his sisters dear to live.

38 Oh, never may those cruel rocks
        Another victim gain.
    Let life ships guard our rocky coast,
        .   .   .   .   .   .

39 To those who perished in the deep
        We give a friendly grave.
    Our joys would aye be greater far
        Had we the power to save.

40　And now that noble steamer,
　　　The *Atlantic*, she is lost,
　　Which o'er the stormy ocean
　　　So oftentimes had passed.

41　And many sad and touching scenes
　　　That never can be told,
　　And many a hundred lives were lost,
　　　And many hearts made cold.

42　Now she will never sail again
　　　Unto that distant shore,
　　To those who look with tearful eyes
　　　For friends who come no more.

43　The dreadful sight will never
　　　From our memories fade away,
　　Till children that surround us now
　　　Are feeble, old, and grey.

44　Oh, angry sea, give up thy dead,
　　　Oh, rocky reefs, sink low!
　　How could you part so many friends?
　　　Why did you cause such woe?

45　Oh, gallant ship that proudly sailed
　　　An hour before the shock,
　　Why did you not keep far away
　　　And shun that sunken rock?

46　With all our friends around us
　　　We close our eyes in sleep,
　　Our thoughts will often wander
　　　Across the dreary deep,

47　In grief for those who closed their eyes.
　　　No thoughts of death were near,
　　But to wake a sinking in the deep,
　　　Shrieks sounding in their ears.

48 So it is with us, my loving friends.
    There's breakers all around,
And in an unexpected hour
    The last great trump will sound.

49 The shrieks and groans and cries of those
    Who fear the chastening rod,
All unprepared must then come forth
    To meet Almighty God!

89

THE *CEDAR GROVE*

FOR such information as I am able to present concerning the wreck of the *Cedar Grove* I am indebted to Mr. Francis J. Audet, Chief of the Index and Information, Public Archives of Canada, who procured the facts from Mr. E. M. Hurst, Collector of Customs at the Port of Canso. The Steamship *Cedar Grove*, of about 2000 tons' register, was wrecked off Canso, Nova Scotia, on the night of November 30, 1882. She had sailed from London, and was bound for St. John, New Brunswick, with a cargo principally of liquors. The captain and two engineers were lost, also a Mrs. Farrell, the only female passenger on board. The particular rock on which the ship split is the so-called Cedar Grove Breaker on the southeast side of St. Andrews Island.

The text that follows was printed in *The Quest of the Ballad*, pp. 201–204. It was taken from the singing and recitation of Harry Sutherland, River John, Pictou County.

1 It's of a noble steamer, the *Cedar Grove* by name,
  She crossed the briny ocean, from London city came.
  She was strongly built on the banks of Clyde, five hundred tons
    or more;
  But her strength it proved of no avail on the rocks of Canso
    shore.

2 The night was dark and stormy, the lookout was at his post;
  The first he saw of danger was breakers on the coast.
  The sailor at the helm, he thought that he could tell
  They were too nigh the land by the heaving of the swell.

3 He wished to give the warning, but thought 't was not his place;
  Discipline must be followed whatever be the case.
  The signal it was given our engines to reverse.
  "To starboard your helm!" the captain cries, "Our ship is off her
    course."

4 But still our noble steamer, she nobly boomed along,
  Till in one moment a dreadful crash brought fear to everyone.
  Two engineers and firemen were hard to work below,
  And by their perseverance it's backward she did go.

5 Once more we gained the deep water, but yet our doom was
    sealed.
  The briny waves rolled in her bows, and then to port she keeled.
  With a heavy weight of water from forward it did flow,
  Burst into aft compartments, and down our ship did go.

6 The saddest of my story which yet it doth remain,
  We had one lady passenger — Miss Farrel was her name.
  For to visit some relations in the city of St. John
  She ventured on the stormy deep, but now she's dead and gone.

7 A sailor said he saw her in the cabin door stand by,
  Did grieve his heart with pity to hear her weep and cry.
  He offered to console her, and said, "You'll not be lost."
  And a moment later that lady's form in the breaking waves was
    tossed.

8 Our steward held her bravely out o'er the ship's dark rail,
  And waiting for the boats to pull up against the gale.
  A giant wave swept over, which did prevail his grip,
  And then that lady's tender form went floating from the ship.

9 The same wave took our captain, and he was seen no more.
  Through heavy mist and darkness the boats still lingered near.
  Two engineers were also lost just as the ship went down.
  Their bodies or the lady's have never yet been found.

10 And now the ill-fated *Cedar Grove* on the bottom she doth lie.
  To save the most of her cargo the divers hard did try.
  A disfigured body was carefully sent on —
  Our aged honoured captain who died while in command.

11 Our cargo was for Halifax from the city of St. John,
  And to the latter port our steamer did belong.
  She was strongly built on the banks of Clyde, five hundred tons
    or more,
  But her strength it proved of no avail on the rocks of Canso shore.

90

CAPTAIN GLEN

THERE is a group of ballads — including "Brown Robyn's Confession" (Child, No. 57), "The Gosport (or Gaspard) Tragedy," "The New York Trader" (No. 91), "The Sailor's Tragedy" (No. 92), and "Captain Glen" — which deal with the motive of a ship containing a criminal who during the voyage is detected by supernatural means and punished for his sins (see Kittredge, *Journal*, XX, 261–264; XXVI, 177–178). In "The Gosport Tragedy" and "The Sailor's Tragedy" this motive appears toward the end and supplies the ideal revenge finale, but in the present ballad, as in "Brown Robyn's Confession" and "The New York Trader" (No. 91) it is dominant, and in each of the three the ship is held back by a storm until the crew discover the criminal and throw him overboard.

For British texts of "Captain Glen" see: Ebsworth, *Roxburghe Ballads*, VIII, 141–143 ("An Excellent New Song, entitled Captain Glen"); Motherwell's *Minstrelsy*, Appendix, XXXI (one stanza with music); Logan, *A Pedlar's Pack of Ballads and Songs*, pp. 47–50 ("Captain Glen's Unhappy Voyage to New Barbary," from a broadside of about 1815, collated with a copy dated 1794); Christie, *Traditional Ballad Airs*, I, 240–241; Greig, CXXX; Ashton, *Real Sailor Songs*, p. 82; Christopher Stone, *Sea Songs and Ballads*, pp. 100–103; Masefield, *A Sailor's Garland*, pp. 199–202. See also *Notes and Queries*, 3d Series, XI, 419–498; *Journal of the Folk-Song Society*, V, 263–265.

In America the song was printed in an early nineteenth-century broadside, "Captain Glen's Unhappy Voyage to New Barbary" (Ford, *Massachusetts Broadsides*, No. 3003); *The Forget Me Not Songster* (New York, Nafis and Cornish), pp. 76–78; the same (Philadelphia and New York, Turner and Fisher), pp. 210–213, and *The Old Forget Me Not Songster* (Boston, Locke and Dubier), pp. 76–78.

"Captain Glen." From the singing and recitation of Alexander Harrison, Maccan, Cumberland County.

1   There was a ship and a ship of fame
     Launch'd off the stocks, bound to the main,
     With a hundred and fifty brisk young men
     Was picked and chosen every one.

2   William Glen was our captain's name.
     He was a tall and brisk young man,
     As bold a sailor as ever went to sea,
     And he was bound to New Barbary.

3   The first of April when we did set sail,
     Blest with a sweet and prosperous gale,
     For we were bound to New Barbary
     With all our whole ship's company.

4   We had not sailed a day but two
     Till all our whole ship's jovial crew

They all fell sick but sixty-three,
As we went to New Barbary.

5 One night the captain he did dream
There came a voice which said to him,
"Prepare you and your company.
To-morrow night you must lodge with me."

6 This wak'd the captain in a fright,
Being the third watch of the night;
Then for his boatswain he did call,
And told to him his secrets all.

7 "When I in England did remain
The holy Sabbath I did profane;
In drunkenness I took delight,
Which doth my trembling soul affright.

8 "There's one thing more I'm to rehearse,
Which I shall mention in this verse,
A Squire I slew in Staffordshire
All for the love of a lady fair.

9 "Now 't is his ghost, I am afraid,
That hath to me such terror bred;
Although the king has pardoned me,
He's daily in my company."

10 "O worthy captain, since 't is so,
No mortal of it e'er shall know;
So keep your secret in your breast,
And pray to God to give you rest."

11 They had not sailed a league but three
Till raging grew the roaring sea;
There rose a tempest in the skies
Which filled our hearts with great surprise.

12 Our mainmast sprung by break of day,
Which made our rigging all give way.
This did our seamen sore affright,
The terrors of that fatal night.

13 Up then spoke our foremost man
As he by the fore-yard did stand.
He cried, "The Lord receive my soul!"
So to the bottom he did fall.

14 The sea did work both fore and aft
Till scarce one sail on board was left;
Our yards were split and our rigging tore.
The like was never seen before.

15 The boastwain then he did declare
The captain was a murderer,
Which did enrage the whole ship's crew.
Our captain overboard they threw.

16 Our treacherous captain being gone,
Immediately there was a calm;
The winds did calm and the raging sea
As we went to New Barbary.

17 Now when we came to the Spanish shore
Our goodly ship for to repair,
The people all were amazed to see
Our dismal case and misery.

18 But when our ship was in repair
To fair England our course did steer;
And when we came to London town
Our dismal case was then made known.

19 Now many wives their husbands lost,
Which they lamented to their cost,
And caused them to weep bitterly
These tidings from New Barbary.

20 A hundred and fifty brisk young men
Did to our goodly ship belong;
Of all our whole ship's company
Our number was but seventy-three.

21 Now seamen all, where'er you be,
I pray a warning take by me:
As you love your life, still have a care
You never sail with a murderer.

22 'T is never more I do intend
For to cross over the raging main;
But I'll live in peace in my own country,
And so I end my tragedy.

91

THE NEW YORK TRADER

"The New York Trader" is one of the group of English ballads in which a criminal on board a ship is detected and punished through supernatural agencies (see note on "Captain Glen," No. 90).

For English texts see Williams, pp. 265–266 ("The Guilty Sea Captain"); Ashton, *Modern Street Ballads*, pp. 268–270; *Journal of the Folk-Song Society*, VII, 2–5 (where it is confused with "Captain Glen"). See also broadsides: Spencer, Bradford (I, 118); George Walker, Durham, No. 110 (II, 31); Catnach (VII, 87); Such, No. 446 (XIII, 140); Catnach (with "Little Jessey" and "Happy Land"); T. Batchelar (with "The Bold Privateer"); Catnach (with "The Bold Privateer").

For American copies see *The Forget Me Not Songster* (New York, Nafis and Cornish), pp. 100–101; *The American Sailor's Songster* (New York, Cozans), pp. 123–124; *The Washington Songster* (New York, Turner and Fisher), pp. 123–124.

From the singing and recitation of Peter Hines, Tatamagouche, Colchester County (printed, *Quest*, pp. 155–157).

1   To a New York trader I did belong.
    She was well built, both stout and strong,
    Well rigged, well manned, well fit for sea,
    Bound for New York in America.

2   Our cruel captain, you do understand,
    Meant to starve us before we made the land;
    At length our hunger grew very great,
    We had but little on board to eat.

3   Being in necessity
    All by our captain's cruelty,
    Our captain in his cabin lay,
    He dreamt a dream, those words did say:

4   "Prepare yourselves and ship's company,
    For to-morrow night you must lie with me."
    Our captain awoke in a terrible fright,
    It being the first watch of that night.

5   Loud for the bos'n he did call,
    And to him related his secret all.
    "Captain," said he, "if this be so,
    O let none of your ship's crew know,
    But keep your secrets in your breast,
    And pray to God to give you rest."

6 "There is one thing more I have to tell:
When I in Waterford town did dwell,
I killed my master, a merchant there,
All for the sake of his lady fair.

7 "I killed my wife and children three
All through that cursed jealousy,
And on my servant laid the blame,
And hangéd he was for the same."

8 Early next morning a storm did rise,
Which caused the seamen much surprise;
The sea broke over us fore and aft
Till scarce a man on the deck was left.

9 Then the bos'n he did declare
Our captain was a murderer.
That so enraged all the ship's crew
They overboard the captain threw.

10 When this was done a calm was there,
Our good light ship homeward did steer;
The wind abated and calmed the sea,
And we sailed safe to America.

11 And when we came to anchor there
Our good light ship for to repair,
The people wondered much to see
What poor distressed shipwreck were we.

92

THE SAILOR'S TRAGEDY

THIS must be the song that intrigued the youthful imagination of George Crabbe when he was a schoolboy in Aldborough. He encountered it there, however, not in the singing of the villagers, but in a sheet of poems and songs attached to a number of *Martin's Philosophical Magazine*, and years afterwards he was in the habit of repeating the couplet which had particularly impressed him,

> The boat went down in flames of fire,
> Which made the people all admire.

(See *The Life and Poetical Works of the Reverend George Crabbe*, edited by his son, London, 1847, p. 5.) If this is actually a couplet from "The Sailor's Tragedy," as it seems to be, the song was current in England at least very soon after the middle of the eighteenth century. Greig prints a version entitled "The Ghost So Grim" (CXXX), which begins, "I am a sailor at home aright." On March 25, 1805, Laurie and Whittle (London) published an engraved and illustrated broadside containing a full text of the English song: "The Sailor and the Ghost: A whimsical Ballad. — As sung by Mr. Moody, Mr. Suett, and Mr. R. Palmer." Thus it appears that the ballad was a favourite on the English stage in the latter part of the eighteenth century. For the same text see *The Universal Songster; or Museum of Mirth* (London, 1834), II, 273 ("The Sailor and the Ghost of his Deserted Deary"). Cf. *Journal of the Folk-Song Society*, VII, 46-47.

At some time in its career — not later than the early nineteenth century — the ballad appeared in a longer form, and in a different style, with the title "Handsome Harry." As this version is to be found only in American broadsides and songsters, it is to be presumed that it originated in the United States. It is more "literary" than the original song, and decidedly less vivid. Quite possibly it was a version specially prepared for the broadside press in Boston. See Ford, *Massachusetts Broadsides*, Nos. 3146-3150, and *The Isaiah Thomas Collection*, Nos. 107-108; Kittredge, *Journal*, XXVI, 177-180.

No local title. From the singing and recitation of Mrs. Ellen Bigney, Pictou, Pictou County (printed in part, in *Quest*, pp. 157-158).

1 I am a seaman . . .
And on the sea I take great delight.
The female sex I did beguile,
And two of them I had with child.

2 I promised to be true to both,
And bound myself under an oath
To marry them if I had life.
The one of them I made my wife.

3 The other being left alone,
Crying, "O false and deluding man,
To me you have done a wicked thing,
Which public shame will upon me bring!"

4   To the silent woods this young maid she goes
Her public shame for to disclose,
And on a tree herself did hang,
Which broke the tender thread of life.

5   Two men of hunting did her see,
Straightway they went and cut her down,
And from her bones her flesh was beastly tore,
Which made these young men weep full sore.

6   And in her bosom a note was found.
These words were written out in large:
"Bury me not, I do you charge,
But on the ground do let me lie,

7   "That every man who passes by
May warning take not to delude poor womankind."
It was often said she vexed him sore,
That on the sea he was forced to go.

8   One day as he was sailing on the mainmast high,
A little boat he chanced to spy;
And in that boat was a ghost so grim,
Which made him tremble in every limb.

9   It's on the deck this young man goes
His mind to the captain for to disclose:
"O captain, captain, stand on my defense,
For here's a spirit coming hence!"

10   It's on the deck the captain goes
To help this young man to face his foes.
"It is well known I was a maid
When first by you I was betrayed.

11   "You betrayed me once. I have you now.
I am a spirit come for you.
And now I've told you my mournful song,
All you who know where love belongs."

12   With great persuasions unto the boat
The young man he was forced to go.
The boat it sunk in a flame of fire,
Which made the ship's crew all admire.

93

GREEN BEDS

THIS is a song popular both in the fo'c's'le and in the cottage. Many versions in recent oral circulation have been recovered in England and America. For references see *Journal*, XXXV, 373; Cox, p. 390.

There are other songs so similar to this in motive that the resemblance must be regarded as due to influence, not to accident. The most important of these is "The Saucy Sailor" (a title also used occasionally for "Green Beds"), in which the ragged sailor, with his pockets full of gold, comes on shore and visits his sweetheart to make trial of her constancy. There is no mother here, and no boarding-house. The test is applied directly to the sweetheart, who is no more disinterested than is the Liverpool landlady, and who is made in the end to endure the same tortures of enlightenment and of abandonment by the gold-laden tar. For versions of this song see Sharp, *Folk-Songs from Somerset*, IV, 42–43 (No. 92), and *One Hundred English Folksongs*, No. 45; Baring-Gould, *Songs of the West*, No. 21; Ashton, *Real Sailor-Songs*, p. 47 ("The Tarry Sailor"); Barrett, *English Folk-Songs*, p. 55; Baring-Gould and Sharp, *English Folk-Songs for Schools*, pp. 76–77; *Journal of the Folk-Song Society*, IV, 342–345. See also the following broadsides: no imprint (V, 63); Ryle (VII, 113); Bebbington, Manchester, No. 350 (X, 96); Such, No. 260 (XII, 105); Catnach (with "Dame Durden"); Ryle and Co. (with "My Skiff is on the Shore" and "A Lowly Youth"); Such (with "Canada I, O"). A Pitts broadside has the song under the title "The Tarry Sailor": here, after the sweetheart fails to meet the test, Jack departs and goes into business as proprietor of a public house. For a short American version see Cox, p. 389.

In another song which also lacks the mother and the boarding-house, the testing of the sweetheart is only the first stage in the progress of a Murder and Retribution ballad. After the sailor goes away jingling the gold in his pockets, the abandoned sweetheart persuades another man to join her; they follow the sailor, murder and rob him, and later are hanged. See Broadwood, *English Traditional Songs and Carols*, pp. 66–67 ("The Little Lowland Maid"); *Journal of the Folk-Song Society*, I, 188–189 ("The Pretty Sailor, or The Lowland Maid").

The final change is rung in a variation with a happy ending. Here the sailor comes to his sweetheart in ragged apparel and with no hint of the gold in his pockets, but the sweetheart, like Emma, shows herself a pattern of constancy, and she is richly rewarded with gold and marriage. See Hammond, *Folk-Songs from Dorset*, pp. 22–23 ("It's of a Sailor Bold"). Along with this happy variant should be mentioned the sentimental song of "The Shipwrecked Tar," in which Jack, with tattered garments and pockets lined with gold, comes ashore and calls successively upon the false jades Poll, Pegg, Doll, and Kitty, who in succession turn him out of doors. Then he goes to Nancy, whom he had formerly deserted for these faithless wenches. She receives him with

> My arms shall be the haven
> For my poor shipwrecked tar,

and her reward is immediate:

> Heaven and my love reward thee.
> I'm shipwrecked but I'm rich.
> All shall with love regard thee,
> Thy love shall so bewitch.

There are broadsides of this song, issued by Pitts and by Jennings (London) on file in the Harvard College Library.

A

"The Liverpool Landlady." From the singing and recitation of Richard Hines, River John, Pictou County (printed, *Quest*, pp. 190–192).

1 I'll tell you a story, I'll not keep you long,
Concerning a sailor whose name it was John.
He had made a gallant voyage to sea and just returned to shore;
He was ragged and dirty as though he was poor.

2 He went to the house where he used to lodge in;
He called for a glass of the very best gin.
"You're welcome home, dear Johnny, you're welcome home
from sea.
Last night my daughter Polly was dreaming of thee.

3 "She dreamed that you made a successful voyage;
She dreamed that you brought home a lot of foreign toys."
O John he sighed and said, "My voyage it had been crossed;
Upon the wide ocean our ship and cargo lost.

4 "Call down your daughter Polly and set her down by me,
And fetch in some liquor for us to have a spree."
"My daughter Polly is busy, John, nor shall she come to thee,
Nor neither will I trust you for a glass, two, or three."

5 O John he being drowsy he hung down his head;
He asked for a candle to light him to bed.
"My beds are all full, John, and has been all the week;
Therefore some other lodgings you must go and seek."

6 "How much do I owe you?" the sailor then he said,
"Come make out your bill and down it shall be paid."
"Five and forty shillings, John, you owed to me of old."
With that he pulled out his two hands full of gold.

7 The sight of the money made the old woman rave,
To see that the sailor had plenty for to gave.
"While you were in earnest, John, I am only in jest.
Of all my old boarders, John, I like you the best.

8 "I'll call down my daughter Polly and set her on your knee;
I'll bring in plenty liquor for you to have a spree.
The green bed is empty, John, and has been all last week,
Where you and my daughter Polly can take a silent sleep."

9 "Before I'd lie in your house I'd lie into my grave.
You thought I had no money. On me you played the knave.
It's when a man's got money he can rant and roar,
With brown jugs and quart mugs and tumblers in galore."

10 Come all you bold sailors that ploughs the rough main,
That do earn your money in cold winds and rain,
When you do get it pray lay it up in store.
Without that companion you're turned out of door.

B

"Green Beds." From the singing and recitation of Robert Langille, Tatamagouche, Colchester County (printed *Quest*, pp. 193–194).

1 'T was of a young sailor
    Who's lately come ashore.
He's ragged in his apparel
    Like one that is poor.

2 He came unto the boarding house
    That he used to board in.
He came unto the old woman
    To see what she would say to him.

3 "You're welcome home, dear Johnnie,
    You're welcome home from sea.
Last night my daughter Mollie
    Was dreaming of thee.

4 "What news, what news, dear Johnnie?
    What news you brought from sea?"
"Bad news, bad news," says Johnnie,
    "For all is gone from me.

5   "The ship has sprung a leaking,
    And all is gone from me,
And the last of my money
    Is drowned in the sea.

6   "Call down your daughter Mollie,
    Call her down to me,
And we'll drink and drown our sorrow,
    And married we shall be."

7   "My daughter she is busy,
    Nor can she come to you;
Neither will I trust you
    With one bowl or two."

8   When Johnnie heard this
    He hung down his head,
And called for a candle
    To light himself to bed.

9   "The green beds are full, John,
    And have been for a week;
So for some other lodgings
    You must go for to seek."

10   When Johnnie heard this
    He hung down his head,
And called for his reckoning
    Which he had to pay.

11   "You owe me thirty shillings, John,
    With something of the old."
With that he pulled out
    His two hands full of gold.

12   When the old woman saw this
    She began to rue,
Saying, "For the future, Johnnie,
    I'm not quite done of you.

13   "If you had been in earnest, John,
    As I was in a jest.
By my reputation, Johnnie,
    I love you the best.

14 "The green beds are empty, John,
       And have been all the week,
   For you and my daughter
       To take a pleasant sleep."

15 "I won't lie in your green beds.
       I'd rather be in the street,
   For when I was in poverty
       Lodgings was for to seek.

16 "But now that I've got plenty
       I'll walk the streets alone,
   With my brown jug and quart mug
       And tumblers in galore."

C

"Green Beds." From the singing and recitation of Mrs. James Campbell,
River John, Pictou County.

1 A story, a story, a story I'll make known
   About a certain young man, his name it was John,
   About a certain young man who's lately come ashore
   In ragged attire like one that was poor.

2 He went to a tavern where he used to lie in,
   To see what the old folks would say unto him,
   To see what the old folks would say unto him.
   "What news, what news, dear Johnny, have you brought from
       sea?"

3 "Bad news, bad news," said Johnny, "have I brought from sea.
   Bad news, bad news," said Johnny, "have I brought to thee.
   Our ship sprung a leak and all have gone but me;
   And all of my money is lost in the sea.

4 "Come take your daughter Molly and sit her on my knee;
   We'll drink and be merry and merry we will be."
   "My daughter Molly is busy, John, and cannot come to you,
   Or neither will I call her for one glass or two."

5 "How much do I owe you and this I will pay;
   How much do I owe you without a word of delay?"
   "You owe me forty shillings, John, with something of the old."
   With that he pulled out his two hands full of gold.

6 'T was then the old woman began for to rue,
And said, "My dearest Johnny, it's what I've done for you.
If you have been a fooling, John, I have only been in jest,
And by my lamentation I love you the best.

7 "I'll take my daughter Molly and sit her on your knee.
You'll drink and be merry, and married you will be.
Our green beds they've been empty, John, and have been all last
     week,
And you and daughter Molly can have a pleasant sleep."

8 "I would n't lie on your green beds, I'd rather lie on the street,
For when I had no money my lodgings was to seek.
But now I've plenty money I'll make the tavern roar,
With my brown jugs and quart mugs and tumblers galore!"

94

FRANK FIDD

FRANK FIDD is one of that brave group of sailors — including such heroes as
Ben Backstay, Tom Bowling, Ben Cable, Harry Hawser, Tom Topsail, Tom
Starboard, Tom Tackle, and Ben Block — whose characters and exploits have
been celebrated by the Dibdens and their imitators. The application of nautical phrases to the activities and attributes of the hero gives a special character
to these biographical songs of seamen; and the reader, who may be presumed
to be familiar at least with the song of Tom Bowling, will observe that the same
phraseological method that is employed there is used also in narrating "The
Life and Death of Frank Fidd."

"Frank Fidd." From the singing and recitation of Richard Hines, River
John, Pictou County (printed, *Quest*, pp. 80–81).

1   Frank Fidd was as gallant a tar
    As ever took reef in a sail;
    And when her lee gun'l lay under
    He laughed at the noise of the gale.

2   His grog he provide against storm,
    While spitting the juice from his quid.
    Aloft, on the yard, or on deck,
    It was all the same to Frank Fidd.

3   One night off the Cape of Good Hope,
    Head winds, our ship lying to,
    The bight of a rope catched Frank's heels,
    And his head bulged on top of the flue.

4   The doctor he sounded his brain
    While the blood from his scuppers run fast.
    While sounding, Frank cried, "It's in vain,
    For death it has broached me at last.

5   "I'm afraid I'll away while I speak.
    Life's capstan's hove taut on my heart.
    My anchor is now short apeak.
    Don't you think I have acted my part?

6   "I never feared danger nor toil
    Whilst a spark of life's blood was on deck,
    But now the last end of my coil
    Is hove through eternity's block.

7   "So, shipmates, no longer delay
    Since life's but a span at the best,
    And since I can cheer you no longer
    I'll mount o'er the truck of the blest.

8   "Safe moored in Felicity Bay
    I'll ride by the Cape of Delight."
    What more can they say of poor Frank?
    He's gone up aloft in a flight.

95

JOLLY SAILORS BOLD

THE source of this song, and of a great many similar ones, is the famous broadside "Ye Gentlemen of England, or When the Stormy Winds Do Blow," composed by Martin Parker, and first issued about 1635. It is thus described: "The Praise of Saylors here set forth, with the hard Fortunes that do befall them on the seas, when Landmen sleep safe on their beds. To a pleasant new tune — *The Jovial Cobler*. Printed at London for C. Wright" (see Ebsworth, *Roxburghe Ballads*, VI, 431). A later seventeenth-century broadside, altered from this one, is entitled "Neptune's Raging Fury; or The Gallant Seaman's Sufferings. Being a Relation of their Perils and Dangers, and of the extraordinary Hazards they undergo in their noble adventures. Together with their undaunted Valour and rare Constancy in all their Extremities, and the manner of their Rejoycing on Shore, at their return home" (Ebsworth, VI, 432–433). Still another version from the latter part of the seventeenth century is "The Jovial Marriner; or, The Sea-man's Renown" (Ebsworth, VI, 369–370). For later versions, with the same topic and point of view but varying considerably in phraseology, see Ashton, *A Century of Ballads*, pp. 213–217 ("Neptune's Raging Fury, or The Gallant Seaman's Suffering"); *The Newcastle Song Book*, I (*The Musical Miscellany*), pp. 11–12; Ashton, *Real Sailor-Songs*, p. 76; Halliwell, *The Yorkshire Anthology*, pp. 257–259 ("The Jovial Sailors' Crew"); *The Essex House Song Book*, part II, p. 10; *Journal of the Folk-Song Society*, VII, 67–68; *Journal of the Irish Folk-Song Society* ("The Sailor's Farewell," two versions); Baring-Gould, *Songs of the West*, 5th ed., No. 38, pp. 76–77 ("The Sailor's Farewell"; here, as in the preceding reference, we find a fusion of the two motives — the Seaman's Suffering and the Sailor's Farewell to his Sweetheart). The song has been printed in America in *The American Singers' Own Book* (Philadelphia, M. Kelly, 1841), pp. 163–164, and in *The American Vocalist* (New York, Richard Marsh, 1856), pp. 163–164.

No title. From the singing and recitation of Richard Hines, River John, who suggested that the song might be called "Jolly Tars" (printed, *Quest*, pp. 78–79).

1   Come all you jovial sailors bold,
      The truth to you I write
  Concerning of the raging sea,
      Which is my heart's delight.
  While the landsmen are on shore
      Little danger do they know,
  While we poor jolly sailors bold
      Must plough the ocean through.

2 They're always with their pretty girls
    A telling them fine tales,
Telling them of the hard day's work
    They done in their corn fields.
It's cutting down the grass and weeds,
    It's all that they can do,
While we poor jolly sailors bold
    Must plough the ocean through.

3 Soon as the sun it does go down
    They'll throw away their hoes,
Saying, "We can work no longer,"
    And homewards they will go.
As soon as ever it gets dark
    It's into bed they'll crawl,
While we poor jolly sailors bold
    Must stand the bitter squall.

4 The night it is as dark as pitch,
    And the wind begins to blow,
The captain comes on the deck:
    "Turn out, boys, from below!
All hands, all hands on deck, my boys,
    And pay your ship regard!
And lay aloft, my lively lads!
    Send down the top-gallant yards!"

5 We'll sail into all parts of the world
    That ever yet was known,
And wo'll bring home all prizes
    From where we do return.
We'll spend our money freely,
    And go to sea for more;
We'll make the town to flourish
    When we return on shore.

96

DIXIE BROWN

THIS song, half narrative and half complaint, seems to be derived from "The Greenland Whale Fishery," which may be found in the following English song collections and broadsides: Ashton, *Real Sailor-Songs*, 83, and *Modern Street Ballads*, pp. 265–267; Sharp and Marsan, *Folk-Songs from Somerset*, III, 54–55 (No. 74); Sharp, *Folk-Songs from Somerset* (*Novello's School Songs*), pp. 10–11; Baring-Gould and Sheppard, *A Garland of Country Song*, pp. 56–57; Greig, LXXXV; broadsides by Pitts, Catnach, Fortey, and Such (No. 292).

For an American version see Colcord, pp. 76–77.

For a different song, which (like "Dixie Brown") is more or less of a complaint as to the hardships of the Greenland whale fishery, see *Journal of the Folk-Song Society*, I, 101–102; II, 243.

"Dixie Brown." From the singing and recitation of Harry Sutherland, River John, Pictou County.

1 As I went walking down the street I met big Dixie Brown.
He looked me in the face, sure, and he eyed me with a frown,
Saying, "The last time you were paid off, with me ran up a score.
Now take my advance, give you a chance, and go to sea once more."

Chorus

Once more, once more,
Once more, brave boys, once more.
I'll take your advance, give me a chance,
And go to sea once more.

2 He shipped me on board a whaler bound for the Arctic seas,
Where the cold winds blow through frost and snow; Jamaica rum would freeze!
But worst of all I had no clothes nor money to buy them on shore;
It's then I wished that I was dead or safe again on shore.

Chorus

Once more, once more,
Once more, brave boys, once more,
It's then I wished that I was dead
Or safe again on shore.

3 Some days while catching devil-fish, the wind would die away,
    With a twenty-five-foot oar stuck in your hand you could pull
      the livelong day;
    And when the shades of night would come on, you would rest on
      your weary way.
    It's then I wished that I was dead or safe again on shore.

Chorus

    Once more, once more,
    Once more, brave boys, once more,
    It's then I wished that I was dead
    Or safe again on shore.

4 Come all you brisk young sailor lads, a warning take by me,
    And when you're off your voyage was long, don't ever get on a
      spree;
    Drink no strong wine, smoke no cigars, save up your money in
      store;
    Get married instead, have all night in, and go to sea no more.

Chorus

    Once more, once more,
    Once more, brave boys, once more,
    Get married instead, have all night in,
    And go to sea no more.

97

SPANISH LADIES

THIS was once a favourite sea song or "forebitter." In some collections it is given as a shanty, with the second stanza repeated as a chorus, but its common use was as a song for nautical entertainment and not as an accompaniment for labour. Its first appearance in print, probably, was in Captain Marryat's *Poor Jack* (chapter XVII), 1840, where it is introduced with the remark, "As this song was very popular at that time [*i.e.*, about 1798] among the seamen, and is now almost forgotten, I shall by inserting it here for a short time rescue it from oblivion." Here, as in the greater number of the collections which I shall cite, it is given, not as a shanty, but as a forecastle song.

For British versions see: Chappell, *Popular Music of the Olden Time*, II, 736–737; J. H. Dixon, *Ancient Poems, Ballads, and Songs of the Peasantry of England* (Percy Society), pp. 235–236; Beckett, *Shanties and Forebitters*, pp. 16–17; Bullen and Arnold, *Songs of Sea Labour*, pp. 32–33; Whall, *Sea Songs and Shanties*, pp. 18–19; L. A. Smith, *The Music of the Waters*, p. 45; Davis and Tozer, *Sailors' Songs or "Chanties*," pp. 94–95; Sharp, *Folk-Songs from Somerset*, V, 62–64, also, *English Folk-Songs*, II, 97–99, and *One Hundred English Folk-Songs*, pp. 205–207; *The Essex House Song Book*, part II, p. 4; *Journal of the Folk-Song Society*, II, 179; Masefield, *A Sailor's Garland*, pp. 180–181; broadsides: Walker, Durham, No. 331; Such, No. 347; Harkness, Preston, No. 387; Such, No. 347; Pitts; Charles Pigott, London. See also *Notes and Queries*, 3d Series, XII, 461; 4th Series, I, 19.

For American versions see S. H. King, *King's Book of Chanties*, p. 24; Frank Shay, *Iron Men and Wooden Ships*, pp. 10–16; Captain John Robinson, "Songs of the Chanty-Man," *The Bellman*, August 4, 1917.

"Spanish Ladies." From the singing and recitation of Nelson Langille, River John, Pictou County.

1 Fare ye well and adieu to the old Spanish ladies!
    Fare ye well and adieu to the ladies of Spain!
For we have received orders to sail for old England,
    And I hope in a short time to see you again.

2 We'll rant and we'll rove like true British heroes,
    We'll rant and we'll rove all on the salt sea,
Until we strike soundings in the Channel of old England.
    From Orean to Scilly is thirty-five leagues.

3 We hove our ship to all for to get soundings.
    We hove our ship to and soundings we got.
In ninety-five fathoms the white sandy bottom,
    We squared our main yards and up channel steered we.

4   The first land we made was called the Dead Man,
    Ram's Head off Plymouth, and the Isle of Wight;
We sailed past Beachy, past Fairlie and Dungunness
    Until we arrived at the South Folding Light.

5   Then the signal was given for this grand ship to anchor.
    Then the signal was given for this grand ship to moor.
Stand by your ringstoppers, let go your shank pointers,
    Have up your clew garnets, stick out tacks and sheets.

6   Let every man drink up a full bumper;
    Let every man toss off a full bowl.
We'll drink and be merry and drown melancholy.
    Here's a health to all pretty girls that love sailors bold.

98

WE'RE ALL AWAY TO SEA

THE usual title of this capstan shanty is "We're All Bound to Go," and it is taken from the usual end-refrain, "Heave away, my Johnny boys, we're all bound to go." How it was transmuted to "We're All Away to Sea" in Dick Hines's version I cannot say. If the shanty could be referred to Dick, an authoritative explanation could be secured; but it is, alas! too late for that. At any rate the song, as I present it, is complete: that is, the full story is told, with only such variations in phraseology as we should expect in any version, for instance, of a popular ballad. And this is the remarkable thing about this particular shanty, that it has a story to tell just as the popular ballad has. The commonest type of shanty has only one even relatively constant factor, *i.e.*, the refrain, and any shantyman may supply fresh lines as his inspiration serves him. In this case alone do we find a fairly consistent, extended, and constant story. And one natural result of this difference is that "We're All Away to Sea" has reappeared on the soil, having suffered a land-change, in the form of a ballad without a refrain. O'Conor, p. 56, so publishes it, under the title "Yellow Meal," and it appears in the same form in *Delaney's Irish Song Book No. 2*, p. 18.

In spite of its ballad-like quality, however, this song was a shanty and not a ballad, and it was apparently impossible for any shanty to keep a secure hold for very long on anything except its refrains. Some of the collections present "We're All Away to Sea" with new lines which have nothing to do with Mr. Tapscott and the Irish girl of the original song.

The "yellow mail" and the "bags of mail" which figure in the song are probably to be regarded as meal — of so old-fashioned a sort that it should be referred to in an old-fashioned pronunciation. Terry (*The Shanty Book*, i, 28) writes it "male" on this supposition. I have written it "mail" since this indicates the regular pronunciation and since it is certain that many sailors, including the one who sang the shanty for me, regarded it as mail and not as meal. As for Mr. Tapscott, his famous packets sailed from Liverpool in 1850 and thereabouts, and the shanty came into existence during the same range of time.

For British versions see Whall, *Sea Songs and Shanties*, p. 56; R. R. Terry, *The Shanty Book*, part I, No. 13, pp. 28–29; L. A. Smith, *The Music of the Waters*, pp. 54–56; Sharp, *Folk-Songs from Somerset*, v, No. 123, pp. 58–61, and *English Folk-Chanteys*, No. 26, p. 30; *Journal of the Folk-Song Society*, v, 308–309; Davis and Tozer, *Sailors' Songs or "Chanties,"* No. 3, pp. 8–9.

For American versions see S. H. King, *King's Book of Chanties*, p. 19; Colcord, *Roll and Go*, pp. 40–41; Shay, *Iron Men and Wooden Ships*, pp. 102–107; Captain John Robinson, "Songs of the Chantyman," *The Bellman*, July 14, 1917.

"We're All Away to Sea." From the singing of Richard Hines, River John, Pictou County (printed, *Quest*, pp. 76–78).

1　One evening as I rambled down by the Clarence dock,
　　Heave away, my Johnnies, heave away!
I overheard an Irish girl conversing with Tapscott.
　　And away, my Johnny boys, we're all away to sea!

2　She says, "Now, Mister Tapscott, come tell me, if you please,
　　Heave away, my Johnnies, heave away!
And have you got a ship of fame to carry me over the seas?"
　　And away, my Johnny boys, we're all away to sea!

3　"O yes, I've got a ship of fame, a ship that does well sail;
　　Heave away, my Johnnies, heave away!
She's lying in the Waterloo dock and taking in the mail.
　　And away, my Johnny boys, we're all away to sea!

4　"We got all things now ready, tomorrow she will sail.
　　Heave away, my Johnnies, heave away!
We've got five hundred passengers and two hundred bags of
　　mail."
　　And away, my Johnny boys, we're all away to sea!

5　For fourteen days we sailed the seas, the wind it proved right
　　true,
　　Heave away, my Johnnies, heave away!
With twenty-seven sailor boys our passengers well knew.
　　And away, my Johnny boys, we're all away to sea!

6　The captain being an Irishman, as you can understand,
　　Heave away, my Johnnies, heave away!
He launched out his little boat on the Banks of Newfoundland.
　　And away, my Johnny boys, we're all away to sea!

7　O then the wind began to blow, it blew from the nor'west.
　　Heave away, my Johnnies, heave away!
And then the seas began to swell, and we could get no rest.
　　And away, my Johnny boys, we're all away to sea!

8　Bad luck to the *Joseph Walker!* she rolled us head and tail.
　　Heave away, my Johnnies, heave away!
And the sailors they broke open the chests and stole our yellow
　　mail.
　　And away, my Johnny boys, we're all away to sea!

9   Well, then we arrived in New York town, the place I thought
        so sweet.
        Heave away, my Johnnies, heave away!
    The very first place I found myself was down on Water Street.
    And away, my Johnny boys, we're all away to sea!

10 Now I'm in Jack Montgomery's, I'll cock my yellow tail.
        Heave away, my Johnnies, heave away!
    So farewell, Mister Tapscott, likewise your yellow mail!
    And away, my Johnny boys, we're all away to sea!

99

SANTY ANNA

THIS was a favourite windlass and capstan shanty in the days when sailors worked to the accompaniment of their music. The hero is the famous Mexican general and politician Santa Anna, who lost a leg during his unsuccessful defense of Vera Cruz against the French in 1838, and who, as the shanty picturesquely records, had replaced this member by a wooden substitute before the time of his second unsuccessful defense of the same town — this time against the American army under General Winfield Scott — in 1847. The shanty presumably came into existence during the latter year or soon after it. Trevine remarks (*Deep Sea Chanties*, p. 18) that many sailors deserted their ships to join Santa Anna and returned to sea after the war.

Several versions have been collected in Great Britain and published, in some cases with the title "Santa [or Santy] Anna," and in others with the title "The Plains of Mexico." See Bullen and Arnold, *Songs of Sea Labour*, No. 16, p. 15; Whall, *Sea Songs and Shanties*, p. 65; R. R. Terry, *The Shanty Book*, part I, No. 8, pp. 18–19, and *Sailor Shanties*, Second Selection, No. 8, pp. 16–17; Smith, *The Music of the Waters*, p. 47; Trevine, *Deep Sea Chanties*, No. 12, pp. 18–19; Davis and Tozer, *Sailors' Songs or "Chanties,"* p. 34; Sharp, *English Folk-Chanteys*, No. 1, p. 2; *Journal of the Folk-Song Society*, III, 237–239; IV, 33.

For American texts see S. H. King, *King's Book of Chanties*, p. 16; Colcord, pp. 34–35; Shay, *Iron Men and Wooden Ships*, p. 91; Captain John Robinson, *The Bellman*, July 28, 1917.

"Santy Anna." From the singing of Richard Hines, River John, Pictou County.

1 O have you heard the latest news?
    Hooray Mexicano!
  The Yankees they took Vera Cruz.
    All on the plains of Mexico!

2 Brave General Taylor gained the day;
    Hooray Mexicano!
  He drove them off from Monterey.
    All on the plains of Mexico!

3 Old Santy Anna with his wooden leg,
    Hooray Mexicano!
  He used it for a wooden peg.
    All on the plains of Mexico!

4   O then we smashed them up and down;
    Hooray Mexicano!
We captured all the Mexican ground.
    All on the plains of Mexico!

5   Then General Walker he came in;
    Hooray Mexicano!
He slaughtered them from limb to limb.
    All on the plains of Mexico!

100

BLOW, BOYS, BLOW

THE three stanzas which I present are fairly constant parts of this halliard shanty — although even here there are plenty of verbal variations to be found, particularly when it comes to the specification of dishes served at the dinner for the crew. In one or two of the published versions, however, the shantyman considers other aspects of the "Yankee ship" and makes no mention of the dinner.

For English versions see: Whall, *Sea Songs and Shanties*, p. 68; Davis and Tozer, *Sailors' Songs or "Chanties,"* No. 21, pp. 40–41; Terry, *Sailor Shanties*, First Selection, No. 7, pp. 13–15, and *The Shanty Book*, part I, No. 15, pp. 32–33; L. A. Smith, *Music of the Waters*, pp. 38–39; Bradford and Fagge, *Old Sea Chanties*, No. 2, pp. 4–5; Bullen and Arnold, *Songs of Sea Labour*, p. 29; Masefield, *A Sailor's Garland*, pp. 318–319; Finger, *Sailor Chanties and Cowboy Songs*, p. 14.

For texts published in the United States see *King's Book of Chanties*, p. 2; Colcord, pp. 7–8; Shay, *Iron Men and Wooden Ships*, pp. 71–72; Captain John Robinson, *The Bellman*, July 14, 1917; Hutchison, *Journal*, XIX, 24.

"Blow, Boys, Blow!" From the singing of Daniel Heighton, Pictou, Pictou County.

1 A Yankee ship going down the river,
    Blow, boys, blow!
A Yankee ship going down the river.
    Blow, my bully boys, blow!

2 What do you think they had for dinner?
    Blow, boys, blow!
What do you think they had for dinner?
    Blow, my bully boys, blow!

3 Ox-tail soup and turkey's liver,
    Blow, boys, blow!
Ox-tail soup and turkey's liver.
    Blow, my bully boys, blow!

101

REUBEN RANZO

THIS is a halliard shanty. As for the origin of the refrain word "Ranzo," Whall suggests, reasonably, that it is a corruption of "Lorenzo," but perhaps this is to enquire too curiously. Whatever its rationale may be, the refrain has a lusty, provocative sound, and it has done service in the hoisting of many a yard and sail.

For British texts see Bullen and Arnold, *Songs of Sea Labour*, No. 28, p. 25; Whall, *Sea Songs and Shanties*, p. 60; R. R. Terry, *The Shanty Book*, part I, No. 22, pp. 46–47, and *Sailor Shanties*, First Selection, No. 3, pp. 6–7; Smith, *The Music of the Waters*, pp. 19–21, 32–33; Davis and Tozer, *Sailor Songs, or "Chanties,"* pp. 38–39; Sharp, *English Folk-Chanteys*, No. 32, p. 37; *Journal of the Folk-Song Society*, v, 38–40; Masefield, *A Sailor's Garland*, pp. 312–313.

For versions published in the United States see *King's Book of Chanties*, p. 8; Colcord, pp. 24–25; Shay, *Iron Men and Wooden Ships*, pp. 100–101; Finger, *Sailor Chanties and Cowboy Songs*, p. 11; Captain John Robinson, *The Bellman*, July 21, 1917.

Three of the lines in the following text are to be found in practically every published version, and one may conclude that they were always, or nearly always, sung when the shanty was raised on shipboard. They are "Poor old Reuben Ranzo," "Ranzo was no sailor," and "He shipped on board a whaler." Among shanties, then, "Reuben Ranzo" may serve as a model of constancy comparable to Griselda among women.

"Reuben Ranzo." From the singing of George Heighton, Pictou, Pictou County.

1 O poor old Reuben Ranzo,
   Ranzo, boys, Ranzo!
O poor old Reuben Ranzo.
   Ranzo, boys, Ranzo!

2 They say he's got lots of money,
   Ranzo, boys, Ranzo!
They say he's got lots of money.
   Ranzo, boys, Ranzo!

3 Ranzo was no sailor,
   Ranzo, boys, Ranzo!
Ranzo was no sailor.
   Ranzo, boys, Ranzo!

4 He shipped on board a whaler,
   Ranzo, boys, Ranzo!
He shipped on board a whaler.
   Ranzo, boys, Ranzo!

102

THE WILD GOOSE

THIS is to be regarded as a halliard shanty, although it apparently served at times for the men who were heaving at the capstan bars. Terry lists it as a windlass and capstan shanty. It is of all shanties the most conspicuous for variability, and the investigator must be guided chiefly by the swing and metre of the lines and refrains and by the appearance of "Ranzo" in one or both of the refrains. Sometimes the "wild goose" figures in the first line; but while this is to be sought for, it is by no means always to be found. Bullen and Arnold (*Songs of Sea Labour*, p. 18) print a version under a title which is also the first line of the song, "Oh, what did you give for your fine leg of mutton?" Terry (*Sailor Shanties*, First Selection, pp. 4–5, and *The Shanty Book*, part I, pp. 26–27) entitles it "The Wild Goose Shanty," and his version begins, "I'm the shantyman of the wild goose nation." Davis and Tozer (*Sailors' Songs*, pp. 50–51) give it the generic title "The Chanty-Man's Song" and present a version which begins with "I'm Chanty-man of the working party." These strangely differentiated versions are all English, and the song seems to have been in use on British ships much more than on American ones. Two versions, however, have been printed in the United States: one by Captain John Robinson (*The Bellman*, July 14, 1917) with the title "Ranzo Ray" and beginning "We've passed the cliffs of Dover in the good old ship the Rover," and one by Colcord, (p. 93) entitled "Huckleberry Hunting" and starting off with "Oh, the boys and the girls went a-huckleberry hunting."

The brief version which follows I secured from Ephraim Tattrie of Tatamagouche, Colchester County. The air is a particularly fine one, of the type which in the eighteenth century was characterized as "wild and melancholy."

> Did you ever see a wild goose floating on the ocean?
>   Ranzo, ranzo, away, away!
> It's just like the young girls when they take the notion.
>   Ranzo, ranzo, away, away!

103

WE 'RE HOMEWARD BOUND

THE well-known capstan or windlass shanty represented by the following stanzas was pretty regularly called upon, in the old days, to aid in the labour of heaving up the anchor when the vessel was homeward bound. Versions of it may be found in the following British collections: Whall, *Sea Songs and Shanties*, p. 49; Davis and Tozer, *Sailors' Songs or "Chanties,"* No. 9, pp. 18–19; Terry, *Sailor Shanties*, Second Selection, No. 3, pp. 5–7, and *The Shanty Book*, part I, No. 3, pp. 6–7; L. A. Smith, *Music of the Waters*, pp. 56–58; Trevine, *Deep Sea Chanties*, No. 2, pp. 4–5; Bullen and Arnold, *Songs of Sea Labour*, p. 7; R. Dunstan, *Sea Shanties*, p. 8.

For texts published in America see *King's Book of Chanties*, p. 14; Colcord, pp. 54–55; Shay, *Iron Men and Wooden Ships*, pp. 133–134; Captain John Robinson, *The Bellman*, August 4, 1917; *Journal*, XIX, 18; Finger, *Sailor Chanties and Cowboy Songs*, p. 12; R. W. Gordon, the *Adventure* magazine.

"We 're Homeward Bound." Sung by Daniel Heighton, Pictou, Pictou County.

1 We're homeward bound, come let us sing,
 Good bye, fare ye well, good bye, fare ye well!
 We're homeward bound, come let us sing,
 Hooray, my boys, we're homeward bound!

2 We're homeward bound for New York town,
 Good bye, fare ye well, good bye, fare ye well!
 We're homeward bound for New York town.
 Hooray, my boys, we're homeward bound!

104

THE RIO GRANDE

This capstan or windlass shanty was steadily requisitioned in the days of wooden ships. Its refrains — with the exception of the changing phrase "my bonny young gal" or "my bonny brown gal" — were practically constant, but its lines were what any shantyman, at any time, chose to make them. Two of the versions below represent two performances, at different times, of the same singer.

For British versions see Sharp, *English Folk-Chanteys*, No. 21, p. 24; Whall, *Sea Songs and Shanties*, p. 54; Davis and Tozer, *Sailors' Songs or "Chanties,"* No. 2, pp. 6–7; Terry, *The Shanty Book*, part I, No. 2, pp. 4–5, and *Sailor Shanties*, Second Selection, No. 6, pp. 12–13; L. A. Smith, *Music of the Waters*, pp. 10–12, 51–52; Beckett, *Shanties and Forebitters*, pp. 2–3; Bradford and Fagge, *Old Sea Chanties*, No. 6, pp. 12–13; Trevine, *Deep Sea Chanties*, No. 3, pp. 6–7; Bullen and Arnold, *Songs of Sea Labour*, p. 13; Masefield, *A Sailor's Garland*, p. 320; R. Dunstan, *Sea Shanties*, pp. 2–3.

For American versions see *King's Book of Chanties*, p. 17; Colcord, pp. 35–36; Shay, *Iron Men and Wooden Ships*, pp. 1–7; Captain John Robinson, *The Bellman*, July 21, 1917; Finger, *Sailor Chanties and Cowboy Songs*, pp. 12–13.

A

"Rio Grande." From the singing of George Heighton, Pictou, Pictou County.

1 O Johnny came over the other day,
        Way, Rio!
    O Johnny came over the other day.
        For we're bound for the Rio Grande!

    Chorus

    Way, Rio!
    Way, Rio!
    Sing fare you well, my bonny brown gal,
    For we're bound for the Rio Grande!

2 "Now give me your hand, my dear lily-white;
        Way, Rio!
    If you'll accept me I'll make you my wife."
        For we're bound for the Rio Grande!

3 "Now Johnny, I love you and don't want you to go;
        Way, Rio!
    And if you will stay I'll love you so so."
        For we're bound for the Rio Grande!

B

"I'm Bound for the Rio Grande." From the singing of Daniel Heighton, Pictou, Pictou County.

"O where are you going, my pretty fair maid?"
    Hay, Rio!
"I'm going a-milking, sir," she said,
    And I'm bound for the Rio Grande! [1]

Chorus
And a hay, Rio!
    O Rio!
Sing fare you well, my bonny young girl,
For I'm bound for the Rio Grande!

C

"Rio Grande." From the singing of George Heighton, Pictou, Pictou County.

I shipped on a vessel the other day,
    Way, Rio!
I shipped on a vessel the other day.
    And we're bound for the Rio Grande!

Chorus
Way, Rio!
Way, Rio!
Sing fare you well, my bonny brown gal,
For we're bound for the Rio Grande!

[1] See Cox, No. 125.

105

ROLLING RIVER

THIS is a windlass and capstan shanty, and is variously entitled "Shenandoah," "Shanadar," "Shanadoah," "Rolling River," and "The Wide Missouri." Several versions have been published in Great Britain. See Bullen and Arnold, *Songs of Sea Labour*, No. 11, p. 10 ("Rolling River"); Whall, *Sea Songs and Shanties*, p. 12 ("Shenandoah"); Bradford and Fagge, *Old Sea Chanties*, No. 8, pp. 16–17 ("Shanadoah"); L. A. Smith, *The Music of the Waters*, p. 47 ("Hurrah, You Rollin' River"); Beckett, *Shanties and Forebitters*, pp. 6–7 ("The Wide Missouri"); Sharp, *English Folk-Chanteys*, No. 11, p. 13, also No. 53, p. 58 ("Shanadar"); Davis and Tozer, *Sailors' Songs or "Chanties,"* No. 4, p. 10; *Journal of the Folk-Song Society*, II, 247–248 ("Shangadore"); V, 44 ("Shanadar"); R. R. Terry, *The Shanty Book*, No. 9, pp. 20–21 ("Shenandoah").

For American versions see Hutchison, *Journal*, XIX, 27; Colcord, pp. 33–34; Shay, *Iron Men and Wooden Ships*, p. 56; *The Bellman*, July 21, 1917; *King's Book of Chanties*, p. 20.

"Rolling River." From the singing of Ephraim Langille, Tatamagouche, Colchester County.

   1   O if I had a dog I would call him Hunter,
            Hooray, my rolling river!
       O if I had a dog I would call him Hunter.
         I'm bound away on the wild Missouri!

   2   And every roll her topsails shiver,
            Hooray, my rolling river!
       And every roll her topsails shiver.
         I'm bound away on the wild Missouri!

106

WHISKY JOHNNY

THE most constant line in this venerable and widely employed halliard shanty was the one ordinarily used to get the song, and the work, under way, — "Whisky is the life of man." The lines that followed, in any given rendition of the shanty, were statements in praise or in reprobation of whisky; within these rather broad limits they might take any form that the shantyman chose to give them.

For English versions see Sharp, *English Folk-Chanteys*, No. 48, p. 53; Whall, *Sea Songs and Shanties*, p. 97; Davis and Tozer, *Sailors' Songs or "Chanties,"* No. 19, pp. 36–37; Terry, *The Shanty Book*, part I, No. 25, pp. 52–53, and *Sailor Shanties*, Second Selection, No. 7, pp. 14–15; L. A. Smith, *Music of the Waters*, p. 31; Bradford and Fagge, *Old Sea Chanties*, No. 5, pp. 10–11; Trevine, *Deep Sea Chunties*, No. 15, p. 22; Bullen and Arnold, *Songs of Sea Labour*, p. 28; Masefield, *A Sailor's Garland*, pp. 307–308.

For American texts see *King's Book of Chanties*, p. 11; Colcord, pp. 6–7; Shay, *Iron Men and Wooden Ships*, p. 82; Robinson, *The Bellman*, July 28, 1917; Hutchison, *Journal*, XIX, 19.

A

"Whisky Johnny." From the singing of George Heighton, Pictou, Pictou County.

1 O Whisky is the life of man,
      Whisky Johnny!
  O whisky is the life of man.
     And it's whisky for my Johnny!

2 O whisky makes you feel so glad,
      Whisky Johnny!
  O whisky makes you feel so glad.
     And it's whisky for my Johnny!

3 I thought I heard the Old Man say,
      Whisky Johnny!
  I thought I heard the Old Man say,
     And it's whisky for my Johnny!

4 O whisky killed my poor old dad,
      Whisky Johnny!
  O whisky killed my poor old dad.
     And it's whisky for my Johnny!

B

"Whisky Johnny." From the singing of Daniel Heighton, Pictou, Pictou County.

1   It's whisky here and whisky there,
      Whisky Johnny!
    It's whisky here and whisky there.
      Whisky for my Johnny!

2   It's whisky makes me wear old clothes,
      Whisky Johnny!
    It's whisky makes me wear old clothes.
      Whisky for my Johnny!

107

BLOW THE MAN DOWN

THIS famous halliard shanty, the classic of sea songs, has been almost as well known, by name, to landsmen as it has been, in its innumerable singing versions, to the toilers of the sea. The regular operation for which it served as stimulus and accompaniment was the hoisting of the squaresails, when the ship was outward bound. It would be impossible to list the various sea tales which have included versions of the song, but it may be found in the following standard British collections: Whall, *Sea Songs and Shanties*, pp. 66–67; Bradford and Fagge, *Old Sea Chanties*, No. 7, pp. 14–15; Terry, *The Shanty Book*, part I, No. 16, pp. 34–35, and *Sailor Shanties*, Second Selection, No. 1, pp. 2–3; Bullen and Arnold, *Songs of Sea Labour*, No. 32, p. 27; L. A. Smith, *The Music of the Waters*, pp. 18–19, 31–32; Trevine, *Deep Sea Chanties*, No. IV, pp. 8–9; Davis and Tozer, *Sailors' Songs or "Chanties,"* pp. 42–43; *The Essex House Song Book*, part II, p. 6; Masefield, *A Sailor's Garland*, pp. 309–311. Sharp (*English Folk-Chanteys*, No. 39, p. 44) has a version with "Knock a Man Down" substituted for "Roll the Man Down."

For American versions see Luce, *Naval Songs*, p. 155; *King's Book of Chanties*, p. 3; Hutchison, *Journal*, XIX, 25; Colcord, pp. 10–14 (three versions); Shay, *Iron Men and Wooden Ships*, pp. 45, 49–50; Robinson, *The Bellman*, July 28, 1917; Finger, *Sailor Chanties and Cowboy Songs*, p. 10.

Version A, so far as it goes, exhibits the most familiar form of the shanty. Version B seems to be entirely original and is a very interesting example of spontaneous composition.

A

"Blow the Man Down." From the singing of Daniel Heighton, Pictou, Pictou County.

1 Blow the man down, bullies, blow the man down!
    Way, hay, blow the man down!
Blow the man down, bullies, blow the man down!
    O give me some time to blow the man down!

2 As I was a walking down Manchester Street,
    Way, hay, blow the man down!
A nice little damsel I chanced for to meet.
    O give me some time to blow the man down!

B

"Blow the Man Down." From the singing of George Heighton, Pictou, Pictou County.

1 Blow the man up and we'll blow the man down!
    To me way, hay, blow the man down!
Blow the man up and we'll blow the man down!
    So give me some time to blow the man down!

2 The Old Man is worried about us, you know,
    To me way, hay, blow the man down!
He worries a lot, but he need worry no more.
    So give me some time to blow the man down!

3 We got full last night and aboard we all came,
    To me way, hay, blow the man down!
I told him we'd never do that again.
    So give me some time to blow the man down!

4 For the Old Man's a good one, and so we all know.
    To me way, hay, blow the man down!
He says, "We'll have a drink and all go below."
    So give me some time to blow the man down!

5 Now he brought out a bottle and gave us a drink,
    To me way, hay, blow the man down!
It was very kind of him, don't you think?
    So give me some time to blow the man down!

6 Paddy West is my boarding-master, you know,
    To me way, hay, blow the man down!
And I've got a record away back, you know.
    So give me some time to blow the man down!

7 When we get to China we'll all let you know
    To me way, hay, blow the man down!
How the Old Man used us, and so and so.
    So give me some time to blow the man down!

108

SALLY BROWN

THE heroine of this windlass and capstan shanty is much given to sudden and startling changes of personality. Ordinarily she is a mulatto, but sometimes she appears as a maid with "blue eyes and curly hair" (Davis and Tozer, *Sailors' Songs or "Chanties,"* No. 1, p. 5), and sometimes she salutes us demurely in the character of a "nice old lady" (Trevine, *Deep Sea Chanties*, No. 6, p. 12). In the following English versions she pretty steadily maintains what we may, with some stretching of terms, describe as her normal personality — that of a "black mulatto" or a "bright mulatter": Sharp, *English Folk-Chanteys*, No. 10, p. 12, and No. 28, p. 33; Whall, *Sea Songs and Shanties*, p. 40; Terry, *Sailor Shanties*, First Selection, No. 4, pp. 8–9, and *The Shanty Book*, part I, No. 7, pp. 16–17; L. A. Smith, *Music of the Waters*, pp. 48–49; Bradford and Fagge, *Old Sea Chanties*, No. 3, pp. 6–7; Bullen and Arnold, *Songs of Sea Labour*, p. 6; Masefield, *A Sailor's Garland*, pp. 315–316.

For American versions see *King's Book of Chanties*, p. 18; Colcord, p. 32; Shay, *Iron Men and Wooden Ships*, pp. 85–86; Robinson, *The Bellman*, July 21, 1917.

A

"Sally Brown." From the singing of Daniel Heighton, Pictou, Pictou County.

1 Sally Brown had a daughter Nellie,
　　Way, hay, roll and go!
　Sally Brown had a daughter Nellie.
　　Spent my money on Sally Brown!

2 Sally Brown was a black mulatto,
　　Way, hay, roll and go!
　Sally Brown was a black mulatto.
　　Spent my money on Sally Brown!

B

"Sally Brown." From the singing of George Heighton, Pictou, Pictou County.

1 I came to the town to see my lady,
　　Way, hay, roll and go!
　I came to the town to see my lady.
　　Spent my money on Sally Brown!

2   And she was dressed up like a baby,
        Way, hay, roll and go!
    And she was dressed up like a baby.
        Spent my money on Sally Brown!

3   Now, she was the fairest in the city,
        Way, hay, roll and go!
    Now, she was the fairest in the city.
        Spent my money on Sally Brown!

4   She was awful sweet, but not so pretty,
        Way, hay, roll and go!
    She was awful sweet, but not so pretty.
        Spent my money on Sally Brown!

109

LOWLANDS

THIS capstan shanty is to be found in two fairly distinct forms. The one — which is probably to be regarded as the earlier — is serious, and, indeed, sombre in tone. It is pretty certainly English in origin, and it makes no reference to the hard task of screwing cotton for an inadequate wage:

> I dreamed a dream the other night,
> Lowlands, Lowlands, away, my John!
> I dreamed a dream the other night.
> My Lowlands, away!

The other places the scene in Mobile Bay, and comments ruefully, but not too seriously, upon the insufficiency of a dollar and a half a day. It seems to be, as Miss Colcord suggests (*Roll and Go*, p. 45), a development or corruption of the English shanty by the negro shanty-singers of Mobile. Whall remarks (*Sea Songs and Shanties*, p. 57): "It [*i.e.*, "Lowlands"] is of American origin and comes from the cotton ports of the old Southern States," but he is obviously considering only the "dollar and a half a day" form of the shanty.

For British versions see Terry, *The Shanty Book*, part I, pp. 12–15; Whall, *Sea Songs and Shanties*, p. 57; Davis and Tozer, *Sailor's Songs or "Chanties."* No. 10; L. A. Smith, *The Music of the Waters*, p. 15; Sharp, *English Folk-Chanteys*, p. 21; Bullen and Arnold, *Songs of Sea Labour*, p. 12; Masefield, *A Sailor's Garland*, p. 305.

For American versions see Luce, *Naval Songs*, pp. 225–226; Robinson, *The Bellman*, July 14, 1917; Colcord, pp. 44–45 (two versions); Shay, *Iron Men and Wooden Ships*, p. 48.

"A Dollar and a Half a Day." From the singing of George Heighton, Pictou, Pictou County.

1. A dollar and a half is very small pay,
   Lowlands low high, my bonny gal!
   A dollar and a half is very small pay.
   A dollar and a half a day!

2. Now I thought I heard the Old Man say,
   Lowlands low high, my bonny gal!
   I thought I heard the Old Man say,
   A dollar and a half a day!

3. We were jamming cotton down in Mobile Bay,
   Lowlands low high, my bonny gal!
   Jamming cotton down in Mobile Bay
   For a dollar and a half a day!

110

CAPTAIN KIDD

THE time of the composition of this song can be specified with a confidence very unusual in such matters. The trial and execution of Captain William Kidd took place in London in May, 1701. On the ninth day of the month his trial was completed and he was sentenced to be hanged for murder and piracy on the high seas; the sentence was carried out on the twenty-third. Between these two dates, we need hardly doubt, the ballad lustily announced its existence in the streets of London. The original version faithfully follows the chief incidents brought out in the trial of Kidd and his associates. See J. F. Jameson, *Privateering and Piracy in the Colonial Period*, pp. 190–257.

Captain William Kidd, who in spite of his protestations of innocence has become the most famous pirate in American history, was born in Dundee in 1654. In 1689 he settled in New York, and the portion of his career which has passed into history and legend began in 1695, when Robert Livingston of New York arranged in London with Lord Bellomont, who had been designated as governor of Massachusetts, for a privateering expedition under Kidd's command. In April, 1696, Kidd sailed in the *Adventure Galley* from England for New York, and in September he sailed from New York for Madagascar and the East Indies with a commission to suppress piracy. Whether he was responsible for the acts of piracy which later were charged against the *Adventure Galley* herself, or whether, as he alleged, he was forced into such acts by his crew, has never been ascertained. At any rate, in 1689 orders were sent to governors of colonies in America to apprehend him as a pirate whenever he should appear, and in 1699, when he returned to Boston, he was arrested and imprisoned. Under the Massachusetts law he could not be condemned to death for piracy, and he was therefore taken to England, where he was tried at the Old Bailey and sentenced to be hanged "infra fluxum et refluxum maris." The sentence was carried out at Execution Dock, Wapping, on the shore of the Thames, May 23d, 1701.

The original broadside of 1701 is in the Crawford collection (*Catalogue*, 1890, No. 843, p. 301), from which it is reprinted in Firth's *Naval Songs and Ballads*, pp. 134–137; "Captain Kid's Farewel to the Seas, or the Famous Pirate's Lament" (see also Jameson, pp. 253–257). Captain Whall refers to the song as a forecastle ballad well known in former days on the English merchant ships, and quotes a few stanzas (*Sea Songs and Shanties*, p. ix; and Masefield (*A Sailor's Garland*, 1906, p. xvii) quotes a fragment which, he says, "may still be heard at sea." See also *Notes and Queries*, 5th Series, I, 268, 375. Most of the existing texts, however, are to be found in American editions. There are several Massachusetts broadside copies from the first half of the nineteenth century, some of them at least as early as 1814 (see Ford, *Massachusetts Broadsides*, No. 3078, and *The Isaiah Thomas Collection*, Nos. 72, 73; Harvard College Library files; E. E. Hale, *New England History in Ballads*, pp. 40–46; H. St. Clair, *The United States Criminal Calendar* (Boston, 1835), p. 29. Early popularity is attested also by a curious parody ("Capt. Kidd's Successor"), which appeared in New England newspapers in 1797 (*The Rising Sun*, Keene, New Hampshire, June 27; *The Kennebeck Intelligencer*, Augusta, Maine, June 30):

> I purchas'd Georgia land, as I sail'd, as I sail'd,
> I purchas'd Georgia land as I sail'd,
> I purchas'd Georgia land, made up of rocks and sand;
> But I paid in notes of hand — and *I failed*.

In 1830 J. F. Watson published a six-stanza version in his *Annals of Philadelphia*, p. 462, "preserved from the recollections of an ancient person." See also *The Forget Me Not Songster* (New York, Nafis and Cornish), pp. 28–32; the same (Philadelphia and New York, Turner and Fisher, about 1840), pp. 192–196; *The Old Forget Me Not Songster* (Boston, Locke and Dubier), pp. 28–32; *The New American Song Book and Letter Writer* (Louisville, C. Hagan & Co., 1847), pp. 102–107; *Robin Hood and Captain Kidd's Songster* (New York, Philip J. Cozans), pp. 186–190; *Elton's Songs and Melodies for the Multitude* (New York, T. W. Strong), p. 76; *Col. Crockett's Free and Easy Song Book*, pp. 271–272; *Father Kemp's Old Folks Concert Music* (Boston, copyright 1874), p. 80 ("Kidd's Lament," with tune); *Howe's 100 Old Favorite Songs* (Boston, Elias Howe Co.), p. 277; H. K. Johnson, *Our Familiar Songs*, pp. 171–173; Pound, No. 72; Colcord, pp. 69–72; Shay, *Iron Men and Wooden Ships*, pp. 73–74. The song is sometimes entitled "Captain Kidd," but more often "Captain Robert Kidd." By what process of transmutation the William Kidd of history became the Robert Kidd of popular balladry is not clear.

There is a curious "Dialogue between the Ghost of Capt. Kidd, and a Kidnapper" in *Poems on Affairs of State*, III (1704), 381–383.

"Captain Robert Kidd." From the singing and recitation of Alexander Harrison, Maccan, Cumberland County.

1 You captains brave and bold, hear our cries, hear our cries,
   You captains brave and bold, hear our cries.
   You captains brave and bold, though you seem uncontrolled,
   Don't for the sake of gold lose your souls, lose your souls,
   Don't for the sake of gold lose your souls.

2 My name was Robert Kidd when I sailed, when I sailed,
   My name was Robert Kidd when I sailed.
   My name was Robert Kidd, God's laws I did forbid,
   And so wickedly I did when I sailed, when I sailed,
   And so wickedly I did when I sailed.

3 My parents taught me well when I sailed, when I sailed,
   My parents taught me well when I sailed.
   My parents taught me well to shun the gates of hell,
   But against them I rebelled when I sailed, when I sailed,
   But against them I rebelled when I sailed.

4 I cursed my father dear, when I sailed, when I sailed,
I cursed my father dear when I sailed.
I cursed my father dear, and her that did me bear,
And so wickedly did swear when I sailed, when I sailed,
And so wickedly did swear when I sailed.

5 I made a solemn vow when I sailed, when I sailed,
I made a solemn vow when I sailed.
I made a solemn vow to God I would not bow,
Nor myself one prayer allow as I sailed, as I sailed,
Nor myself one prayer allow as I sailed.

6 I'd a Bible in my hand when I sailed, when I sailed,
I'd a Bible in my hand when I sailed.
I'd a Bible in my hand by my father's great command,
And I sunk it in the sand when I sailed, when I sailed,
And I sunk it in the sand when I sailed.

7 I murdered William Moore as I sailed, as I sailed,
I murdered William Moore as I sailed.
I murdered William Moore and left him in his gore,
Not many leagues from shore as I sailed, as I sailed,
Not many leagues from shore as I sailed.

8 And being cruel still as I sailed, as I sailed,
And being cruel still as I sailed,
And being cruel still, my gunner I did kill,
And his precious blood did spill as I sailed, as I sailed,
And his precious blood did spill as I sailed.

9 My mate was sick and died as I sailed, as I sailed,
My mate was sick and died as I sailed.
My mate was sick and died, which me much terrified,
When he called me to his bedside, as I sailed, as I sailed,
When he called me to his bedside, as I sailed.

10 And unto me did say, "See me die, see me die,"
And unto me did say, "See me die,"
And unto me did say, "Take warning now by me,
There comes a reckoning day, you must die, you must die,
There comes a reckoning day, you must die.

11 "You cannot then withstand, when you die, when you die,
You cannot then withstand, when you die,

You cannot then withstand the judgment of God's hand,
But bound in iron bands you must die, you must die,
But bound in iron bands you must die."

12 I was sick and nigh to death, as I sailed, as I sailed,
I was sick and nigh to death as I sailed.
I was sick and nigh to death, and I vowed at every breath
To walk in wisdom's ways as I sailed, as I sailed,
To walk in wisdom's ways as I sailed.

13 I thought I was undone, as I sailed, as I sailed,
I thought I was undone, as I sailed.
I thought I was undone and my wicked glass had run,
But health did soon return as I sailed, as I sailed,
But health did soon return as I sailed.

14 My repentance lasted not, as I sailed, as I sailed,
My repentance lasted not, as I sailed.
My repentance lasted not, my vows I soon forgot,
Damnation's my just lot, as I sailed, as I sailed,
Damnation's my just lot, as I sailed.

15 I steered from sound to sound, as I sailed, as I sailed,
I steered from sound to sound as I sailed.
I steered from sound to sound, and many ships I found,
And most of them I burned, as I sailed, as I sailed,
And most of them I burned as I sailed.

16 I spied three ships from France, as I sailed, as I sailed,
I spied three ships from France as I sailed.
I spied three ships from France, to them I did advance,
And took them all by chance, as I sailed, as I sailed,
And took them all by chance as I sailed.

17 I spied three ships of Spain, as I sailed, as I sailed,
I spied three ships of Spain, as I sailed.
I spied three ships of Spain, I fired on them amain
Till most of them were slain, as I sailed, as I sailed,
Till most of them were slain, as I sailed.

18 I'd ninety bars of gold as I sailed, as I sailed,
I'd ninety bars of gold as I sailed.
I'd ninety bars of gold and dollars manifold,
With riches uncontrolled, as I sailed, as I sailed,
With riches uncontrolled, as I sailed.

19   Then fourteen ships I saw, as I sailed, as I sailed,
Then fourteen ships I saw, as I sailed.
Then fourteen ships I saw and brave men they are.
Ah, they were too much for me as I sailed, as I sailed,
Ah, they were too much for me as I sailed.

20   Thus being o'ertaken at last, I must die, I must die,
Thus being o'ertaken at last, I must die.
Thus being o'ertaken at last, and into prison cast,
And sentence being passed I must die, I must die,
And sentence being passed I must die.

21   Farewell the raging main, I must die, I must die,
Farewell the raging main, I must die.
Farewell the raging main, to Turkey, France, and Spain,
I ne'er shall see you again, I must die, I must die,
I ne'er shall see you again, I must die.

22   To Newgate now I'm cast and must die, and must die,
To Newgate now I'm cast and must die.
To Newgate I am cast with a sad and heavy heart,
To receive my just desert I must die, I must die,
To receive my just desert I must die.

23   To Execution Dock I must go, I must go,
To Execution Dock I must go.
To Execution Dock will many thousands flock,
But I must bear the shock, I must die, I must die,
But I must bear the shock, I must die.

24   Come all you young and old, see me die, see me die,
Come all you young and old, see me die.
Come all you young and old, you're welcome to my gold,
For by it I've lost my soul, I must die, I must die,
For by it I've lost my soul, I must die.

25   Take warning now by me, for I must die, I must die,
Take warning now by me, for I must die.
Take warning now by me and shun bad company
Lest you come to hell with me, for I must die, I must die,
Lest you come to hell with me, for I must die.

III

THE *FLYING CLOUD*

THE remorseful hero of the following ballad designates himself by such a variety of names in the different versions of his exploits that one who is unfamiliar with the eccentricities of the folk-song might be inclined to suspect him of seeking refuge behind a series of aliases. In the Scotch version in Greig (CXVIII), he is William Hollander. In a version in *Journal*, XXXV, 370, his "name is Edward Hallahan." Gray (pp. 116–123) prints two texts from Maine in which he is now Edward Hollohan and then Edward Hallahan. Dean's version from Minnesota (*The Flying Cloud*, pp. 1–2) presents him as Willie Hollander. Two other aliases are Edward Hollander (Colcord, pp. 73–75), and Henry Hollinder (Rickaby, *Ballads and Songs of the Shanty-Boy*, pp. 145–149). But his most complete disguise is reserved for the Nova Scotia version, in which he appears as Robert Anderson.

From the singing and recitation of Harry Sutherland, River John, Pictou County, who learned it in one of the lumber-camps where it was, in times past, a particular favourite (printed, in part, in *Quest*, pp. 151–153).

1 My name it is Robert Anderson, I'll have you understand;
   I belong to the city of Waterford, near Erin's happy land.
   When I was young and in my prime and health did on me smile,
   My parents doted on me, I being their only child.

2 My father bound me to a trade in Waterford's own town;
   He bound me to a cooper there by the name of William Brown.
   I served my master faithfully for eighteen months or more,
   Till I shipped on board the *Ocean Queen* bound for Valparaiso's shore.

3 But when I reached Valparaiso's shore, I fell in with Captain Moore,
   Commander of the *Flying Cloud*, belonging to Trimore.
   Most kindly he invited me on a slaving voyage to go,
   To the burning shores of Africa where the sugar-cane doth grow.

4 The *Flying Cloud* was a Spanish ship, twelve hundred tons or more.
   She could easily sail round anything bound down from Baltimore.
   I've often seen that gallant ship with the wind on her after-beam,
   With royals and to'ga'n's 'ls [1] set, running nineteen off the reel.

[1] topgallantsail.

5 The *Flying Cloud* was as fine a ship as ever swam the sea,
Wherever spread a main topsail before a lively breeze.
The sails were as white as the driven snow, and upon them were
no stains.
She had eighteen brass nine-pounder guns she carried by after
main.

6 In the course of a few weeks after we arrived on the African
shore,
With eighteen hundred of those poor slaves from their native
isle we tore.
We marched them down upon our decks, we stowed them in
below.
'T was fourteen inches to a man was all they had to go.

7 And the very next day we put to sea with our cargo of slaves;
It would have been better for those poor souls had they been
in their graves.
For the plague and fever came on board, swept half of them
away;
We dragged their dead bodies on deck, and threw them in the sea.

8 In the course of a few weeks after we arrived on the Cuban shore.
We sold them to the planters there to be slaves for ever more,
For to hoe in the rice and the cotton fields beneath the burning
sun,
Or to lead a sad and lonely life till their career was run.

9 But soon our money it was all spent, we put to sea again,
And Captain Moore he came on deck, and said to us his men,
"There's gold and silver to be had if you with me remain.
We'll hoist the lofty pirate flag and scour the Spanish Main."

10 To this of course we all agreed, excepting five young men;
And two of them were Boston chaps, and two from Newfoundland.
The other was an Irishman belonging to Trimore.
I wish to God I had joined those men and went with them on
shore.

11 We robbed and plundered manys a ship down on the Spanish
Main,
Caused manys a widow and orphan child in sorrow to remain.
Their crews we made them walk the plank, caused them a
watery grave;
For the saying of our captain was that a dead man tells no tales.

12 Pursued we were by manys a ship, by liners and frigates too,
   And manys a time astern of us their burning shells they threw.
   It's manys a time astern of us their cannons loud did roar,
   But 't was all in vain down on the main to catch the *Flying
   Cloud;*

13 Till a man o' war, a Spanish ship, the *Dungeon*, hove in view.
   She fired a shot across our bows, a signal to heave to.
   To this of course we paid no heed, but flew before the wind;
   When a chain-shot took our mizzen down, 't was then we fell
   behind.

14 We cleared our decks for action soon, as the *Dungeon* hove
   alongside;
   And soon across our quarter-decks there ran a crimson tide.
   We fought till Captain Moore was killed, and seventy of his men,
   When a bombshell set our ship on fire; we were forced to sur-
   render then.

15 It's next to Newgate we were brought, bound down in iron
   chains,
   For murdering and plundering of ships at sea down on the
   Spanish Main.
   'T is drinking and bad company that made a wretch of me.
   Come all young men, think of my downfall, and curse to the
   pirate sea.

16 And it's fare you well, you shady bowers, and the girl that I
   adore;
   Her voice like music soft and sweet shall never charm me more.
   No more I'll kiss her ruby lips, or press her lily-white hand,
   For I must die a scornful death, all in a foreign land.

112

GEORGE JONES

GEORGE JONES was one of the group of men who were hanged in Halifax on the 30th of July, 1844, for mutiny and murder on the barque *Saladin*. I have told the story of the mutiny and its sequel in *The Quest of the Ballad*, pp. 213–222, and the same story is told, in greater detail, by MacMechan, *Old Province Tales*, pp. 209–238.

A very good version of the song (from Dartmouth, Nova Scotia) is printed by R. W. Gordon in the *Adventure* magazine for October 20, 1925.

"George Jones." From the recitation of Alexander Brown, River John, Pictou County.

1   George Jones is my name,
    I am from the County Clare.
I quit my aged parents,
    And left them living there.

2   I'd been inclined for roving,
    At home I would not stay,
And much against my parents' will
    I shipped and went to sea.

3   My last ship was the *Saladin*,
    I shudder at her name.
I joined her in Valparaiso,
    All on the Spanish Main.

4   Our ship being heavy loaded,
    Her ship being homeward bound,
With copper ore and silver
    And ore ten thousand pound.

5   Likewise two cabin passengers
    On board of her did come.
The one was Captain Fielding,
    The other was his son.

6   He did upbraid our captain
    Before we were long at sea;
And one by one he inducéd us
    Into a mutiny.

7   It was on one Sunday morning
      When the bloody deed begun,
  And Fielding brought the Bible
      And swore us every one.

8   His attractive prize before his eyes
      He kept it well in view,
  And like a band of brothers
      We were sworn to be true.

9   On the twenty-fourth of April,
      I am sorry to relate,
  We began this desperate enterprise.
      At first we killed our mate.

10   Next we killed our carpenter,
      And overboard him threw.
  Our captain next we put to death,
      With three more of the crew.

11   The watch, they being in their hammocks
      When the work of death begun,
  The watch he called. As they came up
      He killed them one by one.

12   His poor unhappy victims
      Lying in their beds asleep,
  He called them up and murdered them,
      And threw them in the deep.

13   There was two still remaining
      Below and unprepared;
  The hand of God protected them
      And both their lives were spared.

14   By them we were brought to justice,
      And both of them were free.
  They had no hand in Fielding's tribe
      Or in his piracy.

15   We found with Captain Fielding,
      For which he lost his life,
  A brace of loaded pistols,
      Likewise a carving-knife.

16 We suspected him of treachery,
      Which did enrage the crew.
  He was seized by Carr and Galloway
      And overboard was threw.

17 His son he claimed for mercy
      At being left alone,
  But his entreaties were soon cut off;
      No mercy was there shown.

18 We served him like his father,
      Who met a watery grave.
  We buried son and father
      Beneath the briny wave.

19 Our firearms and weapons,
      We threw them in the sea.
  We said we'd sail for Newfoundland,
      Which all we did agree.

20 We squared away before the wind,
      As we could do no more;
  And on the twenty-eighth of May
      We were shipwrecked on the shore.

21 Three of us were confined
      And sentenced for to die.
  The day of execution
      Is the fourteenth of July.

22 Come all ye pious clergymen
      Whom God has pleased to spare,
  I hope you will remember
      Us in your pious prayers.

23 Make appeal to God
      For our departing souls,
  And remember us
      When we decay and mould.

113

CHARLES AUGUSTUS ANDERSON

CHARLES AUGUSTUS (or Gustav) Anderson was one of the unhappy *Saladin* mutineers who were hanged in Halifax on the 30th of July, 1844. See No. 112, above.

"Charles Augustus Anderson." From the singing and recitation of Mrs. James Campbell, River John, Pictou County (printed, *Quest*, pp. 224–226).

1 Come all ye human countrymen, with pity lend an ear,
   And hear my feeling story — you can't but shed a tear.
   I'm held in close confinement bound down in irons strong,
   Surrounded by stony granite walls and sentenced to be hung.

2 Charles Augustus Anderson is my right and proper name;
   Since I came to custody I ne'er denied the same.
   I came of decent parents although I die in scorn.
   Believe me now I much lament that ever I was born.

3 My father was a shipwright, I might have been the same;
   He taught me good examples, to him I leave no blame.
   Likewise my tender mother for me did suffer sore.
   When she hears the sad announcement I'm sure she'll suffer
      more.

4 O dear and loving mother, if I could see your face
   I'd kiss your lips with tenderness and take your last embrace.
   I'd bathe you in my tears of grief before my final hour;
   I'd then submit myself to God, His holy will and power.

5 Farewell, sisters and brothers that's dear unto me,
   So far beyond the ocean whose face I ne'er can see —
   Those happy days I spent with you upon my native shore.
   Farewell, sweet Utavilla, I ne'er shall see you more.

6 If I could recall those days again, how happy I should be
   To bide at home among my friends in love and unity.
   When I think of former innocence and those I left behind,
   'T is God and Him alone that knows the horrors of my mind.

7 No books of consolation are here that I can read.
   I profess the Church of England. By nation I'm a Swede.
   Those words that are addressed to me I can't well understand,
   So I must die like a heathen all in a foreign land.

8 'T was in the town of Gothbury where I was bred and born;
   Here in the city of Halifax I end my days in scorn.
   O pity my misfortunes and a warning take by me
   To shun all bad company and beware of mutiny.

9 Since I left my tender parents 't is but four years ago.
   This awful fate awaited me, but little did I know.
   I got into bad company which has inducéd me
   To become a murderer and a pirate on the sea.

10 They shipped me on board the *Saladin* as you will understand;
   She was bound for Valparaiso, Mackenzie had command.
   We arrived there in safety without the least delay,
   Till Fielding came on board of her. Curse on that fatal day!

11 'T was Fielding who inducéd us to do that horrid crime;
   We might have prevented it if we had thought in time.
   We shed the blood of innocence, the same I don't deny;
   We stained our hands in human blood, for which we have to die.

12 O Lord, I fear Your vengeance, Your judgment much I dread,
   To appear before Your judgment-seat with hands imbrued in
       blood.
   I fear Your indignation, Your pardon still I crave.
   Dear Lord, have mercy on my soul beyond the gloomy grave!

13 The sheriff and his officers all came to him in gaol;
   He knew the fate awaited him but never seemed to fail.
   They placed the final halter on, to end all shame and strife;
   With his own hand he greased the cord that cut the thread of life.

14 They led him to a lonely spot and to that awful stand.
   He viewed the briny ocean and then the pleasant land.
   The rope of justice slipped the ring, which quickly stopped his
       breath.
   Thus ended his career in the violent pains of death.

114

JACK WILLIAMS

VERSIONS of this English stall ballad may be found in *The Newcastle Song Book*, II (*The Minstrel*), 9–10, and in a Harkness broadside (No. 764). For references to other texts, English and American, see *Journal*, XXXV, 378–379. The song was fairly common in English broadsides, and in the middle years of the nineteenth century it was reproduced in many American songsters. Versions have been found recently in Kentucky, Nebraska, and Ohio.

"Jack Williams." From the singing and recitation of Richard Hines, River John, Pictou County.

1   I am a boatman by my trade,
        Jack Williams is my name;
    And by a false deluding girl
        I was brought to grief and shame.

2   In London town where I did dwell
        The people did me know;
    I fell in love with a handsome girl
        That proved my overthrow.

3   I went a robbing night and day
        To maintain her fair and gay;
    And what I got I valued not,
        I brought to her straightway.

4   At length to Newgate I was sent,
        Bound down in irons strong,
    With a rattling chain around my leg,
        And she longed to see it on.

5   I wrote a letter to my love
        Some comfort for to find;
    Instead of proving friend to me
        She proved to be unkind.

6   "You robbed and stole to keep me gay;
        The truth I don't deny.
    You made your bed, young man," said she,
        "Down on it you must lie."

7   'T was then I stood my trial
     And boldly made my plea;
And then I was transported
     Far away to Botany Bay.

8   If ever I do return again,
     A solemn vow I'll make
To shun all evil company
     For that false woman's sake.

115

THE WEXFORD GIRL

THIS ballad is to be found in several English broadsides of the early nineteenth century, and Belden (*Journal*, XXV, 11) surmises that it is derived from the eighteenth-century broadside ballad of "The Berkshire Tragedy, or, The Wittam Miller." Versions have been found in oral circulation in Virginia, Tennessee, Missouri, Kentucky, and Mississippi. For references to texts, both English and American, and for two additional versions from West Virginia, see Cox, pp. 311–321.

The titles ordinarily used to designate the song are "The Wexford Girl" and "The Cruel Miller." In Nova Scotia it is commonly entitled "The Wexford Girl," but Daniel Brown of River John, the singer who gave me the following version, called it "Waterford Town."

1   It was in the town of Waterford,
  Where I was bred and born.
 It was in the city of Baltimore
  That I owned a flowered farm.

2   I courted manys a Wexford girl
  With dark and rolling eyes.
 I asked her for to marry me,
  And "Yes," was her reply.

3   I went up to her father's house
  About eight o'clock one night;
 I asked her for to take a walk,
  Our wedding day to appoint.

4   We walked along quite easily
  Till I came to level ground.
 I broke a stake out of the fence,
  And I beat this fair maid down.

5   Down on her bended knee she fell;
  In mercy she did cry,
 "O Willie dear, don't murder me,
  For I'm not prepared to die!"

6   He heeded not the words she said,
  But he beat her all the more,
 Till all the ground for yards around
  Was in a bloody gore.

7 I went up to my mother's house
      About twelve o'clock that night;
   My mother she'd been sitting up,
      She took an awful fright.

8 "O son, dear son, what have you done?
      What bled your hands and clothes?"
   The answer that I made to her
      Was, "Bleeding of the nose."

9 I asked her for a candle
      To light my way to bed,
   Likewise a handkerchief to wrap
      Around my aching head.

10 I tied it and I twisted it,
      But no comfort could I find;
   The flames of Hell shone round me,
      And my true love not far behind.

11 It was in about three weeks after,
      This fair maid she was found
   A floating down the river
      That leads to Wexford town.

12 And all that saw her said she was
      A beauteous handsome bride,
   That she was fit for any lord, duke, or king,
      Or any squire's bride.

13 I was taken on suspicion,
      And placed in Wexford gaol,
   Where there was none to pity me,
      Or none to go my bail.

14 Come all ye royal true lovers,
      A warning take by me,
   And never treat your own true love
      To any cruelty.

15 For If you do you'll rue like me
      Until the day you die;
   You'll hang like me, a murderer,
      All on the gallows high.

116

PETER AMBELAY

WHEN I published *The Quest of the Ballad* (1919) I was able to quote, from my recollection of a deceased singer's performance, the first stanza of this song, but at that time I knew of no one in Nova Scotia who could reproduce the full traditional version. The song, as I now present it, was collected in the summer of 1926.

Gray prints three versions from Maine in *Songs and Ballads of the Maine Lumberjacks*, pp. 63–69.

"Peter Ambelay." From the singing and recitation of Paul Brown, River John, Pictou County.

1 My name is Peter Ambelay,
      I give you to understand.
   I belong to Prince Edward Island,
      In that gay and virtuous land.

2 In eighteen hundred and eighty-one,
      When the flowers they were valiant to view,
   I left my native country
      My fortune to pursue.

3 I landed in New Brunswick
      In that lumbering counteree;
   I hired to work in the lumbering woods
      A south of Miramichi.

4 I hired to work in the lumbering woods
      Where they cut the tall spruce down;
   In loading two sleds from the yard
      I proved my deathly wound.

5 There is danger on the ocean,
      Where the waves roll mountain high;
   There is danger in the battle-field,
      Where the angry bullets fly.

6 There is danger in the lumbering woods,
      Where they cut the tall spruce down,
   For I have fell a victim
      In that great monstrous snare.

7 Here's adieu to my father,
     It was him that drove me here;
  I thought it very hard of him,
     His treatment so severe.

8 It is not right to force a boy
     Nor to try to keep him down,
  For it leaves him to ramble
     When he is far too young.

9 Here's adieu to my nearer friend,
     I mean my mother dear;
  She has raised a son who fell in love
     As he left her tender care.

10 How little did my mama think
     When she sang tra la la,
  What countries I might travel through,
     What death I had to die.

11 There's only one thing I've got to say
     Before I pass away,

   .   .   .   .
     .   .   .   .

117

WHEN THE BATTLE IT WAS WON

From the singing and recitation of John Brown, River John, Pictou County.

1 Come all you aged people, I pray you lend an ear,
You'll hear my feeling story, you can't but shed a tear.
'T was of an aged couple that had one only son;
He was shot as a deserter when the battle it was won.

2 He was tall, neat, and handsome, his countenance was fair;
Red and rosy was his cheeks, and dark brown was his hair.
He stood and gazed around the crowd and gave one heavy sigh:
"If it was not for my mother I would not fear to die."

3 The morning I was leaving home my mother said to me,
"It is the breaking of my heart to see you go away.
You know you are my darling, my dear and only son.
May the Lord restore you home again when the battle it is won."

4 About six weeks thereafter, while standing on the field,
A letter was put in my hand, and dark brown was the seal.
I quickly tore it open, and the first lines caught my eye,
"Come home and see your mother once more before she dies."

5 O who could shun those dying words all from a mother dear?
Before the dawning of next day at her bedside stood near.
She threw her arms around my neck, which gave to her much
joy:
"Behold, I see you home again, my own and soldier boy!"

6 I scarce had time to press her lips when a heavy step I heard,
And turning round to learn the cause an officer I spied.
He said, "You cowardly rascal, from the battle-field you've run.
You'll be shot as a deserter when the battle it is won."

7 And turning from her bedside: "Take care, sir, what you say.
My mother she is dying, on her death-bed doth lay.
I don't care if you shoot me, I'll never leave her so
Until she do recover, or to her grave doth go!"

8 He called his men around me and took me right away
Before I had time to defend myself or had a word to say.
They put me in the guard-house where many have gone before,
And it's my dying mother I'll never see no more.

118

THE BATTLE OF FREDERICKSBURG

THIS threnodic and somewhat overwrought composition may have come into existence as early as the second year of the Civil War, when the Union army, under General Burnside, was defeated with heavy slaughter by the Confederates, under General Lee, at Fredericksburg. For a version very like the following one see Dean, *The Flying Cloud*, pp. 14–16 ("The Charge at Fredericksburg"). The song is listed by Shearin and Combs, p. 14 ("The Battle of Gettysburg") and by Pound, p. 39 ("The Last Fierce Charge"). An air is published in *Journal*, XXIII, 70, by Barry, who refers to a text which appeared in "Everybody's Column" in the *Boston Globe*, August 19, 1912. Barry's text is included in his MS. collection (in the Harvard College Library).

No local title. From the singing and recitation of Daniel Brown, River John, Pictou County.

1 It was just before that last great charge,
    Two soldiers drew their rein,
  With a clasp of hand and parting words —
    They might never meet again.
  One had dark blue eyes and curly hair,
    Nineteen but a month ago,
  Red on his cheeks down to his chin,
    He was only a boy, you know.

2 The other was tall, dark, straight, and proud,
    Whose fate in this world was dim.
  He only trusted no more to roam;
    She was all this world to him.
  They rode on manys a road together,
    And marched for manys a mile,
  But never till now did they meet their foe
    With a calm and peaceful smile.

3 They glared in each other's eyes
    With a terrible glassy gloom.
  The tall dark man was the first to speak,
    Saying, "Charlie, our hour is come.
  We will ride up this hill together,
    But you will ride down alone.
  I'll promise a little trouble to take
    For me when I am gone.

4   "There on my breast you'll find a face;
     I'll wear it in this fight.
It is dark blue eyes and curly hair,
    And smile like the morning light.
Like the morning light was her love to me,
    Till the hour of trouble has come.
O what care I for the turn of fate,
    If she'd promise to be my own?

5   "Dear Charlie, write to her when I am gone,
.   .   .   .
And tell her gently where I died,
    And where is my resting place.
Tell her my soul shall weep for her
    In the bordering lands between
Heaven and earth, until we meet.
    It won't be long, I fain!"

6   The tears bedimmed the eyes of this blue-eyed beaut;
    His voice was low with pain:
"I'll do your bidding, comrade of mine,
    If I return again;
But if you ride back and I remain,
    You must do the same for me,
For I have a mother who waits for her boy,
    You must do the same tenderly.

7   "One after another her loved ones is gone,
    She's buried a husband and son;
And I being the last to leave my country,
    She kissed me and sent me on.
She'll weep and wail like a wavering saint,
    Her heart will be filled with woe;
And now my head feels dizzy and faint;
    I'll see her soon I know."

8   Just then the orders came to charge.
    With an instant touch of hand,
Were ordered out upon the road
    In that great devoted band.
Straightway for the crest of the hills
    Were rebels with shots and shells,
With terrible debts on our drearied ranks
    We cherished them as they fell.

9 As we were sorely riding back
       From the fields we could not gain,
   And those that were not doomed to die
       Rode sadly back again.
   But amongst the dead lie on the field,
       Was the boy with the curly hair,
   And the tall dark man that rode by his side
       Lie dead beside him there.

10 There was no one to write to that fair-haired girl
        The words that her lover said,
    And the mother that waits for her boy at home
        Will learn that he is dead.
    No more she'll weep in peace nor woe;
        There's no one to ease her pain,
    Until she crosses the river of death
        And stands by his side again.

119

THE BAD GIRL'S LAMENT

THE relationship between this song and "The Dying Cowboy" is obvious. Both of them are derived from the English broadside song of "The Unfortunate Rake" or "The Unfortunate Lad." See *Journal*, XXIV, 341; *Journal of the Folk-Song Society*, IV, 325; V, 193; Cox, p. 242. A version of "The Bad Girl's Lament," from Antigonish, Nova Scotia, was contributed by Barry to *Journal*, XXV, 277. In the Sharp MS. of *Songs from the Southern Appalachians* (Harvard College Library), p. 807, there is a fragment entitled "St. James's Hospital," in which the bad girl is replaced by "my son":

> I found my son, my only son,
> Wrapped up in white linen as cold as the clay.

"The Bad Girl's Lament." From the singing and recitation of Mrs. Ellen Bigney, Pictou, Pictou County.

1 As I walked out of St. James's Hospital,
   St. James's Hospital one early morn,
I spied my only fairest daughter
   Wrapped up in white linen as cold as the clay.

   Chorus

So beat your drums and play your pipes merrily,
   And play the dead march as you bear me along.
Take me to the churchyard and throw the ground o'er me;
   I'm a young maiden. I know I've done wrong.

2 Once on the street I used to look handsome;
   Once on the street I used to look gay.
'T was first to the ale-house, then down to the dance-hall,
   From the dance-hall to the poor-house, then down to my grave.

3 O come, dear mother, and sit down beside me,
   And sit down beside me and pity my case,
For my head it is aching, my heart it is breaking,
   With sore lamentations I know I've done wrong.

4 O send for the minister to pray o'er my body;
   O send for the doctor to heal up my wounds;
O send for the young man that first came a courting me,
   That I may see him before I am gone.

5 O send for young sailors to carry my coffin;
   O send for young Ganders to sing me a song;
And one of them with a bunch of red roses
   To place on my coffin as you carry me along.

120

THE DYING COWBOY

THIS song is sometimes entitled "The Dying Cowboy" and sometimes "The Cowboy's Lament." It is an American song derived, apparently, in some fashion from the English broadside song "The Unfortunate Rake" or "The Unfortunate Lad" (see Barry, *Journal*, XXIV, 341). For full references see Cox, p. 242.

"The Dying Cowboy." From a manuscript of songs copied down by Mrs. Willard Thompson of River John from the singing of neighbours.

1   One early morning as I rode over,
     As I rode over to Larnos fair home,
   I chanced to spy a dashing young cowboy
     All robed in white linen and ready for the grave.

Chorus

"So beat your drums slowly, and play your pipes lowly,
     And play the dead march as they bear me along.
So take me to the prairies and lay the sod o'er me,
     For I'm a young cowboy and I know I've done wrong.

2   "'T was once in the saddle I used to go riding;
     'T was once in the saddle I used to go gay.
I first took to drinking and then to card-playing;
     I got shot in the bosom and now I must die.

3   "Will some one go tell my dear aged mother,
     And break the news gently to sister dear?
But there is another far dearer than mother
     Would bitterly weep if she knew I was here.

4   "Will some one go bring me a cup of cold water?
     A cup of cold water?" the poor fellow cried.
But when they returned the spirit departed
     And back to the Maker — the cowboy was dead.

121

THE PRISONER'S SONG

THIS plaintive song has been current for many years throughout Canada and the United States, though it has not often found its way into print. Pound, p. 34, reports a version from Nebraska, and R. W. Gordon prints a text in the *Adventure* magazine for January 1, 1927.

"The Prisoner's Song." From the singing and recitation of Miss Greta Brown, River John, Pictou County.

1 It's hard to be locked up in prison,
    Far from your own heart's delight,
  With cold iron bars all around you,
    And a stone for your pillow at night.

Chorus

  Lonely and sad, sad and lonely,
    Sitting in my cell all alone.
  I've been thinking of the days that have gone by me,
    The days when I know I have done wrong.

2 Once I had a father and a mother,
    Living in a cottage by the sea;
  Once I had a sister and a brother,
    I wonder if they ever think of me.

3 Seven long years I have been in prison,
    Seven long years I have got to stay,
  For knocking down a man in the alley,
    And stealing all his greenbacks away.

4 It's hard to be locked up in prison,
    Thinking of the days that are gone by,
  Thinking of the days that are gone by you,
    The days when I know I have to die.

5 I wish I had the wings of an eagle,
    I wish I had the wings of a dove
  I would fly to the feet of my true love,
    And there I would lay down and die.

122

VAN DIEMAN'S LAND

THIS doleful ballad has been sung extensively in England, Scotland, and Ireland, and the names of the *dramatis personae*, their provenience, and the scenes of their earlier activities have been varied so as to domesticate the song practically wherever it happened to be current. Greig (XXXIII) has a version ("The Gallant Poachers") which begins,

> Come all ye gallant poachers
> That ramble free from care,

and introduces the following persons:

> There was poor Tom Brown from Glasgow
> Jack Williams and poor Joe,
> . . . .
> There came a girl from Scotland,
> Susan Stuart was her name.

The English versions usually specify Nottingham, or Nottingham Town, as the scene of the first events in the tale, though they do not all agree in the naming of the characters. A broadside by J. Cadman, Manchester (No. 234) shows a curious attempt to add verisimilitude to the story by the use of initials: "Poor A-B- from Nottingham, C-D-, and poor Joe," and, "There was a girl from Birmingham, S-W- was her name." But most of the English versions introduce "Poor Tom Brown of Nottingham Town, Jack Williams, and poor Joe," who are sent to Warwick gaol, then to Van Dieman's Land, and are befriended by Susan Summers.

For English texts see Williams, pp. 263–264; Broadwood, *English Traditional Songs and Carols*, pp. 2–3; Ashton, *Modern Street Ballads*, pp. 361–363; *Journal of the Folk-Song Society*, I, 142–143. See also broadsides: J. Gilbert, Newcastle, No. 125 (IV, 111); Harkness, Preston, No. 366 (VI, 98); J. Cadman, Manchester (VI, 229); Catnach (VII, 184); Bebbington, Manchester (IX, 165); Such, No. 335 (XIII, 28).

The invocation in my text seems to be the result of a fusion of the opening lines of the usual version of "Van Dieman's Land," *i.e.*, "Come all ye gallant poachers that ramble free from care," with the invocation of the ballad of "Botany Bay," which is, "Come all you men of learning, a warning take by me, or "Come all young men of learning, a warning take by me."

For versions of "Botany Bay" see Ashton, *Modern Street Ballads*, pp. 359–360; Barrett, *English Folk-Songs*, No. 52; Sharp, *One Hundred English Folk-Songs*, pp. 198–199; *Journal of the Folk-Song Society*, V, 85–86; Such broadside, No. 499. The same invocation appears in the stall ballad of "Young Johnston," which tells the story of a young man who was hanged for forgery (broadside, Forth, Pocklington, III, 155).

Dean prints a version of "Van Dieman's Land" from Minnesota in *The Flying Cloud*, p. 95.

"Van Dieman's Land." From the singing and recitation of James Langille, Marshville, Pictou County (printed, *Quest*, pp. 39–40).

1 O come all ye men of learning, and rambling boys beware!
It's when you go a hunting take your dog, your gun, your snare.
Think on lofty hills and mountains that are at your command,
And think on the tedious journey going to Van Dieman's Land.

2 O there was three men from Galloway town, Brown, Martin, and
  Paul Jones.
They were three royal comrades; to their country they were
  known.
One night they were trapanded by the Keeper of the strand,
And for seven long years transported unto Van Dieman's Land.

3 O Brown he had a sweetheart, Jean Summer was her name;
And she was sent to Dublin town for the playing of her game.
Our captain fell in love with her and married her out of hand,
And the best of treatment she gave us going to Van Dieman's
  Land.

4 O the place we had to land upon was on some foreign shore,
The people gathered around us about five hundred score.
They yoked us up like horses and sold us out of hand;
They chained us to a chain, boys, to plough Van Dieman's Land.

5 O the place we had to sleep upon was built of sods and clay,
And rotten straw for to lie upon and dare not a word to say.
The people gathered all round us saying, "Slumber if you can,
And think on the Turks and tigers that's in Van Dieman's Land."

6 O one night as I lay upon my bed I dreamed a pleasant dream;
I dreamed that I was in old Ireland down by a spurling stream,
With a handsome girl upon my side and she at my command,
When I woke quite broken-hearted all in Van Dieman's Land.

123

JACK DONAHUE

It is ordinarily supposed that "Jack Donahue" is an Irish ballad, but the invocation and the narrative details both suggest an Australian rather than an Irish origin. A comparison with "Van Dieman's Land" (No. 122) will bring out some differences which may be rather indistinct but which are undeniably significant. In the latter song all the internal evidence points to English or Irish provenience, and the listener is invited to "think of the tedious journey going to Van Dieman's Land," a far-away country concerning which he learns little in the course of the song except that it is inhabited by "Turks and tigers." In "Jack Donahue," on the other hand, we hear nothing of the hero's parent land except that "in Dublin city of renown his first breath ever he drew." There is no mention of a long voyage to Australia, as there should be if Australia were a distant land. As soon as the invocation and preliminary explanations are over the listener finds himself in Australia with Jack on his way to the Sydney gaol, which happily he does not reach; and, after that, he feels equally at home among the newspapers and constables of Sydney and the wolves and kangaroos of the wild woods.

Once, when I was a schoolboy, I met and devoured a paper-covered novel of Australian adventure named *Captain Stormalong*. One of the characters, an old Australian, was sitting by the camp-fire with his companions one night discoursing of various matters, and during the conversation he spoke of a native bard (by the name, I think, of Skinner) who had in his time made many good songs, including one about the highwayman Jack Donahue. The tale passed in and out of my active consciousness long before I became interested in the song myself, but I am sure of everything about my reference except the name of the bard, and such questions of fact are likely to be pretty reliable in literature of the local and adventurous sort. At any rate my recollection, unconvincing as it may be to others, hardens me in my belief that "Jack Donahue" is not an Irish ballad, and that "its first breath ever it drew" in Australia.

I have found no printed text of the song which can compare, in length or in narrative interest, with the Nova Scotia version. In comparison with it the following texts are incomplete or fragmentary: O'Conor, pp. 22–23; Wehman broadside, No. 751; Pound, *American Ballads and Songs*, pp. 158–159; Lomax, pp. 64–65.

In *Johnny Roach's New Variety Songster* (New York, Frank Starr & Co.), one of the popular song-books of the late sixties, there is a version of this ballad — "as sung by Johnny Roach, with great success" — which is a palpable remaking to suit the music hall and the requirements, in particular, of its Irish patrons. The ballad is shortened, a chorus is added, —

With me hale kom hale come lay me down lay, etc., —

and the "patriotic" note is sounded in the following stanza:

The likes of bold Jack Donahue was not in this country.
For maintaining of the people's laws he fought so manfully.
Sure he had rather roam the wild world through like a wolf or a kangaroo
Than to live in British slavery, says bold Jack Donahue.

The same made-over version is included in *Wehman's Irish Song Book No. 4*, 1893, p. 12.

"Jack Donahue." From the singing and recitation of Richard Hines, River John, Pictou County (printed, *Quest*, pp. 66–68).

1 Come all you gallant bushrangers and outlaws of disdain,
   Who scorn to live in slavery or wear the brands of chains.
   Attention pay to what I say, and value it if you do.
   I will relate the matchless fate of bold Jack Donahue.

2 This bold undaunted highwayman, as you shall understand,
   He was banished for his natural life from Erin's happy land.
   In Dublin city of renown his first breath ever he drew,
   And his deeds of valour entitled him of bold Jack Donahue.

3 He scarcely there had reached his fate on the Australian shore
   When he took to the highway as he had done before.
   There was Mathew Mar and Jack Woods, and Warbly, and
       Wangelo too;
   They were the four associates of bold Jack Donahue.

4 He happened to be taken in the middle of his prime
   And banished for his natural life for that outrageous crime;
   But he left all the constables of Sydney in a stew,
   And before they reached the Sydney gaol they lost Jack Donahue.

5 He scarcely had made his escape till a robbing he went straight-
       way;
   The people were frightened to travel the roads by night and day;
   And every day the newspapers would publish something new
   Concerning of that highwayman they called Jack Donahue.

6 As Donahue and his companions walked out one afternoon
   Little thinking of the brands of death that would afflict them
       soon,
   To their surprise the horse-police well arméd came in view,
   And in quick time they did advance to take bold Donahue.

7 Said Donahue to his companions, "If you'll stand true to me
   This day I'll fight for liberty and that right manfully.
   To be hanged upon a gallows I never intend to do.
   This day I'll fight until I die!" cried bold Jack Donahue.

8 "Oh no," said cowardly Wangelo, "such things can never be.
　Don't you see there's eight or ten of them? It's time for us to
　　flee.
　And if we wait we'll be too late, and the battle we'll surely rue."
　"Then begone from me, you cowardly dogs!" cried bold Jack
　　Donahue.

9 The sergeant said to Donahue, "Discharge your carabine!
　Or do you intend to fight with us or unto us resign?"
　"To surrender to such cowardly dogs I never intend to do.
　This day I'll fight for liberty!" cried bold Jack Donahue.

10 "Now if they had been true to me I would recall their fame,
　But people will look on them with scorn and great disdain.
　I'd rather range the wild woods round like a wolf or kangaroo
　Than I'd work one hour for government!" cried bold Jack
　　Donahue.

11 The sergeant and the corporal they did their men divide,
　Some men fired behind him and others at his side.
　The sergeant and the corporal they both fired at him too,
　Till at length a ball it pierced the heart of bold Jack Donahue.

12 Nine rounds he fired and shot five police before the fatal ball
　That pierced the heart of Donahue and caused him for to fall.
　And as he closed his struggling eyes he bade the world adieu.
　Kind Christians all, pray for the soul of bold Jack Donahue!

124

BRENNAN ON THE MOOR

THIS is an Irish song, though it was as popular in Scotland, seventy-five years ago, as in Ireland, and it has also had considerable currency in England. The hero, William Brennan, acquired some celebrity as a highway robber in the first years of the nineteenth century. He was hanged in County Cork in 1804. See the letter of Frank Kidson, quoted in *Folk-Songs of Somerset*, p. 70.

In my text of the song, stanza 3 is not connected with its immediate context. In the version printed in Ford's *Vagabond Songs* this stanza comes later and explains how Brennan makes his escape from the Mayor of Caskell.

For British versions see Ford, *Vagabond Songs and Ballads of Scotland*, II, 56–61 (two versions, to the second of which my version corresponds fairly closely); Kidson, *Traditional Tunes*, pp. 123–126 (with music); Sharp and Marson, *Folk-Songs from Somerset*, I, 52–53 (with music); Gillington, *Eight Hampshire Folk Songs*, No. 4, pp. 7–9 (with music); Sharp, *Folk-Songs from Somerset*, Set 2, pp. 18–19 (in *Novello's School Songs*). See also broadsides: Bebbington, Manchester, No. 401 (x, 144); Such, No. 68 (xi, 68); W. Fortey, Catnach Press (with "Nancy Till"); Such, No. 68 (with "The Limerick Races").

The ballad is included in the following American song books: *The "Walking Down Broadway" Songster* (New York, Robert M. De Witt, 1869), pp. 28–29; *"The Rovin' Irish Boy" Songster* (De Witt, 1870), pp. 58–59; *Wehman's Irish Song Book No. 1*, 1887, p. 106. It appeared as a De Marsan broadside (List 15, No. 15), and as a Wehman broadside (No. 133). See also *Singer's Journal*, I, 21; *Delaney's Irish Song Book No. 1*, p. 13; O'Conor, p. 59; Sharp MS. of *Songs from the Southern Appalachians*, p. 781 (Harvard College Library).

"Brennan on the Moor." From the singing and recitation of David Rogers, Pictou, Pictou County.

1 It's of a highway robber a story I will tell.
His name was Will Brennan and in Ireland he did dwell.
It was on the Sibburd Mountain he first took his wild career,
And many a wealthy gentleman before him shook with fear.

Chorus

Brennan on the Moor,
Bold and undaunted stood young Brennan on the Moor.

2 It's with a brace of pistols he travelled night and day;
He never robbed a poor man all on the king's highway;
He always took it from the rich like robber in distress,
And always did divide it with the widow in distress.

3 Willie's wife had been to town some provisions for to buy.
It's when she seen her Willie she began to weep and cry.
"Come, hand me that [tenpenny ¹]" — those very words he
　spoke —
And she handed him a blunderbuss from underneath her cloak.

4 Willie met a packman all on the king's highway,
They rode along together until the break of day.
When the packman found that his watch was gone
It's then he encountered Brennan and robbed him back again.

5 When Willie saw the packman as good a man as he,
He took him for his comrade until his dying day;
When Willie's forefinger was shot off by a ball,
And Willie and his comrade was taken after all.

6 Here's a health unto my wife, my little children three;
Likewise unto my mother, who will shed tears for me;
Likewise unto my father; his old gray locks will cry,
Saying, "I wish, young Willie Brennan, in your cradle you had
　died."

¹ Word supplied from Ford's version.

125

DICK TURPIN AND THE LAWYER

THE notorious highwayman Dick Turpin plied his trade on the roads of England chiefly during the middle years of the fourth decade of the eighteenth century. He was hanged on the 10th of April, 1739. Several ballads dealing with his professional exploits and his famous ride to York were current in the eighteenth century. The longest of these begins with the Lawyer episode, as in my version, then proceeds to similar experiences with an Exciseman and a Judge, passes from these to a lament, and closes with an account of the hanging that ended Turpin's career (Logan, *A Pedlar's Pack*, pp. 115–121). Logan collates his own version with a chapbook version of about 1796. Whether the episode of the robbing of the lawyer was originally treated in a separate ballad, or whether it originally served as the opening episode in the longer ballad, is not quite clear, though the latter supposition seems more reasonable for an eighteenth-century composition. We may in that case, and if we please, imagine a process the reverse of that employed in the composition of the "Gest of Robin Hood." But whatever the story of its beginnings may be, the ballad of "Dick Turpin and the Lawyer," in its single state, has had a wide popularity in England. It was sometimes entitled "Turpin Hero" and sometimes "O Rare Turpin."

For other versions of the longer ballad see chapbook entitled *The Dunghill-Cock, or Turpin's Valiant Exploits*, printed by J. & M. Robertson, Glasgow, 1809, No. 28, in the collection by John Bell, Newcastle, Harvard College Library, 25252.19; Cadman broadside (25242.27, fol. 137).

For English versions of "Turpin and the Lawyer" ("O Rare Turpin") see *Journal of the Folk-Song Society*, II, 279–281; Moffat, *The Minstrelsy of England*, p. 160; E. Duncan, *The Minstrelsy of England*, II, 36; Williams, pp. 99–100 (two versions). See also broadsides: T. Birt, London; no imprint (v, 175); C. Croshaw, York (with "The Rainy Night"); J. Cadman, Manchester.

In America the song is reported by Pound, p. 12.

"Dick Turpin and the Lawyer." From the singing and recitation of Richard Hines, River John, Pictou County (printed, *Quest*, pp. 157–158; reprinted, Pound, No. 70).

1　As Turpin was a riding across the moor
　There he saw a lawyer riding on before.
　Turpin, riding up to him, said, "Are you not afraid
　To meet Dick Turpin, that mischievous blade?"

　　Chorus

　Singing Eh ro, Turpin I ro.

2　Says Turpin to the lawyer for to be cute,
　"I hid my money into my boot."
　Says the lawyer to Turpin, "He can't find mine,
　For I hid it in the cape of my coat behind."

3   They rode along together to the foot of the hill,
When Turpin bid the lawyer to stand still,
Saying, "The cape of your coat it must come off,
For my horse is in want of a new saddle-cloth."

4   Turpin robbed the lawyer of all his store;
He told him to go home and he would get more;
"And the very first town you do come in
You can tell them you was robbed by Dick Turpin."

126

MY POOR BLACK BESS

THE central incident in this mournful summary of adventures is Dick Turpin's famous (though apparently apocryphal) ride from London to York. W. Harrison Ainsworth, in the romance *Rookwood*, retails the exploits which made up the Turpin legend, and, in particular, furnishes a highly exciting narrative of the great ride which terminated in the death of Black Bess. See also the *Dictionary of National Biography* for a colder scrutiny of the legend and for references.

For British broadside texts see, for instance, Ryle (VII, 78); Bebbington, Manchester, No. 179 (IX, 173); Such, No. 450 (XIII, 143); Harkness, Preston, No. 505 (with "The Troubadour" and "Woman Rules the Day"); another sheet, very much ornamented, but without imprint; Pitts (sheet entitled "Turpin's Garland"; contains also "Bill Jones" and "The Smuggler King"). See also "The Lover's Harmony," 1840, pp. 387–388.

The song was printed in America as a De Marsan broadside (List 9, No. 82). See also *Singer's Journal*, I, 262; Lomax, pp. 194–196.

"Dick Turpin's Ride." From the singing and recitation of Richard Hines, River John, Pictou County.

1 When Fortune's blind goddess had fled my abode
   My friends proved unfaithful; I took to the road
   To plunder the wealthy and relieve my distress.
   I brought thee to aid me, my poor Black Bess.

2 No vile whip or spur did your sides ever gall,
   For none didst thou need, thou wouldst bound at my call.
   To fair Hounslow Heath thou unwilling came guest,
   The minions of Fortune, my poor Black Bess.

3 When the dark sable midnight its mantle had thrown
   O'er the bright face of nature, so oft we have gone.
   No poor man I plundered nor herd did I press,
   The widow or orphan, my poor Black Bess.

4 How gently thou stood when a carriage I stopped,
   The gold and the jewels the inmates have dropped.
   Thou wert always so kind and never distressed,
   Thou wert always so faithful, my poor Black Bess.

5 When Argus' high justice [1] did me hotly pursue,
   From London to York then like lightning we flew;
   No toll-bar could stop thee, through the river did breast.
   In twelve hours we reached it, my poor Black Bess.

[1] Corruption of "*Argus-eyed justice.*"

6   The bloodhounds are approaching, they never shall behave
The breast that so noble, so faithful and brave.
You must die, my dumb friend, though it does me distress.
There now, I have shot you, my poor Black Bess.

7   And after ages, when I am dead and gone,
This tale will be handed from father to son.
Some will think it a pity, but still will confess
In kindness I shot you, my poor Black Bess.

8   It's now I am taken, despair is my lot.
The laws I have broken, the cock I have shot.
I will die like a man and I'll soon be at rest;
So farewell forever, my poor Black Bess.

127

JACK SHEPPARD

JACK SHEPPARD was born in 1702 in the parish of Stepney, near London. As a lad he was apprenticed to a carpenter, but it was not long before he developed the skill in manipulating locks and the predilection for "Edgeworth Bess" which seem to have been jointly responsible for his early downfall. By 1724 he was a noted criminal in London, and in August of that year he was committed to Newgate and sentenced to death. He escaped from prison, however — not only on this occasion, but also on a second one, a few weeks later, after he had been recaptured and sentenced on additional indictments. Because of his inability to leave his favourite haunts in London or to abandon the profession of burglary, he found himself for a third time within the walls of Newgate in September, and this time he was successfully conveyed to Tyburn and hanged by the neck.

Logan (*A Pedlar's Pack*, pp. 152–154) reproduces a short song of "Jack Shepard" in thieves' cant. It has nothing in common with the song that I present except its subject and its fitness for the music-hall stage.

"Jack Sheppard." From the singing and recitation of Richard Hines, River John, Pictou County.

1 Some years ago, perhaps a hundred,
  Jack Sheppard lived, the bold and free.
 A smarter chap ne'er cracked a crib, sir,
  Nor swung upon old Tyburn tree.

2 Now, William Woods he was Jack's master,
  And a carpenter by trade.
 He made all sorts of wooden boxes,
  And Jack to him was apprentice made.

3 Then Jack he courted his master's daughter,
  But she jilted him, I must confess.
 Then Jack he married two wives after,
  Emma Maggot and Edgeworth Bess.

4 One day Jack, being short of money,
  He took it in his precious head
 All for to rob his late employer
  After they had gone to bed.

5 Now, William Woods slept very soundly,
  But Missus Woods did only doze,
 And when Jack Sheppard made his entry
  Madame Woods kicked off the clothes.

6   She rose and caught Jack by the breeches,
     And Jack he would have gone to prison,
But Mister Blueskin, Jack's accomplice,
     Madame Woods cut through the weasand.

7   Then Jack was taken and put in prison,
     In irons strong he was bound down,
But Jack he swore he'd break his fetters
     If they weighed a thousand pound.

8   His wife went to him in the prison,
     Which circumstance to him did please;
And to escape out of the window
     He tore the tail off her chemise.

9   Now three times he was put in prison,
     For three times he had got away.
He being tired of escaping,
     They hung him up on a summer's day.

128

THE WILD COLONIAL BOY

A VERSION of this song is printed by R. W. Gordon in the *Adventure* magazine for December 20, 1925.
From the singing and recitation of Louis Gratto, River John, Pictou County.

1 Of a wild colonial boy, Jack Davis was his name,
He was born in South Australia, a place called Castlemain.
He was his father's comfort and his mother's only joy,
And dearly did those parents love their wild colonial boy.

2 At the early age of sixteen Jack left his native home,
And through Australia's sunny isle he was inclined to roam.
He robbed the rich to save the poor and their farms he did destroy,
And a terror to Australia was the wild colonial boy.

3 At the early age of eighteen Jack commenced his wild career,
With a heart that dared all danger, 't was new to him to fear.
O he robbed those wealthy squires, and their farms he did destroy;
They bodily gave their gold up to the wild colonial boy.

4 One day upon the prairie as Jack was going along,
All listening to the mocking birds singing their joyful song,
Three mounted police, Kelly, Davis, and Fitz-Ryan,
Rode up. They thought to capture of the wild colonial boy.

5 "Surrender now!" says Kelly. "You see we're three to one.
Surrender in the queen's name! You are our plundering son."
"O it's little time I'll have to fight and then you'll me destroy,
But ne'er will I surrender," cried the wild colonial boy.

6 O he fired a shot at Kelly that brought him to the ground,
And then he turned to Davis where he received his mortal wound.
And then a bullet sharp from the pistol of Fitz-Ryan
Pierced his poor heart, so they captured the wild colonial boy.

129

ZILLAH

The broadside versions of this song have the title "Sylvia's Request and William's Denial." In the versions more recently found in England the heroine has lost her stately former name and has become "Sovie" or "Sovay." This might seem to indicate an intermediate "Sophia" or "Sophie," but I suspect that the later name is a direct modification of the original one. In the "Zillah" of my version A we have, plainly enough, a nineteenth-century domestication of "Sylvia."

For broadside texts see Pitts (with "At Close of Day" and "Behold the Man that is Unlucky"); Jackson and Son, Birmingham (with "Young Edwin in the Lowlands Low"). See also *Journal of the Folk-Song Society*, III, 127–129 ("Sovie, Sovie; or The Female Highwayman"); Sharp and Marson, *Folk-Songs from Somerset*, II, 10–11 ("Sovay, Sovay").

A

"Zillah." From the singing and recitation of Mrs. James Campbell, River John, Pictou County.

1　As Zillah on a certain day
　　She dressed herself in men's array;
　　With sword and pistol by her side,
　　To meet her true love away did ride.

2　She met her true love on the plain;
　　She stepped up to him and bade him to stand.
　　"Stand and deliver, kind sir," said she,
　　"Or this very moment your life I'll have!"

3　He delivered to her his watch and gold,
　　But still she cried, "There's one thing more,
　　There's a diamond ring I saw you wear —
　　Deliver it to me, your life I'll spare."

4　"That diamond ring is a token given.
　　Before I'll give it, my life I'll lose!"
　　She was tender-hearted like a dove.
　　She rode away from her own true love.

5　Next morning in a garden green,
　　Like turtledoves these two lovers were seen.
　　He saw his watch hang down by her clothes,
　　Which made him blush like any rose.

6 "What makes you blush, you silly thing?
　　I fain would had your diamond ring;
　　But since you have so loyal been,
　　Here, take your watch and gold again!"

7　"I think that was a bold attempt of you.
　　If I had had my pistol too,
　　Had I my pistol loaded with powder and ball,
　　I would have fired and ruined all."

B

"The Diamond Ring." From the singing and recitation of David Rogers,
Pictou, Pictou County.

1　It's of a handsome young lady gay,
　　She dressed herself up in men's array;
　　A sword and pistol by her side,
　　　　Rode out to meet him,
　　Rode out to meet her own true love.

2　She saw him out all on the plain,
　　Rode up unto him, bid him to stand.
　　"Stand and deliver, kind sir," said she,
　　　　"Or this very moment,
　　Or this very moment your life I'll have."

3　He delivered to her his watch and gold,
　　But still she said, "There is one thing more,
　　There's a diamond ring that I saw you wear —
　　　　Deliver it to me,
　　Deliver it to me and your life I'll spare."

4　"That diamond ring is a token give.
　　Before I give it my life I'll lose!"
　　She was tender-hearted as a dove.
　　　　She rode away,
　　She rode away from her own true love.

5　Next morning in the garden green,
　　Like turtle-doves those two lovers were seen.
　　He saw his watch laying by her clothes,
　　　　Which made him blush,
　　Which made him blush like e'er a rose.

6 "What makes you blush, you silly thing?
I'm sure you've kept that diamond ring.
But since you have so royal been,
    Here is your watch,
Here is your watch and your gold again."

7 "Was not that a bold attempt of you?
Had I not my pistols too?
If they'd been loaded with powder and ball,
    I would have fired,
I would have fired and ruined all."

130

THE BOX UPON HER HEAD

THERE were many titles for this brave old song of the Dauntless Maid, and some of them will be noted below. The stall version issued as "The Staffordshire Maid" is likely to be a bit more "literary" than the others (see broadside, without imprint, on file in the Harvard College Library).

For British texts see Baring-Gould MS. (Harvard College Library), Article 1; Greig, xxxv ("The Maid and the Robber"); Williams, pp. 280–281 ("It's of a Pretty Fair Maid"); Broadwood and Maitland, *English County Songs*, pp. 60–61 ("The Beautiful Damsel, or The Undaunted Female"); broadside in collection numbered 25242.18, Harvard College Library — R. Evans, Printer, Foregate Street, Chester ("The Undaunted Female"); Percy broadsides (Harvard College Library), III, 44 ("The Staffordshire Maid," "Sold by S. Gamidge, in High-street, Worcester; W. Lloyd, in Mortimer-Cleobury; Mr. Taylor, in Kidderminster; and S. Harward, in Tewkesbury"); "Street Ballads" (Harvard College Library, 25242.27, fol. 63, 299); also Harvard College Library, 25242.17: Ryle (VII, 153); Bebbington, Manchester, No. 201 (IX, 194); Such, No. 23 (XI, 23); Pitts (with "The Lovely Sailor"); Elias Keys, Devonport (with "George Barnwell"); Harkness, Preston, No. 426 (with "The Irish Girl"); Mason, Belper (with "You Shan't Come Again"); W. M'Call, Liverpool (with "The Boys of Kilkenny"); W. S. Fortey, at the Catnach Press (with "Speak of Man as You Find Him"); Catnach; Pitts (with "The Lovely Sailor").

"The Box upon Her Head." From the singing and recitation of David Rogers, Pictou, Pictou County.

1 It's of a rich merchant in London did dwell,

. . . .

And he had a servant for many long years,
And what followed after you quickly shall hear.

2 One night as she lay in her bed she dreamed a dream —
She dreamed that her father was making sad moan.
It's early next morning she so quickly arose,
She demanded her wages, her box, and her clothes.

3 With her box upon her head she marched it along
Until that she met with a noble gentleman.
He says, "My pretty fair maid, if you'll come along with me,
I will show you a nigh way across the country."

4 She walked along with him till they came to a lonesome place,
And when he got there, O he bid her for to stand.
He says, "My pretty fair maid, since you're come along with me,
Now deliver your money and then you may go free."

5 O the tears from her eyes like crystals did run;
She wrung her hands and so bitterly did cry.
He stooped to his bundle to take out a knife,
And while he was a stooping she killed him with his staff.

6 With her box upon her head she marched it along
Until that she met with another gentleman.
He says, "My pretty fair maid, where are you going so late?
Come tell to me what noise was that I heard at yonder gate.

7 "To your master or your mistress you have done some wrong;
To your master or your mistress this box does belong.
To your master or your mistress you have done some ill;
For one moment from trembling you cannot stand still."

8 "To my master nor my mistress I have done no ill,
But I'm afraid in my heart that a young man I've killed."
She turned back with him to show him the place,
And when they got there he lay bleeding on his face.

9 He opened the bundle to see what was in.
There was a knife and a whistle and manys a precious thing,
Likewise a brace of pistols, some powder and some ball,
Likewise a whistle more robbers for to call.

10 He put the whistle to his mouth, he blowed both loud and shrill,
When four strapping robbers came tripping o'er the hill.
He shot one of them and that speedily,
Which well became the woman — she shot the other three.

11 He says, "My handsome fair maid, for the honour you have done,
I'll make you my bride and that very soon."

131

DONALD MUNRO

A BROADSIDE containing this song (together with "Napoleon's Farewell") was printed by James Wright, Edinburgh. Logan (*A Pedlar's Pack*, pp. 413–415) prints a version taken "from a chap-book of songs, circa 1778." The English title is "Munro's Tragedy."

For American versions see R. W. Gordon, *Adventure* magazine, July 30, 1925 (a text from Seattle, Washington, from a singer whose grandfather learned it in Ontario); Barry, *Journal*, XXVI, 183–184 (from a singer in Boston who learned it in Nova Scotia); Rickaby, pp. 185–187 (from Michigan). It seems probable that all versions of the song to be found in the United States came from Scotland by way of Canada.

"Donald Munro." From the singing and recitation of Alexander Murphy, Cape John, Pictou County (printed, *Journal*, XXV, 184–185).

1 Ye sons of North Britain, you that used to range
In search of foreign countries and lands that was strange,
Amongst this great number was Donald Munro.
Away to America he likewise did go.

2 Two sons with his brother he caused them to stay,
On account of their passage he could not well pay.
When seven long winters were ended and gone
They went to their uncle one day alone,

3 To beg his consent to cross o'er the main
In hopes their dear parents to meet with again.
Their uncle replied then and answered them, "No,
Thou hast no money wherewith thou canst go."

4 And when they were landed in that country wild,
Surrounded by rebels on every side,
There being two rebels that lurked in the wood,
They pointed their pistols where the two brothers stood.

5 And lodging a bullet in each brother's breast,
They ran for their prey like two ravenous beasts.
"You cruellest monsters, you blood-thirsty hounds,
How could you have killed us until we hath found,

6 "Found out our dear parents whom we sought with much care!
I'm sure when they'll hear us they'll die in despair,
For they left us in Scotland seven twelvemonths ago.
Perhaps you might know them — their names were Munro."

7   "O curse to my hands, O what have I done?
    O curse to my hands, I have murdered my sons!"
    "Is this you, dear father?   How did you come by?
    And since I have seen you, contented I'll die."

8   "I'll sink into sorrow till life it is o'er
    In hopes for to meet you on a far brighter shore,
    In hopes for to meet you on a far brighter shore,
    Where I'll not be able to kill you no more."

132

KATE AND HER HORNS

EBSWORTH (*Roxburghe Ballads*, VIII, 430–431) prints this song ("Crafty Kate of Colchester") as a broadside issued by John White at Newcastle-upon-Tyne, and states that this is a reprint of an earlier broadside of date 1689–90. He also shows by quotation that it is related to the ballad of "The Politick Maid of Suffolk; or, the Lawyer Outwitted" (Madden Collection, III, 638), in which a maid reclaims her recreant lawyer by disguising herself as the devil.

"Kate and Her Horns" has close affiliations, also, with another ballad, "The Jealous Husband Outwitted," in which a hosier of Leicester has a handsome wife whom he persecutes because of jealousy. She procures as accomplices two chimney-sweeps well stained with professional soot, disguises herself as the devil, and the three lie in wait in the house one night when the husband is to return at a late hour. When he enters he is seized by the devil and his attendant imps, who threaten to carry him off to hell as a punishment for his ill-treatment of his wife. He begs off with abject promises of reform, and they finally leave him. The chimney-sweeps agree to keep the secret, and the wife sheds her devil-disguise and returns to a chastened husband. (For versions of this ballad see Logan, *A Pedlar's Pack*, pp. 384–387; broadside on file in the Harvard College Library, printed by Jennings, London, "The Jealous Husband Well Fitted.")

The Harvard College Library has three early nineteenth-century Boston broadsides of "Kate and Her Horns" (Nathaniel Coverly, Jr., Milk Street); two others without imprint (see Ford, *Massachusetts Broadsides*, Nos. 3199–3201, and cf. *The Isaiah Thomas Collection*, Nos. 131, 132). See also *The Forget Me Not Songster* (New York, Nafis and Cornish), pp. 145–147; *The Old Forget Me Not Songster* (Boston, Locke and Dubier), pp. 145–147; *The Popular Songster* (Philadelphia and New York, Fisher and Brother); *Home Sentimental Songster* (New York, T. W. Strong), pp. 325–326; Sharp MS. of *Songs from the Southern Appalachians*, p. 614 (Harvard College Library). The song is reported by Belden, No. 46; by Shearin and Combs, p. 30; and printed by Combs, *Folk-Songs du Midi des États-Unis*, 1925, pp. 157–158.

"Kate and Her Horns." From the singing and recitation of Peter Hines, Tatamagouche, Colchester County (printed, *Quest*, pp. 146–149).

1 You that in merriment delight
Pray listen now to what I write,
So shall you satisfaction find
Will cure a melancholy mind.

2 A damsel sweet in Colchester,
And there a clothier courted her
For three months' space, both night and day,
But yet the damsel still said nay.

3   She said, "Were I to love inclined
     Perhaps you soon might change your mind
     And court some other damsel fair,
     For men are false, I do declare."

4   He many propositions made,
     And like a royal lover said,
     "There's none but you shall be my wife,
     The joy and comfort of my life."

5   At length the maid gave her consent
     To marry him, and straight they went
     Unto their parents then, and woe,
     Both gave their leave and liking too.

6   But see the curséd fruits of gold,
     He left his royal love behind,
     With grief and love encompassed round,
     Whilst he a greater fortune found.

7   A lawyer's daughter fair and bright,
     Her parents' joy and whole delight,
     He was resolved to make his spouse,
     Denying all his former vows.

8   And when poor Kate she came to hear
     That she must lose her only dear,
     All for the lawyer's daughter's sake,
     Some sport of him Kate thought she'd make.

9   Kate knew when every night he came
     From his new love, Nancy by name,
     Sometimes at ten o'clock or more.
     Kate to a tanner went therefore,

10 And borrowed there an old cowhide
     With crooked horns both large and wide;
     And when she wrapped herself therein
     Her new intrigue she did begin.

11 Kate to a lonesome field did stray.
     At length the clothier came that way,
     And he was sore a scared at her,
     She looked so like old Lucifer.

12 A hairy hide, horns on her head,
    Which near three feet asunder spread;
    With that he saw a long black tail.
    He strove to run, but his feet did fail.

13 And with a grum and doleful note
    She quickly seized him by the throat,
    And said, "You'd leave poor Kate, I fear,
    And hold a lawyer's daughter dear.

14 "Now since you've been so false to her,
    You perjured knave of Colchester,
    You shall, whether you will or no,
    Into my gloomy regions go!"

15 This voice did so affrighten him
    He, kneeling on his trembling limbs,
    Cried, "Master Devil, spare me now,
    And I'll perform my former vow.

16 "I'll make young Kate my lawful bride."
    "See that you do," the devil cried,
    "If Kate against you doth complain,
    Soon shall you hear from me again!"

17 It's home he went, though very late.
    He little thought that it was Kate
    That put him into such a fright;
    Therefore next day by morning light

18 He went to Kate and married her,
    For fear of that old Lucifer.
    Kate's friends and parents thought it strange
    That there was such a sudden change.

19 Kate never let her parents know,
    Nor any other friend or foe,
    Till they a year had married been,
    She told it at her lying-in.

20 It pleased the women to the heart,
    They said she fairly played her part;
    Her husband laughed as well as they,
    It was a joyful merry day.

133

BILL THE WEAVER

This forthright narrative of a triangular situation was current in England and Scotland in the eighteenth century ("Will the Weaver"): see, for example, *A New Garland* (Preston, printed by E. Sergent, *ca.* 1793: Harvard College Library, 25276.43.58, No. 67). It was included in a chapbook printed between 1823 and 1829 by E. Johnstone, Stirling (Harvard College Library, 25276.23). It appeared also on broadsides: Such, No. 483 (with "The Punch Ladle"); W. Armstrong, Banastre St., Liverpool (with "Ground for the Floor"). See also Williams, pp. 106–108.

"Will the Weaver" occurs in Coverly broadsides (Boston, about 1814) and in other American broadsides of about the same time (see Ford, *Massachusetts Broadsides*, Nos. 3405–3406, and *The Isaiah Thomas Collection*, Nos. 289–290). See also Shoemaker, *North Pennsylvania Minstrelsy*, 2d ed., 1923, pp. 130–131); Sharp MS. of *Songs from the Southern Appalachians* (Harvard College), pp. 592, 679. Cf. Rickaby, pp. 205–206.

"Bill the Weaver." From the singing and recitation of John Brown, River John, Pictou County.

1 "Mother, mother, now I'm married,
   Don't you wish I'd longer tarried?
   For the women they do say
   Men and riches wear away."

2 "Son, O son, O don't discover,
   But go home and dearly love her;
   Give the ladies once their due,
   Let me hear no more from you."

3 I went home. I met a neighbour
   All on purpose for to vex me.
   "Neighbour, neighbour, do you know
   Who I saw with your wife just now?

4 "I saw her and Bill the Weaver,
   They were standing close together.
   They were standing on the door,
   They went in and I saw no more."

5 I went home in raging wonder,
   Knocking on the door like thunder.
   "Who is there?" the weaver cried.
   "'T is my husband. You must hide."

6   In the house I quickly entered,
    Through the rooms I quickly ventured,
    Searching all the corners round.
    Nothing of him could be found.

7   Up the chimney hole I gazéd,
    There I saw the wretch amazéd,
    There I saw the wretched soul
    Come to stuff my chimney hole.

8   I cracked on a raging fire,
    All to please my own desire.
    My wife cried out with right good will,
    "Husband dear, a man you'll kill!"

9   I put on a little more fuel.
    My wife cried out, "My own dear jewel,
    Since I am your lawful wife,
    Take down that man and spare his life!"

10 I took him down and so merrily did I shake him,
    And severely did I strike him.
    Every blow these words I spoke,
    "Never come back to stuff my smoke."

11 If you ever see a chimney-sweeper
    Half as black as Bill the Weaver,
    Hands and clothes and face likewise,
    Sent him off with two black eyes.

134

DUNCAN CAMPBELL

THIS song, with the title "Duncan Campbell" or "Erin-Go-Bragh," is an old favourite in Scotland. It is not Irish, as might at first appear, but Scotch. The natives of the Western Highlands and islands of Scotland speak with an accent very similar to that of the people of the north of Ireland, and the song records the vicissitudes of a native of the Shire of Argyle who visited Edinburgh and was there mistaken for an Irishman. This misapprehension, as the references below will indicate, was communicated to the broadside versions, which sometimes presented the hero as "Pat Murphy."

For British versions see Greig, CXXVII ("Erin-Go-Bragh"); Ford, *Vagabond Songs*, I, 47–49; see also the following broadsides (Harvard College Library): Such, No. 148, with "Pat Murphy" as the hero (25242.71); no imprint (25242.17), III, 55, and IV, 174; Bebbington, Manchester, No. 107 (IX, 103); and, in the files, Harkness, Preston, No. 298 (with "The Jolly Ranger"); W. & T. Fordyce, Newcastle and Hull, No. 154 (with "The Jolly Ranger"); Hodges (late Pitts), with "Pat Murphy" as the hero, rather inconsistently averring "It's I'm no Paddy though to Ireland I've been" (with "The Pirate of the Isles").

The song was printed in New York as a De Marsan broadside, List 11, No. 17 ("Daniel Campbell's Trip to England"), and in *Delaney's Irish Song Book No. 3*, p. 9 ("Daniel Campbell").

"Duncan Campbell." From the singing and recitation of John Brown, River John, Pictou County.

1   My name is Duncan Campbell from the town of Argyle.
    I've travelled this country for manys the long mile;
    I've travelled this country, old England and all,
    And the name that I go by is Erin go bragh.

2   One night in old England as I walked down the street,
    A sassy policeman I happened to meet.
    He stared me in the eyes and he give me some jaw,
    Saying, "There's a bold Paddy from Erin go bragh."

3   "I am not a Paddy though in Ireland I've been;
    I am not a Paddy though old Ireland I've seen;
    And although I'm a Paddy that's nothing at all,
    For there's manys the bold hero from Erin go bragh."

4   "I know you're a Paddy from the cut of your hair;
    I know you're a Paddy from the clothes that you wear;
    And you've left your own country for breaking the law.
    You'll see all old stragglers from Erin go bragh."

5 A stick of Irish hazel I held in my fist;
Sure around his stout body I made it to twist,
While the blood from his knuckles I quickly did draw.
"And it gives him inflammation," cries Erin go bragh.

6 They gathered around me like a flock of wild geese,
Saying, "Catch that bold Paddy or he'll kill our police."
And for every friend I had, sir, I'm sure he had twa.
"It's pretty tough fighting," cried Erin go bragh.

7 I run to the river and I jumped in my boat.
Sure I hoisted my sail and away I did float,
Saying, "Good-bye, old England, policemen and all.
May the devil be with you!" said Erin go bragh.

135

MORRISSEY AND THE RUSSIAN

JOHN MORRISSEY (1831–1878), "the Irish boy who fought his way to fame and fortune," is celebrated in American broadsides as the hero of many epic encounters. For references to the various songs recounting his victories and to accounts of his life see Kittredge's note in Rickaby's *Ballads and Songs of the Shanty-Boy*, p. 226.

From the singing and recitation of Harry Sutherland, River John, Pictou County.

1 It's being tried in Fugee[1] in South America
   Where the Russian challenged Morrissey and unto him did say:
   "I hear you are a fighting man and wear the belt, I see.
   What would you think if you'd consent to have a round with me?"

2 Now up speaks bold Morrissey with a heart bold, stout, and true:
   "I am that gallant Irishman that never did subdue,
   For I can fight the Yankee or the South Sea Russian Bear,
   In, on, or off bold Erin's isle, and still the belt I'll wear."

3 Now this enraged the Russian all on a Yankee land,
   For to see that he would be put down all by an Irishman.
   "I think you are too light a man, and that's without mistake;
   I would have you to resign your belt before your life I take."

4 Then these two bullies stripped in the ring most glorious to be
       seen,
   While Morrissey clapped on his belt bound round with shamrocks
       green.
   They sparred a time around the ring up till the eleventh round,
   When Morrissey received a blow which brought him to the ground.

5 For a minute and a half this hero lie before he did arise.
   The news went all around the ring. "He's dead," was all their
       cries.
   While Morrissey arose again on coming from the ground;
   From that until the twenty-eighth the Russian boy came down.

[1] Corruption of *'T was in Tierra del Fuego*.

6 The twenty-eighth decided. The Russian felt his mark,
For Morrissey gave him a blow which touched him on the heart.
He called upon his second to give him a glass of wine,
While Morrissey he turned and said, "The battle is surely mine."

7 Now to hear the shouts of those Irish folks which grieved these
Yankees sore,
For to see that there eighteen-stone pounder — his height was six
feet four.
They drank a health to Erin's isle and made the taverns roar
In honour to bold Morrissey, and still the belt he wore.

136

MORRISSEY AND THE BLACK

From the singing and recitation of Harry Sutherland, River John, Pictou County.

1   Come all you true Irish boys, please listen to me.
     I will sing you the praises of John Morrissey,
     Who has lately been challenged for ten thousand pounds
     For to fight Ned the black of Mulberry town.

2   At six in the morning the fight to behold
     There were thousands assembled with silver and gold.
     'T was fourteen to one was the cry on black Ned,
     That Morrissey the Irishman he would be killed dead.

3   At six in the morning this fight to begin,
     Stripped off to the buff and jumped into the ring.
     "Come lay your belt down," the black he did say,
     "Or your life I will have in the ring on this day."

4   Then Morrissey bold in the ring like a bear,
     Saying, "Here stands the bones of an Irish hero
     Who has never been conquered by black, white, or brown,
     While known to his country and Irish all round!"

5   The first round being over, the second did say,
     "Success to the country that raised you, my boy.
     It's never for bribery your country disown,
     For all we are worth we will bet on your bones."

6   The third, fourth, and fifth round, and up to the tenth,
     When Morrissey received seven blows on the belt;
     From that till the fourteenth severely knocked down;
     He bled at the ears as he lay on the ground.

7   Refreshed by his second, John Hanan so prime,
     And Morrissey into the ring like a lion,
     And as they fought up to the twenty-fourth round,
     And every blow the black came to the ground.

8 The twenty-fifth round being fought in grand style,
Morrissey turned to the Irish and smiled;
Coming down on the black with a mightiful stroke,
He left him for dead with three ribs of him broke.

9 Here's a health to John Morrissey, that hero of fame,
Who has conquered their bruisers from over the main.
He's a true Irish hero and was never put down;
He belongs to Tipperary and Templemore town.

137

DARLING OLD STICK

THIS swashing old Irish song was a favourite one both in Great Britain and in America, if one may judge by the number of times it appeared in song-books and on broadsides in both countries during the middle years of the nineteenth century.

For British texts see *The People's Song-Book* (London, Jordan, Jackson, and Wood, 1847), pp. 257–259; *The Sprig of Shillelah*, compiled by Dinny Blake (David Bryce, Paternoster Row, London, 1852), pp. 120–122; broadsides by H. Pratt, Birmingham; J. Harkness, Preston (No. 421: "Written and sung by Mr. J. Kearney, at the Castle Tavern"); Bebbington, Manchester (No. 229); J. Cadman, Manchester (No. 222); and one, without imprint (25242.71), "written and sung by Mr. J. Kearney, at the Castle Tavern."

For texts published in America see Patrick Donahoe, *The Irish Comic Songster* (about 1850), pp. 42–45; *The Shamrock, or, Songs of Old Ireland* (New York, Dick and Fitzgerald, 1862), pp. 62–64; *The Charley O'Malley Comic Songster* (Dick and Fitzgerald, 1864; included in the *Encyclopedia of Popular Songs* by the same publishers); *The "Wearing of the Green" Songster* (New York, Robert M. De Witt, 1866), pp. 35–36; *Conner's Irish Song Book* (San Francisco, D. E. Appleton & Co., 1868), pp. 17–18; *The "Love Among the Roses" Songster* (De Witt, 1869), p. 12; *Dan Bryant's "Shaun the Post" Songster* (De Witt, 1870), p. 175; *The Irish Comic Songster* (New York, Dick and Fitzgerald), pp. 62–64; Andrews and De Marsan broadside, List 2, No. 8; *Wehman's Irish Song Book No. 3* (New York, 1891), pp. 50–51; *Delaney's Irish Song Book No. 3*, p. 21; O'Conor, p. 51.

"Bull Morgan McCarthy." From the singing and recitation of John Brown, River John, Pictou County.

1　Now me name is Bull Morgan McCarthy from Thrim,
　　Sure I've just one relation, that's me brother Jim,
　　And he's gone soldierin' way out to Carfoul
　　And I'm afraid he's laid low from a lickin' the school.
　　Sure, it's livin' or dead or be livin',
　　A prayer o'er his soul I'll be givin',
　　And to send it right home to heaven,
　　That he's left me his darlin' ould stick.

2　Now if this stick could speak, it would tell ye fine tales,
　　How it battered the countenance of the O'Neils.
　　It's made pieces of skulls fly about in the air,
　　And it was the promoter at Finnegan's fair.
　　For I'll swear by the toe-nails of Moses
　　That it's oft-times broke bridges of noses,
　　And whoever now dare to oppose it,
　　It's meself and me darlin' ould stick.

3   Now the first time I used it 't was on Saint Patrick's day:
    Larry Fagins and I we got onto the spree.
    We went to a ball way up the Tyne,
    And before it was out I kissed Kate Magavine.
    Then her true love went out for his cousin.
    With that, sure, he brought in a dozen.
    O what a nice humbug he got us in
    If it had n't been for the cane end of me stick!

4   Now when war was the word, when the affections came in,
    For to lather us well, we peeled off to our skin,
    And I stood like a hurdle, just for the attack,
    And the first man came in, I laid him on his back.
    And I popped out Pat Glancy,
    Who once humbugged my sister Nancy;
    And Kate, sure, she took quite a fancy
    To meself and me darlin' ould stick.

5   Now I lathered her true love until he was black,
    And she tipped me the wink; we was off to a crack
    Way up to a house at the tother end of the town,
    Where we cheered up our spirits by lettin' some down.
    It's when I got her snug in a corner,
    It's then the whisky commenced for to warm her,
    And she swore her true love was an informer,
    It's then I said first to me stick.

6   Now before the judge, when she swore to the fact,
    Yes, before we left we were decently whacked;
    But the judge he havin' more feelin's than sense,
    He said all Kate swore was in my own offense.
    But there was one swore ag'in me named Terry.
    That night he lay in Tipperary,
    And he swore that a coal-porter was canary
    For to transplant me and me stick.

7   Now early next mornin' when I went to the dock,
    Sure, a lot of gay fellows around me did flock,
    And a pain in me shoulder for shakin' hands so often,
    "Arrah bedad," said one, "I thought I seen your coffin."
    But I went and I bought this gold ring, sir,
    And Kate to the priest I shall bring, sir,
    And when I return I shall sing, sir,
    The affections of me and me stick.

138

DORAN'S ASS

THERE are English broadsides of this Irish song in the Harvard College Library: 25242.17, X, 70 (Bebbington, Manchester, No. 332); XI, 45 (Such, London, No. 45); sheet on file, without imprint, numbered 882.

For texts printed in America see *The Shamrock, or, Songs of Old Ireland* (Book IV of *The Universal Book of Songs*, published by Dick & Fitzgerald, New York, 1864); Wehman broadside, No. 413; O'Conor, p. 43; Dean, pp. 38–39.

"Paddy Doyle." From the singing and recitation of Alexander Murphy, Cape John, Pictou County.

1   One Paddy Doyle lived in Killarney;
  He courted a girl called Biddy O'Toole.
 Her tongue was tipped with a bit of the blarney;
  The same to Pat was a golden rule.
 Day and dawn she was his colleen.
  Pat was often heard to say,
 "Arrah, what's the use of me walking faster?
  Biddy, she will meet me on the way."

   Chorus

     Whack fol loora loora lido
     Whack fol loora loor I day

2   One heavenly night in dull November,
  The moon shone clearly from above —
 The night it was I don't remember —
  Pat sought out to meet his love.
 This boy to-day had drunk some liquor,
  His spirits being light and gay.
 Fatigue and whisky overcome him;
  Pat lay down upon the way.

3   Pat lay down in gentle slumber,
  Thinking of his Bridget dear,
 Dreaming of pleasures without number,
  Thinking of her coming near.
 But he was not long without a comrade,
  And one that could toss up the hay,
 For an old jackass had smelled of Paddy,
  And he laid beside him on the way.

4 Pat snugged and he hugged this hairy devil,
   And threw his head to the world of care.
Says Pat, "She's mine, may the heavens bless her!
   But by my soul she's like a bear."
Pat put his head on the donkey's forehead,
   And then the ass began to bray.
Pat he yelled and screamed out, "Murder!
   Who has served me in such a way?"

5 Pat jumped up and off he ran
   At railroad speed and faster too.
He never stopped neither hand nor foot
   Till he arrived at Bridget's door.
By this time it was getting morning.
   Pat fell on his knees to pray,
Saying, "Open the door, my Bridget darling!
   I'm killed, I'm murdered on the way!"

6 Pat told his story mighty civil
   While Biddy prepared a whisky glass —
How he hugged and he snugged that hairy devil.
   "Go along," says Biddy. "It was Doran's ass."
"I knew it was, my Bridget darling."
   They both got married that same day,
But Pat he never saw his old straw hat,
   For the jackass eat it on the way.

139

LARRY McGEE

The Irish song "Larry Magee's Wedding" is so similar in metre and plot to the one which I present that there is pretty certainly a tie of relationship. The former song is to be found in the following collections of Irish songs, all published in America: *The Donnybrook Fair Songster* (New York, Dick & Fitzgerald, 1863), pp. 22–23; *Delaney's Irish Song Book No. 3*, p. 4; O'Conor, p. 83, and *John N. Conroy's Tipperary Christening Songster* (New York Popular Publishing Co.), pp. 12–13. I have found no exact parallel to the Nova Scotia version.

"Larry McGee." From the singing and recitation of John Brown, River John, Pictou County.

1 Now it was in the county of Wicklow lived Larry McGee,
And the devil's own boy for diversion was he.
O he had a donkey and pig, but he had no wife;
Now rich was his home but lonely his life.
There was one Missus Brady, who was reared up a lady.
"By the holy Saint Patrick, she's the girl to suit me."
O be darrahs O kester be darrahs! He coaxed her
To change her name from Missus Brady to Mistress McGee.

Chorus

Arrah wheedle O me dad, what a wedding we had!
    Such eating and drinking you never did see!
And the neighbours came flocking to throw up the stocking,
    And to dance at the wedding of Larry McGee.

2 Now to keep the wedding up, sure the whisky went round,
While hot steaming punch you might have been drowned.
Now the peraties were cooked and the fish were boiled,
All in their jackets for fear they would spoil.
The neighbours so frisky they smoked and drank whisky,
They gathered together like leaves on a tree.
While the young hearts did mingle, the old ones did jingle
For to dance at the wedding of Larry McGee.

3 Now it was out beyond the house where the stable you see,
And all in the straw there did lie Larry McGee.
O he was not alone for his donkey was there —
That was the ass he used to ride down to Donnybrook Fair.

He begun tricking, the beast begun kicking,
The neighbours all laughed as they witnessed the spree.
"Arrah be easy," says Larry, "O why did you marry?"
And he thought that the donkey was Missus McGee.

4 Now things went on nice till Missus Shandy you see,
Stepped right on the toe-nail of Missus McGee.
He begun swearing in defense of his darling,
With a shillalah in hand he welcomed the fray.
But it's old Tommy Shandy with the bedposts so handy,
With a clout knocked the wind out of Larry McGee.

140

THE WEDDING OF BALLYPOREEN

THIS was one of the most popular of the rough-and-tumble Irish wedding songs. For British versions see *The Sprig of Shillelah*, compiled by Dinny Blake (David Bryce, Paternoster Row, London, 1852), pp. 324–327; Greig, XLVIII. See also broadsides: W. Midgley, Halifax (I, 147); Ryle (II, 192); no imprint (VI, 11); Ryle (VII, 7); Ryle (with "The Shop on Fire"); Pitts, No. 92; Swindells.

For American publication, see, for example, *Berry's Comic Songs* (Philadelphia, A. Winch, 1856), p. 60; *Rodey Maguire's Comic Variety Songster* (New York, Dick and Fitzgerald, 1864), pp. 44–46; *Delaney's Irish Song Book No. 1*, p. 13; O'Conor, p. 63.

"The Wedding of Ballyporeen." From the singing and recitation of Alexander Murphy, Cape John, Pictou County.

1 Long life and success to a true Irish bawd,
    She'll sing you a song and she'll send you a hod,
    She'll sing you a song about music and health,
    A song ready made, she composed it herself,
    About maids, boys pressed in a wedding,
    A supper, good cheer, and a bedding,
    A crowd you could scarce poke your head in,
    Assembled at Ballyporeen.

2 One fine summer's morn about twelve in the day,
    When the birds fell a singing and asses did bray,
    There was Patrick the bridegroom and Ocheney the bride,
    With their best tukes and tukens sat out side by side.
    The pipers played first in the rear, sirs.
    The maids blushed, the bridegroom did swear, sirs.
    O dear, how the spalpeens did stare, sirs,
    At the wedding of Ballyporeen!

3 They were soon tacked together, for home did return,
    To make ready the day by the sign of the churn.
    They sat down together, a frolicsome group,
    For the banks of old Shannon ne'er saw such a troop.
    There were turf-cutters, swaddlers, and ailers;
    There were peddlers, smugglers, and nailers;
    There were pipers, fiddlers, and sailors
    Assembled at Ballyporeen.

4 They all sat down to meat, Father Murphy said grace.
Smoking hot were the dishes and eager each face.
Knives and forks did rattle and platters did play,
While their elbows enjostled and walloped away,
Until mountains of beef were cut down, sirs.
They demolished until the bare bones, sirs.
O dear, how the spalpeens did roar, sirs,
At the wedding of Ballyporeen!

5 There was bacon and greens, but the turkey was spoilt,
There was potatoes both ways, both roasted and boilt,
Plum pudding, red herring, — the priest got the snipe, —
Cole cannon, cold dumpling, cold cow-heel and tripe.
They ate till they could eat no more, sirs.
The whisky came pouring galore, sirs.
O dear, how the spalpeens did roar, sirs,
At the wedding of Ballyporeen!

6 The whisky went round and the songsters did roar;
Tim sung "Paddy O'Kelly," and Nell sung "Molly Astore";
But soon they got a hint for their songs to forsake.
Every man take his sweetheart his trotters to shake,
When pipers and couples advancing,
Pumps, brogues, and bare feet a prancing.
Such fiddling, piping, and dancing
Was never at Ballyporeen!

141

THE ROSE OF TRALEE

For this song see "The Rose of Tralee. Words by E. Mordaunt Spencer. Music by Charles W. Glover" (Harvard College); O'Conor, p. 80. In a De Marsan broadside (List 15, No. 42; List 19, No. 70) the song is modified to a warning against the Rose of Tralee.

From the singing and recitation of Alexander Harrison, Maccan, Cumberland County.

1 The pale moon was rising o'er yonder high mountain,
    The sun was declining beneath the blue sea,
  When I strayed with my love to a clear crystal fountain
    That flowed through the beautiful vale of Tralee.

Chorus

  She was lovely and fair as the roses in summer,
    It was not her beauty alone that won me,
  But O it was truth in her eyes that was burning
    That made me love Mary, the rose of Tralee.

2 The cool shades of evening her mantle was spreading,
    As Mary in silence sat listening to me,
  And the moon through the valley her pale light was shedding.
    It was there I won Mary, the rose of Tralee.

3 To the green church of Erin I went with my Mary,
    In fear that some other might win her from me.
  'T was there we were married. 'T was in green she appearéd.
    And I won the heart of the rose of Tralee.

142

THE POOR MAN'S LABOUR'S NEVER DONE

THE ensuing lament was printed as an Irish song by Michael Joseph Barry in *The Songs of Ireland* (Dublin, 1845), p. 99, and by Manus O'Conor in *Old Time Songs and Ballads of Ireland* (New York, 1901), p. 31. The versions in these editions are much alike, and they both differ a good deal from mine in phraseology. All versions, however, unite in the expression of what may be regarded as the thesis of the song:

> For woman's ways they must have pleasure [or, be pleaséd],
> The poor man's labour's never done.

For English texts see Sharp, *Folk-Songs from Somerset*, IV, 60–61 (No. 101), also, *One Hundred English Folk-Songs*, pp. 156–157, and *English Folk-Songs*, II, 60–61 (in each case with music, and under the title "The Brisk Young Bachelor").

"The Old Bachelor." From the singing and recitation of Christopher Brown, River John, Pictou County.

1 I am an old bachelor, early and early,
　　　Seek my mind was this content.
　I married a wife to lie close by her,
　　　And she did grieve my heart full sore.

2 Must I become a servant to her,
　　　Milk the cows and errands run?
　Women's ways must be pleaséd,
　　　A poor man's labour's never done.

3 The very first year that we were married,
　　　Scarcely a wink of sleep I got.
　She scratched my shins till the blood came sprinkling.
　　　She cried, "Husband, stretch your feet!"

4 When I asked her what was the matter,
　　　She cried, "Husband, come, come, come!"
　Women's ways must be pleaséd,
　　　A poor man's labour's never done.

5 The very second year that we were married,
　　　A new-born babe she brought forth.
　Sat me down beside the cradle,
　　　Give it gruel when it need.

6   When it cried she bitterly scolded me;
     Out of doors I was forced to run
  Without hat, coat, wig, or waistcoat.
     A poor man's labour's never done.

7   His old mother, sitting in the corner
     Where she was weeping all alone:
  "Ah son, ah son, there is women plenty.
     Why should you be tied to one?

8   "Marry the second and you'll try her,
     And if you find she will not do,
  Marry the third, fourth, and the fifth one;
     Then your sorrows will renew."

143

WHEN I WAS SINGLE

THIS song is contained in a garland entitled *The Careless Batchelor's Garland* (No. 1 in a collection numbered 25252.6 in the Harvard College Library). Here its title is "The Careless Batchelor." Under the title "Oh, When I Was Single Again" it appears in a broadside, without imprint, in the same library (together with "The Converted Army," "On Guard," and "Home Again"). Alfred Williams prints a version in *Folk-Songs of the Upper Thames* (p. 111).

Miss Mason prints a song entitled "When I Was a Maiden" (*Nursery Rhymes and Country Songs*, p. 42), which is in very much the same style as this one, except for a change in the sex of the complainant. It was probably composed as a reprisal. The first stanza is:

> When I was a maiden, O then, and O then!
> When I was a maiden, O then!
> Lovers many had I as the stars in the sky,
> And the world it went very well then, and O then;
> The world it went very well then.

Versions of "When I Was Single" are reported by Belden, No. 48; by Shearin and Combs, p. 31, and Pound, p. 58. There are two copies in the Sharp MS. of *Songs from the Southern Appalachians* in the Harvard College Library (pp. 351, 421). See also Pound, No. 98; *Delaney's Song Book No. 6*, p. 22.

"When I Was Single." From the singing and recitation of Mrs. Ellen Bigney, Pictou, Pictou County.

1 When I was single, O then,
  When I was single, O then,
  When I was single my pockets did jingle,
  I wish I was single again.

Chorus

  Again and again and again,
  Again and again and again,
  When I was single my pockets did jingle,
  I wish I was single again.

2 I married a wife, O then,
  I married a wife, O then,
  I married a wife, she's the plague of my life,
  I wish I was single again.

3 My wife took the fever, O then,
  My wife took the fever, O then,
  My wife took the fever, I hope it won't leave her,
  I wish I was single again.

4　My wife she did die and O then,
　My wife she did die and O then,
　My wife she did die, not a tear did I cry,
　And I'll never get married again.

5　I went to her funeral, O then,
　I went to her funeral, O then,
　The music it played, and I danced on the way,
　And I'll never get married again.

6　I walked in the garden one day,
　I walked in the garden one day,
　I walked in the garden, I saw a maid passing,
　I wished to get married again.

7　I married another, O then,
　I married another, O then,
　I married another, she's worse than the other,
　I wish I was single again.

8　All you that have wives, O then,
　All you that have wives, O then,
　Be good to the first, the next is far worse,
　I wish I'd my old one again.

144

THE POOR HARD–WORKING MAN

O'Conor (p. 128) prints a song, entitled "Pat Malony's Family," which corresponds roughly in character and point of view to this one. It begins:

My name is Mike Malony, I'm a carpenter by trade,
I married Molly Higgins, who all my trouble made;
She'd as many of relations as fishes in the sea,
They ate me out of house and home, and destroyed me family.

No local title. From the singing and recitation of John Brown, River John, Pictou County.

1 O I am a poor hard-working man,
  I laboured every day.
I have to work so very hard
  To keep my family.
There's eleven children and my wife;
  Two of them are small.
Just give me your attention,
  And I'll tell you of them all.

Chorus

 Arrah, there's Mick, and there's Tim,
 There's little Tom and Jim,
 Mathew, Mark, Luke, John, and Paul.
 There's Rosanna and Joanna,
  That thumps the grand piano;
 And my wife she often told me
 I am the daddy of them all.

2 O Mick and Tim are boot-blacks,
  Will shine them for a dime.
Tom and Jim are dancers,
  They have their business fine.
Mathew, Mark, Luke, and John,
  Their stage is off Broadway,
And Paul's a dancing barber.
  The girls they sing and play.

3   O the girls they are the eldest
        Of all the family.
     Rosanna is twenty-five,
        And Joanna's twenty-three.
     I wish they would get married,
        For the devil the tap they'll do
     But dance and play and sing all day,
        And skip the toora loo.

145

THE FELLOW THAT LOOKS LIKE ME

THIS song is in the Sheet Music Collection in the Harvard College Library, "By J. F. Poole. Copyright by Frederick Blume. District Court, Southern District, New York, 1867." It was much esteemed in the late sixties as a popular song and as a choice bit of music-hall entertainment, and it was included in several of the songsters of the period. See, for instance: "*The Fellow That Looks Like Me*" *Songster* (New York, Robert M. De Witt, 1867), pp. 5–6; *Tony Pastor's 201 Bowery Songster* (New York, Dick and Fitzgerald, 1867); "*The Irish Boy's Return*" *Songster* (New York, The American News Co., 1868), pp. 9–10; *Howe's Comic Songster* (Boston, Elias Howe), pp. 35–36; *William H. Lingard's "On the Beach at Long Branch" Song Book* (Dick and Fitzgerald, 1868), pp. 116–117; *The "Walking Down Broadway" Songster* (De Witt, 1869), pp. 38–39.

From the singing and recitation of Alexander Murphy, Cape John, Pictou County.

1 In sad despair I wandered, my heart was filled with woe,
　　While on my grief I pondered; what to do I did not know,
　Since cruel Fate has on me frowned, and trouble seems to be
　　That there is a fellow in this here town the very image of me.

Chorus

O would n't I like to catch him, whomever he may be!
Would n't I give him particular fits, the fellow that looks like me!

2 One evening as I started up Central Park to go,
　　I was met by a man upon the road, saying, "Pay me the bills
　　　you owe."
　In vain I said, "I owe you naught," but he would not let me free
　　Till a crowd came round and the bills I paid for the fellow
　　　that looked like me.

3 One night as I went walking through a narrow street uptown,
　　I was met by a man upon the road, saying, "I've caught you,
　　　Mister Brown.
　You know my daughter you have wronged" — though his girl
　　　I never did see —
　　But he beat me till I was black and blue, for the fellow that
　　　looked like me.

4 And to a ball I went one night. When just enjoying the sport,
    A policeman caught me by the arm, saying, "You're wanted
      down to court.
  You've escaped us thrice, but this here time I'm sure you shan't
      get free."
    So I was arrested and dragged to jail for the fellow that looked
      like me.

5 I was tried next day, found guilty too, just to be taken down,
    When another policeman just stepped in with the right crimi-
      nal, Mister Brown.
  They locked him up and set me free. O wasn't he a sight to see!
    The ugliest wretch that ever I saw was the fellow that looked
      like me.

Chorus

O wasn't I glad they caught him, for he was a sight to see!
The ugliest wretch that ever was on earth was the fellow that
    looked like me!

146

BETSY BAKER

THIS song was popular both in Great Britain and in America during the second and third quarters of the nineteenth century. The version in *The American Songster* (noted below) is thus introduced: "A comic song, sung by Mr. Sloman, with enthusiastic applause, at the Baltimore Theatre. Tune — 'Yankee Doodle.'"

The Harvard College Library has a chapbook copy of this song, printed by J. Neil, Glasgow, 1829 (25276.23), and the following broadside copies: 25242.17, I, 140 (Spencer, Bradford); II, 44 (George Walker, Durham, No. 111); III, 144 (no imprint); VII, 2 (no imprint); — in the files, Catnach (two copies, each with "The Soldier's Gratitude"); T. Birt (with "Love Among the Roses"); Harkness, Preston, No. 432. See also Williams, p. 219.

For American texts see *The American Songster* (New York, Nafis and Cornish), pp. 69–73; *Howe's Comic Songster* (Boston, Elias Howe); *The People's Free-and-Easy Songster* (New York, Wm. H. Murphy), p. 59; *Rodey Maguire's Comic Variety Songster* (New York, Dick and Fitzgerald, 1864), pp. 46–48.

The following version was recollected by Frank McNeil of Little Harbour, Pictou County, from the singing of old people in the community during his boyhood.

1 From noise and bustle far away,
    Hard work my time employing,
How merrily I spent each day,
    Content with health enjoying.
The birds did sing and so did I,
    As I flew o'er each acre,
And I vowed if ever I did wed
    'T would be with Betsy Baker.

Chorus

Li toora loora loora lay
Li toora loora lilo
Li toora loora lay
Li toora loora lilo

2 In church I saw her dressed so neat,
    One Sunday, being hot weather.
With love my heart began to beat
    As we sang psalms together.
How piously she hung her head,
    And while her voice did shake her,
I vowed if ever I would wed
    'T would be with Betsy Baker.

3   .   .   .   .
    I found from conversation,
She had just come home from boarding-school
    And finished her education.
But love made me speak out more free;
    Says I, "I have many an acre.
Will you give me your company?"
    "I won't," said Betsy Baker.

4   So when I found she'd served me so,
    I thought it best to leave her.
I got no sleep all that long night,
    And love brought on a fever.
The doctor came with his glasses and cane,
    And his long face like a Quaker.
Says he, "Young man, where is your pain?"
    Says I, "With Betsy Baker."

5   So when I was not bad enough,
    He bled me and he pilled me;
And if I'd taken half his stuff
    I'm certain sure he'd have killed me.
So then to preserve my life,
    'Twixt me and the undertaker,
I thought the best thing I could do
    Was go to Betsy Baker.

6   Straight to Miss Betsy then I went,
    Resolved with love to take her;
But in the meantime she had fell in love
    With a rattling mad play actor.
He said if she would marry him
    A lady he would make her;
So then, poor girl, was led astray,
    And I lost Betsy Baker.

147

COURTING IN THE KITCHEN

IF the Clown could have heard this song he would not have been frustrate of his desire to listen to "doleful matter merrily set down"; and the air is as rollicking as the jingle of the printed lines. The earliest version which I have found is in *The Sprig of Shillelah*, "compiled by Dinny Blake" and printed by David Bryce, Paternoster Row, London, in 1852 (pp. 214–216).

Among the Andrews and De Marsan broadsides there is one entitled "The Man Who Lost his Breeches" (List 8, No. 48), to be sung to the "Tune of 'Courting in the Kitchen.'"

From the singing and recitation of Richard Hines, River John, Pictou County.

1 Come all you belles and beaux,
　　I pray you give attention.
For love, it plainly shows,
　　Is the devil's own invention.
Once in love I fell
　　With a maid who smiled bewitching;
Miss Henrietta Bell,
　　Lived in Captain Phipps's kitchen.

Chorus

Ri to loora lay
Ri to loora lido
Ri to loora lay
Ri toora loora lido

2 At the age of seventeen
　　I was bound unto a grocer
Not far from Stephen's Green
　　Where Miss Bell for tea did go, sir.
Her manners were so free
　　They set my heart a twitching.
Then she invited me
　　To a blow-out in the kitchen.

3 Sunday being the day
　　That we was to have the flare-up,
I dressed myself quite gay,
　　I frizzed and oiled my hair up.

The captain had no wife
　　And he was out a fishing.
Then we kicked up high life
　　Down below stairs in the kitchen.

4　At the hour of six o'clock,
　　　Then we set down to table.
She handed me both cakes and tea,
　　　I eat while I was able;
I eat cakes, drank wine and tea
　　　Till my side it got a stitch in.
The hours flew quick away
　　　While courting in the kitchen.

5　She sat down on my knee,
　　　We kissed, she hinted marriage,
When rolling to the door
　　　Came Captain Phipps's carriage.
Her looks showed me full well
　　　That moment she was wishing
I was with Old Nick in hell,
　　　Or somewheres from the kitchen.

6　Right off my knee she flew,
　　　Full five-foot-six or higher,
And then head first she threw me
　　　Right slap bang in the fire.
My new repealing coat
　　　That I got from Master Stitchem,
And a twenty-shilling note
　　　Went a blazing in the kitchen.

7　She grieved to see my duds
　　　All bedaubed with smoke and ashes;
Then a tub of dirty suds
　　　Right over me she dashes.
While I lay on the floor
　　　The water she kept pitching
Till the footman broke the door
　　　And walked into the kitchen.

8　He said, "What brought you here?"
　　　"Sir," said I, "I was invited."
On assault they did indict me
　　　And I was brought to trial.

They'd take bail to no amount,
    To get home then I was itching.
I had to give some account
    What brought me in the kitchen.

9 I said, "She did invite me,"
    But she gave flat denial.
Then the judge he says to me,
    "Stand up, young man, for trial."
She swore I spoilt her character,
    In spite of all her screeching.
I got six months on the wheel
    For courting in the kitchen.

148

KIRTLE GAOL

THE gaol which looms so large in this robust ditty of the music hall and the forecastle is called by many names and assigned to many places in the various broadside versions which deal with the daily life within its walls. These variations, however, need surprise no one who has noted the geographical inconsistencies of "The Butcher Boy" or of "Van Dieman's Land."

In several texts the house of detention is merely "County Gaol." See broadsides: Ryle & Co. (II, 127); no imprint (IV, 152); Ryle & Co. (V, 229); W. S. Fortey (Catnach Press). O'Conor, p. 121, has this same "County Gaol" version. The first stanza usually ends:

> They piped into a railroad mail,
> And carried me off to County Gaol.

In another version the hero is conducted to "Bellevue Gaol." (In every case the title corresponds to the name of the gaol, a circumstance which adds a complication to the tracing of the song.) See broadsides: no imprint (VI, 71); Bebbington, Manchester, No. 132 (IX, 127). Here the first stanza ends:

> They put me in the Bridewell mail,
> And whipped me off to Bellevue Gaol.

A third version appears in a broadside printed by Harkness, Preston (No. 582): "A New Song on Wakefield Gaol." The lines closing the first stanza are:

> From the Town Hall they did me trail,
> And whipped me into Wakefield Gaol.

Another Harkness broadside (No. 481) I have reserved for final consideration, since it probably explains the name of the prison house in the Nova Scotia version. It is entitled "Kirkdale Gaol," and its first stanza ends:

> They put me in a railroad mail,
> And whipped me off to Kirkdale Gaol.

The "Kirtle" of my version is a contraction, or corruption, of "Kirkdale." A stranger circumstance is the combining of elements from various broadside versions in the shibboleth of the concluding couplet of my first stanza:

> From the Town Hall and the Bridewell Mail
> They took me off to Kirtle Gaol.

No fewer than three different broadside texts are here represented — in the three component phrases "the Town Hall," "the Bridewell Mail," and "Kirtle [i.e., Kirkdale] Gaol."

For American copies of "County Jail" see "That's the Style for Me, Boys," Songster (New York, copyright 1869), pp. 12–13; The "We Won't Go Home till Morning" Songster (New York, copyright 1869), pp. 32–33; The Old Clown's "W-h-o-a January" Songster (New York, 1870), pp. 36–37; "My Father Sould Charcoal" Songster (New York, 1870), pp. 58–59; Yankee Robinson's "Beautiful Amazon" Songster (New York, 1870), pp. 48–49; Singer's Journal, I, 167; De Marsan broadside, List 12, No. 12 ("as sung by E. Dugan"); Wehman's Irish Song Book No. 3 (New York, copyright 1891), pp. 71–73. Cf. Belden, No. 109.

"Kirtle Gaol." From the singing and recitation of Richard Hines, River John, Pictou County.

1 Good people all, give ear, I pray,
And mark you well what I do say.
To my misfortunes great and small
Come listen and I will tell you all.
I used to live a joyous life,
Devoid of care, devoid of strife;
I could go to bed and fall asleep,
No evil spirits around me creep.
But O the touts of Cupid's gad,
They nearly drove me ramping mad.
From the Town Hall and the Bridewell Mail
They took me off to Kirtle Gaol.

2 When I got to the end of the rout
The turnkeys turned my pockets out
To see if I'd got any such stuff
As blunt,[1] black tobacco, or snuff.
They took me down to try my size,
Colour of hair, colour of eyes,
The length of my nose from root to tip;
To see if I had more than one top lip.
Then straight into the yard I goes;
They give to me a suit of clothes.
The kids come out and did me hail,
"Here's another new cock for Kirtle Gaol!"

3 One of them with a roguish sneer:
"Me Jakie kiddie, what brought you here?"
"It's who do you think you're going to lout?
What brought me here if it wasn't a tout?"
Then they all gathered round like so many fools,
Till one old cock spoke up the rules:
That each new cock would sing a song,
Or tell a tale, Bob knows how long,
Or break his wind and give a whack,
Or else be tied up to a black-jack,
And then be walloped too, and wale
With a big wet towel in Kirtle Gaol.

[1] Slang term for ready money.

4   I walked and trotted about the yard
Thinking my case was wonderful hard,
When all of a sudden I heard a ding.
'T was deputy wardsmen, "All fall in!"
O then it was as stiff as starch,
Right about face and then quick march,
Some clinking of clogs, some in their minds,
Some with their pantaloons tore showed their behinds.
To lie on a cushion as hard as a nail —
It would kill the devil in Kirtle Gaol.

5   On Sunday morning we did turn out;
Each stoned his cell and cleaned his pot,
And then around the yard did lurch
Till we all fell in to go to church.
O then such dresses you might view —
One leg was yellow, the other was blue,
One sleeve was yellow, the other was gray.
When the parson came out to preach and pray,
Saying, "Elijah he went up in a cloud,
Lazarus walked about in a shroud,
And Jonah lived inside of a whale."
That's a damn sight better than Kirtle Gaol.

149

THE FENIAN SONG

THE so-called Fenian Brotherhood was formed in New York in 1857. Its main purpose, apparently, was to "set Ireland free," but among its subsidiary projects was an invasion of Canada from the United States. In Canada there was for a time a good deal of excitement accompanied by the drafting and training of young men for the purpose of sweeping back the threatening tide. The inconsiderable fragment which I present is all that remains — for me, at least — of what was probably a Canadian recruiting song.

From the singing and recitation of Ephraim Tattrie, Tatamagouche, Colchester County.

> If you happen to walk out
> Some one in your ears are humming,
> And they'll ask you if you know
> When the Fenians are a coming.

> *Chorus*
> To me merser inka day
> To me merser inka taddie
> To me merser inka day
> O ware o re laddie

> They dare not 'vade our soil,
> Nor try to work us wrongful.

150

THE LUMBERMAN'S LIFE

It is probable, though not certain, that this complaint had its beginnings in the woods. Its earliest known appearance in print is in a De Marsan broadside (List 5, No. 98): "Composed and Written by Geo. W. Stace, La Crosse Valley, Wis." Gray, pp. 53–57, prints a version from Maine and remarks, "The ballad is well known in Maine, but is probably of New Brunswick origin." See also Dean, *The Flying Cloud*, pp. 87–88 (Minnesota); Rickaby, pp. 43–47 (Minnesota). The version which I present is only a poor fragment.
From the singing of Ephraim Tattrie, Tatamagouche, Colchester County.

1 O a lumberman's life is a wearisome life.
　　Some say it is free from care.
　O the winding of an axe, O from daylight until dark,
　　And the wild forests we must steer.

2 When our camps they are dark and the piercing winds do blow,
　　And our limbs they are almost froze;
　When our camps they are dark and the piercing winds do blow
　　And our limbs they are almost froze.

3 O every rapid that we run they think it is great fun,
　　And they don't know the dangers we're in;
　O every rapid that we run they think it is great fun,
　　And they don't know the dangers we're in.

4 O the lumbering I'll give o'er and contented stay on shore,
　　And live with a smiling little wife.
　O the lumbering I'll give o'er and contented stay on shore,
　　And live with a smiling little wife.

151

McLELLAN'S SON

THIS is a native song, made in commemoration of an accidental shooting over half a century ago in Pugwash. The Reverend John Warner of Parrsboro, Nova Scotia, informs me that it was composed immediately after the accident by his mother, who lived in Pugwash and was acquainted with the details.

From the singing and recitation of Mrs. James Palmer, Waldegrave, Colchester County (printed, *Quest*, pp. 197–198).

1 It was on September the eighteenth day
. . . .
  A gun was heard, a mournful sound,
  Like thunder rolled and shook the ground.

2 The people crowded to the spot
  From which there came that mournful shock,
  And there in death's cold fetters bound
  A victim bleeding on the ground.

3 It's there they saw a man and gun
  Who had this dreadful murder done;
  With rolling eyes cast on the ground
  He told the truth to all around.

4 "It's I took up this cursed gun
  To snap it off in careless fun,
  When this poor boy with spirits large
  Came up the hill and met the charge.

5 "I'll tell you what I'd have you do —
  Take this same gun and shoot me too.
  Where shall I hide my guilty head?
  I wish to God I too was dead.

6 "It's take poor Daniel on a door,
  And lay him on the bar-room floor.
  Send for a justice very soon,
  And let the jury fill the room."

7 The parents of this murdered boy
Has given up all hopes of joy,
To think their son to man had grown
To die by folly not his own.

8 Take warning, all you careless youths,
Be always sure and speak the truth.
Take warning by McLellan's son,
Mind how you trifle with a gun!

152

THE BEAR RIVER MURDER

THIS edifying mixture of narrative, moralistic comment, and good counsel was compounded in 1895 by one S. Smith on the occasion of the murder of Annie Kempton by Peter Wheeler at Bear River, Digby County. The text is reproduced from a broadside in the possession of Dr. George H. Cox of New Glasgow. At the top of the sheet the composer issues an imperative summons to all readers, reminds them of a truth so tenacious that it has become proverbial, and then reveals his identity, thus:

Stop! Look! Read!
A Friend in Need is a Friend Indeed.
S. Smith, Author.

It is comforting to know that the stern pronouncement at the conclusion of the first stanza did not go entirely unheeded, and that the murderer was, at least, hanged.

1   About a brutal murder
    I now say a word,
    I mean that Bear River murder,
    No doubt of it you've heard.
    "If Wheeler is the murderer,
    It's gibbeted he ought to be,
    For hanging is too good for him!"
    Said Detective Power to me.

2   God bless Annie Kempton,
    I hope she is in Heaven above
    With those little angels,
    The ones we all do love.
    Such a brutal murder I never heard of before,
    And I hope in the name of our Maker
    I'll never read of no more!
    "So it's boys, guide your tempers,
    And fight for sweet liberty.
    I think my words are true,"
    Said Detective Power to me.

3   I think he's the murderer, and it does seem to me
    As if he done the murder before he went to tea.
    Next morning when she was found
    She was laid upon the floor,

And the pot of beans in the oven
She had placed there the day before.
Now he got Judge and Justice,
And sentenced in the Court;
And sentence it was passed on him
Where he had to be hanged by the throat.
"So it's boys, guide your tempers,
And fight for sweet liberty.
There is no freedom now in prison,"
Said Detective Power to me.

4   On the eighth of September
He has to be hung
For that cruel murder
Which he's confessed that he's done.
"So boys, take my advice,
And fight for sweet liberty;
I think my words are true,"
Said Detective Power to me.

153

GERRY'S ROCKS

THE song of the tragedy of Young Munro and his sweetheart Clara Vernon
grew out of the actual event (which is said to have taken place during a lumber
drive on the Penobscot River in Maine) and spread throughout the United
States and Canada. It has also found its way into Scotland (Greig, CXXXII).
See Gray, p. 3; Cox, p. 236; Dean, pp. 25–26 (Minnesota); Rickaby, pp. 11–19.

A

"The Jam on Gerry's Rocks." From the singing and recitation of Miss
Susan Forbes, Cape John, Pictou County.

1 Come all you bold shanty boys and list while I relate
Concerning a young river man and his untimely fate,
Concerning a young shanty boss, so handsome, true and brave;
'T was on the jam on Gerry's Rocks he met his watery grave.

2 It was on a Sunday morning, as you will quickly hear,
Our logs were piled up mountains high, they could not keep them
clear.
Our foreman said, "Turn out, brave boys, with hearts devoid of
fear;
We'll break the jam on Gerry's Rocks and Ellingstown will steer."

3 Now, some of them were willing and some of them were not;
To work on jams on Sunday they did not think they ought —
Till six of our Canadian youths did volunteer to go
To break the jam on Gerry's Rocks with our foreman young
Munro.

4 They did not roll off many logs till they heard his young voice say,
"I warn you, boys, be on your guard, for the jam will soon give
way."
These words were scarcely spoken when the jam did break and go,
And it carried off these six fine youths with their foreman young
Munro.

5 When the rest of those young shanty boys the sad news they did
hear,
In search of their brave comrades to the river they did steer.
Meanwhile their mangled bodies a floating down did go,
While dead and bleeding near the bank was that of young Munro.

6 They took him from his watery grave, brushed back his raven hair.
There was one fair girl among them whose sad cries filled the
air —
There was one fair girl among them that came from Saginaw
Town,
Her cries and moans rose to the skies. Her true love had gone
down.

7 Fair Clara was a noble girl, the river men's true friend,
Who with her widowed mother dear lived near the river's bend.
The wages of her own true love the boss to her did pay,
And the shanty boys made up for her a generous purse next day.

8 They buried him in sorrow's depths — 't was on the first of May.
In a green mound by the river side there grew a hemlock gray.
Engraved upon that hemlock that by the grave did grow
Was the name and date and the sad fate of their foreman young
Munro.

9 Fair Clara did not long survive, her heart broke with her grief.
'T was scarcely six months afterwards death came to her relief.
And when the time at last had come when she was called to go
Her last request was granted, to be laid by young Munro.

B

"Gerry's Rocks." From the singing and recitation of Alexander Brown,
River John, Pictou County.

1 'T was on one Sunday morning,
As you shall quickly hear,
The logs they piled up mountains high;
We could not keep them clear.

2 The boss did say, "Turn to, brave boys,
Without one dread of fear,
And we'll break the jam on Gerry's Rocks,
And Eggartown we'll steer."

3 Some of them were willing,
While others did hang back;
It's for to work on Sunday.
They did not think it right.

4   Six Canadian shanty-boys
        Did volunteer to go,
    For to break the jam on Gerry's Rocks,
        With their foreman, young Munro.

5   They had not rolled off many logs
        When the boss to them did say,
    "Brave boys, you must be on your guard,
        For the jam will soon give way."

6   Those words were scarcely spoken
        When the jam did break and go,
    Carrying six of those brave shanty-boys
        And their foreman, young Munro.

7   The rest of those bold shanty-boys
        Those tidings came to hear.

    .   .   .   .
        .   .   .   .

8   For to search for their dead bodies
        To the river side did go;
    And cut and mangled on the beach
        Lie the body of young Munro.

9   They took him from the river side,
        Smoothed down his waving hair.
    There was one fair form among them,
        Whose moans did rent the air.

10   There was one fair form among them,
        A maid from Signal Town,
    Whose moans and cries did rent the sky
        For her lover who was drowned.

11   We buried him quite decent,
        All on the third of May.
    The boss to Miss Clara
        Her lover's wages paid.

12   Likewise a cheque of a thousand pounds
        She received the very next day.

    .   .   .   .
        .   .   .   .

13　Poor Clara, she did n't survive,
　　　Her heart was filled with woe.
　　·　·　·　·　·　·　·
　　　　·　·　·　·　·　·

14　And less than three months after
　　　She was called to go.
　　Her last request was granted —
　　　To be buried by young Munro.

15　It 's graved upon a hemlock tree,
　　　By the river side did grow,
　　The age, the date, and the drowning
　　·　Of foreman young Munro.

16　Come all ye royal shanty boys
　　　That wish to go and see,
　　There is a mound by the river bank,
　　　Likewise this hemlock tree.

17　The shanty boys cut the woods all down,
　　　Those lovers they lie low,
　　Handsome Clara from Signal Town,
　　　And foreman young Munro.

154

THE GIRL WHO WAS DROWNED AT ONSLOW

ONSLOW is a farming community at the head of Cobequid Bay in Colchester County. The tale runs that the girl whose fate is lamented in the following true song was preparing to return home one night with her brother, and that their sleigh was by accident backed into the water; the brother escaped, but in the darkness and confusion his companion was swept away by the current and drowned.

From the singing and recitation of Alexander Harrison, Maccan, Cumberland County.

1   What mournful news that we did hear
From Onslow Town which did appear!
A damsel fair just in her bloom,
A blooming flower cut down at noon!

2   Just in the height of youthful blood,
Cut off the stage by icy flood,
Bound downward by a frozen stream,
Her tender body's life to end.

3   The screech of her surviving breath
Unto her mother did appear,
Which woke her in a sad surprise,
To hear the screeches and dismal cries.

4   Her father in sad surprise,
With wringing hand and watery eyes,
That night he spent in grief and tears
A looking for his daughter dear.

5   They searched the river far and near,
But nothing of her could they see,
Till the third day with watery eyes
Her tender body they did spy.

6   When her true love came to hear
That he had lost his dearest dear:
"Ah, must we, must we, shall we part?
These thoughts distracts and breaks my heart."

7 Oh, parents dear, dry up your tears;
Weep not for your daughter dear.
We hope to meet her on that shore
Where she and you will part no more;
Where she and you and I must spend
Eternity that has no end.

155

A FROG HE WOULD A WOOING GO

FOR texts of this song see, for example, the *Journal of the Folk-Song Society*, II, 226; Campbell and Sharp, No. 119; Sharp, *Nursery Songs from the Appalachian Mountains*, No. 1; *Journal*, XXVI, 134; XXXV, 392–394; Cox, pp. 470–473; Wyman and Brockway, *Twenty Kentucky Mountain Songs*, pp. 86–93; Scarborough, *On the Trail of Negro Folk-Songs*, p. 46; Odum and Johnson, *Negro Workaday Songs*, p. 187; Payne, *Publications of the Texas Folk-Lore Society*, V; Barnes, *The West Virginia Review*, December, 1926, pp. 74–75. For an exhaustive study of the history of the song see Kittredge, *Journal*, XXXV, 394–399.

I reproduce the song from my own recollections of singing by housemaids during my childhood. My text is a form of the comedian Liston's *rifacimento* of the antique ditty (cf. Ford, *Massachusetts Broadsides*, No. 3120, and *The Isaiah Thomas Collection*, No. 92).

1   A frog he would a wooing go,
      Heigho! says Rowley O.
  A frog he would a wooing go
  Whether his mother would let him or no.
  With a rowley, powley, gammon and spinach,
      Heigho! says Anthony Rowley.

2   So off he set with his opera hat,
  And on the way he met with a rat.

3   They soon arrived at the mouse's hall,
  They gave a loud knock and they gave a loud call.

4   "O pray, Mistress Mouse, are you within?"
  "O yes, kind sirs, I am sitting to spin.

5   "O pray, Mister Frog, won't you give us a song?
  And let it be something that's not very long."

6   "I pray you, excuse me," says Mister Frog,
  "I've got a bad cold that I caught in a bog."

7   As they were in glee and making a din,
  A cat and her kittens came tumbling in.

8   The cat she seized the rat by the crown,
  The kittens they pulled the little mouse down.

9   This put Mister Frog in a terrible fright,
      He picked up his hat and he bid them good-night.

10   As froggie was crossing over a brook,
      A lily-white duck came and gobbled him up.

11   So this is the end of one, two, three —
      The rat, the mouse, and the little froggie!

156

THE TAILOR AND THE CROW

THE oldest known form of this song was found by Halliwell in Sloane MS. 1489 (which is a "collection of miscellaneous verses" written down in 1627: see E. J. L. Scott, *Index to the Sloane Manuscripts*, 1904, p. 427). Halliwell printed it in *The Nursery Rhymes of England*, 2d ed., 1843, p. 57 (No. 87), as follows:

> Hic hoc, the crow,
> For I've shot something too low:
> I have quite missed my mark,
> And shot the poor old sow to the heart;
> Wife, bring treacle in a spoon,
> Or else the poor old sow's heart will down.

See also Halliwell, *Popular Rhymes and Nursery Tales*, 1849, p. 12. Dearmer and Shaw, *Song Time*, p. 2, inadvertently date this "early version" 1489, mistaking the number of the manuscript for the year of our Lord. The most elaborate version is that published by J. Pitts in an engraved broadside of about 1830. Since it is little known and very curious, I reproduce it (as C). Between the two falls the standard nursery version printed by Rimbault with tune (see B), of which the Nova Scotia text (A) is a variant. For other variants of this standard form see Halliwell, *Nursery Rhymes*, 2d ed., Nos. 85, 86, p. 56 (cf. 5th ed., No. 176, pp. 115–116; A. Lang, *The Nursery Rhyme Book*, p. 163); Baring-Gould, *A Book of Nursery Songs and Rhymes*, No. 26, pp. 39–40; Baring-Gould and Sheppard, *A Garland of Country Song*, pp. 102–103 (with a tune different from Rimbault's); Baring-Gould and Sharp, *English Folk-Songs for Schools*, pp. 98–99.

Part of an adaptation from Nebraska is printed by Pound, p. 13. Belden (No. 95) has two Missouri variants, one of which contains a stanza corresponding to the seventh stanza of the Pitts version (C). A North Carolina fragment (Campbell and Sharp, No. 121) has a touch of this same stanza. Cf. "Sly Young Crow" in *Hathaway's Select Songster* (Philadelphia, 1840, pp. 240–241).

A

"The Tailor and the Crow." From the singing and recitation of David Rogers, Pictou, Pictou County.

1 It's of a tailor who was cutting out a coat.
    To me lang dum dilly dum coy me
He saw a crow a sitting on an oak.
    To me lang dum dilly dum coy me

Chorus

Coy me leero kill my care O
Coy me leero coy me
To me lump jump jump talla lalla ling
To me lang dum dilly dum coy me

2 And he said to his wife, "Hand me down my old carabang,
   Till I shoot that crow right through the wing!"

3 He fired and he missed his mark,
   And shot his old sow right through the heart.

4 "Now my old sow is dead and gone,
   And the devil may sing her funeral song.

5 "Now my old sow is dead and cold,
   And the little pigs praying for the old sow's soul."

B

"The Carrion Crow." The standard English nursery version. From E. F. Rimbault, A Collection of Old Nursery Rhymes, with Familiar Tunes (London, Chapell & Co.), pp. 10–11. See the same version and the same tune in John Graham, *Traditional Nursery Rhymes*, p. 32, and in Dearmer and Shaw, *Song Time*, p. 2.

> A carrion crow sat on an oak,
>   Derry, derry, derry, deeco;
> A carrion crow sat on an oak,
> Watching a tailor shape his cloak.
>   Sing heigh ho, the carrion crow,
>   Derry, derry, derry, deeco.
>
> O! wife, bring me my old bent bow,
>   Derry, derry, derry, deeco;
> O! wife, bring me my old bent bow,
> That I may shoot yon carrion crow.
>   Sing heigh ho, the carrion crow,
>   Derry, derry, derry, deeco.
>
> The tailor shot, and he miss'd his mark,
>   Derry, derry, derry, deeco;
> The tailor shot, and missed his mark,
> And shot his own sow through the heart.
>   Sing heigh ho, etc.
>
> Oh! wife! Oh, wife! some brandy in a spoon,
>   Derry, derry, derry, derry, deeco;
> Oh, wife! bring me some brandy in a spoon,
> For our old sow is in a swoon.
>   Sing heigh ho, etc.

The old sow died, and the bells did toll,
    Derry, derry, derry, deeco;
The old sow died, and the bells did toll,
And the little pigs pray'd for the old sow's soul.
    Sing heigh ho, etc.

C

"Carrion Crow." From an engraved and illustrated broadside of about 1830, "Sold by J. Pitts, Great St. Andrew St." (Harvard College Library). The same text is in *The Lover's Harmony* (London, Pitts, [1840]), p. 184. A variant of six stanzas is printed by Williams, p. 227.

1 As I went forth one May morning, fol de rol, &c.
  As I went forth one May morning,
  'T was all for to hear the little birds sing,
  To my high ho, the carrion crow, sung croak, croak dol de rol, &c.

2 This curst carrion crow it sat upon an oak,
  This curst carrion crow it sat upon an oak,
  And espy'd a poor taylor a cutting out a coat,
  To my high ho, &c.

3 I'll be shot, says the taylor, I'll be with you by & by,
  I'll be shot, says the taylor, &c.
  And I'll pop my yard right thro' & thro' your eye.
  To my high ho, &c.

4 Wife go fetch me my arrow and my bow,
  Wife go fetch me, &c.
  That I may have a shot at this old carrion crow.
  To my high ho, &c.

5 The taylor he shot but he miss'd his mark,
  The taylor he shot, &c.
  And he shot his neighbour's old sow quite thro' and thro' the heart.
  To my high ho, &c.

6 Wife go and fetch me some treacle on a spoon,
  Wife go and fetch me some treacle, &c.
  For our neighbour's old sow is in a terrible swoon.
  To my high ho, &c.

7 Hang me, says the taylor, if I care a louse,
   Hang me, says the taylor, &c.
   For we shall have black puddings, nice chitterlings and souse,
   To my high ho, &c.

8 Now the bells they did ring, and the bells they did toll,
   Now the bells they did ring, &c.
   And the little pigs squeak'd for the old sows soul,
   To my high ho, the carrion crow sung croak, croak, fol de rol, &c.

157

LITTLE JOHNNY GREEN

THIS song, under the title "My Grandma's Advice," or "My Grandmother's Advice," was very popular in the middle of the last century. It is a modification of the eighteenth-century English song, "The Old Maid" (*The Lover's Harmony*, No. 17, p. 134 (Pitts [1840]). For references see *Journal*, XXXV, 402; Cox, p. 469.

I reproduce the song from my own recollection of the singing of a housemaid during my childhood.

1 My grandmother lived on yonder little green,
As fine an old lady as ever was seen;
And she often cautioned me with care,
Of all false young men to beware.

Chorus

Timmy I, timmy O, timmy umpa tumpa tay,
Of all false young men to beware.

2 The first that came a courting was little Johnny Green,
As fine a young man as ever was seen;
But the words of my grandma so rung in my head
That I could n't attend to a word that he said.

Chorus

Timmy I, timmy O, timmy umpa tumpa tay,
That I could n't attend to a word that he said.

3 The next that came a courting was young Ellis Grove.
Him I received with a joyous love,
With a joyous love that could n't be afraid.
Better get married than die an old maid!

Chorus

Timmy I, timmy O, timmy umpa tumpa tay,
Better get married than die an old maid.

4 O dear, what a fuss these old folks make!
I think there must be some mistake,
For if all the boys and girls had been afraid,
Grandma herself would have died an old maid.

Chorus

Timmy I, timmy O, timmy umpa tumpa tay,
Grandma herself would have died an old maid.

158

THE QUAKER'S WOOING

THIS antiphonic song, imported from England, has had wide currency in
Canada and the United States. In *Journal*, XVIII, 55–56, Barry prints two
versions from Massachusetts and refers to Newell's *Games and Songs of American Children*, 1884, pp. 94–95 for a complete copy. See also *Journal*, XXIV,
341–342; Pound, p. 44, and No. 108; Rosa S. Allen, *Family Songs*, 1899, p. 14
(with tune); *Focus*, III, 276.

I reproduce the song from my own recollection of the singing of a housemaid — Adeline Langille, of Marshville, Pictou County.

1   "Madam, I have come a courting,
       Mm, O dear!
   Not for fun or idle sporting.
       Mm, O dear!"

2   "You may sit and court the fire,
       Teedle eedle ing ting tay!
   A man like you I don't admire.
       Teedle eedle ing ting tay!"

3   "I've a ring and twenty shillings,
   You may have them if you're willing."

4   "I don't want your ring and money,
   I'll marry a man that'll call me honey."

5   "I will change my religion,
   I will be a Presbyterian."

6   "Just like all you foolish Quakers,
   Always up to some such capers!"

7   "I'll go home and tell my daddy
   That you're not inclined to marry."

8   "You and your dad may go to the Harry,
   A man like you I'll never marry!"

159

THE BUILDING OF SOLOMON'S TEMPLE

In English and American song collections and broadsides may be found an interesting assortment of songs in glorification of freemasonry. Some of these deal at large with Biblical history, and some, like the ensuing example, confine themselves for the most part within the precincts of the Temple. It has been rather generally claimed by the singers that these songs, rightly understood, convey significant information about the society, and this has been as generally denied by others. That must be as it may. I am chiefly interested in my recollection of the assurance that was given me by the old sailor who sang the song for me and his conviction that it was one of extraordinary dignity and importance.

In the shape in which the song has come to me there are some names which have become somewhat cryptic — though they have lost nothing in sonority — by slight deviations from the authorized forms. For this reason it may not be amiss to add a brief explanation or two. Hiram Bereaf, the "gay cunning craftsman" of stanza 5, is the Hiram Abiff of masonic tradition, the ingenious worker in brass from Tyre, who (according to I Kings, vii, 14) was "a widow's son of the tribe of Naphtali," and (according to II Chronicles, ii, 14) was "the son of a woman of the daughters of Dan." Ahalabus and Bazaleel, who fashioned the great pillars of stanza 7, were ancient craftsmen highly endowed and trained "to devise cunning works, to work in gold, and in silver, and in brass, and in cutting of stones, to set them, and in carving of timber, to work in all manner of workmanship." They were actually employed in the building, not of the Temple, but of the Tabernacle which preceded it, and their wisdom and skill are recorded in the 31st chapter of Exodus, where they are named, respectively, Aholiab the son of Ahisamach and Bezaleel the son of Uri. Their importance in masonic tradition accounts for their presence here. And, finally, the "gold of Purvail" (in stanza 11) is that pure "gold of Parvaim" with which the house of the Lord at Jerusalem was garnished and overlaid.

Printed texts of this particular song are rather rare. For English versions see Greig, CXLVIII; broadside, "The Freemason's King," T. Bloomer, 10 High St., Birmingham (Harvard College Library). There is a Boston broadside of the piece in the Harvard College Library ("Solomon's Temple," with "The Grand Sweeper") which has the following imprint (and advertisement): "*The greatest collection of Songs and Ballads in New England may be found at the corner of Marshall and Hanover Streets, Boston. — Also, Books at Auction Prices.*" A version may be seen in *Howe's 100 Old Favorite Songs* (Boston, Elias Howe Co.), p. 262. See Ford, Massachusetts Broadsides, No. 3345.

"The Building of Solomon's Temple." From the singing and recitation of Richard Hines, River John, Pictou County.

1 In history we read of a freemason king,
The glory of Israel, his praise let us sing!
He who built a great fabric, as we understand,
On the Mount Moriah in Jerusalem.

2 He who conquered Goliath, as in history we find,
And purchased the ground for to raise that design,
Then ordered King Solomon, as he was his son,
To finish the building that he had begun.

3 King Solomon in order to erect that great plan,
He numbered all the workmen that was in the land.
Seventy thousand to bear burden he them did reserve;
Eighty thousand on the mountain to hew, cut, and carve.

4 Three thousand six hundred he ordered to be
The masters of workmen for to oversee.
And if you believe me I tell you it's true,
He clothéd them all in the orange and blue.

5 Then straightway to Tyre a letter did send,
Requesting King Hiram for to be his friend;
And finding him willing to grant him relief,
Sent a gay cunning craftsman called Hiram Bereaf.

6 He being a son of a widow of the daughters of Dan,
In every particular he acted the man.
In all things put to him he did nothing amiss.
He exceeded them all in the casting of brass.

7 He cast two great pillars would dazzle your sight,
They were full fifty cubits. He stood them upright,
That all Israel might see them as they went to church.
They stood one on each side of King Solomon's porch.

8 He cast two great pillars of an immense worth;
They spread forth their wings for to cover the earth.
They stood better there than they would in the field;
They were made by Ahalabus and great Bazaleel.

9 And the molten sea thirty cubits about,
And the brazen oxen without any doubt,
And manys the vessel this Hiram did cast,
And lots of fine vessels I'm sure we have missed.

10 And the place where he cast them I will explain:
It was in a valley they called Jordan's plain.
Between Succoth and Zarthan that place it was found;
Those vessels was all cast in that clayey ground.

11 And now the bold craftsmen the stone did it square,
All ready for building before they came there;
And on proper carriages they were all brought down,
That on that great temple no hammer should sound.

12 They put on the top of that beautiful pile,
There were three golden rods lest the birds should defile,
And a place made for worship in his holy name.
It was all overlaid with the gold of Purvail.

13 When the Queen of Sheba she heard of his fame,
She unto King Solomon then instantly came.
The report of his wisdom through the nations did pass,
For he was King Solomon, the grandson of Jess'.

14 When bright Phoebe in the morning her light doth expel,
Such a beautiful building I'm sure it looked well;
When light stands against light in three ranks doth shine
Such a beautiful temple was ne'er seen in time.

15 Jerusalem is a city of walls great and high;
It's a wonder to all strangers that do it pass by.
I'm sure it's a type of that vision was seen
On the Isle of Patmos by John the divine.

16 When our brethren do meet in a lodge for to shine,
Each man he is clothed in a garment so fine;
And likewise our master who sits in the chair,
And rules all our actions by the compass and square.

17 Then come, all my dear brethren, join chorus with me.
Here's a health to all masons that's honest and free!
King Solomon's wisdom and Hiram's also —
Come, fill up our glass! Let us drink, then we'll go.

160

THE LOVELY BANKS OF BOYNE

THIS ballad was sung for me after my collection had gone to press, and it could not be put in its proper place — in group 21–71, which contains songs dealing with lovers and their vicissitudes. The special variety of doleful matter which it sets forth (*i.e.*, the lament of a deserted maid), although it is incidental to a good many of the ballads, is not often the main theme. Among the numbers of this collection "The Butcher Boy" is probably the one which most nearly resembles the present song.

From the singing and recitation of Neil O'Brien, Pictou, Pictou County.

1 I am a gay young lassie and I love my Jimmy well.
   My heart was ever true to him, far more than tongue can tell.
'T was at my father's castle where he gained this heart of mine,
   And he causes me to wander from the lovely banks of Boyne.

2 He courted me some length of time and promised me to wed,
   Until he gained my favors and away from me he fled.
His love it flew like the early dew when the sun begins to shine,
   And he soon forgot poor Flora on the lovely banks of Boyne.

3 I understand this false young man to England sailed away.
   I did pack up my jewelry upon that very day.
I left my home and friends so dear in sorrow to repine,
   And I quickly followed after him from the lovely banks of
      Boyne.

4 I understand this false young man arrived at London town,
   And wed there with a lady fair, and her of high renown.
Young girls beware; mark what I say; mind how you spend your
      time;
   Think on the fate of Flora on the lovely banks of Boyne.

5 O fare ye well, ye purly streams that now flow far away,
   Where me and my bonny boy for pleasure used to stray.
Here in the walls of Dublin I will spend my youthful time,
   Far from my home I loved so dear on the lovely banks of Boyne.

161

THE BANKS OF NEWFOUNDLAND

IF I had found this song in time I should have placed it next to "Dixie Brown" (No. 96), the song which, in this collection, it most resembles in subject-matter and tone. Much more interesting, however, than its general similarity to "Dixie Brown" is its remarkable resemblance, in details of incident and phraseology, to "Van Dieman's Land" (No. 122). The invocation and warning of the first stanza, the dream that follows, the benevolence of the warm-hearted Irish girl, Cassie Higgins — these all have their counterparts in the woeful ballad of Brown, Martin, and Paul Jones. Colcord prints a text of the song (pp. 92–93).

From the singing and recitation of Neil O'Brien, Pictou, Pictou County.

1 Ye rambling boys of Erin, ye rambling boys beware.
　　When you go on board of a merchant ship, blue dungaree jump-
　　　ers wear.
　Lay aside your working jackets, keep them at your command,
　　And beware of the cold nor'westers on the Banks of Newfound-
　　　land.

2 I had a dream the other night, I dreamt that I was home.
　　I dreamt that me and my true love were in old Marylebone,
　That we were on old England's shore with a jug of ale in hand,
　　But when I woke my heart was broke on the Banks of New-
　　　foundland.

3 We had on board two Irish lads, Mike Murphy and Pat Moore.
　　In the year of eighteen forty-four those sailors suffered sore.
　They pawned their clothes in Liverpool and sold their notes of
　　　hand,
　　Not thinking of the cold nor'westers on the Banks of New-
　　　foundland.

4 We had on board an Irish girl, Cassie Higgins was her name.
　　'T was her I promised to marry, on me she had a claim.
　And she tore up her dresses to make mittens for my hands
　　Before she'd see her true love freeze on the Banks of New-
　　　foundland.

5 It's now we're passing the Virgin Rocks and stormy winds do
  blow,
    With a crowd of sailors on the deck a shoveling off the snow.
  We'll wash her down, we'll scrub her decks with holystone and
    sand,
      And we'll bid adieu to the Virgin Rocks on the Banks of New-
        foundland.

6 It's now we're passing Sandy Hook and the cold winds they still
  blow,
    With a tug-boat right ahead of us, into New York we'll go.
  We'll fill our glasses brimming full with a jug of rum in hand,
      For while we're here we can't be there on the Banks of New-
        foundland.

162

THE WRECK OF THE *GLENALOON*

THIS song, also a late acquisition, belongs with "The Wreck of the *Atlantic*" and "The *Cedar Grove*" (Nos. 88 and 89). In spite of its self-conscious and occasionally thwarted attempts to achieve emotional intensity through the power of description it is, on the whole, a very effective tale. Its model, apparently, is not the popular ballad, but rather the literary narrative poem in which the story is subordinated to description and introspection. There is too much insistence upon the sombre accompaniment of night, but the scene is somehow realized; and the fourth stanza, at least, serves as a link to bind the song to the poetry of the folk.

From the singing and recitation of Neil O'Brien, Pictou, Pictou County.

1 'T was only a ripple and just a puff that stirred our old brown
  sails,
  Or like the breath of a sick man's lips that flutters awhile
  and fails.
  And after a time the wind was dead as we rolled on the oily sea,
  Like a weary man in a fever fit, moving uneasily.

2 No headway on our old ship now; she might have been a log.
  Three leagues away the land lay hid in a bank of cold grey fog,
  And two points on our starboard bow. 'T was a summer's night
  in June,
  Where the water and skies seemed joined in one, lit up by a
  red full moon.

3 O bloody red, but it silvered soon with a faint and glimmering
  light,
  Stretched from our bark to the ocean's edge, wavering broad
  and bright.
  There's something in a shiny belt about a league away,
  Like the shapeless mass of a rugged rock on the face of the
  water lay.

4 There was no rock or reefs laid down on the chart just thereabout.
  I looked through my night glass steadily, but could not make
  it out.
  I kept my eye on the ugly thing as I walked the quarter deck,
  And ordered my crew to lower a boat, for perhaps it was a
  wreck.

5 As we rowed away to that shapeless mass as it loomed against
　　the moon,
　　I read on the bow of that mastless brig her name, the *Glenaloon.*
　I hailed, but never a voice replied, there was no one on the deck;
　　So we shipped our oars and touched her side, then climbed
　　upon the wreck.

6 There was a rubbish of splintered spars, her fore and main mast
　　gone,
　　Shattered boats on her littered decks, but human beings none.
　Surely that is a human form a crouching on the deck,
　　With an old sou'wester and guernsey frock, "Shipmates, one
　　of the wreck!"

7 'T was sadly I raised the old chap's hat — I remember the moon
　　was full —
　　I startled back as the bright rays shone on a glimmering
　　ghostly skull.
　And making my way through sails and spars muddled with
　　shade and light,
　　Five more skeletons we found, bleached to a deathly white.

8 In walking aft the deck was flush; to the cabin I made my way.
　　Stretched on a locker in full length the skeleton captain lay.
　In his bony hands a paper clutched, I read what it said next day:
　　"We are wrecked, boats stove, and food all gone; we can but
　　wait and pray."

9 As we rowed away from that mastless brig in the light of the
　　pitiful moon,
　　I read again that fatal name, that queer name *Glenaloon.*
　And faster and faster into the water the blades of our stout oars
　　fell,
　　For her deck seemed swarmed with shadowed forms waving a
　　wild farewell.

10 Next day the sun shone bright and clear as we buried that flesh-
　　less crew,
　　Shrouded and sheeted one by one as they sank in the water
　　blue.
　And I never look back on a summer's night on the face of a red
　　full moon
　　But I think of the horrors we once revealed on the wreck of
　　the *Glenaloon.*

Folk Tunes

FOLK TUNES

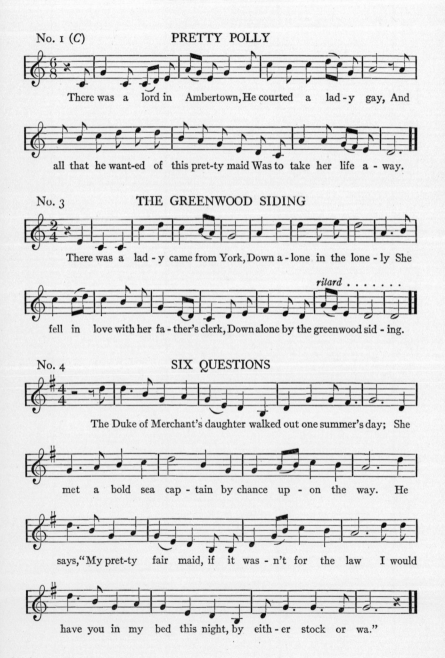

No. 1 (C)   PRETTY POLLY

There was a lord in Ambertown, He courted a lad-y gay, And
all that he want-ed of this pret-ty maid Was to take her life a - way.

No. 3   THE GREENWOOD SIDING

There was a lad - y came from York, Down a - lone in the lone - ly She
fell in love with her fa - ther's clerk, Down alone by the greenwood sid - ing.

ritard . . . .

No. 4   SIX QUESTIONS

The Duke of Merchant's daughter walked out one summer's day; She
met a bold sea cap - tain by chance up - on the way. He
says, "My pret-ty fair maid, if it was - n't for the law I would
have you in my bed this night, by eith - er stock or wa."

No. 5 (all versions)   **LORD BATEMAN**

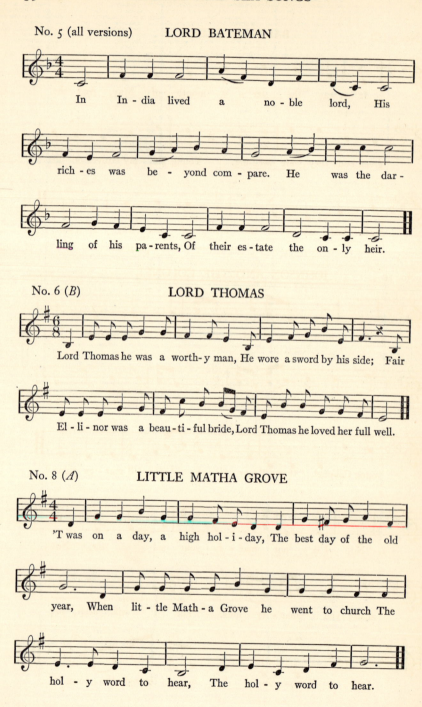

In In-dia lived a no-ble lord, His rich-es was be-yond com-pare. He was the dar-ling of his pa-rents, Of their es-tate the on-ly heir.

No. 6 (*B*)   **LORD THOMAS**

Lord Thomas he was a worth-y man, He wore a sword by his side; Fair El-li-nor was a beau-ti-ful bride, Lord Thomas he loved her full well.

No. 8 (*A*)   **LITTLE MATHA GROVE**

'T was on a day, a high hol-i-day, The best day of the old year, When lit-tle Math-a Grove he went to church The hol-y word to hear, The hol-y word to hear.

No. 9 (C)   BARBARY ELLEN

It was the ver-y month of May, And the green buds they were swell-ing. Young Jim-my Groves on his death bed lay For the love of Bar-b'ry El-len.

No. 10   JOHNSON AND THE COLONEL

1. As John-son and the young Col-onel To-geth-er were drink-ing wine, Says John-son to the young Col-onel, "If you'll mar-ry my sis-ter I'll mar-ry thine."

2. "No, I'll not mar-ry your sis-ter, Nor shall you mar-ry mine, For I will keep her for a miss As I go through the town."

No. 11 (*A*)   SIR JAMES THE ROSE

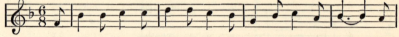

Of all the Scot-tish northern chiefs Of high and war-like name, The

brav-est was Sir James the Rose, A knight of muck-le fame.

No. 13   BOLENDER MARTIN

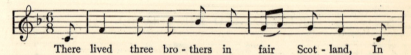

There lived three bro-thers in fair Scot-land, In

Scotland there lived bro-thers three. And they drew lots to

see which would go A rob-bing all on the salt sea.

No. 19 (*A*)   THE SEA–CAPTAIN

It was of a sea-cap-tain that fol-lowed the sea. Let the

winds blow high or blow low O, "I shall die, I shall die," the sea-

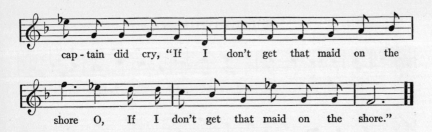

cap - tain did cry, "If I don't get that maid on the

shore O, If I don't get that maid on the shore."

No. 20   SIR NEIL AND GLENGYLE

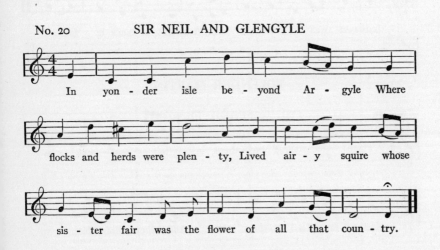

In yon - der isle be - yond Ar - gyle Where

flocks and herds were plen - ty, Lived air - y squire whose

sis - ter fair was the flower of all that coun - try.

No. 21   THE GOLDEN GLOVE

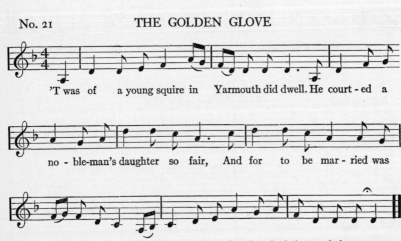

'T was of a young squire in Yarmouth did dwell. He court - ed a

no - ble-man's daughter so fair, And for to be mar - ried was

all their in-tent, When friends and re - la - tions had giv - en their con-sent.

No. 22   **THE LADY'S FAN**

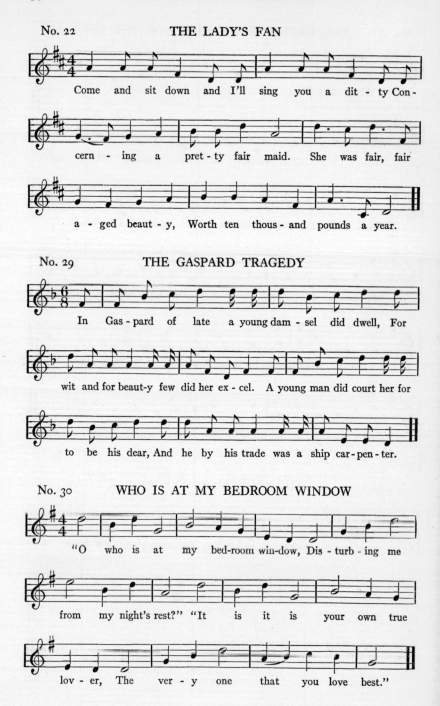

Come and sit down and I'll sing you a dit - ty Con-

cern - ing a pret - ty fair maid. She was fair, fair

a - ged beaut - y, Worth ten thous - and pounds a year.

No. 29   **THE GASPARD TRAGEDY**

In Gas - pard of late a young dam - sel did dwell, For

wit and for beaut-y few did her ex - cel. A young man did court her for

to be his dear, And he by his trade was a ship car - pen - ter.

No. 30   **WHO IS AT MY BEDROOM WINDOW**

"O who is at my bed-room win-dow, Dis - turb - ing me

from my night's rest?" "It is it is your own true

lov - er, The ver - y one that you love best."

No. 47 THE GREEN MOSSY BANKS OF THE LEA

When first from my coun-try, a strang-er, cur-i-os-i-ty caused me to roam, O-ver Eu-rope I re-solved to be a rang-er, when I left Phil-a-del-phia my home. I quick-ly sailed o-ver to Ire-land, where forms of great beau-ty doth shine. It was there I be-held a fair dam-sel, and I wished in my heart she was mine.

No. 54 THE CHIPPEWA STREAM

As I went a walk-ing one even-ing in June, A view-ing the ros-es, they were in full bloom, I met a pret-ty fair maid as I passed a-long. She was washing some lin-ens by the Chippe-wa Stream.

No. 56   THE DAWNING OF THE DAY

As I walked out one morn-ing fair all in the month of June, Each bush and tree was decked in green and the flowers were in their bloom. Re-turn-ing home all from a walk through a field I took my way; I chanced to see a pret-ty fair maid at the dawn-ing of the day.

No. 59 (*A*)   THE BUTCHER BOY

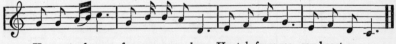

In Lon-don town where I did dwell, A butcher boy I loved him well. He court-ed me for man-y a day; He stole from me my heart a-way.

No. 72 (both versions)   THE BONNY BUNCH OF ROSES

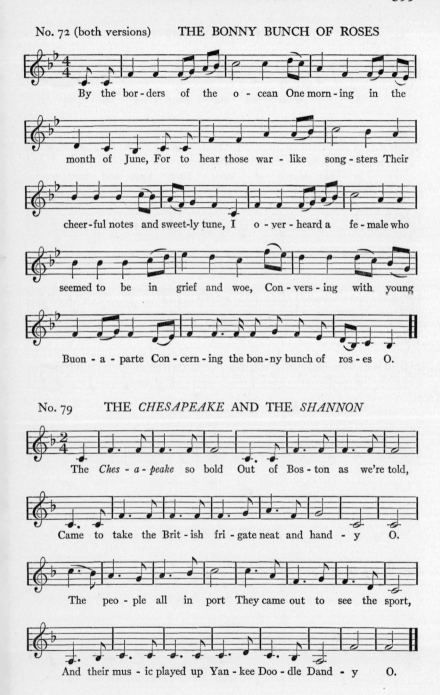

By the bor - ders   of   the   o - cean One morn - ing   in   the
month of   June, For   to   hear those war - like   song - sters Their
cheer-ful notes and sweet-ly tune, I   o - ver - heard a   fe - male who
seemed to   be   in   grief and woe, Con - vers - ing with young
Buon - a - parte Con - cern - ing the bon - ny bunch of   ros - es   O.

No. 79   THE CHESAPEAKE AND THE SHANNON

The Ches - a - peake so bold   Out   of Bos - ton as we're told,
Came to take the Brit - ish fri - gate neat and hand - y   O.
The   peo - ple all   in   port They came out to   see the sport,
And their mus - ic played up Yan - kee Doo - dle Dand - y   O.

No. 81 (*B*)   KELLY THE PIRATE

Ad-miral Kel-ly gave or-ders on the first of May To cruise in the chan-nel for our en-e-my, To pro-tect our com-merce from that dar-ing foe, And all our mer-chant-ships where they would go. Then it's

Chorus

O Brit-ons stand true, Stand true to your col-ours, stand true!

No. 93 (*A* or *C*)   GREEN BEDS

A stor-y, a stor-y. a stor-y I'll make known A-bout a cer-tain young man, his name it was John, A-bout a cer-tain young man whose late-ly come a-shore In rag-ged at-tire like one that is poor.

No. 94

FRANK FIDD

Frank Fidd was as gal-lant a tar as ev-er took reef in a

sail, And when her lee gun - 'l lay un - der He

laughed at the noise of the gale. His grog he pro-vide a-gainst

storm, While spit-ting the juice from his quid; A-

loft, on the yard, or on deck, It was all the same to Frank Fidd.

No. 102

THE WILD GOOSE

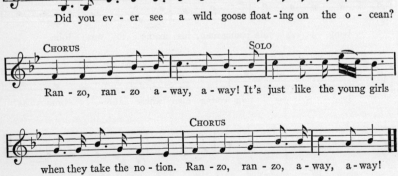

Solo

Did you ev - er see a wild goose float-ing on the o - cean?

Chorus   Solo

Ran - zo, ran - zo a - way, a - way! It's just like the young girls

Chorus

when they take the no - tion. Ran - zo, ran - zo, a - way, a - way!

No. 104 (all versions)   RIO GRANDE

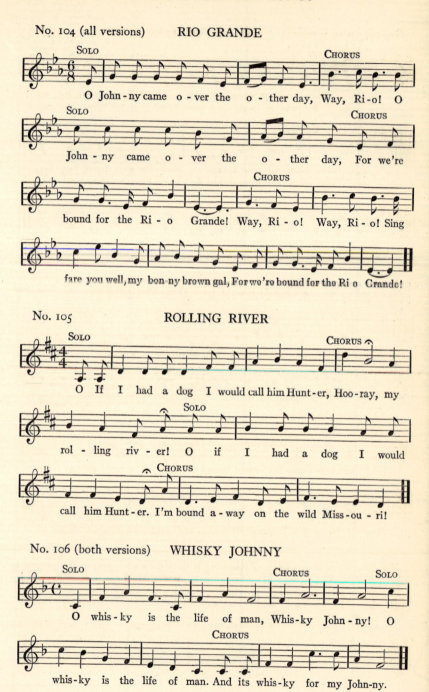

O John-ny came o-ver the o-ther day, Way, Ri-o! O John-ny came o-ver the o-ther day, For we're bound for the Ri-o Grande! Way, Ri-o! Way, Ri-o! Sing fare you well, my bon-ny brown gal, For we're bound for the Ri o Grande!

No. 105   ROLLING RIVER

O If I had a dog I would call him Hunt-er, Hoo-ray, my rol-ling riv-er! O if I had a dog I would call him Hunt-er. I'm bound a-way on the wild Miss-ou-ri!

No. 106 (both versions)   WHISKY JOHNNY

O whis-ky is the life of man, Whis-ky John-ny! O whis-ky is the life of man. And its whis-ky for my John-ny.

No. 107 (both versions) BLOW THE MAN DOWN

Blow the man down, bul-lies, blow the man down, To me
As I was a walk-ing down Man-ches-ter Street, To me

way, hay, blow the man down! Blow the man down, bul-lies,
way, hay, blow the man down! A nice lit-tle dam-sel I

blow the man down. O give me some time to blow the man down!
chanced for to meet. O give me some time to blow the man down!

No. 113 CHARLES AUGUSTUS ANDERSON

Come all you hu-man country-men, with pit-y lend an ear, And

hear my feel-ing stor-y— you can't but shed a tear. I'm

held in close con-fine-ment bound down in i-rons strong, Sur-

round-ed by ston-y gran-ite walls and sentenced to be hung.

No. 121 THE PRISONER'S SONG

It's hard to be locked up in pri-son, Far from your

own heart's de-light, ... With cold i-ron bars all a-

round you, And a stone for your pil - low at night.

CHORUS

Lone - ly and sad, sad and lone - ly, Sit - ting in my

cell all a - lone. I've been thinking of the days that have gone

by me, . . . The days when I know I have done wrong.

No. 122   VAN DIEMAN'S LAND

Oh come all ye men of learn - ing, and ramb-ling boys be-

ware! It's when you go a hunt - ing take your

dog, your gun, your snare. Think on loft - y hills and

moun - tains that are at your com - mand, And think

on the te - dious journ - ey go - ing to Van Die - man's Land.

No. 123 JACK DONAHUE

Come all you gal - lant bush - rang - ers and out - laws of disdain, Who scorn to live in slav - er - y or wear the
bonds of chains, At - ten-tion pay to what I say and val-ue it if you
do. I will re - late the matchless fate of bold Jack Don - a - hue.

No. 143 WHEN I WAS SINGLE

When I was single, O then, When I was single, O then,
When I was single my pock - ets did jingle I
CHORUS
wish I was single a - gain. A - gain and a - gain and a - gain, A-
gain and a - gain and a - gain, When I was single my
pock - ets did jingle, I wish I was single a - gain.

No. 147   COURTING IN THE KITCHEN

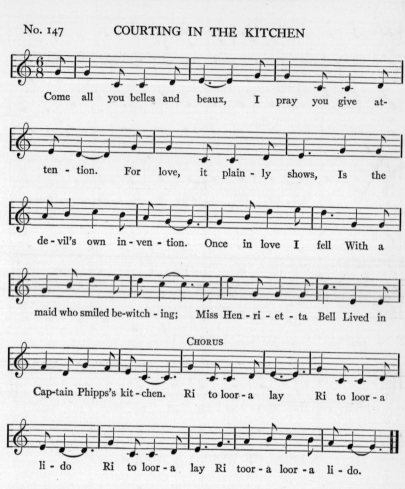

Come all you belles and beaux, I pray you give at-
ten - tion. For love, it plain - ly shows, Is the
de - vil's own in - ven - tion. Once in love I fell With a
maid who smiled be-witch - ing; Miss Hen - ri - et - ta Bell Lived in

CHORUS

Cap-tain Phipps's kit - chen. Ri to loor - a lay Ri to loor - a
li - do Ri to loor - a lay Ri toor - a loor - a li - do.

No. 148   KIRTLE GAOL

Good peo - ple all, give ear, I pray, And mark you well what
I do say. To my mis - for - tunes great and small Come

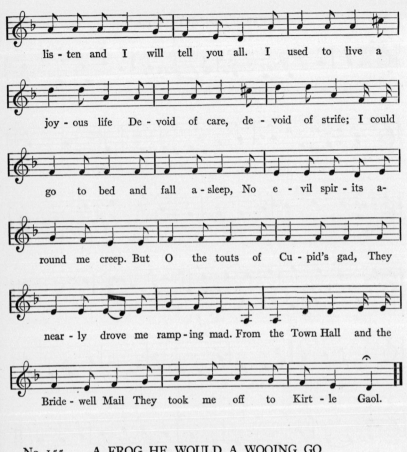

lis - ten and I will tell you all. I used to live a

joy - ous life De - void of care, de - void of strife; I could

go to bed and fall a - sleep, No e - vil spir - its a -

round me creep. But O the touts of Cu - pid's gad, They

near - ly drove me ramp - ing mad. From the Town Hall and the

Bride - well Mail They took me off to Kirt - le Gaol.

No. 155   A FROG HE WOULD A WOOING GO

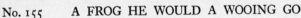

A frog he would a woo - ing go, Heigh - o! says Row - ley O. A

CHORUS

frog he would a woo - ing go Whether his mother would let him or no. With a

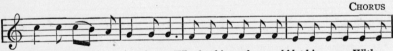

row - ley, pow - ley, gammon and spinach, Heigho! says Anthony Row - ley.

No. 157 LITTLE JOHNNY GREEN

My grandmother lived on yonder little green, As fine an old lad-y as

ev-er was seen. And she of-ten cau-tioned me with care Of

CHORUS

all false young men to be-ware. Tim-my I, tim-my O, tim-my

um-pa tum-pa tay, Of all false young men to be-ware.

No. 158 THE QUAKER'S WOOING

Slow

Mad-am, I have come a court-ing, Mm, O dear!

Not for fun or id-le sport-ing, Mm, O dear!

Lively

You may sit and court the fire, Tee-dle eed-le ing ting tay A

man like you I don't ad-mire. Tee-dle eed-le ing ting tay.

No. 159   THE BUILDING OF SOLOMON'S TEMPLE

In his-t'ry we read of a free-ma-son king, The

glor-y of Is-rael, his praise let us sing; He who built a great fab-ric, as

we un-der-stand, On the Mount Mo-ri-ah in Je-ru-sa-lem.

No. 160   THE LOVELY BANKS OF BOYNE

I am a gay young lass-ie and I love my Jim-mie

well. My heart was ev-er true to him far more than tongue can

tell. . . 'T was at my fath-er's cas-tle where he

gained this heart of mine, And he caus-es me to

wan-der from the love-ly banks of Boyne

INDEXES

INDEX OF TITLES

INDEX OF FIRST LINES

DATE DUE

Unless this book is returned on or before the last date stamped below a fine will be charged. Fairness to other borrowers makes enforcement of this rule necessary.

MAR 1 1930			
DEC 19 1932			
NOV 27 1942			
MAY 3 1 1959			
MAY 1 1 1960			